Learning, Curriculum and Life Politics

In the **World Library of Educationalists**, international experts themselves compile career-long collections of what they judge to be their finest pieces – extracts from books, key articles, salient research findings, major theoretical and practical contributions – so the world can read them in a single manageable volume. Readers will be able to follow themes and strands of the topic and see how their work contributes to the development of the field.

Professor Ivor F. Goodson has spent the last 30 years researching, thinking and writing about some of the key and enduring issues in education. He has contributed over 40 books and 600 articles to the field.

In *Learning, Curriculum and Life Politics*, Ivor Goodson brings together 19 key writings in one place. Starting with a specially written Introduction, which gives an overview of his career and contextualises his selection within the development of the field, the chapters cover:

- curriculum history and policy
- classroom pedagogy and strategies for professional development
- life history, narrative and educational change.

This book not only shows how Ivor's thinking developed during his long and distinguished career; it also gives an insight into the development of the fields to which he contributed.

Ivor F. Goodson has recently joined the Von Hugel Institute at St Edmunds College, University of Cambridge. He is also Professor of Learning Theory at the Education Research Centre, University of Brighton. Currently he is Professor in residence at the University of Barcelona.

He is the founding editor of the *Journal of Education Policy* and European Editor of *Identity*. He will be presented with the Michael Huberman Award for his educational research at the American Educational Research Association meeting in San Francisco in 2006. The work in this volume can be linked with the webpage www.ivorgoodson.com which contains a range of additional information and articles.

Contributors to the series include: Richard Aldrich, Stephen J. Ball, John Elliott, Elliot W. Eisner, Howard Gardner, John K. Gilbert, Ivor F. Goodson, David Labaree, John White and E.C. Wragg.

World Library of Educationalists series

Learning, Curriculum and Life Politics

The selected works of Ivor F. Goodson

Ivor F. Goodson

Routledge
Taylor & Francis Group

LONDON AND NEW YORK

First published 2005
by Routledge
2 Park Square, Milton Park, Abingdon, Oxon OX14 4RN

Simultaneously published in the USA and Canada
by Routledge
270 Madison Ave, New York, NY 10016

Routledge is an imprint of the Taylor & Francis Group

© 2005 Ivor F. Goodson

Typeset in Sabon by
Newgen Imaging Systems (P) Ltd, Chennai, India
Printed and bound in Great Britain by
MPG Books Ltd, Bodmin, Cornwall

British Library Cataloguing in Publication Data
A catalogue record for this book is available
from the British Library

Library of Congress Cataloging in Publication Data
Goodson, Ivor.
    Learning, curriculum and life politics: the selected works
of Ivor F. Goodson/Ivor F. Goodson.
        p. cm.
    1. Curriculum planning – History. 2. Education – Curricula –
Social aspects. 3. Teachers – History. I. Title.
    LB2806.15.C664 2005
    375'.001–dc22   2005005630

ISBN 0–415–35219–3 (hbk)
ISBN 0–415–35220–7 (pbk)

To Andy

For the good times,
with all of my love.

DAD

CONTENTS

ACKNOWLEDGEMENTS

To my colleagues at the Education Research Centre at the University of Brighton and the Von Hugel Institute at St Edmunds College, University of Cambridge. I should also like to thank the research assistants that have worked with me in a variety of research projects over the last decade or so notably: Martha Foote, Michael Baker, Dr Marshall Mangan, Dr Valerie Rea and Dr Chris Anstead. They have been invaluable collaborators and friends in the wide range of work undertaken during this time and their work fully informs many of the articles in this volume.

I should also like to thank my secretary Anna Winskill for her good humour and patience during the compilation of this volume. It is a difficult and sometimes tedious task to compile such a large volume of collected work and she has endured this with a fine sense of humour, tenacity and skill.

For readers requiring more information on collected work please visit my webpage which is www.ivorgoodson.com or contact me at I.F.Goodson@brighton.ac.uk or ivorgoodson@yahoo.co.uk

The following articles have been reproduced with the kind permission of the respective journals

Becoming an Academic Subject. *British Journal of Sociology of Education*, 1981, 2(2): 163–180.

Coming to Curriculum: Extract from 'Reconstructing Aspects of a Teacher's Life'. Article in process.

Learning and The Pedagogic Moment: Extract from 'The Pedagogic Moment'. Article in process.

Long Waves of Educational Reform: Extract from 'Report to the Spencer Foundation'. Submitted September 2003.

Nations at Risk and National Curriculum. *Journal of Education Policy*, 1991, section in *Handbook of the American Politics of Education Association*, pp. 219–232.

On Curriculum Form. *Sociology of Education*, 1992, 65(1): 66–75.

Preparing for Post-modernity: Storying the Self. *Educational Practice and Theory*, 1998, 20(1): 25–31.

Representing Teachers: Bringing Teachers Back In. *Teaching and Teacher Education: An International Journal of Research and Studies*, 1997, 13(1).

Sponsoring the Teacher's Voice. *Cambridge Journal of Education*, 1991, 21(1): 35–45.

The Story of Life History. *Identity: An International Journal of Theory and Research*, 2001, 1(2): 129–142.

The Story So Far. *The International Journal of Qualitative Studies in Education*, 1995, 8(1): 89–98.

Towards a Social Constructionist Perspective. *Journal of Curriculum Studies*, 1990, 299–312.

The following chapters have been reproduced with the kind permission of the respective publishers

Action Research and the Reflexive Project of Selves. In International Action Research: A Casebook for Education Reform, S. Hollingsworth (ed.), *Action Research Reader*, London: Falmer Press, 1997.

Chariots of Fire: Etymologies, Epistemologies and the Emergence of Curriculum. *The Making of Curriculum, 2nd edition*, London: Falmer Press, 1995.

History, Context and Qualitative Methods. In R.G. Burgess (ed.), *Strategies for Education Research*, London: Falmer Press, 1985.

Scrutinizing Life Stories. In N. Bascia, D. Thiessen and I. Goodson (eds), *Making a Difference about Difference*, Canada: Garamond Press, 1996, pp. 123–138.

The Making of Curriculum. *The Making of Curriculum, 2nd edition*, London: Falmer Press, 1995.

The Personality of Educational Change. *Professional Knowledge, Professional Lives: Studies in Education and Change*, Maidenhead: Open University Press, 2003.

Towards an Alternative Pedagogy. In J. Kincheloe and S. Steinberg (eds), *Unauthorized Methods: Strategies for Critical Teaching*, London: Routledge, 1998.

A poor boy hobbled forth to give a reply. He was lame and humpbacked, and his wan, emaciated face told only too clearly the tale of poverty and its consequences – but he gave forthwith so lucid and intelligent a reply to the question put to him that there arose a feeling of admiration for the child's talents combined with a sense of shame that more information should be found in some of the lowest of our lower classes on matters of general interest than in those far above them in the world by station. It would be an unwholesome and vicious state of society in which those who are comparatively unblessed with natures gifts should be generally superior in intellectual attainments to those above them in station.

(Lord Wrottesley, 1860)

True education is not for every man the scrap of paper he leaves school with. Dare we as teachers admit this? Dare we risk our existence by forcibly expressing our views on this? While we pause after the first phase of our acceptance, are we to rely on examinations for all to prove ourselves worthy of the kindly eye of the State? Dare we allow to leave some of our charges who have been once more neglected and once more squeezed into a heap of frustrating unimportance?

(P.L. Quant, 1967)

People must be educated once more to know their place (English Civil Servant talking about the new National Curriculum).

(John Pilger in *Heroes*, 1986
(South End Press))

INTRODUCTION
Learning, curriculum and life politics

The compilation of a set of collected works brings with it the problem of developing criteria for selection; what lines of thought are to be favoured or downplayed or deleted. For after thirty years or so of writing, the shape of ones thinking only really emerges fully with this advantage of hindsight. But this itself is to privilege the retrospective selection over the full developmental diversity of avenues of investigation. For in truth our studies go off in many directions – some prove fruitful, some rapidly become cul-de-sacs; some lie dormant and then accelerate rapidly, whilst others blossom early but then fade gradually. All of this only becomes clear later.

This collection tends to work backwards in some ways from my current work on life histories, professional life and work, and life politics; but to counter this whiggishness it also tries to work in the opposite direction following the chronology of scholarly concerns with learning, pedagogy and curriculum and following these through to the present day.

My recent research location has been rather fortunate and quite unexpected. Having spent five years working on the Spencer Foundation project Change Over Time (1998–2003) I have completed a set of essays and books that pull together a range of research on professionalisation and life history. This work was undertaken whilst at the University of Western Ontario in Canada and mostly at the Warner Graduate School in the University of Rochester in New York State.

Upon returning to work in my home country, apart from the considerable joy at home-coming, I was planning to write a number of books which summarised my educational thinking. For the moment this has been forestalled by the award of two large longitudinal research grants. The first is part of the UK Governments Teaching and Learning Programme and is funded by the Economic and Social Research Council, the project *Learning Lives: Learning, Identity and Agency in the Life-Course* is concerned to understand learning in a variety of milieu across the life course and employs a life history methodology in pursuit of this data.

Alongside this the European Union has funded a complimentary four-year project which studies *Professional Knowledge* in eight European countries. Again a life history approach is employed.

Hence in the years through until 2008/09 the work on learning, curriculum and life politics will be grounded within two highly generative research programmes. Hopefully therefore these themes will achieve greater focus and clarity as a result.

At the heart of so much of my research is a belief that we have to understand the personal and biographical if we are to understand the social and political. This far from unique insight nonetheless allows us to scrutinise the educational enterprise from a highly productive vantage point. So much of recent writing on educational and social change, and likewise so many new governmental initiatives, across Western societies have proceeded in denial or ignorance of the personal missions and biographical trajectories of key personnel. Whilst this often provides evidence of 'symbolic action' to electorates or professional audiences the evidence at the level of service delivery is often far less impressive. Sometimes the symbolic enshrinement of targets, tests, and tables whilst winning wide constituency support at the outset proves later to have had often negligible or even contradictory effects at the point of delivery. The point of contradiction is often the ignorance or denial of personal missions and biographical mandates. These therefore seem a good place to locate our studies (and indeed our policies) not reluctantly at the end of a process but enthusiastically at the beginning.

For this reason, above all, I have tried to practice what I preach by beginning with some autobiographical fragments. This can perhaps help the reader in seeing, often quite literally, 'where I'm coming from'. If this works, although it runs the risk of seeming self indulgent; it nonetheless can validate the notion that we should start by understanding and honouring peoples biographical trajectories and proclivities.

Chapters 1 and 2 therefore focus on extracts from longer articles which cover my personal hinterland. My background, has substantially informed my angle of, and approach to, social investigation and therefore a few autobiographical segments might provide useful information for those reading selected work. The 'ancestral voices' of region and class, one might say of 'tribe', have always spoken loudly to me and this has not receded in the face of social and geographical mobility. I have tried to explain this modality of 'holding on' in other works (see Goodson, 1997).

Certainly the legacy of 'Cobblers City' spelt out in Chapter 1, has an enduring importance for me. To grow up among a community of independent labourers who existed beyond the direct power of the squire and his estate managers bred a fierce sense of independent judgement and a compelling sense of the frequent inauthenticity of dominant social orders. I still see social orders, even 'new world orders' from that angle, my judgements remain not pre-determined or pre-ordained but in aspiration still, 'independent'.

In Chapter 2, some of my early experiences of learning and teaching are outlined. As the chapter on *Long Waves of Reform* makes clear the period 1968–74 was one of great social innovation in many parts of the Western world. It was a particularly interesting time for those concerned to explore the parameters of and possibility of strategies for social inclusion. In England comprehensive schools had been introduced in the mid-1960s and were developing serious experiments in the broadening of the social base of educational success. Certainly the schools in which I taught took this social mission seriously and provided a wide range of insights into the social order of schooling.

Chapter 3 explores the kind of pedagogic terrain which emerged in many of the more experimental comprehensive schools. These initiatives sought to explore educational endeavours as a dialectic or dialogue between teacher and learner; alongside this a more personalised process of learning was explored, so many of these new learning modes offered very promising avenues of education for traditionally less advantaged school clienteles. In due course more prescriptive centralised curricula were introduced which had the effect of closing off these avenues of potential advancement and inclusion.

Chariots of Fire looks in some detail at the history of curriculum as a concept. The origin of the definition of curriculum linked to the emergence of state schooling are investigated. The power of curriculum to designate and differentiate and the linkage to school subjects is seen as a relatively recent invention. As Thompson argues 'all education which is worth the name involves a relationship of mutuality, a dialectic' (1968, p. 16).

By the end of Chapters 2 and 3 the reader can perhaps begin to see how a project focussing on curriculum history had started to emerge. Chapter 4 was written as a speculative essay trying to link the origins of curriculum definition to the emergence of state schooling. The paper was written for a quite wonderful symposium organised at the University of British

Colombia in the summer of 1985. This was the time when I was starting to think about leaving my homeland and some of the incipient nostalgia no doubt comes through in the text. This was, we should note, a rotten time in England. The miners strike was dividing the country in a horrendous way, inequality was back on the increase sponsored by a range of government policies and practices, the national curriculum was being hatched, the universities were being cut. Only later would these interlinked phenomena emerge as part of a clear world movement towards a new world economic order yet one subject to ongoing contestation.

In *Chariots of Fire*, the relations between curricula and the social order are scrutinised in a historical manner. Through historical study we can begin to glimpse the importance not just of the rhetoric of reform but of the continuities of curriculum and social stratification. These never proceed in a determinist way nor are they part of some well thought out conspiracy by agents of the rich and powerful. We have to understand continuity and change within each historical context in which they are embodied and embedded.

Becoming an Academic Subject aims to show how by scrutinising in historical detail the emergence of an academic subject, geography, a range of sociological and philosophical explanations can be interrogated. The process that emerges is less domination by dominant interest groups, more solicitous surrender by subordinate groups. It is important to distinguish between domination and structure and between mechanism and mediation. What historical study points us to is the complexity of these processes and to the fact that social forces have to work and re-work the configurations of curriculum in each historical time and place. As Chapter 9 points out, we can discern historical conjunctures at particular periods but these are never pre-determined or historically inevitable. Becoming an academic subject looks at the ongoing contests and struggles over school knowledge.

Interestingly, at about the time the article on which this chapter is based came out, my first book, *School Subjects and Curriculum Change* appeared. As an unlooked-for spin-off from the book a publisher, Falmer Press, contacted me. The plan was to define a series of books on curricular history to be called *Studies in Curriculum History*. So began an intellectual project that covered twenty years and allowed a wide range of historical studies to be not only undertaken but published. If ever there was a lesson about historical contexts, this was it. At that time in university schools of education, historical studies of education and indeed philosophical, psychological and sociological studies were all being undertaken and published. These studies often developed the link between social and historical context and educational possibilities. In subsequent years paradoxically, a growing emphasis on practical, and particularly subject, knowledge was to obscure these links – our understandings of the social construction of schooling and curriculum began to be paved over. Social inclusion was to become a rhetoric uncoupled from systematic social investigation or historical elucidation. The curriculum so unambiguously implicated in social exclusion was to be unproblematically adopted as a part of the apparatus for pursuing social inclusion. This is what often happens when history is consigned to the dustbin: a case of reinventing the square wheel.

Chapter 7 looks at the importance of how the curriculum is socially constructed for the ongoing maintenance of the social order. In some ways this chapter asks questions that would be relevant for the interrogation of current educational policies: for instance 'why is the dominant form of subject-based curriculum treated by policy makers as a "timeless given" '; more pressingly 'why are so many contemporary educational theorists accepting this as they follow the trajectory of current policies?' Perhaps the appeal is itself part of the diagnosis of this chapter that 'the internalisation of differentiation effectively masks the social process of preferment and privilege'.

In *The Making of Curriculum*, I examine the socio-political process by which school subjects become 'timeless givens' in the grammar of schooling. In fact the 'traditional subjects' turn out to be examples of the 'invention of tradition' as is so much else in our social world. Traditions which endure in the arena of schooling and curriculum must appeal to powerful 'constituencies' and without that support new challenges can never gain traction. The tradition of school subjects therefore are broadly harmonised with the external constituencies of power. Curriculum approaches that might seek to educate more disadvantaged groups must 'run the gauntlet' of the powerful external constituencies. Sustainability in the world of the school curriculum is therefore closely equated with the resonance achieved with external constituencies.

I noted earlier the distinction between domination and structure, and mechanism and mediation. This means that any assertion about curriculum must be located within the historical period in question. At certain points new structures are established which set up new 'rules of the game'. Whilst this establishment of new structures might be viewed as domination, the period that follows such legislation is one of mediation. Hence as we noted in earlier sections, the period of the 1960s and early 1970s was one of social innovation in much of the Western world. In this period there were social missions and social movements aiming at social justice and social inclusion. These missions and movements, again as noted in earlier chapters, led to serious pedagogic and schooling experiments to broaden social inclusion. My point in covering some of these alternative pedagogies was not to argue that these provided an answer to the perennially elusive project of social inclusions but to delineate the purposes, pedagogies and practises that were developed as part of this social movement. In later periods 'social inclusion' again surfaced but this time as an uncoupled political rhetoric located within a far more stratifying strategy of educational provision. Since this rhetoric showed little interest in the earlier experiments and social movements it was difficult to believe in its serious purpose. Schools are weighted with contextual inertia and to completely ignore history in this way is to be either naïve or duplicitous, it is certainly not to be properly informed or strategically purposeful.

But this is to run ahead, for by the millennium much had changed and the reversals of the period following Thatcher's election in 1979 and Reagan's in 1980 have been well-documented. The chapter *Nations at Risk and National Curriculum* looks at the reversal in the field of curriculum. For instance in England the similarity between the 1904 structure of secondary education and the 1988 National Curriculum is pointed up. I note that the 1904 structure embodied that curriculum offered to the grammar school clientele as opposed to the curriculum being developed in the Board Schools and aimed primarily at the working class. At this point dominant interest groups were acting to favour one segment or vision over another. In the years following the Second World War and culminating in the 1960s more egalitarian forces at work in a different economic climate brought the creation of comprehensive schools where children of all classes came under one roof. As we saw earlier, come curriculum initiatives sought to redefine and challenge the hegemony of the grammar school curriculum and associated pattern of social prioritising. It was to defeat this challenge that some of the policies of the Thatcher government were formulated, notably the National Curriculum. 'Seeking in turn to challenge and redirect these reforms and intentions the political right has argued for the rehabilitation of the "traditional" (i.e. grammar school) subjects. The national curriculum can be seen as a political statement of the victory of the forces and intentions representing these political groups. A particular vision, a preferred segment of the nation has therefore been reinstated and prioritised, and legislated as "national".'

The changing configuration of curriculum provides us with a valuable litmus test of social and political intentions and purposes. As we can see these configurations change as the balance of social forces and the underlying economic landscape undergo cyclical change. In *Long Waves of Reform*, using an extensive archive of data generated by the Spencer Foundation project 'Change over Time', I try to delineate the long cycles of educational reform. Looking at the USA and Canada there is a remarkable similarity in the main 'conjunctures' of change in curriculum and pedagogy. A similar pattern of experimentation in pursuit of social justice to that witnessed in Britain can be seen in the period of the late 1960s and early 1970s. All schools were affected by the progressive desire to build a 'Great Society', characterised by social inclusion and social justice. Whilst some schools pursued 'root and branch' revolutionary change (as with the comprehensive schools mentioned in Chapters 1 and 2) others pursued social inclusion within a more conventional grammar of schooling.

The pattern of reversal noted in the previous chapter was similarly evident with the introduction of standards-based testing and new patterns of systems differentiation (e.g. Magnet Schools). This was part of a world movement to transform schooling, often in ways that resonated with the emerging new economic world order. Some commentators have called this 'market fundamentalism', bringing in a competitive business ethos around notions of school effectiveness and school choice. This accelerating marketisation of schooling had many implications, one was to side-line the significance of the struggle over kinds of curriculum. Differentiation of life chances through curriculum was progressively passed over to the work of the market in disbursing resources according to particular school sites and systems, related increasingly closely to patterns of residential location.

The seismic social and political changes at the end of the twentieth century, which are echoed in the educational transformations noted above, pose a challenge for those concerned to investigate them. The changing positionality of curriculum as a distributor of life chances and the salience of tests, targets and tables has moved the focus of social and political action. Our studies therefore need to reflect this transformation and reconceptualise both the substantive focus of inquiry and the methods employed.

From the beginning I have argued that we have to understand the personal and biographical if we are to understand the social and political. This is nowhere more true than in the relevance of personal biography in the choice of research focus and method. I have tried to show 'where I am coming from' and this illuminates a clear predisposition in favour of strategies for social inclusion and social justice. But I have also tried to provide a historical context for understanding social possibilities. Hobsbawm's golden age of egalitarianism which culminated in the 1960s and 1970s has clearly passed and some personal nostalgia is patently evident in some of my accounting (Hobsbawm, 1994). But I do seek to avoid and warn against golden age reminiscences for, as Lasch has reminded us, nostalgia is the abdication of memory (Lasch, 1979). I should therefore note a few of the myths of the golden age. Many public services, schools included, developed a culture which favoured service providers rather than clients and customers and at time, trade union action sometimes exacerbated the problem. Public and professional groups can hijack resources for their own purposes just as other groups can. And progressive practices can develop areas of looseness, non-accountability and professional self-aggrandisement if so permitted. In many ways Britain in the 1970s provided a case study of such, ending as it did in a 'winter of discontent' among workers and trade unions which ushered in the Thatcher government.

The exhumation of the conflicts of the 1970s, the attribution of blame and delineation of causes is an ongoing task for historians. Their importance for the arguments in this book is to point out that all was not as it should be in the public services before the more recent reforms and restructuring. Whilst the best professionals adopted a 'caring vocationalism' in providing social inclusion many examples of self-serving professionalism could be found. The task as always was to try to understand both the larger social movements of reform but also their specific embodiment and embeddedness in personal biographies.

This book has sought to employ this focus from the beginning and in the later sections will make both the methodological and substantive argument for an increasing focus on 'life politics': I believe the new world order makes this even more important than it was in the earlier periods examined above. This is partly because of the triumph of 'the individualised society' – more than ever, in this context, individual life politics becomes the site of social contestation. Once the focus was on collective social movements, say for school or curriculum change. Now a primary strategy for understanding social change should focus on the individuals' life politics.

As Reeves has contended:

> The individual is steadily replacing the collective as the site of political action, analysis and conflict. The point here is not that everyone is becoming more selfish, but that the self is becoming a more important unit of politics than the class or group. In part this is because of the greater choice of lifestyle on offer and the breaking of hereditary voting patterns. More important has been the steady erosion of stable political affiliations; hence Labour winning more of the middle-class vote than the Tories in 1997. This is neither a progressive nor a regressive trend; it is simply a fact.
>
> One of the consequences has been what one seasoned political observer calls 'the privatisation of anger'. People get angry a lot, but generally as individuals, rather than in a group. Once we had Jarrow marchers; now we have road rage. Once we had trade unions; now we have therapists. Many of the major battles under way – for example, between work and life, healthy living and obesity, good and abusive parenting – are being fought within individuals, rather than between them.
>
> (Reeves, 2004, p. 24)

In the chapters that follow a number of papers pursue the relevance of life history methods to our understanding of the social world. The vital difference between life stories and narratives and fully developed life histories is that the story or narrative is located in the historical context in which lives are embodied and embedded. The storylines and scripts by which we recount our lives are related to the conditions and possibilities current in particular historical periods. It is therefore important to develop social constructionist perspectives to understand and develop changing historical contexts.

The first chapter in the methods section therefore looks at an early attempt to define Social Constructionist Perspectives for the study of curriculum. As Esland has noted: 'trying to focus the individual biography in its socio-historical context is in a very real sense attempting to penetrate the symbolic drift of school knowledge, and the consequences for the individuals who are caught up in it and attempting to construct their reality through it'. Mills has argued that social science ideally deals with 'problems of biography, history and of their intersections within social structures'. Hence the chapter argues that social constructionist study should focus on the individual life history and career; the group or collective; professions, categories, subjects or discipline that evoke rather as social movements over time. Likewise schools and classrooms develop patterns of stability and change; and finally the various relations between individuals and between groups and collectives, and between individuals, groups and collectivities over time.

This approach is further developed in the next chapter on *History, Context and Qualitative Methods*. A major part of the chapter presents one teachers life history and does so because 'this episode in a subject teachers life illustrates the way that the collection of life histories and elucidation of the historical context can combine'. I argue that:

> Above all the strength of beginning curriculum research from life history data is that from the outset the work is firmly focused on the working lives of practitioners... In articulating their response to historical factors and structural constraints, life storytellers provide us with sensitising devices for the analysis of these constraints and the manner in which they are experienced.

The Story of Life History provides a brief summary of the historical emergence of the life history tradition particularly at the University of Chicago in the 1920s. In its first incarnation 'the life history approach fell from grace and was largely abandoned by social scientists'. At first this was because of the increasingly powerful advocacy of statistical methods but also because the qualitative nature of the method undercut sociology's claim to scientific status. Moreover even among ethnographically inclined sociologists, more emphasis came to be placed on inter-active situations than on biography as the basis for understanding human behaviour.

In the 1970s a re-emergence of life history methods gathered force and with the new 'condition of post-modernity' this led to a large-scale rehabilitation of life history study. The current concern with understanding identity and subjectivity means that having failed the 'objectivity tests' under modernism, life history work is now very much back on the agenda. As we shall see later in the 'individualised society' we need new strategies for exploring peoples 'life politics' and indeed their 'moral careers'. The next section of this volume turns to these matters.

In *Preparing for Post-modernity*, I argue that 'life politics, the politics of identity construction and ongoing identity maintenance' will become a major and growing site of ideological and intellectual contestation with the progressive marketisation or privatisation of so many institutional settings. This means that these institutional sites may no longer be the central and most significant arenas for contestation and it also means that the methodological genres, which focus solely on institutional analysis and theorising, may be similarly diminished.

But if institutional life is being penetrated by marketisation and globalisation this does not mean that the individual's life politics remain in any way beyond the fray. The outreach of these world movements acknowledges no boundaries, indeed as the struggle around the Genome Project has highlighted our own bodies and genes are now within range. In *The Story So Far* we note how in the cultural logic of corporate rule, the life story, represents a form of cultural apparatus to accompany a newly aggrandising world order. The story then comes to stand as a form of commentary in itself, often divorced from any provision of contextual commentary. This strategy is increasingly evident in the media and overwhelmingly present in what some commentators now call the 'narrative politics' of America. In the new politics it is not the policies or programme that the voters recognise but the story, hyper-real as it may be, that they are told.

The relationship of the story line to scripts and social context is reviewed in *Scrutinising Life Stories*. The chapter argues that 'the collection of stories especially the mainstream stories that live out a prior script, will merely fortify patterns of domination. We shall need to move from life stories to life histories, from narratives to genealogies of context, towards a modality that embraces "stories of action within theories of context" '. The chapter provides examples of mid-life progress narratives and scholarship boy stories which show 'the intimate relationship between social circumstances and cultural storylines. In a real sense social structures push storylines in particular directions and the stories then legitimate the structures – and so on, in a self-legitimating circle'. But I add that the relationship between social structure and the story is 'loosely coupled and stories can resist as well as enhance the imperatives of structure'.

Action Research and the Reflexive Project of Selves grows from a series of life history interviews with key proponents of the educational movement called Action Research. The picture that emerges adds new perspectives as to how educational and social movements gain their adherents. A conventional view might be that new recruits to a social movement are converted by reading the main texts or hearing keynote lectures from the main advocates. What emerges from our interviews is rather more extended than such ready 'conventions'. A personal set of transitions are seen in process and the ongoing construction of identity projects and lifestyles plays an important part.

The final three chapters concentrate on ways of representing the world of the teacher. In *Representing Teachers* the popular genre of teachers stories and narratives is reviewed. The genre is located in the historical period of its emergence. It is argued that with the end of ideology, the end of the Cold War, we see the emergence of a cult of personality and celebrity. Associated with this has been a growing movement towards personal narratives and stories, not least in the field of educational study. 'Once again the personal narrative, the practical story, celebrates the end of the trauma of the Cold War and the need for a human space away from politics, away from power. It is a thoroughly understandable nirvana, but it assumes that power and politics have somehow ended.' In the period following the Cold War we have soon moved on to the war on terror. In a recent television programme made by Richard Curtis called 'The Power of the Nightmares' he asserts that politicians having failed to deliver our dreams with the collapse of ideologies have now set themselves up to protect us from our nightmares. The retreat into the personal domain is therefore likely to continue apace and our paradigms of educational study in pursuing an antidote should provide new ways to connect back in to collective history and socio-political context.

Sponsoring the Teachers Voice provides a set of guidelines for investigating life histories as a way of exploring the teachers life and work. The development of teachers life histories provides a contextual background to the teachers practice, and to the changes over time. An increasing range of work is building our understanding of the teachers life and work:

> Much of the work that is emerging on teachers lives throws up structural insights which locate the teachers life within the deeply structured and embedded environment of schooling.

The Personality of Change provides further evidence for this contention. The work grows out of the wide range of life history interviews conducted on the Spencer Project in the USA and Canada, called *Change Over Time*. The study was set up to explore school change over a 30 to 40 year period. Our interviews covered three cohorts of teachers (although some teachers cover all three periods): the teachers from the 1950s and 1960s (Cohort 1); the 1970s and 1980s (Cohort 2) and the teachers from the 1990s through to the projects end in 2001.

If you are lucky, research has its epiphanic moments – mostly delivered at unexpected times in unpredicted ways! For me, in this project it was trying out some interview schedules with Cohort 3 teachers. We had added a final question to try to get some sense of where teaching work was placed in the full spectrum of the activities of a life, 'are there any projects or interests outside your work that you would like to tell us about?' With some exceptions many Cohort 1 and 2 teachers had provided stories which placed their teaching as a central life project, a 'passion' or a 'vocation', even a 'calling'. Teaching was their 'life work and a source of enduring meaning and commitment in their lives'. Moreover, and this was often very clearly stated, teaching gave their life personal meaning within a collective project or vocation that expressed firmly held beliefs and values.

For Cohort 3 teachers this latter sense was seldom present. In the early stages of the interview, they often defined their teaching as 'just a job', 'only a pay cheque', 'I turn up and do what I'm told between 8 and 5', 'I follow the rules'. Others went on to say that they did a good job, and some that they enjoyed the work, but not one linked their work to a broader public or social vision. My epiphany came when they talked about 'other interests or projects'. There the change of body language was deafening; they leaned forward in their seats, their eyes shone, their hand movements were animated. 'Did they have other interests?' 'Oh yes, I'm planning to get out in the next two years and start a beauty clinic . . . I'm so excited'; 'I'm training in the evenings to become an occupational therapist,

I cant wait to begin my life', 'I'm saving up so as to retire at 50 – its only five years away . . . then my life will begin.'

For these teachers it would seem their work and its meaning are being transformed and uncoupled from wider collective visions and public purposes. Other research for instance the work of Robert Putnam and Richard Sennett points to a similar pattern: a growing range of studies illustrate a crisis of personal meaning and collective, public purpose at the heart of Western life. It seems the New World Order is failing to deliver personal meanings and narratives linked to wider public purposes. It is losing the battle for the hearts and minds of its own citizens in the intimate heartlands of their own stories. This may be calamitous for the delivery of better public services and a reinvigorated public life. In the life histories of ordinary people the effects have yet to be fully seen for these are early days in the global warming of human storylines. Our continuing study of life histories and life politics will provide vital evidence as to whether these patterns are consolidated or reversed.

References

Goodson, I.F., 1997, Holding on together: conversations with Barry. In P. Sikes and F. Rizvi (eds), *Researching Race and Social Justice Education – Essays in Honour of Barry Troyna* (Staffordshire: Trentham Books).

Hobsbawm, E., 1994, *The Age of Extremes* (London: Michael Joseph).

Lasch, C., 1979, *The Culture of Narcissism* (New York: Norton).

Reeves, R., 2004, Big Ideas – the triumph of the 'I'. In *New Statesman*, 26th July, pp. 23–24.

Thompson, E.P., 1968, *Education and Experience*. Fifth Mansbridge Memorial Lecture (Leeds: Leeds University Press).

PART 1

LEARNING AND CURRICULUM

CHAPTER 1

LEARNING AND THE PEDAGOGIC MOMENT

Extract from 'the pedagogic moment'

Article in process

From early on in my life I have always focused on particular phrases or incidents which seemed to offer the promise of breakthroughs in meaning or experience. Sartre has called these 'spontaneous moments', others have named them 'critical incidents' or in the 1960s 'happenings' or 'teachable moments'. For my own part, I have sought out these moments and have called them in my own journals and thoughts 'pedagogic moments'.

When I started teaching in a comprehensive school in the Midlands of England in 1970, I did so with a strong sense of a cultural mission. I was voyaging out from the working class village I had grown up in to another working class community to teach children very similar to those I had grown up with. At that time, the sense of stability and continuity in English working class life was less fragmented and assaulted than the world ordinary people now inhabit. I was, and remain, proud of the people I grew up amongst and wished to remain among them as a teacher. A few months into my teaching career, I returned to my home village and on Friday night went where I always went, to the local pub, 'The Bull and Chequers'. There, for the last 14 years, I had met the young women and men I grew up with so I immediately bumped into Brian Leeming, the boy whom I sat next to throughout primary school. He had been a real mate to me, helping me to learn to read in the large class where the teacher always seemed so distracted and busy:

Me:	Hey Brian! How are you doing kid?
Brian:	Not so bad – still slaving away in the factory.
	What you at? Haven't seen you around lately.
Me:	I'm teaching.
Brian:	(Look of confusion and suspicion.) Teaching! Teaching what?
Me:	I'm teaching history.
Brian:	Teaching history, kid! I'm making history.

Later, I thought a lot about this exchange. It was, of course, an emotionally loaded encounter. The mate, who had helped me learn to read and with whom I had grown up, was one of the brightest and best of my gang of friends. His confusion was part of the general ambivalence we had all felt towards teachers. But the challenge he posed was more substantial. For, if teaching history was fully divorced from making history, I was doomed to living out a life of instrumental operation, disengaged from the folks I cared about. I suppose, in searching for pedagogic moments, I have been searching for evidence that the rupture Brian mentioned, essentially the rupture between teaching as a life and living a life, was not inevitable. In the pedagogic moment, the rupture between teachers and taught is healed and a dialectic, an exchange, takes place, which affects not just beliefs but the very heart of the matter of living and experience.

The roots of pedagogy

Searching for roots in the postmodern Diaspora, whilst fashionable, is a deeply elusive process. In some ways, though, it is a natural search for me at this moment: my mother is 98 and for the past two Christmases I have watched as my son peppers his grandma with questions about the family history. At New Year she brought out all the family photo albums and got down to serious business.

As the process got underway, I began to realise what a deeply oral culture I grew up in. My mother is quite simply a great storyteller. Neither she, nor my dad, were very much at ease with writing but she can 'tell' stories brilliantly. This storytelling tradition is central to the roots of pedagogy as I practice and understand it.

One paper cutting which she produced this Christmas was the obituary of my granddad, James. James fathered 13 children but appears, on all birth certificates but two, as 'unemployed'. He apparently grew vegetables and sold them around the village from his tricycle which had a large basket at the back (like my father and myself and my son he was a slow learner with transport technology such as the bicycle!). Another paper cutting says James was one of the most popular fellows in the village. In the local hostelry he was everybody's favourite storyteller.

One of the other documents my mother uncovers is my father's deeds of *Indenture*. Here, the 13-year-old boy is signed over as an apprentice to the Reading Gas Company. At the bottom, somebody has scribbled my father's name in pencil and in a shaky hand the young boy has gone over the signature in pen (he could not write). Thereby, he signed on for a job that lasted 52 years. James had to countersign the 'handing over' of his son. This he did with a firm 'X'. (He had run away from home at 11 years of age and never mastered any writing or reading skills.)

My grandmother was also a wonderful storyteller. Since she lived to the age of 98, I remember her well. Whilst James sold his vegetables and told his stories in the pub, she took in laundry. She taught herself to read and write and kept the family finances written in a great ledger book. She also founded the family motto. When she fell pregnant for the 13th time at the age of 50, having delivered 12 daughters, the midwife came to aid the birth in the bedroom of the cottage. The midwife screamed out: 'Mrs. Goodson, it's a boy!' She apparently replied calmly: 'Yes, I know ... we're a very persistent family.' Indeed, we are and the family motto inscribed in the family stories reflects this.

On my mother's side, it was a similar story. My grandfather, like James, was a younger son growing up on a farm. With *primogeniture*, he inherited nothing and made his living in a succession of shops – mostly butchers' shops, and finally a working man's café in Reading. He also was a legendary storyteller and a man of stridently independent views. The combination of oral culture and independent views is something I have recently come to understand. A book on the village I grew up in has described *Woodley in the Nineteenth Century*. Originally, the village comprised a number of cottages that were 'small owner–occupier tenements' (p. 14), but as the 18th Century progressed, the local 'lord' or landlord, James Wheble, began to enclose the land and buy the cottages. 'As the cottages were acquired by Wheble, they were let out to labourers on his estate' (p. 14).

Wheble purchased Woodley Park and the existing estate to the side of his land, from Henry Addington in 1801 (the year Addington became Prime Minister of the country).

One area of Woodley, the 'old village', stood beyond Whebler's enclosures, outside his estate. In the 1830s, they were mainly freelance agricultural labourers, but the Rev. James Sherman noted: 'almost every labourer in that village was a poacher' (p. 39). The village he alluded to was my grandfather's village – the cottages and tenements (and beer houses) along Crockhamwell Road, on Wheelers Green and in Cobblers City and Woodley Green. Given the control of nearly all the land by Squire Wheble: 'new building had to take place either on the few remaining owner-occupier sites in Cobblers City and Woodley Green, or on the lands of the squires with their approval' (p. 59).

Independent spirits, therefore, gravitated to Woodley Village where my grandparents' cottage was located. Only in Cobblers City was a fiercely independent group of labourers able to stay outside the influence of the Squire and his estate managers:

> The most fascinating aspect of the area was the concentration of so many phases of social and economic development, reflected in the building, into one tiny corner of the Liberty. A city of cottages, sheds and workshops, created by the independent labourers of Woodley as they did what their forefathers had done before them – survived within the social and economic framework created by other more powerful hands around them.
>
> (p. 76)

Independent survival in the face of a socio-economic order that has sought to control and possess land and rights is an enduring part of Cobblers City. It is also therefore a part of my birthright and my scholarly and pedagogic posture. I do not start from the assumption that new world orders are well intentioned and benign nor that they are inevitably malign. I am deeply aware from my ancestral voices that certain groups face dispossession and displacement when new economic orders emerge. Certainly when Squire Wheble began to enclose the land around Woodley my forefathers had to respond rapidly. Most labourers in the village accepted the dispossession involved: That my own family chose to resist this economic order by locating in Cobblers City speaks of an enduring independence of spirit. This spirit hopefully informs my own chosen vocation and my pedagogic moments in the new era which David Harvey has characterized as 'accumulation by dispossession' (Harvey, 2003). Patterns of dispossession and displacement it seems endure. As to independent responses, well, we shall see . . . .

References

Harvey, D., 2003, *The New Imperialism* (New York: Oxford University Press), pp. 137–182.
Lloyd, F., 1977, *Woodley in the Nineteenth Century* (Reading Borough Council: Reading Libraries).

CHAPTER 2

COMING TO CURRICULUM

Extract from 'reconstructing aspects of a teacher's life'

Article in process

Extracts from a diary, 1973

1   For several years I have had a recurrent dream:

> It was the staff party and each member of staff was asked to entertain for fifteen minutes. The contributions were predictable – shop-windowing the various talents of a professional community. The music teacher played a short piece on the cello, the English teacher read some of his own poems, a group of teachers presented a short play highlighting many staffroom jokes and rumours, the head gave a short morale-boosting speech and so on – shades of my own school speech days. In the middle however, the lights had gone down and a rock 'n roll band started playing – heavy saxophone, subversive lyrics – some of the most troublesome pupils were playing on drums and guitar – three of the cutest girls were singing 'ooh-wahs' to the side and there singing was – oh my God – a teacher.
>
> After two songs – one a Little Richard, one a Larry Williams – the curtain closes. The school staff talk in embarrassed whispers. It is as if an alien has visited; the tribe close ranks. The authenticity and excitement of an alternative culture has been glimpsed – then rapidly purged from the memory. The staff party continues.

2   What I encounter in schools when I am wearing my W.C. (i.e. working class) culture or youth culture hats is a group of people (teachers) whose life-style contradicts or ignores those criteria most central to my existence.

Since beginning to join them as a group and since changing my life-style towards theirs, I have experienced a sense of anti-climax so monumental that it leaves me with an existence which feels hollow and worthless.

(Personal diary, 1973)

Life before teaching

I was born in 1943 in Woodley near Reading in Berkshire. My father was a Gas Fitter and my mother was at the time working in a munitions factory. My dad was the youngest of 13 children and was preceded by 12 sisters. His father appears on most of the children's birth certificates as 'unemployed labourer', but twice, in moments of fortune, as 'railway platelayer'. He died (in the old workhouse) before I was born. The mother took in laundry and lived to be 98 years old. On my mother's side, there were seven children. Her mother and father worked in a variety of jobs and in 1929 they were running a cafe in a working class district of Reading where my mum and dad met.

When I first went to school at the age of six I could not read. But I did find school a fascinating as well as disturbing experience. In my village you did not go to school gladly. I still remember that long walk to school on the first day and seeing one of my mates, Paul Sharp, clinging to the gatepost of his house and screaming blue murder as his mum tried to detach him and take him off to his first day of 'state edification' (an uncle's phrase!).

A few years ago, I tried to summarise my 'personal points of entry' into studies of schooling. So let me continue the story with an extended quote:

> My own parents viewed the achievement of 'their' Labour government after the war as most clearly demonstrated by the new schooling, which was offered to me and to other working people's children. Here, I was told, was the chance to learn, a chance to start to understand the world in which I was growing up.
>
> Yet, from the beginning I experienced odd contradictions, for while I was supposed to learn, most of the questions for which I sought answers were not on the school's agenda. They were, it is true, mainly childish questions but they turned on my understanding of the world at the time. They were things that we talked about at home: Why did my father work so hard? Why did I not see him in the mornings, or until late in the evening? Why did my mother go to work to 'support me'? Why were all the fields I played in being developed by more and larger 'council estates'? Why did we have to walk (or later, ride) more than three miles to school? Why was the school in a 'posh' village and not in my village? Why were the children from my village treated differently to the children from the immediate school locality?
>
> These then were aspects of my world; but why did we never talk about them let alone learn about it at school?
>
> My concerns about schooling increased when I went to secondary school. I passed the '11-plus' and was sent off to a grammar school (again, miles away from my village). All my friends now went to *our* village's school: a secondary modern. The long ride to the grammar school through the council estates wearing a blue 'Venetian' blazer and a hat with a yellow tassel cemented an incurable fascination with schooling. (The fascination lasted longer than the blazer and hat, which I took to packing in my bike saddle bag and putting on in the school's bike shed.)
>
> At the grammar school the curriculum made my sense of dichotomy at the primary school seem churlish. Here, not only was the content alien and dull but the very form of transmission and structure (the discursive formation no less) utterly bewildering. I experienced schooling as one learning a second language. A major factor in this cultural displacement was the school's curriculum.
>
> At the school I languished: taking nine 'O' level exams and failing eight. At fifteen I was at work in a crisp factory. Later however (through the intervention of one teacher) I returned to school and, though still burdened with a sense of alienation from the subject matter, began to perform the tests of rote learning and memory which were rewarded with exam passes.
>
> A degree (in Economic History) and a period of doctoral work (Irish immigrants in Victorian England) followed but in 1968 the continuing sense of dichotomy between 'life' and 'study' led me to abandon all thought of an academic career. The starting points were two articles – one by Basil Bernstein

in New Society, 'Open Schools, Open Society'; the other by Barry Sugarman on secondary school pupil cultures (*British Journal of Sociology*, 1967).

These articles showed me that there were modes of academic study where the everyday experiences of ordinary pupils and people might be investigated. In short, where my experience of life and my intellectual questions about that experience might be finally reconnected. But, just as before, I had had to abandon my intellectual interests to pass examinations; now once again, I had to abandon an academic career so that self and study might be reinvested with some degree of authenticity.

The decision to abandon my academic career was essentially a positive redirection. Once I had identified the kind of work epitomized in Bernstein and Sugarman, I saw the newly-organizing comprehensive schools as the place where I wanted to work. Here, my own class background and experience might engage with that of my pupils in a 'common language' of dialogue between teacher and taught. For the new generation of pupils from working homes there might be something beyond the pervasive alienation I had experienced at school.

These then, were the hopes I set off with as I left my working class home in a Berkshire village to settle in another village in Leicestershire and begin teaching in a 'comprehensive school'.

(Goodson, 1988)

One point that is not sufficiently covered in this account is my increasing commitment to a youth culture focussing on a general hedonism and immersion in pop music. This commitment – as the aforementioned Sugarman article noted – often went hand-in-hand with the rejection of grammar schools by working class students. At the time of my teenage years, 1956–62, Rock 'n Roll was a major presence in Reading – The Rolling Stones were a local band (Marianne Faithful, Mick Jagger's girlfriend, went to a local school), the Who and the Animals played there regularly. They and a variety of local bands began to develop a brand of indigenous Rock, which later emerged as a force in much of the Western world. When I moved to university in London my interest continued (coincidentally Mick Jagger was at the London School of Economics at the same time and I remember several good evenings in the Three Tuns pub with him). I spent a lot of time at the Marquee Club watching bands like The Who perfect their art and would spend weekends at the Ricky Tick Club in Windsor where Eric Clapton and Jimmy Page (then with the Five Dimensions) would play.

On moving to Leicester, I encountered another vigorous Rock scene. The Il Rondo Club was superb and many national and local bands played there. Two local bands, Family and Showaddywaddy, emerged from this scene to become widely popular. The local pub in Countesthorpe, the Railway Tavern, had a wonderfully stocked jukebox and here in the evening working class youth culture of the sort as I had known since the age of 13 held the stage.

Teaching in Leicestershire

So the story reaches a small village in the flat plains south of Leicester. I had seen the following advertisement in the *Times Educational Supplement* and applied for the job. At the time I knew nothing of the significance of the school. I remember going up to the interview in Leicester with my girlfriend at the London School of Economics, Anna Bicat. I was interviewed at 2.30 p.m. by Tim McMullen and

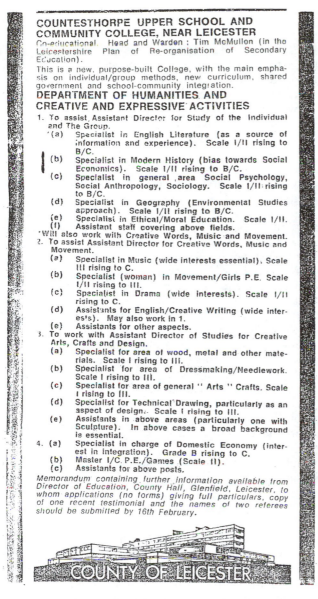

Times Educational Supplement Advertisement (7 January 1970).

Mike Armstrong. They had obviously just had a convivial lunch in County Hall and the interview went pretty well. When Anna and I got back to our flat in Hampstead there was a telegram waiting (I still have it – historical sources, item 203!) which said 'would like to appoint you. Please telephone acceptance'. I loved their style and immediately phoned back.

As the papers about the school came through I began to realise this was an unusual and highly innovative school (McMullen, 1970).

Countesthorpe College

The main aims

1   For those of school age: to give them the widest possible set of abilities, achievements and attitudes to enable them to find those actions – intellectual, emotional, social – that will bring the greatest satisfactions to their life as adults which will lie between the years 1975–2025.

2   For those who have left school: to provide opportunities for them, both as individuals and groups, to find greater satisfactions from the life they lead now and will lead in the future.

   The full interpretation of these general aims will be worked out by the staff, students and community over the years; however, certain considerations are clear from the beginning:

   i   It will be necessary to fit people to take part in the 'superstructure' of society – the economic and political section – education must be appropriate to rapidly changing technological and social patterns, to a world where industry and commerce demand increasingly high-grade technologists, middle-grade technicians, executives, planners and administrators rather than skilled, semi-skilled, or unskilled workers; to an increasing demand for 'service' occupations of all kinds, involving mainly human relations; to a world where, for perhaps the majority, the length of time spent on 'work' and the interest of it will decline sharply.

   ii   It will be as necessary – or even more so – to fit people for a richer individual and group life outside the 'superstructure' of society, both because economically this is now possible and also because pressures show that we are increasingly dissatisfied with a purely 'technocratic' approach to society; that fewer people will get satisfaction from work; and that work will occupy a smaller part and less time in our lives.

Both of these 'directions' imply a re-examination of, and a change in, curriculum, methods, authority relationships, and organisation.

General lines of development

1   The development of the college as a community in which the Upper School students, the staff – professional and others – and the adults from the local community work together rather than in compartments. This implies: 'participatory' rather than 'authoritarian' making of decisions; the blurring of the lines separating school and community and an actual mixing of adults and students in an extended school and community day.

2   The re-thinking and selection of the curriculum in terms of its relevance. This may involve: different content for certain subjects, for example, maths, physics; development of interdisciplinary problem-based rather than subject-based work in some areas – particularly in humanities and creative arts; the introduction of new specialisms perhaps as parts of interdisciplinary areas, for example, sociology, psychology and the disappearance of – or considerable lessening of importance of – others.

3   A re-thinking of organisation in terms of who makes decisions and at what level, and a new academic organisation in 'areas' rather than in subject departments.

4   A re-thinking of the methods by which students learn and the size of the groups into which they are organised, with an emphasis on more individual or small group learning, more 'independent' time available for student-chosen activities, more co-operation between teachers, and more use of new media.

5   The development of an organisation which will allow the development of individuals along lines suited to them personally and at a speed appropriate to them without classifying children more than is essential into 'able' and 'less able' groups.

6   A pastoral organisation which will be the *main* contact for parents by which an overall responsible master or mistress controls approximately 200 students helped by a team of tutors who also teach the students for at least one subject.

7   The development of a form of government both within the school section and the wider community, by which, those who take part in the life of the college, determine the *policy* to be adopted (McMullen, 1970).

As the character of the school began to emerge I could see why the references from my tutors might have helped in getting me appointed to the school. The references had been clear about strengths and weaknesses:

> Mr Goodson's great strength is his ability to make relationships with individual pupils. He treats children seriously when it is important to do so; he listens to what they say and encourages them to say a great deal, even when they would normally be reluctant. He is also capable of indicating that their standards are not what they should be without arousing antagonism. He has a strong sense of humour and can banter with pupils without losing their respect.

Although 'he was a popular student and has a great deal of charm':

> He can sometimes appear off-hand to people who 'go by the book'. He offended one or two teachers at Hammersmith in this way: but it is worth emphasizing that the 'injured' parties felt threatened by the success of Mr. Goodson's teaching methods which had involved pupils in a manner never achieved by their own lecturing techniques.
>
> (*Education Tutor*, 1970)

This emerging pedagogy was practised in a direct grant school in Hammersmith, Latymer Upper, where I undertook my 'teaching practice' for the PGCE at the Institute of Education. A very conventional, conservative school. Yet the ingredients of a pedagogy that was more consciously defined at Countesthorpe are quite clear, I think. In fact, I am surprised at how prophetic the reference is. Moreover I had assumed that my informal style and use of humour had in a sense 'emerged' at Countesthorpe. Clearly this was not the case, although the open environment there and the general ethos must have encouraged me to 'come out' more. Lifestyle and pedagogy became interdependent.

Early on at the school an ethnographic researcher spent some time watching a few of us teaching. He captured the essence of my pedagogy at the time with great economy. I still marvel at how quickly he could see that which so many pupils sensed but so few educators could understand:

> As I watch him teaching it does seem to me that there is something about him different to other teachers, even the other jokesters like Liz. Ivor doesn't seem to *represent* school like other teachers do. He gives the impression of simply

being there because it's a job. In some subtle and indefinable way he conveys a kind of insolence that pupils frequently convey, but never teachers. There is something confident, arrogant and deeply irreverent about the way he acts. He seems to carry no responsibility for the ethos and culture of teaching. It's not just that he swears, most teachers in the school do and some much more. Not that he jokes because other teachers joke. Not his dress or appearance which is conventional alongside many of the staff. It's a quality of presence, something in his total personal style.

(Walker, 1973)

He likewise captured my lifestyle. I seem to remember the poor devil had to sleep several times on a mattress in a room he later described in his report to the Ford Foundation (so much for life 'in the field'):

Ivor shares the flat with two (?) other teachers. His room is fairly chaotic. An enormous hi-fi system (much admired by his pupils who are often found using it). A collector's collection of rock records (no jazz) of which 10 or 11 LP's seemed in more or less constant use. Magazines piled up around the room, the most used of which was *Let it Rock* which contained several of Ivor's articles. Books on local industrial history (Ivor was a joint author of one), on Russia and a scattering of sociology (Bernstein's *Class, Codes and Control*, Nell Keddie). Most of the floor space was taken up by an old mattress, the rest by socks, a tennis racquet, gym shoes (once white?), a big trunk, assorted letters (one applying for the post of 'geography teacher'). On the fading wallpaper a Beatles poster and a school report made out in Ivor's name and signed by a pupil ('Could do better if he tried harder').

(Walker, 1973)

But how do personal lifestyle and pedagogy interact? What of the person carries over into the teacher role? Here the theme of indivisibility emerges:

Often teachers do feel the contradictions between themselves as teachers and themselves as persons. Hence the teacher who is friendly in the playground or in the corridor but freezes in the classroom, or the teacher who allows a relaxed atmosphere in some parts of the lessons but who knows when to be serious. We detect nothing of this in Ivor and nor do those who know him better than we do. He seems the same in almost any situation.

(Walker, 1973)

In a series of notes and letters written in 1973, I tried to spell out why I favoured such a pedagogy and what was missing in this and other ethnographic accounts:

I think you have to spell out much more about youth culture. It looks just like a red-herring that you just drop in.

Surely the important point is that for my whole generation (and yours!) youth culture was the way into a whole radical alternative lifestyle. It genuinely acted to break down class and other stereotypes.

Now given that this is so. Given that I subscribe to that lifestyle. It should follow that if teachers who have experienced youth culture carry that over into their teaching then normal stereotypes might dissolve.

Youth culture and WC (working class) culture are broadly similar in whole areas. This is particularly true, I would say, in reference to authority.

Therefore a teacher who has experienced youth culture *and* carries it over into his teaching (whether he or she be a week-end beatnik or a life-styler!) should find himself well-placed and in empathy with WC kids.

You see it's interesting that you mention Lennon and Best – they typify one strand in youth culture and WC culture – the *rebel* (in this case with a cause I think!).

I find it hard to believe that many WC kids will take teachers seriously who take school seriously. I mean this solely in the sense of 'image'. Something you've not touched on – and yet it's part of the vocabulary of many WC kids.

Schools are 'hate objects' in the internal language of the WC. You go to them in much the same spirit you go to the factory – by the time you are a teenager that is. You learn to hate every hypocrisy and fallacy that they stand for. A teacher who fully identifies with the school therefore encounters a similar response.

(Letter to Walker, 1973)

Two other notes I found on old bits of paper from 1972 spell out more of the approach and pinpoint my predominant concerns at this stage in my life in teaching.

For the WC child

1   The person comes before the role in deciding if you learn from a teacher. Learning will only go on if the person is accessible and acceptable. It is the first threshold.
2   The person can be adjudged at a number of levels. Certain factors seem to predispose the kids in liking teachers.

  (a)   An ability to joke and be joked with – a classic WC 'testing' mechanism (Scwartz calls it 'sounding' among black youth in New York).
  (b)   An irreverence, rebelliousness like their heroes.
  (c)   A general acceptance of laughs and fun as essential ingredients of life.

There are other symbols which might imply an empathy with the culture based on ways of walking and moving and acknowledgements of 'distancing' in certain defined situations (e.g. the teacher in the lunchtime disco).

Since the teachers' role is tied up with the commodity he is purveying much depends on the commodity. Most find few points of reference or relevance in his 'subject'. So the only way for the WC child to come to terms with school is through the teacher's own person divorced from his role. Only in the relationship that he has with his teacher can the child explore the alien world of the school. The teacher must exist and define a social context and relationship which the child finds sympathetic. This implies the teacher is sufficiently aware of the child's culture to include a number of familiar symbols which can render the world of classroom sufficiently familiar to the child.

1   What I think one is saying is that the first stage in the learning process is the establishment of a 'knowing' relationship. The socio-pastoral threshold precedes the academic threshold. Though for most WC kids that relationship is assumed, suspended in expectation of instrumentality.
2   Without this relationship, *whatever* the pedagogy, transmission or transfor- mation, there will be undue numbers of failures. Simply because they never

'came to terms' with what the teacher was about. So what he elicits will be nothing to do with the child's potential.

3   But the relationship is not just the prerequisite for transmission. It should by its establishment affect the nature of that transmission. The critical point is that at which the child ENGAGES, from then on exploration is cooperative. Learning becomes a possibility (Personal notes 1973–74).

The most obvious point to emerge from my journals, scribblings, and recorded conversations is what we might call my '*chronology of concern*' or '*sequence of concern*'. Quite clearly, in the first few years at the school, my concerns were primarily classroom focussed – how do we engage children in learning, particularly the majority of the children who were from working class homes. In finding my feet in teaching, in carving out a 'style', these were the first concerns. At the heart of the process of becoming a teacher for me was this question of pedagogic orientation. But I believe the question of pedagogic orientation carried an implicit amalgam of other values and positions. Pedagogic orientation clearly, I think, derived a good deal from personal strengths and weaknesses, as well as crucial matters of background such as social class and regional origins. But most importantly, I believe questions of pedagogic orientation crucially anticipate and circumscribe subsequent judgements about styles of curriculum, school governance and organisation right down to basic political judgements such as which sorts of schools, which types of pupils should be chosen and sponsored.

I should note that I am not here concerned to present evidence as to the quality of my classroom practice: about whether I was a good or bad teacher. My concern is to characterise my evolving *view* of pedagogic style and orientation and the juxtaposition of personal style and pedagogic style. The argument I wish to make is that this pedagogic orientation and interdependent sense of personal lifestyle is a crucially important consideration in the styles of curriculum, governance and schooling to which one gives allegiance. In short, in the interplay between personal lifestyle and pedagogic orientation there are many of the origins of teacher predispositions. Predispositions that are to support particular versions of subjects of syllabuses, curriculum projects, assessment procedures, as well as administrative decisions, political decisions, and issues of pastoral and community concern.

Coming to curriculum

In the first years in teaching then my major concern was clearly with 'classroom matters' – with developing a pedagogic style and orientation. But in developing this pedagogic orientation, I was implicitly developing and furthering an allegiance to styles of curriculum, assessment, and schooling.

In part, this 'coming to curriculum', this requirement to examine and question existing styles of curriculum was part of an institutional search that went on at Countesthorpe in the early years. For if the radical relationships and pedagogies pioneered at the school were to survive, new styles of curriculum and assessment were necessary. Hence even probationary teachers like myself were involved in drawing up new syllabuses for examination at Mode 3.[1] A primary concern in developing curriculum was the need to *engage* students – as we have seen this was my major concern in the classroom, so it was inevitable that it would feed through into curriculum planning. In the classroom, the 'mixed ability' classroom, we sought to involve *all* students – so we sought a curriculum that reflected this 'comprehensive' intention.

Writing in November 1973, I tried out a few of my tentative ideas: for instance on the issue of student autonomy.

> After these generalised prophetic justifications, a final justification is that student autonomy may serve to solve some of the educational problems facing contemporary education. The problems of teaching mixed ability groups from differing backgrounds are many and various. Most of these problems, however, are connected with the lack of motivation of students to learn and, closely allied, the questionable relevance of what they are asked to learn. As we have seen, even after new curriculum developments, teachers still consider that they should control every aspect of the student's learning situation. This total monopolisation by teachers I believe to be a major cause of the sense of alienation and disinterest among students. The Monopoly must be broken for student interest to be engaged. To take one instance: teachers are increasingly aware that 'relevance' is an important criterion for consideration in school studies. Teachers are divided from their students by a fast-widening generational gulf and, normally, by the broad abyss of class differences. In this light it is surely manifestly absurd for the teacher to insist on deciding which things are going to appeal to the students on the basis of relevance. Relevance is only one of a number of reasons for learning but, as with many other things, students are better placed than teachers to make judgements upon it. One is not saying that the student should be given the right to decide everything about the learning situation but that the present teacher monopoly of such decisions should be broken. What is needed is a view of learning which sees it as a negotiable, collaborative exercise between teacher and student. The curriculum can then be seen as something that evolves from, on one side, the students' demand for something relevant, useful and interesting, and on the other, the teachers' demand for something which broadens the students' horizons and offers entrance to new ways of understanding.
>
> (Goodson, 1973a, p. 8)

The 'students' demands for something relevant did however lead to finite, relatively clear, clusters of interest. One area was their interest in developments within their own community. Major changes were happening in Leicester and the surrounding countryside at this time and the students were eager to know what was happening and to investigate the causes of change. This led on to series of urban and community studies investigations, which I described in some detail at the time (Goodson, 1973b).

My perception of matters at the time was evident in the articles I wrote. These were pioneering comprehensive schools – our chance was to define new curricula which engaged all pupils and could lead towards 'education of all'. I believed passionately (and of course still do) in the right of *all* children to a full education. I also believed the rhetoric of comprehensive schooling, the provision of equal educational opportunities for all abilities and social classes. Given this (no doubt naive) belief the task before us was clear. We had to define a new range of school curricula and new examination syllabuses that would cover content and themes which engaged all pupils. My own involvement in defining new curricula in urban and community studies was part of this optimistic project of re-definition.

When I moved to take up a new post as Head of the Faculty Humanities in Milton Keynes, I spent a great deal of time defining new curricula in this way. A new 'O' level in Community Studies was defined and accepted by the examination board in the first year. My outline plan for the Faculty was fairly explicit about my curriculum values at this time.

The prerequisite for involvement in the academic work of the faculty, or in the community within and without the school, is a sense of personal confidence and dignity. Hence we place the student and his experience at the centre of the learning process; we acknowledge that we cannot teach without him learning, cannot devise objectives without considering his motivation.

The Faculty of Humanities has two main objectives:

1   In giving the student a sense of their own uniqueness and dignity to aid their self-knowledge and self confidence. This requires:

   (a) some exploration of the student's own life experience so far; and
   (b) the use of learning strategies which allow the student some autonomy in directing their own learning.

2   To involve the students in the emerging communities of Milton Keynes and the school. To aid them in identifying with their new environment and in using its communal facilities.

   This presumes exploration of the communities of Milton Keynes and district at a number of levels.

   The learning strategies associated with these broad objectives involve two kinds of skills:

   (a) Social skills, for example an understanding of the concept of 'sharing'.
   (b) Academic skills.

The Faculty would hope to take a major part in 'training for life' on the campus and in the emerging community outside and in giving meaning to the underlying philosophy of sharing (Goodson, 1974).

But by 1974–75 it was becoming increasingly clear that the new curricula defined in pursuit of 'education for all' were meeting great opposition. The Black Papers, first launched in 1969, began to work through a critique of the new initiatives and a call for a return to traditional subjects and teaching. The new curriculum initiatives pioneered in these new comprehensive schools were not of course without flaws and inadequacies, but by this time it was abundantly clear that we were up against major structural barriers.

In a way I believe we were pursuing the rhetoric of 'comprehensive education', 'education for all', to its logical conclusion. But we were to learn that logic and politics collided fairly early on in the proceedings. Curriculum and assessment became the terrain where 'education for all' collided with 'O' levels for the top 20 per cent'. In short, when egalitarian practice collided with inherited meritocratic intent. In 1976 the Ruskin Speech by a Labour Prime Minister, James Callaghan, made it conclusively clear that the comprehensive experiment was not to be seriously pursued. Subsequent events have of course confirmed this.

My increasing sense of personal frustration in the face of this political restructuring led me in 1975 to join a project at Sussex University concerned with urban and community environmental education. A chance in short to explore in more depth my growing interest in promoting the new curricula I had defined in the two comprehensive schools in which I had worked. But the project gave me a chance to do much more than this. It allowed me to study in detail (for a PhD) the politics of curriculum change. In the first year, I sat down to write up my beliefs about curriculum and my dawning awareness of links between knowledge and control. My first paper derived from an article I had finished whilst teaching in 1974. In this I had still seemed optimistic about curriculum change and comprehensive education (this optimism/naivety was a strong feature in all my journal entries until mid-1974).

> In contemporary English secondary schools perhaps the most common definition of curriculum is as that 'package of courses of study offered by the school'; the curriculum is something 'evolved by the staff'. The definition of the package which constitutes the curriculum is undertaken by the head, initially influenced by a variety of factors ranging from ideologies to examinations to interest groups. The individual teacher stands as the receiver of this curriculum package: his task will normally be to teach just one aspect of the package. He is handed a syllabus, given some classes and allocated a number of periods on the timetable. In short, the curriculum plan is transmitted to the teacher who is expected to receive and carry out the decisions made about the curriculum by those above him.
>
> This process is repeated in the way that the child receives the curriculum. He is given his 'package of courses', told when he will do what, and with whom. Similarly, at the classroom level, the child is told how each course will be organized, what content he will be asked to cover and by what method he will learn it. In the classroom we see the 'teacher's curriculum' in operation: all the decisions and definitions about the curriculum are made by the teachers *before* direct transmission to the child.
>
> The assumptions upon which the teachers' curriculum are based are increasingly in conflict with a whole range of developments in contemporary society and education. At all levels of society, traditional authority figures are under question: parents, clergymen, politicians, managers, but none more so than the teacher. 'No longer does student response depend upon a mutually acceptable relationship between the teacher and taught.' But as the comprehensive system spreads, the problems of the teachers' authority become more than just an aspect of general societal questioning. The teachers' curriculum depends upon a social contract between teacher and taught which reflects a mutual instrumentality. Comprehensive schools contain pupil populations that cover a broad range of abilities and inclinations which must be reflected in a spectrum of potential instrumental relationships. Faced with this diversity the teachers' curriculum would seem, even in theory, far too simplistic; the mutual instrumentality, the single social contract on which the teachers' curriculum depends, will never exist in the comprehensive school even were the intention there.
>
> Fundamentally the teachers' curriculum seems totally out of spirit with emergent patterns of authority and schooling. Moreover the very nature of the knowledge transmitted through the teachers' curriculum is a source of further conflict because of its class-based and obsolescent characteristics. In this situation the choice would appear to be between using more repressive methods in school in an attempt to reverse the emerging patterns, and testing new curriculum models.
>
> (Goodson, 1975)

By 1976 this optimistic posture had been redefined to a much more defensive tone – ruminating about 'the substantial forces maintaining transmission as the dominant pedagogy' (see Chapter 3).

Making connections

The argument in this paper begins to make links between my involvement in pedagogic and curriculum reform, my growing frustration at the more general obstruction of reform efforts and an emerging understanding of patterns of social and political organisation and control in British society in the mid-1970s. This emerging sense of the link between knowledge and control was of course partially derived from the current work in the new Sociology of Knowledge but it also, as we have seen, was driven by a strong sense of personal quest. Interestingly a review I did at the time of Whitty and Young's *Society, State and Schooling* speculated on this juxtaposition commenting on their contention that:

> Neither the old-Left, nor the Fabian social democrats, seem to take seriously the suggestion that the educational policies they support merely provide more efficient means of maintaining the status quo. Certainly neither group seems to have recognised that we need to examine 'what counts as education', and thus the way in which prevailing definitions of it sustain just that form of society which those on the Left, albeit in varying degrees wish to change.

I wrote:

> To any working-class person who has experienced grammar school and university education (in this case both as child and teacher) this contention strikes one with all the force that a statement of the obvious can muster. As Williams noted nearly two decades ago, when the University Local Examinations Boards that led to 'O' and 'A' levels were first established they were titled 'Middle class examinations'. Significantly it was this examination system which survived and that was built into the fabric of secondary education. The alternative tradition developed by the working class in the mechanics Institutes and in adult education stressed all those things that the middle class examinations of abstract and classical knowledge played down-the relation of school knowledge to contemporary life, the students role in choosing and directing study, equality between general discussion and expert tuition.
>
> Anyone scrutinising contemporary comprehensive schools will find this alternative tradition alive and well. Unfortunately a closer look will show that it is only the 'less able' of 'CSE and non-examination' students who receive the alternative curriculum. The 'O' level and 'A' level examinations continue to stress precisely those traditional views of knowledge derived from the grammar school. So, if it's the working class alternative view of knowledge that turns you on take your place in the CSE and non-examination stream, otherwise take the schizophrenic route through 'O's and 'A's, BA's and PhD's away from home and kinship, away from roots and class.
>
> (Goodson, 1979)

My sense of biography was no doubt heightened by the teaching I undertook at the University of Sussex in 1975–77. I was asked to teach a 'contextual' course on 'working class lifestyles'. The course was optional but attracted a large number of students, mostly working class. In the course the students were encouraged to write up their reminiscences of life and schooling in line with the course rhetoric 'that the most important resource will be the life histories of course participants'. The course forced me to think long and hard about class, culture and curriculum and since I was at the time developing a scheme for my doctoral work the two tasks converged. I certainly realised that my own views about pedagogy and curriculum were projected through a prism of social class that had much in common with other working class peoples' experiences. I came across Albert Hunt's interesting book about his working class experience of schooling.

Hunt blamed above all the teacher's assumption that because he is deeply involved with a particular subject that subject must be of value and interest to everybody else. So a subject is placed at the 'centre of all education' – and a failure to make that subject come to life becomes the teachers' failure. But in Hunt's experience, as in mine and that of my students at Sussex, initially it was the subjects themselves which ensured nothing came to life:

> Virtually nothing in the whole of my formal educational experience had ever connected with me in a way that involved me – me as a person. I had feelings, convictions, commitments to ideas and people. None of these seemed related to my work...Everything existed for me in fragments.
>
> (Hunt, 1976)

Hence I began to develop a broader sense of working class experience of curriculum. Yet the poignancy of these emerging personal insights developing in Britain in 1976–77 was in many ways too bitter to bear. For just as one grasped the full alienating potential of traditional subjects for working class students, so the political pendulum began to secure rehabilitation of these very subjects.

Again by a twist of biographical fate I was able to watch this at first hand. I had been asked in 1976 to act as Chairman of a Subject Advisory Committee for one of the main Examining Boards. By chance it was the same Board that accepted my student-centred Community Studies 'O' level at Mode 3. Yet I was an observer at a committee meeting where that very Mode 3 examination was closed down – the reasons given were twofold: it was not 'cost effective' to have so many Mode 3's and there had been a 'proliferation of subject titles' (an argument that later was used to underpin the arguments in favour of an National Curriculum). So on the grounds of such apparent pragmatism, such expediency, a whole sub-culture of pedagogy and curriculum was effectively purged.

My commitment to my doctoral studies deepened as my work on the origins of school subjects and on the fate of urban and environmental studies as a innovatory new curriculum area became focussed. I was therefore able to re-focus my investigations on the politics of curriculum in a way that would offer illumination to my own experience of schooling and that of my class. Since that time I have spent most of my academic life searching for a more finely grained understanding of the history and politics of curriculum.

But the catalyst in this emerging exploration of the world of schooling has been my lived experience in school. Without this experience I believe my scholasticism would be arid and unproductive. Consistently I seek connections back to the life stories of colleagues and cohorts and to my own experience of schooling as a child and as a teacher, for it is there that the process of 'coming to know' began.

Note

1   Mode 3 exams were those where the teachers played a central part in defining the syllabus and conducting the assessment.

References

Education Tutor, Institute of Education, University of London, 1970.
Goodson, I.F., 1973a, Curriculum Development and Student Autonomy, *Transcript*, No. 2, November.
Goodson, I.F., 1973b, Developing Contexts for Autonomous Learning, *Forum*, May.
Goodson, I.F., 1974, Man in Time and Place, Outline Plan, Stantonbury Campus.
Goodson, I.F., 1975, The Teacher's Curriculum and The New Reformation, *Journal of Curriculum Studies*, November, pp. 150–161.
Goodson, I.F., 1979, Review of M. Young and G. Whitty (eds), Society, State and Schooling. In *Socialism and Education*, March.
Goodson, I.F., 1988, Personal Points of Entry. Notes for I.F. Goodson, *The Making of Curriculum* (Falmer: London, New York, and Philadelphia, PA).
Hunt, A., 1976, Hopes of Great Happenings (Eyre Methuen). See Goodson, I.F. – 1987, Introduction, *School Subjects and Curriculum Change* (Falmer: London, New York, and Philadelphia, PA).
Letters to Rob Walker, 3 March 1973.
McMullen, T. (Probable author), 1970. Briefing papers, Countesthorpe College.
Personal diary, 1973.
Personal notes circa, 1973–74.
Times Education Supplement, 7 January 1970.
Walker, Rob, 1973, Teaching that's a Joke, SAFARI Occasional Paper, No. 4, University of East Anglia.

CHAPTER 3

TOWARDS AN ALTERNATIVE PEDAGOGY

J. Kincheloe and S. Steinberg (eds), *Unauthorized Methods: Strategies for Critical Teaching*, London: Routledge, 1998

Current classroom practice is largely derived from the belief that the teacher's basic task is the 'transmission of knowledge'. At one level this statement is obviously true – any pedagogy is concerned with the transmission of values and ways of knowing – but at the level of rhetoric 'transmission' has come to characterize a particular view of practice and an associated view of knowledge as a commodity. The distinction between transmission as an aspect of pedagogy and transmission *as* pedagogy is in this sense crucial. What may seem a superficial confusion in educationists' language might mark a deeper confusion of considerable importance. Implicit in the notion of transmission is a one-way communication; it is to 'pass on, hand on' (*Concise Oxford Dictionary*) knowledge *from* the teacher *to* the pupil. In this paper I take 'transmission' as characterizing any educational incident which sets the learning of knowledge *previously* planned or defined by the teacher as the basic objective. In thus characterizing transmission I am echoing practice derived from this model in that curricula and lessons centre on the prior definition of knowledge *for* transmission. The transmission pedagogue works to defend this prior definition against interactive redefinition.

By this definition a broad spectrum of teaching styles – 'chalk and talk', 'question and answer', 'discovery projects', 'discussion', 'individualized worksheets' – might be seen as following the transmission model. Hence in 'chalk and talk' the teacher will have decided beforehand what content, concepts or skills he wants to get across: in the 'question and answer' he will have decided what answers are the right ones that he is after: in 'discovery' he will know what he is aiming to help the child discover. In all cases the style of the encounter and the outcome are previously prescribed.

This chapter will argue that if the intention of teaching is to involve *all* pupils in learning then transmission, with its dependence on the viability of pre-planned educational incidents and outcomes, is particularly ill suited. In arguing this way I am not wishing to imply that pupil/teacher interaction should go on without using previously defined ideas, material and conceptual structures, or that at no stage should ideas and content be transmitted from teacher to pupil. I am, however, arguing that it is misguided to set transmission as the basic role of the classroom teacher.

The substantial forces maintaining transmission as the dominant pedagogy only partly explain why the development of radical alternatives has largely gone in default. In spite of the enormous validity of its critique of transmission teaching, child-centred progressivism remains for most a negative creed: sure that to transmit to an unwilling child is pointless, but unsure what to do instead. As a result, the 'failure' of the transmission classroom often becomes the 'problem' of the progressive teacher. By only reacting negatively to transmission pedagogy, progressivism is in danger of becoming an extension of it.

It is time to move on from the negativity of progressivism to the definition of a positive alternative pedagogy. To do so might transform educational debate from the present 'no contest' between ideologies which both faithfully reproduce the social system into a dialectic concerned with educational priorities. Much is to be gained by teachers exploring the possibilities of changing their classroom practice, but to do so they need to move beyond the potent but frustrated plea: 'OK, but what's the alternative?' This article pursues a tentative search for an answer.

Classroom learning

The assumption which underpins transmission pedagogy is that what is decided in the pre-active context can be made to work in the interactive context (Jackson, 1968, p. 152; see also Keddie, 1971). I want to question this assumption and argue that what is decided at the pre-active stage of curriculum planning is commonly contradicted and subverted at the interactive stage.

The assumption that pre-active decisions can and should be made to work in the interactive context is inevitably allied to the belief that learning consists of the child coming to accept and understand the teacher's expositions and definitions. In arguing that pre-active decisions seldom stand up in the interactive context I am by implication arguing for a new model of classroom learning. Modern studies of learning show how information is idiosyncratically processed by each learner. Recognition of the uniqueness of individual processing and of the variability of interests is the prerequisite of any understanding of classroom life and of any move to describe a new pedagogy. The new pedagogy would seek to define a strategy which sensitized the teacher to individual processes and interests and positioned his response to these at the centre of his teaching: broad collective plans and decisions would be ancillary to this central response.

In many ways the new pedagogy would be seeking to formalize at the theoretical (pre-active) level what already sometimes goes on at classroom (interactive) level: as we have argued, transmission is commonly subverted in the classroom. Studies of classroom interaction offer boundless evidence of such recurrent subversion. Philip Jackson's studies of *Life in Classrooms* are widely regarded for their authentic flavour:

> As typically conducted, teaching is an opportunistic process. That is to say, neither the teacher nor his students can predict with any certainty exactly what will happen next. Plans are forever going awry and unexpected opportunities for the attainment of educational goals are constantly emerging. The seasoned teacher seizes upon these opportunities and uses them to his and his students' advantage . . . in the classroom as elsewhere, the best laid schemes suffer their usual fate.
>
> (Jackson, 1968, p. 166)

The unpredictability of classroom life described by Jackson explains the most common classroom phenomena: one group of children working along the lines the teacher has laid down (e.g. listening, answering or filling in the worksheet); some just going through the motions by copying out bits or doodling, and another group thoroughly alienated, talking among themselves, staring out of window, thinking of last night at the disco.

This range of responses is what most teachers will readily recognize as the 'reality' of their classrooms. The myth of transmission has it that it is only the teacher's inadequacy that explains why more children are not working along pre-determined lines. I am arguing that the recurrent failure to involve so many children in class-room learning can be most convincingly explained by fundamental flaws in the transmission model. A pedagogy so firmly situated in the pre-active vacuum can only expect partial success, given the variabilities of interactive reality; no pedagogy so all – dependent on prediction could hope to encompass the diversity of the classroom.

Even more disturbingly, the fatal flaws of transmission pedagogy mean that teachers' expectations inevitably come to fit the partial successes which are transmission's inevitable achievement:

> The most wasteful and destructive aspect of our present educational system is the set of expectations about student learning each teacher brings to the begin-ning of a new course or term. The instructor expects a third of his pupils to learn what is taught, a third to learn less well, and a third to fail or just 'get by'. These expectations are transmitted to the pupils through school grading policies and practices and through the methods and materials of instruction. Students quickly learn to act in accordance with them, and the final sorting through the grading process approximates the teacher's original expectations. A pernicious self-fulfilling prophecy has been created.
>
> (Bloom, 1971, p. 47)

If the involvement of all students is to be our aim, and this article takes that view, then a pedagogy firmly situated in the interactive reality of the classroom is required: a pedagogy that accepts and works with the individual interests and processes which are at the centre of classroom learning.

Alternative theories and practice

In discussing an alternative pedagogy I am conscious that I am merely presenting a pedagogy in embryo, yet it is an embryo with a long history. Central to an alternative theory is the focus of investigation upon the *individual* process of learning. Each individual pupil exhibits the most positive response in the learning process when the information being dealt with somehow 'meshes' with what he is interested in. 'A child's education (as opposed to schooling) can only proceed through the pursuit of his interests since it is only these which are of intrinsic value', and fur-ther, 'whatever enables him to appreciate and understand his interest more fully and to pursue it more actively and effectively is education' (Wilson, 1971, p. 67). Over half a century ago Dewey was similarly disposed to focus on the individual experiences of the pupil. He saw: the need of reinstating into experience the subject matter of the studies, or branches of learning. It must be restored to the experience from which it has been abstracted. It needs to be psychologized, turned over, trans-lated into the immediate and individual experiencing within which it has its origin and significance... (Dewey, 1971, p. 22). If the subject matter of the lessons be such as to have an appropriate place within the expanding consciousness of the child, if it grows out of his own past doing, thinking and suffering and grows into application in further achievements and receptivities, then no device or trick or method has to be restored to in order to enlist 'interest'. The psychologized is of interest – that is, it is placed in the whole of conscious life so that it shares the work of that life. But the externally presented material, conceived and generated in standpoints and attitudes remote from the child, and developed in motives alien to him, has no such place of its own. Hence the recourse to adventitious leverage to push it in, to factitious drill to drive it in, to artificial bribe to lure it in (Dewey, 1971, p. 27).

Acknowledgement of the crucial role of each individual pupil's interests and experience in the learning process is only a starting point for exploring a possible new pedagogy. Certainly such acknowledgement could be, and often is, used in amplifying transmission method pedagogies. 'This regard for children's interests in teaching has more relevance to the method of teaching than to its content... Children's existing interests can be used as a starting point from which they can be led on to take an interest in realms of whose existence they never dreamt' (Peters and Hirst, 1970, pp. 37–38). By this argument the child's interest can be used as a method but has little relevance to content: the teacher defines the content and uses the child's interest to transmit it to him. Acknowledgement of the importance of the child's experience and interests *and* acceptance of these as valid knowledge content in classroom learning can lead to two distinctive alternative pedagogies. The first pedagogy, child-centred progressivism, would centre on the child's interest, *and* in doing so conclude that the pedagogy should aim to allow him to personally direct his own learning. W.H. Kilpatrick's views are closest to advocating this pedagogy; for him education starts where the child is so as to capitalize on the child's personally directed activity springing from his real interest:

> It is what pupils do of themselves that brings the best learning results, both in direct learning and in concomitant learnings. We can thus say, paradoxically, that the teacher's aim is to give as little help as possible, that is, to give the least degree of direct help consistent with the best personal work on the part of the pupils.
>
> (Kilpatrick, 1951, p. 307)

A similar style of pedagogy is described by Charity James:

> at its most elementary, if a group of students is engaged on Interdisciplinary Enquiry, within the area of investigation (say, some aspect of life in a techno-logical society, or of human growth and development in childhood and adolescence) students formulate the questions they want to answer, identify the problems which they want to solve, create hypotheses for their solutions, test them and revise the hypotheses.
>
> (James, 1968, pp. 65–66)

For James, as for Kilpatrick, the teacher is seen 'as a consultant to students in their self-directed enterprise' (James, 1968, p. 65).

Whilst sympathetic to the emphasis of Kilpatrick and James, I think the pedagogy they recommend is over-dependent (one might say solely dependent) on 'what pupils do themselves' (Kilpatrick, 1951, p. 307). Such an emphasis seems to be ill suited to the interactive character of classroom learning in two ways:

1   A major part of the rationale for classroom learning must surely turn on those aspects the pupil learns in interaction with his peers and his teacher. This interactive dimension in learning can aid the development of the pupil's

interests and ideas into other areas from those he might independently explore. Learning associated with the kind of pedagogy Kilpatrick and James advocate seems to miss most of the potential present in classroom interaction.

2   A further aspect of classroom interaction is that the pupil's independent studies may well be subject to a good deal of interruption. The Kilpatrick model never seems to come to grips with the question of 'control' within the classroom. Any pedagogy that fails to address this question is surely doomed. This is not because the class-room teacher is an irremediable authoritarian by nature but because part of his/her job must be to ensure that pupil's work can go on uninterrupted. This means that he must be more than a consultant in his classroom. A viable pedagogy must acknowledge that in the classroom 'the crowds remain' to pull at the student's attention and divert the teacher's energy (Jackson, 1968, p. 111).

A second pedagogy based on the child's individual interests and experiences addresses itself to the interactive potential and reality of the classroom. Acknowledgement of the paramount role of individual process is self-sufficient. The paramountcy of individual process in learning does not preclude the role of external challenge and collaboration in that process; rather, it argues for such a role to be at the centre of the teacher's actions.

Towards an alternative pedagogy

A number of accounts of the introduction of innovation teaching courses, besides underlining the pervasive flaws of transmission, also indicate how an alternative pedagogy could remedy such flaws. The following quotation refers to a fourth-year Humanities course in a comprehensive school:

> A theme is chosen, strategies worked out to relate it to the pupil's experience and interest, materials prepared, resources mobilized. The process is intensely exciting, above all, I think because it incites us to pursue ourselves to the course of study we are preparing to advocate to our pupils. Ironically, by the time the programme is ready to be presented to the pupils for whom it is intended, our own enthusiasm as teachers if often half-spent, or else has become so self-absorbing that we cannot appreciate that it will not be shared by everyone else. We have become our own curriculum's ideal pupils; our resources are beautifully designed to satisfy not our pupils' intellectual demands, but our own!
>
> (Armstrong, 1974, p. 51)

An account of a first-year undergraduate course in economics makes the same points:

> One puzzling factor in the situation was that, whilst students appeared to get very little out of the Demand Theory Package, the members of faculty who prepared it felt that they had learnt a lot. In preparing the Factor Pricing package, therefore, our attention began to shift towards the problem of getting the students to share the experience which the faculty had had. It became clear that it was the process of 'sorting it all out', so important and necessary in developing self-instructional materials, which was the key to this problem.

> In presenting the students with a completed analysis we were concentrating their attention on predetermined solutions at the expense of focusing it on either the nature of the problem or the analytic process itself.
>
> (Eraut *et al.*, 1975)

From these two accounts it becomes apparent that what is needed is to involve the student in the process of 'sorting it all out' – what Dewey called 'the need of reinstating into experience the subject matter'. The need is to move the pedagogic focus from the pre-active situation where it is divorced from the pupils to the interactive situation where the pupils are involved. By so changing the focus learning becomes less a matter of mastering externally presented material – more a case of actively reconstructing knowledge.

We have stated before that moving the pedagogic focus from implementing the pre-active to interpreting the interactive does not imply an absence of planning (or for that matter, evaluation). As before, the teacher will be concerned to plan for his lessons but in the new situation will seek to ensure that the predictive does not become the prescriptive. E.W. Eisner comes near to the spirit of such a plan in describing expressive objectives: 'An expressive objective describes an educational encounter: it identifies a situation in which children are to work, a problem with which they are to cope, a task in which they are to engage; but it does not specify what from that encounter situation, problem or task they are to learn' (Popham *et al.*, 1969, pp. 15–16). In short, planning is concerned with the process of learning and does not prescribe what is going to be produced.

A number of examples of work based on this kind of pedagogic ideal are already in operation. An important minority of 'progressive' teachers in British primary schools and a growing body in middle schools already work an alternative pedagogy:

> At her best the primary school teacher working in a more or less progressive English primary school is perhaps the only contemporary polymath, even if to herself she seems more like a 'jack of all trades'. She is something of an expert in the psychology of learning and the nature of childhood, passionately committed to intellectual exploration within the most widely ranging areas of experience, rarely afraid to tackle, at the invitation of her pupils, new disciplines, and often the master of some particular part of experience which she teaches – art or nature or language. Doubtless to put it so badly is to idealize, but it is an idealization drawn from life.
>
> (Armstrong, 1974, p. 56)

The guiding principle of this primary school tradition is 'intellectual exploration' – a working plan of principles of procedure will be needed to facilitate such exploration together with predictions as to worthwhile activities and useful resources.

The American Social Science Curriculum, *Man: A Course of Study*, on which Bruner acted as consultant goes some way towards defining principles of procedure for an alternative pedagogy:

1   To initiate and develop in youngsters a process of question-posing (the inquiry method).
2   To teach a research methodology where children can look for information to answer questions they have raised and used the framework developed in the course (e.g. the concept of the life cycle) and apply it to new areas.

3   To help youngsters develop the ability to use a variety of first-hand sources as evidence from which to develop hypotheses and draw conclusions.
4   To conduct classroom discussions in which youngsters learn to listen to others as well as express their own view.
5   To legitimate the search: that is, to give sanction and support to open-ended discussions where definitive answers to many questions are not found.
6   To encourage children to reflect on their own experiences (Hanley *et al.*, 1970, p. 5).

Whilst not wishing to recommend the whole of Bruner's curriculum package as exemplifying an alternative pedagogy, this definition of principle does offer useful guidelines of a broad plan of interaction.

As well as broad principles of procedure it is also useful for teachers to have a working list of likely criteria for judging classroom activities. Raths recently attempted to produce such a list which included, for example, 'All other things being equal, one activity is more worthwhile than another if it permits children to make informed choices in carrying out the activity and to reflect on the consequences of their choices' (Raths, 1971). But clearly lists of procedural principles and worthwhile activities might fall into the trap whereby pre-active definition prescribes interactive interpretation. To avoid this it is important to try to 'catch the spirit' in which such lists should be used. 'The problem is to produce a specification to which teachers can work in the classroom, and thus to provide the basis for a new tradition. That specification needs to catch the implication of ideas for practice' (Stenhouse, 1975).

What might fulfil this need is a description of the kind of encounter which best characterizes the new tradition: an exemplar of the pedagogy in interaction. Peter Medway and I attempt to define an exemplar of what, for want of a better phrase, we called cooperative learning (Goodson and Medway, 1975, p. 17) and which is derived from our teaching experiences.

Unauthorized methods

Imagine this situation in a secondary school. A male teacher with a group in his classroom. He spends two mornings and two afternoons with them each week. He has set up a room that reflects many of his own interests and his predictions of what might grab his kids. There are charts and paintings on the wall, a trolley of assorted materials in the corner, some records, filmstrips, paint and brushes, and so on. It is an environment deliberately set up for learning.

It's noticeable that the teacher is relating very differently to different groups and individuals. Some he leaves alone; with others he sits down and looks at what they have done and makes vague situation-maintaining remarks, 'yes, that's good, go on'; with others he's engaged in specific and animated point-by-point argument, explanation, planning, disagreement.

This situation exemplifies cooperative learning – cooperative, that is, between teacher and student. There may well also be cooperation between students, but we want to single out for attention here the type of relationship between the teacher and either individual students or small groups of friends. It is cooperative in that teacher and student look together at a topic, each presenting to the other his own perception of it, both feeling their way through dialogue towards a common perception. Cooperation is not a euphemism, a gentler way of doing the same old thing by persuasion rather than imposition. We take the implied equality seriously, and the learning relationship, starting on the teacher's side with a commitment to the principle of reciprocity, progresses to the point where reciprocity is experienced as a reality.

A cooperative learning enterprise that reaches the crucial learning threshold might pass through three stages:

First stage

The student says 'I want to do something on the second world war' and gets the reply, 'OK, get started. Here's some books and magazines, there is a filmstrip you can look at'. During the following period the teacher may feel quite anxious about what's going on: There may be a lot of copying out of books, drawing of pictures, collecting of unrelated bits and pieces of knowledge – useless knowledge it may seem, and so indeed it may sometimes turn out to be. But what *may* be going on is a process of exploration in which the student, often unconsciously, feels around the topic to locate the real source of its attraction – some problem or worry or preoccupation or powerful feeling related to it.

Second stage

The teacher, after watching all this and trying to detect underlying themes and concerns in the students busy activity, while very gently maintaining it and restraining himself from criticism, and the student, who is beginning to understand why the topic holds his interest, get together to bring it into focus. 'So what you're really on about is the casual, pointless way people could get killed, in ways that couldn't make any sense to them – you live your whole life, have an education, a family, fillings in your teeth, and end up in a ditch after some minor skirmish with an unimportant enemy outpost that was going to withdraw one minute later anyway.' The teacher goes on to suggest further ways of exploring the central interest.

Third stage

The student is now experiencing the satisfaction of successfully investigating a topic alone and bringing it under control. The student has developed tenacity and perseverance, is making statements he or she can back up, is hypothesizing with confidence, and can improvise from knowledge. The project is out of the intensive care unit and the teacher can speak his mind about it without fear of killing it stone dead or putting the student down. The relationship has become robust and stimulating to both sides. The student enjoys the teacher's company and finds it challenging. The teacher has become interested in the student *and* in the topic – about which he or she now knows a lot more. The teacher takes the student's challenges and suggestions seriously, and now experiences the co-operation which started off as abstract ideal.

This is the stage of synthesis. The student has a perspective on the whole topic that may be expressed in a piece of writing that integrates generalizations, facts, attitudes, and the students' whole view of the world. The final writing or presentation will express the dynamic vigour of the reconstruction of knowledge that has gone on.

If, as I intend, this description is taken as characterizing a new pedagogy at work, a number of important implications need to be clearly enunciated. Firstly, learning will often involve *individual* negotiation between pupil and teacher: the teacher learns alongside his pupils, an adult learner among young learners, though with additional responsibilities to those of his charges. The teacher helps the child isolate a problem which is puzzling him (the example given related to the Second World War), together they devise a plan for investigating the problems, the investigation promotes a number of hypothesis, these are worked through and reformulated, and together the teacher and child discus and define a mutually acceptable solution. In this case the teacher's energy, resource preparation and stock of commonsense and specialist knowledge is used in facilitating the child's inquiry into something he has become interested in. (In transmission the teacher puts much of his energy and resources into preparation *before* confronting the variety of children's interest – a fatiguing gamble which too seldom pays off.)

Secondly, the pedagogy implies a radical re-ordering of the way in which knowledge is defined. The rhetoric of transmission schools maintains that the child gets a balanced 'diet' of 'subjects' which cover the main disciplines of knowledge. But this must be recognized as rhetoric: the knowledge which teachers transmit has *never* been 'received' by most children. That is why there are 2 million acknowledged adult illiterates, why I can do no mathematics and speak no foreign languages (not even Latin), why in many schools only the minority are even *offered* subject transmission while the rest do 'Parentcraft', 'Personal Development' and 'Motor Cycle Maintenance'. Knowledge, as transmitted in schools, has been described by Barness: 'School knowledge which someone else presents to us. We partly grasp it, enough to answer examination questions, but it remains someone else's knowledge, not ours. If we never use this knowledge we probably forget it' (Barnes, 1976, p. 81).

Although optimistic (how many pupils even sit exams, let alone answer the questions successfully?), this description catches the essence of school knowledge and Barnes goes on to argue for a new view of knowledge known as 'action knowledge':

> In so far as we use knowledge for our own purposes...we begin to incorporate it into our view of the world, and to sue parts of it to cope with the exigencies of living. Once the knowledge becomes incorporated into our view of the world on which our actions are based, I would say it has become 'action knowledge'.
>
> (Barnes, 1976, p. 81)

Only if the teacher gives the child access to 'action knowledge' can learning take place. An alternative pedagogy would seek to offer the child such an opportunity whilst transmission pedagogy pre-empts it. In placing the individual pupil in such a central position in defining the approach to knowledge there is not only a psychological rationale (which some traditionalists concede) but a logical rationale too. All subject matter begins with an original attempt to solve problems and it is this unitary process of knowledge creation that should be the focus of pedagogy, not the transmission of its differentiated products. Only by involvement in this process can the pupil begin exploration of the wider fields and forms of knowledge: that successive broadening and deepening of knowledge which is the only route to a 'balanced curriculum' for each child.

Some constraints and problems

The most obvious constraint to centring a pedagogy around the pupil's inquiry in cooperation with the teacher is that pupils have to attend school and the teacher is responsible for such attendance. Yet this is the constraint within which any style of classroom learning has to operate; it is not a constraint which I see as advocating a transmission model, rather that an alternative pedagogy would better accommodate this fact of classroom life.

A more specific problem relates to the nature of classroom life, for 'the crowds remain to pull at the student's attention and to divert the teacher's energy'. There are two problems associated with an alternative pedagogy. (a) Is 'individual negotiation' possible in the hurly-burly of the classroom? (b) Does a role as an equal learner interfere with the teacher's control capacity? Undoubtedly most people would answer 'yes' at this stage and move on to conclude that only transmission can cope with classroom realities. A number of facts indicate that his could be an outdated perception. In a number of primary school classrooms with 40 or 45 pupils, of often noisy and mobile inclination, an alternative pedagogy has been made to work quite successfully. Exceptional teachers, perhaps, but what of the average teacher? In the upper secondary school the average teacher works in an organization which maximizes his opportunity for short, specialized sessions of transmission. As widely reported, it is at this level that 'control' is most difficult: where transmission is maximized 'control' problems are greatest. Even as a 'survival technique' it would appear that transmission is outmoded: the pedagogy and associated organizational structure work against the establishment of those individual and personal relationships which as well as alleviating 'control' problems might serve to increase the educative potential of the teacher.

The contradictions in transmission pedagogy have already encouraged new developments in our classrooms. Clearly the development of an alternative pedagogy can only be part of a much larger scheme of transformation, but acknowledgement of the enormity of the task should not inhibit developments, for this would seem one important place to begin. By exploring an alternative pedagogy in their classrooms, teachers can clarify what is possible in schools, what purposes schools serve in our society, and perhaps bring new understandings of the rhetoric of transmission. That is a long way from accepting that transmission *is* teaching.

For 'progressive' models of education the development of an alternative pedagogy would provide that coherent and positive view of the teacher's involvement that has so far seemed lacking. Active challenging of and collaboration with the child might then have been seen as criteria for a successful pedagogy, rather than an outmoded pattern of teacher domination. Further, an alternative pedagogy should move beyond the individual negotiations that this chapter has concentrated on; collective and group aspects need to be developed. From an individual knowledge of and relationship with each student the teacher can then and only then, broaden his curriculum and group involvement. And from a clear definition of pedagogy new definitions of school and classroom might begin.

References

Armstrong, M., 1974, The Role of the Teacher. In P. Buckman (ed.), *Education Without Schools* (London: Souvenir Press).

Barnes, D., 1976, *From Communication to Curriculum* (Harmondsworth: Penguin).

Bloom, B.S., 1971, Mastery Learning. In J.H. Block (ed.), *Mastering Learning: Theory and Practice* (New York: Holt, Rinehart and Winston).

Concise Oxford Dictionary.

Dewey, J., 1971, *The Child and the Curriculum* (Chicago, IL: University of Chicago Press). [I share the severe reservations about Dewey expressed most recently in the work of Clarence Karier.]

Eraut, M., Mackenzie, N. and Papps, I., 1975, The Mythology of Educational Development, *British Journal of Educational Technology*, 6(3) (October).

Goodson, I. and Medway, P., 1975, The Feeling is Mutual, *Times Educational Supplement* (20 June).

Hanley, J.P., Whitla, D.K., Moo, E.W. and Walter, A.S., 1970, *Curiosity, Competence and Community. Man: A Course of Study* (Cambridge, MA: Education Development Center).

Jackson, P.W., 1968, *Life in Classrooms* (New York: Holt, Rinehart and Winston).

James, C., 1968, *Young Lives at Stake* (London: Collins).

Keddie, N., 1971, Classroom Knowledge. In M.F.D. Young (ed.), *Knowledge and Control* (London: Collier-MacMillan). Using Jackson's distinction, what the teacher does before the lesson in the empty classroom is pre-active; when the children enter the classroom it is interactive. Nell Keddie has drawn attention to a similar dichotomy between the 'educationist context' and the 'teacher context'.

Kilpatrick, W.H., 1951, *Philosophy of Education* (New York: MacMillan).

Kincheloe, J. and Steinberg, S. (eds), 1998, *Unauthorized Methods: Strategies for Critical Teaching* (New York and London: Routledge), pp. 35–37.

Peters, R. and Hirst, P., 1970, *The Logic of Education* (London: Routledge and Kegan Paul).

Popham, W.J., Eisner, E.W., Sullivan, H.J. and Tyler, L.L., 1969, *Instructional Objectives* (Chicago, IL: Rand McNally).

Raths, J.D., 1971, Teaching Without Specific Objectives, *Educational Leadership* (April), pp. 714–720.

Stenhouse, L., 1975, Defining The Curriculum Problem, *Cambridge Journal of Education*, 5(2) (Easter).

Wilson, P.S., 1971, *Interest and Discipline in Education* (London: Routledge and Kegan Paul).

CHAPTER 4

CHARIOTS OF FIRE

Etymologies, epistemologies and the
emergence of curriculum

The Making of Curriculum, 2nd edition, London: Falmer Press, 1995

The problem of reconceptualising our study of schooling can be partially illustrated in the basic etymology of curriculum. The word curriculum derives from the Latin word *currere*, which means to run, and refers to a course (or race-chariot). The implications of etymology are that curriculum is thereby defined as a course to be followed, or most significantly, presented. As Barrow notes 'as far as etymology goes, therefore the curriculum should be understood to be "the presented content" for study' (Barrow, 1984, p. 3). Social context and construction by this view is relatively unproblematic for by etymological implication the power of 'reality-definition' is placed firmly in the hands of those who 'draw up' and define the course. The bond between curriculum and prescription then was forged early; it has survived and strengthened over time. Part of the strengthening of this bond has been the emergence of sequential patterns of learning to define and operationalise the curriculum as prescribed.

From its Latin origins it is important to trace the emergence of curriculum as a concept which began to be used in schooling. According to Hamilton and Gibbons 'the words class and curriculum seem to have entered educational discourse at a time when schooling was being transformed into a mass activity' (Hamilton and Gibbons, 1986, p. 15). But the origins of the class/curriculum juxtaposition can be found earlier and at the higher education level. From Mir's analysis of the origins of 'classes' as first described in the statutes of the College of Montaign we learn:

> It is in the 1509 programme of Montaign that one finds for the first time in Paris a precise and clear division of students into *classes*...That is, divisions graduated by stages or levels of increasing complexity according to the age and knowledge required by students.
>
> (Hamilton and Gibbons, 1986, p. 7)

Mir argues that the College of Montaign actually inaugurated the Renaissance class system but the vital connection to establish however is how organisation in classes was associated with curriculum prescribed and sequenced for stages or levels.

Hamilton provides further evidence from Glasgow where the *Oxford English Dictionary* locates the earliest source of 'curriculum' in 1633. The annexation of the Latin term for a racecourse is clearly related to the emergence of sequencing in schooling but the question 'Why Glasgow?' remains. Hamilton believes, that 'the sense of discipline or structural order that was absorbed into curriculum came not so much from classical sources as from the ideas of John Calvin (1509–64)':

> As Calvin's followers gained political as well as theological ascendancy in late sixteenth century Switzerland, Scotland and Holland, the idea of discipline – 'the very essence of Calvinism' – began to denote the internal principles and external machinery of civil government and personal conduct. From this perspective there is a homologous relationship between curriculum and discipline: curriculum was to Calvinist educational practice as discipline was to Calvinist social practice.
>
> (Hamilton and Gibbons, 1986, p. 14)

We have then an early instance, if these speculations carry weight, of the relationship between knowledge and control. This works at two levels with regard to curriculum definition. Firstly there is the social context in which knowledge is conceived of and produced. Secondly there is the manner in which such knowledge is 'translated' for use in particular educational milieu, in this case classes but later classrooms. The social context of curriculum construction must take account of both levels.

The evidence of Paris and Glasgow in the sixteenth and seventeenth centuries can be summarised as follows and makes a fairly clear statement of the interlinked nature of the emerging mode of curriculum and patterns of social organisation and control:

> the notion of classes came into prominence with the rise of sequential programmes of study which, in turn, resonated with various Renaissance and Reformation sentiments of upward mobility. In Calvinist countries (such as Scotland) these views found their expression theologically in the doctrine of predestination (the belief that only a preordained minority could attain spiritual salvation) and, educationally, in the emergence of national but bipartite education systems where the 'elect' (i.e. predominantly those with the ability to pay) were offered the prospect of advanced schooling, while the remainder (predominantly the rural poor) were fitted to a more conservative curriculum (the appreciation of religious knowledge and secular virtue).
>
> (Hamilton, 1980, p. 286)

This quote sets up the unique significance of curriculum as it developed. For soon after as its power to designate what should go on in the classroom was realised, a further power was discovered. Alongside the power to *designate* was the power to *differentiate*. This meant that even children who went to the same school could be given access to what amounted to different 'worlds' through the curriculum they were taught.

Hamilton contends that 'the "class" pedagogies pioneered at Glasgow University had a direct influence on those adopted in the elementary schools of the nineteenth Century' (Hamilton, 1980, p. 282). The general connection between 'class' pedagogies and a curriculum based on sequence and prescription is clear but to move towards the 'modern' duality of pedagogy and curriculum involves the transition from class to classroom system.

In analysing the historical transition from 'class' to classroom system the shift in the initial stages of the Industrial Revolution in the late eighteenth and early nineteenth century 'was as important to the administration of schooling as the concurrent shift from domestic to factory production was to the management of industry'. Indeed, as Smelser has shown the two were intimately related:

> in the pre-industrial family of a craftsman, the parents themselves are responsible for teaching the child minimum occupational skills, as well as for his emotional moulding during his early years. When a growing economy places demands for greater literacy and more technical skills, the pressure is for this multi-functional family to give way to a new, more complex set of social arrangements. Structurally distinct educational institutions appear and the family begins to surrender some of its previous training functions to these new institutions, having lost these functions, accordingly, the family becomes more specialised, focusing relatively more on emotional conditioning in the early childhood years and relatively less on its former economic and educational functions.
>
> (1968, p. 79)

In the 'domestic-putter out' system then the family unit remained at home and education, albeit rather more in the guise of training and apprenticeship, could therefore take place in the home. With the triumph of the factory system the associated break-up of the family opened up these roles to subsequent penetration by State schooling and to their replacement by the classroom system where large groups could be adequately supervised and controlled. Hence 'the change from class to classroom reflected a more general upheaval in schooling – the ultimate victory of group-based pedagogies over the more individualised forms of teaching and learning' (Hamilton, 1980, p. 282).

If we specifically turn to the development of schooling in England at this stage the intersection of pedagogy and curriculum begins to resemble more 'modern' patterns. As Bernstein has argued pedagogy, curriculum and evaluation considered together constitute the three message systems through which formal educational knowledge can be realised, in this sense they constitute a modern epistemology (Bernstein, 1971, p. 47). In the 1850s the third prong was pioneered with the founding of the first university examination boards. The centennial report of the University of Cambridge Local Examinations Syndicate states:

> The establishment of these examinations was the universities response to petitions that they should help in the development of 'schools for the middle classes'.
>
> (University of Cambridge, 1958)

Also at this time the features of curriculum mentioned earlier, the power to differentiate, was being institutionalised. The birth of secondary *examinations* and the institutionalisation of curriculum *differentiation* were then almost exactly contemporaneous. For instance the Taunton Report in 1868 classified secondary schooling into three grades depending on the time spent at school. Taunton asserted:

> The difference in time assigned makes some difference in the very nature of education itself; if a boy cannot remain at school beyond the age of 14 it is useless to begin teaching him such subjects as required a longer time for their proper study; if he can continue till 18 or 19, it may be expedient to postpone some studies that would otherwise be commenced earlier.

Taunton noted that 'these instructions correspond roughly but by no means exactly to the gradations of society'. (This statement could as we shall see, be equally well applied to the Norwood Report nearly a century later.) In 1868 schooling till age 18 or 19 was for the sons of men with considerable incomes independent of their own exertions, or professional men, and men in business whose profits put them on the same level. These received a mainly classical curriculum. The second grade up to age 16 was for sons of the 'mercantile classes'. Their curriculum was less classical in orientation and had a certain practical orientation. The third grade till age 14 was for the sons of 'the smaller tenant farmer, the small trades-men, (and) the superior artisans'. Their curriculum was based on the three 'R's but carried out to a very good level. These gradations cover secondary schooling. Meanwhile most of the working class remained in elementary schools where they were taught rudimentary skills in the three 'R's. By this time the curriculum functioned as a major identifier of and mechanism for social differentiation. This power to designate and differentiate established a conclusive place for curriculum in the epistemology of schooling.

By the turn of the century the epistemology, with which we are familiar, was emerging. Thus:

> By the 20th Century, the batch production rhetoric of the 'classroom system' (for example, lessons, subjects, timetables, grading, standardisation, streaming) had become so pervasive that it successfully achieved a normative status – creating the standards against which all subsequent educational innovations came to be judged.
>
> (Hamilton, 1980, p. 282)

The dominant epistemology, which characterised state schooling by the beginning of the twentieth century, combined the trilogy of pedagogy, curriculum and evaluation. The last of the pieces in the trilogy was the establishment of university examination boards and here the side effects on curriculum were to be both pervasive and long lasting. The classroom system inaugurated a world of timetables and compartmentalised lessons; the curriculum manifestation of this systemic change was the school subject. If 'class and curriculum' entered educational discourse when schooling was transformed into a mass activity in England 'classroom system and school subject' emerged at the stage at which that mass activity became a state-subsidised system with a secondary sector. And in spite of the many alternative ways of conceptualising and organising curriculum the convention of the subject retains its supremacy. In the modern era, in secondary schooling, we are essentially dealing with the *curriculum as subject*.

Whilst this system was inaugurated in the 1850s it was established on the present footing with the definition of the Secondary Regulations in 1904 which list the main subjects, followed by the establishment of a subject-based 'School Certificate' in 1917. From this date curriculum conflict began to resemble the existing situation in focusing on the definition and evaluation of *examinable* knowledge. Hence the School Certificate subjects rapidly became the overriding concern of grammar schools and the academic subjects it examined soon established ascendancy on these schools' timetables. In 1941 Norwood reported that:

> a certain sameness in the curriculum of schools resulted from the double necessity of finding a place for the many subjects competing for time in the curriculum and the need to teach these subjects in such a way and to such a standard as will ensure success in the School Certificate examination.

The normative character of the system is clear and as a result of 'these necessities' the curriculum had 'settled down into an uneasy equilibrium, the demands of specialists and subjects being widely adjusted and compensated' (The Norwood Report, 1943, p. 61). The extent to which university examination boards thereby influenced the curriculum through examination subjects is evident. The academic subject-centred curriculum was in fact strengthened in the period following the 1944 Education Act. In 1951 the introduction of the General Certificate of Education allowed subjects to be taken separately at 'O' level (in the School Certificate blocks of 'main' subjects had to be passed); and the introduction of Advanced level increased subject specialisation and enhanced the link between 'academic' examinations and university 'disciplines'. The academic subjects which dominated 'O' and especially 'A' level examinations were then closely linked to university definitions; but even more crucially they were linked to patterns of resource allocation. Academic 'subjects' claiming close connections to university 'disciplines' were for the 'able' students. From the beginning it was assumed that such students required 'more staff, more highly paid staff and more money for equipment and books' (Byrne, 1974, p. 29). The crucial and sustained line between 'academic' subjects and preferential resources and status was therefore established.

But if this system was predominant with regard to staffing and resources for academic subjects in grammar schools, the implications for the other schools (and styles of curriculum) should not be forgotten. Echoing Taunton, Norwood in 1943 had discovered that schooling had created distinctive groups of pupils each of which needed to be treated 'in a way appropriate to itself'. This time the social and class basis of differentiation remained the same but the rationale and mechanism for differentiation was significantly different. Before the argument had focussed on time spent at school now the emphasis was on different 'mentalities' each recognising a different curriculum. Firstly 'the pupil who is interested in learning for its own sake, who can grasp an argument or follow a piece of connected reasoning'. Such pupils 'educated by the curriculum commonly associated with grammar schools have entered the learned professions or have taken up higher administrative or business posts'. The second group whose interests lie in the field of applied science or applied arts were to go to technical schools (which never developed very far). Thirdly, the pupils who deal 'more easily with concrete things than with ideas'. The curriculum would 'make a direct appeal to interests, which it would awaken by practical touch with affairs'. A practical curriculum then for a manual occupational future.

We see then the emergence of a definite pattern of *prioritising* of pupils through curriculum; what emerges I have called elsewhere 'the triple alliance between academic subjects, academic examinations and able pupils'. Working through patterns of resource allocation this means a process of pervasive 'academic drift' afflicts sub-groups promoting school subjects. Hence subjects as diverse as woodwork and metalwork, physical education, art technical studies, book-keeping, needlework and domestic science have pursued status improvement by arguing for enhanced academic examinations and qualifications. Likewise schools defined as different from grammar schools, the technical schools and secondary modern schools also were ultimately drawn into the process of academic drift both ending up competing for success through academic subject based styles of examination.

The manner in which this structure effects the definition of the school curriculum as subjects are defined, promoted and redefined is examined in some detail in the later chapters. In a way the evolution of each subject reflects in microcosm a struggle over alternatives over time, which is not dissimilar to the overall pattern discerned as State schooling is established and defined. Hence Layton sees the initial stage as one where 'the learners are attracted to the subject because of its bearing on matters of concern to them. At this point the teachers are seldom trained as subject specialists but do 'bring the missionary enthusiasms of pioneers to their task'. Significantly at this stage 'the dominant criterion is relevance to the needs and interests of the learners'. However as the subject 'progresses' (a subject at any point in time resembling a coalition which veneers a sub-set of warring factions) the role of the universities becomes more and more important. This is not least because subject groups employ a *discourse* where they argue increasingly for their subject to be viewed as an 'academic discipline' (thereby claiming the financial resources and career opportunities which accrue). The corollary of this claim is the university scholars must be given control over defining the 'discipline' (the aspiration to the rhetoric of 'the discipline' is related to acceptance of this hierarchical pattern of definition so in this sense the discursive formation is critical). Jenkins has noted that:

> one detects a certain embarrassment in teachers who not unnaturally feel the difference between forms, disciplines and subjects are in part differences of status.
>
> (Jenkins and Shipman, 1976, p. 102)

In effect the differences are over *who* can define 'disciplines' – essentially this is presented as the characteristic activity of university scholars.

The progressive refinement of an epistemology suited to State schooling then embraces the trilogy of pedagogy, curriculum and examination. Until recently the 'triple alliance' of academic subjects, academic examinations and able students have been able to enjoy a clear hierarchy of status and resources. Thus our under-standing of curriculum has to focus mainly on analysing the dominant convention of the school subject and the associated examination by university boards. The linking of resources to 'academic' subjects places a priority on subjects that can be presented as 'academic disciplines' and this places further power in the hands of the universities. Not that the power of the universities over curriculum is unchal-lenged, the challenges are recurrent. Reid has noted that a major area of conflict is between the external constraints arising from university requirements and the internal pressures which have their origins in the school:

> Schools are, however, poorly equipped to resist university pressures. To a large extent they allow the legitimacy of the university demands, and have evolved an authority structure which is linked to them.
>
> (Reid, 1972, p. 106)

Such recurrent conflict is of course likely as the school subjects 'progresses' away from Layton's early stage where 'the dominant criterion is relevance to the needs and interests of the learners'. But as we have seen an epistemology has been institutionalised and resourced which places the academic 'discipline' at the top of the curriculum apex. Not surprising the culminating stage in the establishment of an 'academic' subject celebrates the power of scholars to define the disciplines' field. In this culminating stage however Layton argues that related to this change in who defines school knowledge 'Students are initiated into a tradition, their attitudes approaching passivity and resignation, a prelude to disenchantment' (Layton, 1972).

The final stage of Layton's model summarises (and comments upon) the kind of political 'settlement' with regard to curriculum, pedagogy and evaluation in operation. Plainly however there are recurrent conflicts and the 'achievement' of this 'settlement' has been a painstaking and deeply contested process. It is important when assessing the contribution of scholars of education to establish how their work resonates with the contested nature of education generally and curriculum specifically. As always there is a danger of accepting that which is worked for and achieved as a *fait accompli*, a given. Nothing could be further from the truth.

Antecedents and alternatives

The epistemology and institutionalised system of State schooling briefly described above was in sharp contrast to antecedent forms of education and to the involvement of the State in schooling at this earlier stage. Rothblatt for instance describes education in Georgian England as follows:

> The State was not interested in 'national education' – indeed the idea had not yet occurred. The Church, which was interested in education, because of its continuing rivalry with Dissent, still did not have a firm policy and left the direction of studies to local or personal initiatives, or to the forces of the market. The demand for education and the demand for particular levels of education varied radically from period to period and from group to group, depending upon social and economic circumstances, occupational distributions, and cultural values. Countless persons, lay as well as clerical, opened schools, tried out various educational experiments and programmes in an effort to retain a fickle or uncertain clientele. And home tuition, where adjustments in curricula could be made quickly and easily according to the learning ability of the pupil, certainly remained one of the most important means of elementary and secondary education throughout the nineteenth century.
>
> (Rothblatt, 1976, p. 45)

Such a personal and local mode of educating could well have allowed response to the experience and culture of the pupils even in situations less ideal than home tuition 'where adjustments could be made quickly and easily according to the learning ability of pupil'. But among working class groups certainly in the sphere of adult education such respect for life experience in curriculum was a feature at this time and later. This contribution can be summarised as: 'the students' choice of subject. The relation of disciplines to actual contemporary living and the parity of general discussion with expert instruction' (Williams, 1975, p. 165). Above all there is the idea of curriculum as a two-way *conversation* rather than a one-way *transmission*.

Likewise different patterns of education and attendance characterised the working class private school, which thrived in the first half of the nineteenth century and continued into the second half in many places even after the 1870 act. Harrison has described these schools and the views that State inspectors held of them:

> Government inspection and middle class reformers condemned such schools as mere baby-minding establishments. They noted with strong disapproval the absence of settled or regular attendance. The pupils came and went at all times during the day. School hours were nominal and adjusted to family

needs – hence the number of two- and three-year olds who were sent to be 'out of the way' or 'kept safe'. The accommodation was over-crowded and sometimes stuffy, dirty and unsanitary. The pupils were not divided into classes, and the teacher was a working man or woman...

As well as not being arranged in classes, the curriculum was often individualised rather than sequential. Harrison describes 'Old Betty W's School' where; 'on fine days the little forms were taken outside her cottage and placed under the window. The children had their books, or their knitting and the old lady, knitting herself incessantly, marched backwards and forwards hearing lessons and watching work' (Harrison, 1984, p. 290).

These working class schools were effectively driven out by the version of state schooling which followed the 1870 act. Thompson has argued that the watershed for such schools, certainly such styles of working class education, were the fears engendered by the French Revolution. From now on the State played an increasing role in the organisation of schooling and of curriculum:

> attitudes towards social class, popular culture and education became 'set' in the aftermath of the French Revolution. For a century and more most middle class educationalists could not distinguish the work of education from that of social control: and this entailed too often, a repression or a denial of the life experience of their pupils as expressed in uncouth dialect or in traditional cultural forms. Hence education and received experience were at odds with each other. And those working men who by their own efforts broke into the educated culture found themselves at once in the same place of tension, in which education brought with it the danger of rejection of their fellows and self-distrust. The tension of course continues.
>
> (Thompson, 1968, p. 16)

The disjuncture then between common cultural experience and curriculum can be estimated, for working class clienteles, as developing after the moral panics associated with the French Revolution. From this date on the school curriculum was often overlaid by social control concerns for the ordinary working populace.

For other classes at the time this overlay of closely structured, sequenced and presented curriculum was not always deemed necessary. We learn that the public schools 'followed no common pattern of education, though they agreed on the taking of Latin and Greek as the main component of the curriculum. Each evolved its own unique forms of organisation with idiosyncratic vocabularies to describe them' (Reid, 1985). In so far as the curriculum depended on a learning of texts it was not judged essential that the teacher taught the text – a highly individualised form of curriculum. Moreover 'where students were divided into "forms" (a term referring originally to the benches on which they sat) this was done in a rough and ready manner for the convenience of teaching and not with the idea of establishing a hierarchy of ability or a sequence of learning' (Reid, 1985, p. 296).

Hence coherent alternative forms of education and curriculum developed in a wide range of schools for all classes prior to the Industrial Revolution and even after industrial transformation were retained in the public schools for the 'better classes' (and indeed for the working class were retained and defended in pockets such as 'adult education'). The model of curriculum and epistemology associated with State schooling progressively colonised all educational milieu and established itself some time in the late nineteenth century as the dominant pattern.

The subsequent linking of this epistemology to the distribution of resources and the associated attribution of status and careers stands at the centre of the consolidation of this pattern. The assumption that the curriculum should be primarily academic and associated with university disciplines has been painstakingly worked for and paid for. We should beware of any accounts that present such a situation of 'normal' or 'given'.

At root such a hierarchical system is often seen as denying the dialectic of education, the notion of dialogue and flexibility which some viewed (and view) as central to the way we learn. If 'subject matter is in large measure defined by the judgements and practice of the specialist scholars' and 'students are initiated into a tradition' their attitudes approach passivity and 'resignation' this mutuality is deliberately denied. The rhetoric of the 'discipline' and the academic subject might therefore be seen as characterising a particular mode of social relations.

Educationists concerned with establishing a more egalitarian practice and curriculum are driven to constantly assert the need for dialogue and mutuality and with it to argue for 'reconstruction of knowledge and curriculum'. For if the opinions cited are right the very fabric and form of curriculum (as well as the content) assumes and establishes a particular mode of social relations and social hierarchy. Seen in this way to argue only for changing the teaching method or the school organisation is to accept a central mystification of hierarchical structure through curriculum which would actively contradict other aspirations and ideals. Hence where pockets of alternative practice exist they present a similar case for egalitarian practice: in liberal adult education the following argument is presented:

> All education which is worth the name involves a relationship of mutuality, a dialectic: and no worthwhile educationalist conceives of his material as a class of inert recipients of instruction – and no class is likely to stay the course with him – if he is under the misapprehension that the role of the class is passive. What is different about the adult student is the experience that he brings to the relationship. This experience modifies, sometimes subtly, and sometimes more radically, the entire educational process: it influences teaching methods, the selection and maturation of tutors, the syllabus: it may even disclose weak places or vacancies in received academic disciplines and lead on to the elaboration of new areas of study.
>
> (Thompson, 1968, p. 9)

By this view then the disciplines cannot be taught as final 'distillations' of knowledge unchallengeable and unchanging and should not be taught as incontestable and fundamental structures and texts. This would provide a deeply flawed epistemology, pedagogically unsound and intellectually dubious, for in human scholarship 'final distillations' and 'fundamental' truths are elusive concepts. We are back with the dual face of socially contexted knowledge – both because knowledge and curriculum are pedagogically realised in a social context and are originally conceived of and constructed in such a context.

The alternatives to such a dominant view continue to surface. In past debates we can find certain radical teachers pursuing the comprehensive ideal seriously and arguing that in such a milieu knowledge and curricula must be presented as provisional and *liable to reconstruction*. Armstrong writes that his 'contention is that the process of education should imply a dynamic relationship between teacher, pupil and task out of which knowledge is reconstructed, for both teacher and pupil, in the light of shared experience' (Armstrong, 1977, p. 86).

Conclusion

In this chapter some of the origins of curriculum have been speculatively scrutinised. In particular we have seen that the notion of curriculum as structured sequence or 'discipline' derived a good deal from the political ascendancy of Calvinism. From these early origins there was a 'homologous relationship between curriculum and discipline'. Curriculum as discipline was allied to a social order where the 'elect' were offered the prospect of advanced schooling and the remainder a more conservative curriculum.

Out of these origins we have seen how this concept of curriculum became appended to a new notion of discipline. This time, (so we are to believe) 'fundamental' disciplines of 'the mind'. The juxtaposition of curriculum with (newly defined) 'discipline' intersects with a remarkably similar social configuration. This time the 'elect' are recruited by their capacity to display a facility for those academic 'subjects' allied to the 'disciplines'; their 'election' is signified by going on to study the 'disciplines' in the universities where they are defined and institutionalised.

References

Armstrong, M., 1977, Reconstructing Knowledge: An Example. In J. Watts (ed.), *The Countesthorpe Experience* (London: George Allen and Unwin).

Barrow, R., 1984, *Giving Teaching Back to Teachers: A Critical Introduction to Curriculum Theory* (Brighton: Wheatsheaf and Althouse).

Bernstein, B., 1971, On the Classification and Framing of Educational Knowledge. In M.F.D. Young (ed.), *Knowledge and Control* (London: Collier Macmillian).

Byrne, E.M., 1974, *Planning and Educational Inequality* (Slough: NFER).

Hamilton, D., 1980, Adam Smith and the Moral Economy of the Classroom System. *Journal of Curriculum Studies*, Vol. 12(4) October–December.

Hamilton, D. and Gibbons, M., 1986, Notes on the Origins of the Educational Terms Class and Curriculum. Paper presented at the *Annual Convention of the American Educational Research Association*, Boston, MA, April.

Harrison, J.F.C., 1984, *The Common People* (London: Flamingo).

Jenkins, D. and Shipman, M., 1976, *Curriculum: An Introduction* (London: Open Books).

Layton, D., 1972, Science as General Education, *Trends in Education* (London: HMSO).

Reid, W.A., 1972, *The University and the Sixth Form Curriculum* (London: Macmillan).

Reid, W.A., 1985, Curriculum Change and the Evolution of Educational Constituencies: The English Sixth Form in the Nineteenth Century. In Ivor Goodson (ed.), *Social Histories of the Secondary Curriculum: Subjects for Study* (Lewes: Falmer Press).

Rothblatt, S., 1976, *Tradition and Change I English Liberal Education: An Essay in History and Culture* (London: Faber and Faber).

Smelser, N., 1968, *Essays in Sociological Explanation* (New Jersey: Prentice Hall).

The Norwood Report, 1943, *Curriculum and Examinations in Secondary Schools*. Report of the Committee of the Secondary School Examinations Council, appointed by the President of the Board of Education in 1941 (London: HMSO).

Thompson, E.P., 1968. *Education and Experience*, Fifth Mansbridge Memorial Lecture, (Leeds: Leeds University Press).

University of Cambridge, Local Examinations Syndicate, One Hundredth Annual Report to University, 29 May 1958.

Williams, R., 1975, *The Long Revolution* (London: Penguin).

CHAPTER 5

BECOMING AN ACADEMIC SUBJECT

British Journal of Sociology of Education, 1981, 2(2): 163–180

Sociological and historical perspectives

Contemporary accounts of school subjects arise from two major perspectives – the sociological and the philosophical. Sociological accounts have followed a suggestion made in 1968 by Musgrove that researchers should:

> examine subjects both within the school and the nation at large as social systems sustained by communication networks, material endowments and ideologies. Within a school and within a wider society subjects as communities of people, competing and collaborating with one another, defining and defending their boundaries, demanding allegiance from their members and conferring a sense of identity upon them...even innovation which appears to be essentially intellectual in character, can usefully be examined as the outcome of social interaction.
>
> (Musgrove, 1968, p. 101)

Musgrove remarked that 'studies of subjects in these terms have scarcely begun at least at school level'.

A more influential work in the field of the sociology of knowledge was the collection of papers in Knowledge and Control edited by M.F.D. Young in 1971. The papers reflect Bernstein's contention that 'how a society selects, classifies, distributes, transmits and evaluates the educational knowledge it considers to be public, reflects both the distribution of power and the principles of social control' (Bernstein, 1971, p. 47). Young likewise suggests that 'consideration of the assumptions underlying the selection and organisation of knowledge by those in positions of power may be a fruitful perspective for raising sociological questions about curricula' (Young, 1971, p. 31). The emphasis leads to general statements of the following kind:

> Academic curricula in this country involve assumptions that some kinds and areas of knowledge are much more 'worthwhile' than others: that as soon as possible all knowledge should become specialised and with minimum explicit emphasis on the relations between the subjects specialised in and between specialist teachers involved. It may be useful therefore, to view curricular changes as involving changing definitions of knowledge along one or more of the dimensions towards a less or more stratified, specialised and open

organisation of knowledge. Further, that as we assume some patterns of social relations associated with any curriculum, these changes will be resisted insofar as they are perceived to undermine the values, relative power and privileges of the dominant groups involved.

(Young, 1971, p. 34)

The process whereby the unspecified 'dominant groups' exercise control over other presumably subordinate groups is not scrutinised although certain hints are offered. We learn that a school's autonomy in curriculum matters 'is in practice extremely limited by the control of the sixth form (and therefore lower form) curricula by the universities, both through their entrance requirements and their domination of all but one of the school examination boards'. In a footnote, Young assures that no direct control is implied here, but rather a process by which teachers legitimate their curricula through their shared assumptions about 'what we all know the universities want' (Young, 1971, p. 22). This concentration on the teachers' socialisation as the major agency of control is picked up elsewhere. We learn that:

The contemporary British educational system is dominated by academic curricula with a rigid stratification of knowledge. It follows that if teachers and children are socialised within an institutionalised structure which legitimates such assumptions, then for teachers high status (and rewards) will be associated with areas of the curriculum that are (1) formally assessed (2) taught to the 'ablest' children (3) taught in homogeneous ability groups of children who show themselves most successful within such curricula.

(Young, 1971, p. 36)

Young goes on to note that it 'should be fruitful to explore the syllabus construction of knowledge practitioners in terms of their efforts to enhance or maintain their academic legitimacy'.

Two papers by Bourdieu in *Knowledge and Control* summarise his considerable influence on English sociologists of knowledge (Bourdieu, 1971). Unlike many of the other contributors to *Knowledge and Control*, Bourdieu has gone on to carry out empirical work to test his theoretical assertions. His recent work – through concentrated at university, not school, level – looks at the theme of reproduction through education and includes an important section on 'the examination within the structure and history of the educational system' (Bourdieu and Passeron, 1977). Young also has come to feel the need for historical approaches to test theories of knowledge and control. He wrote recently: 'one crucial way of reformulating and transcending the limits within which we work, is to see...how such limits are not given or fixed, but produced through the conflicting actions and interests of men in history' (Young, 1977, pp. 248–249).

Certainly the most undeveloped aspect of *Knowledge and Control* in respect to school subjects is the scrutiny of the process whereby unspecified dominant groups exercise control over presumably subordinate groups in the definition of school knowledge. Moreover if the dominant groups in question are related to the economy one would expect high status knowledge to be of the sort Apple refers to 'for the corporate economy requires the production of high levels of technical knowledge to keep the economic apparatus running effectively and to become more sophisticated in the maximisation of opportunities for economic expansion' (Apple, 1978, p. 380). In fact high status groups have tended to receive 'academic' rather than 'technical' knowledge: a point that maybe contributes to the continuing dysfunctionality of the UK economy. We need to explore how this apparent contradiction developed and has been maintained in the school curriculum. Young's work, lacking in empirical evidence, develops horizontally in this exploration, working out from theories of social structure and social order to evidence of their application. Such macro-sociological theorising is very different, although far from inimical, to studying social groups actively at work in particular historical instances. In this respect the examination of the process of 'becoming a school subject' should generate useful historical insights.

The second school of explanation, which might almost be called the 'establishment view', is essentially philosophical and has preceded and stood in contradiction to sociological perspectives. The philosophical view has been attacked by Young because, he argues it is based on 'an absolutist conception of a set of distinct forms of knowledge which correspond closely to the traditional areas of the academic curriculum and thus justify, rather than examine, what are no more than socio-historical constructs of a particular time' (Young, 1977, p. 23). Even if we largely accept Young's critique, however, it is important to know that in fact school subjects themselves represent substantial interest groups. To view subjects as 'no more than socio-historical constructs of a particular time', whilst correct at one level, hardly serves to clarify the part played by those groups involved in their continuance and promotion over time.

The philosophical perspective is well summarised by the work of Hirst and Peters, and also Phenix. Hirst's position begins from a series of convictions that he defined in 1967 in a Schools Council Working Paper:

> No matter what the ability of the child may be, the heart of all his development as a rational being is, I am saying, intellectual. Maybe we shall need very special methods to achieve this development in some cases. Maybe we have still to find the best methods for the majority of the people. But let us never lose sight of the intellectual aim upon which so much else, nearly everything else, depends. Secondly it seems to me that we must get away completely from the idea that linguistic and abstract forms of thought are not for some people.
> (Hirst, 1967)

Hirst and Peters argue that 'the central objectives of education are developments of mind' and that such objectives are best pursued by the development of 'forms of knowledge' (a definition later broadened to include 'fields' of knowledge). From these forms and fields of knowledge so defined, school subjects can be derived and organised. Hence what is implied is that the intellectual discipline is created and systematically defined by a community of scholars, normally working in a university department, and is then 'translated' for use as a school subject.

This interpretation of Hirst's and Peters' work is commonly drawn, although not by the authors themselves. Other philosophers are more explicit. Phenix for instance states that: 'the general test for a discipline is that it should be the characteristic activity of an identifiable organised tradition of men of knowledge, that is of persons who are skilled in certain specified functions that they are able to justify by a set of intelligible standards' (Phenix, 1964, p. 317). The subsequent vision of school subjects as derived from the best work of specialist scholars, who act as initiators into scholarly traditions, is generally accepted both by educationists and laymen. It is a view supported by spokesmen for governmental and educational agencies, subject associations and, perhaps most significantly, the media.

In questioning the consensus view that school subjects derive from the intellectual disciplines or forms of knowledge it is again important to focus on the historical process through which school subjects arise. This investigation may provide evidence of a considerable disparity between the political and philosophical messages which seek to explain and legitimise the 'academic tradition' of school subjects and the detailed historical process through which school subjects are defined and established. Once a discipline has established an academic base it is persuasively self-fulfilling to argue that here is a field of knowledge from which an 'academic' school subject can receive inputs and general direction. This version of events simply celebrates a *fait accompli* in the evolution of a discipline and associated school subject. What is left unexplained are the stages of evolution towards this position and the forces which push aspiring academic subjects to follow similar routes. To understand the progression along the route to academic status it is necessary to examine the social histories of school subjects and to analyse the strategies employed in their construction and promotion.

Closer analysis of school subjects uncovers a number of unexplained paradoxes. First, the school context is in many ways starkly different from the university context – broader problems of pupil motivation, ability and control require consideration. The translation from discipline to school subject therefore demands considerable adaptation and as a result, 'many school subjects are barely disciplines let alone forms of thought. Many are unclear about their most fruitful concepts, forms of explanations and characteristic methodology' (Jenkins and Shipman, 1976, p. 107). Secondly, school subjects are often either divorced from their discipline base or do not have a discipline base. Many school subjects therefore, represent autonomous communities. Esland and Dale have noted:

> Teachers as spokesmen for subject communities are involved in an elaborate organisation of knowledge. The community has a history, and, through it, a body of respected knowledge. It has rules for recognising 'unwelcome' or spurious matter, and ways of avoiding cognitive contamination. It will have a philosophy and a set of authorities, all of which give strong legitimation to the activities which are acceptable to the community. Some members are accredited with the power to make 'official statements' – for instance, editors of journals, presidents, chief examiners and inspectors. These are important as 'significant others' who provide models to new or wavering members of appropriate belief and conduct.
>
> (Esland and Dale, 1972, pp. 70–71)

The degree of isolation or autonomy of the school subject can be seen on closer analysis to be related to the stages of the subjects' evolution. Far from being derived from academic disciplines some school subjects chronologically *precede* their parent disciplines: in these circumstances the developing school subject actually brings about the creation of a university base for the 'discipline' so that teachers of the subject can be trained.

Layton has analysed the development of science in England from the nineteenth century, suggesting a tentative model for the emergence of a school subject in the secondary school curriculum. He has defined three stages in this process. In the first stage:

> the callow intruder stakes a place in the timetable, justifying its presence on grounds such as pertinence and utility. During this stage learners are attracted to the subject because of its bearing on matters of concern to them. The teachers are rarely trained specialists, but bring the missionary enthusiasm of pioneers to their task. The dominant criterion is relevance to the needs and interests of the learners.

In the interim second stage:

> a tradition of scholarly work in the subject is emerging along with a corps of
> trained specialists from which teachers may be recruited. Students are still
> attracted to the study, but as much by its reputation and growing academic
> status as by its relevance to their own problems and concerns. The internal
> logic and discipline of the subject is becoming increasingly influential on the
> selection and organisation of subject matter.

In the final stage:

> the teachers now constitute a professional body with established rules and val-
> ues. The selection of subject matter is determined in large measure by the
> judgements and practices of the specialist scholars who lead inquiries in the
> field. Students are initiated into a tradition, their attitudes approaching
> passivity and resignation, a prelude to disenchantment.
>
> (Layton, 1972)

Layton's model warns against any monolithic explanation of subject and disciplines. It would seem that, far from being timeless statements of intrinsically
worthwhile content, subjects and disciplines are in constant flux. Hence the study
of knowledge in our society should move beyond the a-historical process of philosophical analysis towards a detailed historical investigation of the motives and
actions behind the presentation and promotion of subjects and disciplines.

In examining the historical process of becoming a school subject the next section
provides a brief case study of Geography. The subject's development is traced
largely through the publications of the Geographical Association, which means that
the focus of the study is on one aspect of the 'rhetoric' of subject promotion rather
than on the 'reality' of curriculum practice. The elucidation of the relationship
between 'rhetoric' and 'reality' remains one of the most profound challenges for
future curriculum histories. (In one sense this relates to the broader problem of the
historians' dependence on written and published documentary sources.) This argues
that subsequent studies are required to examine how far promotional activity
affects the 'small print' of examination syllabuses and the content and practice of
classrooms. Earlier work has, I think, evidenced that the promotional rhetoric
employed by rural studies to validate its claims to be an academic discipline
substantially modified the small print of an 'A' level syllabus.

The establishment and promotion of geography

In the late nineteenth century geography was beginning to establish a place in the
curricula of public, grammar and elementary schools. The subject was emerging
from the initial birth pangs when it appears to have been little more than a dreary
collection of geographical facts and figures which Mackinder contended 'adds an
ever-increasing amount to be borne by the memory' (Mackinder, 1887). This early
approach (which clearly precedes the somewhat idealised version of Layton's stage
one), has been called the 'capes and bay' period. Very soon however the subject
began to attract more inspired teachers, as a former pupil recalls: 'Later, however,
in a London secondary school "capes and bays" were dramatically replaced by
"homes in many lands" and a new world opened to us, through our non-graduate
"specialist teacher"' (Garnett, 1969, p. 36).

The non-graduate label was at this time inevitable as geography remained outside the universities. It was partly to answer this problem that one of the founding fathers of geography, H.T. Mackinder, posed the question in 1887 'How can geography be rendered a discipline?' Mackinder was aware that the demand for an academic geography to be taught in universities could only be engendered by the establishment of a more credible position in schools. Essentially it was in the public and grammar schools that geography needed to establish its intellectual as well as pedagogical credibility.

In these schools, without full-fledged academic status, the subject's position as an established part of the curriculum remained uncertain. As a Rochester headmaster noted, 'the over-crowding in the school timetable makes it impossible to give more than one and at most two lessons per week in geography' (Bird, 1901). In the elementary schools geography was rapidly seen as affording utilitarian and pedagogic possibilities in the education of the children of working people. Hence the take-up of the subject grew considerably in the period following the 1870 Education Act. In 1875 'elementary geography' was added to the main list of class subjects examined in elementary schools.

Given the limited base in the elementary and secondary school sector the promoters of geography began to draw up plans for a subject association. Hence in 1893 the Geographical Association was founded 'to further the knowledge of geography and the teaching of geography in all categories of educational institutions from preparatory school to university in the United Kingdom and abroad' (manifesto). The formation of the Association in 1893 was extremely well-timed and it rapidly began to operate as a vocal lobby for the subject. Two years later the Bryce Commission reported and its recommendations were built into the 1902 Education Act. Further the 1904 Secondary Regulations effectively defined the traditional subjects to be offered in secondary schools; geography's inclusion in the regulations was a major staging-post in its acceptance and recognition and in the broad-based take-up of external examinations in geography in secondary schools. The emergence of external examinations as a defining factor in secondary curricula around 1917 is clearly reflected in the sharp increase in the Association's membership around this date. At this stage geography was included in many Examination Board regulations both at School Certificate and Higher School Certificate as a main subject. Certain Boards, however, included geography only as a 'subsidiary subject'.

For those teachers involved in promoting geography the founding of a subject association was only a first stage in launching the subject; what was also required was an overall plan aimed at establishing the subject in the various educational sectors mentioned in the constitution. At a discussion on geographical education at the British Association in September 1903, Mackinder outlined a four-point strategy for establishing the subject:

> Firstly, we should encourage university schools of geography, where geographers can be made . . .
>
> Secondly, we must persuade at any rate some secondary schools to place the geographical teaching of the whole school in the hands of one geographically trained master . . .
>
> Thirdly, we must thrash out by discussion and experiment what is the best progressive method for common acceptation and upon that method we must base out scheme of examination.
>
> Lastly, the examination papers must be set by practical geography teachers.
> (Mackinder, 1903)

This strategy reads very much like a plea for monopoly rights or for a closed shop. The geography teacher is to set the exams and is to choose exams which satisfy the criteria of broad 'acceptation' of the subject (there is not even the facade that the pupils interest should be the central criterion); the teaching of geography is to be exclusively in the hands of trained geographers and the universities are to be encouraged to establish schools of geography 'where geographers can be made'.

In the immediate period following this pronouncement the Council of the Geographical Association continued the earlier rhetoric about the subject's utility; a changeover was only slowly implemented. Thus in 1919 we learn that: 'In teaching geography in schools we seek to train future citizens to imagine accurately the interaction of human activities and their topographical conditions...The mind of the citizen must have a topographical background if he is to keep order in the mass of information which he accumulates in the course of his life and in these days the background must extend over the whole world' (The Geographical Teacher). Eight years later we hear that 'travel and correspondence have now become general; the British dominions are to be found in every clime and these facts alone are sufficient to ensure that the subject shall have an important place in the school timetable' (Board of Education, 1927).

Alongside the utilitarian and pedagogic claims, as we shall see, the Geographical Association began to mount more 'academic' arguments. But the problems of the more utilitarian and pedagogic emphases had by now surfaced. Thus in the 1930s the Norwood Committee was concerned by the way geography appeared effortlessly to change direction and definition, thereby intruding on the territory of other subjects and disciplines. Above all, the committee was concerned with the temptation afforded by what it called the 'expansiveness of geography', for 'environment is a term which is easily expanded to cover every condition and every phase of activity which makes up normal everyday experience'. Hence, 'enthusiasts for geography may be inclined sometimes to extend their range so widely as to swallow up other subjects; in so doing they widen their boundaries so vaguely that definition of purpose is lost, and the distinctive virtues inherent in other studies closely pursued are ignored in a general survey of wide horizons' (The Norwood Report, 1943, pp. 101–102).

The results of such 'expansiveness' in school geography were later reported by Honeybone who argued that by the 1930s geography 'came more and more to be a "world citizenship" subject, with the citizens detached from their physical environment'. He explained this partly by the spread 'under American influence' of 'a methodology, proclaiming that all education must be related to the everyday experience of children'. Hence, 'in terms of geography, they insisted that the approach must always be through life and the work of men. This is a premise with which many teachers of geography will agree, but when put in the hands of people untrained in geography or trained without a proper sense of geographical synthesis, it frequently meant that geography in school started with the life and work of man and made no real attempt to examine his environment'. Thus through the work of those teachers untrained or badly trained in the subject, 'by 1939 geography had become grievously out of balance; the geographical synthesis had been abandoned; and the unique educational value of the subject lost in a flurry of social and economic generalisations' (The Norwood Report, 1943, p. 87).

The central problem therefore remained the establishment of departments in universities where geographers could be made and the piecemeal changes in pursuit of pupil relevance and utility could be partially controlled. To further this objective the Geographical Association began to promote more academic arguments for the subject. This increasingly academic presentation of the school subject provided more pressure on the universities to respond to the demand for the training of geography specialists. As a recent president of the Geographical Association has noted, 'the recognition of our subject's status among university disciplines...could never have been achieved without remarkable stimulus and demand injected from out of schools' (Garnett, 1969, p. 387). The contention, whilst correct, contains the origins of the status problems geography has encountered in universities. As David Walker has noted, 'some senior members of our ancient universities can still be found who dismiss it as a school subject' (Walker, 1975, p. 6). As a result until recently geographers remained a frustrated university profession because of what Wooldridge described as 'the widespread belief among our colleagues and associates that we lack academic status and intellectual respectability. What has been conceded is that geography has a limited use in its lower ranges. What is implicitly denied by so many is that it had any valid claim as a higher subject' (David, 1973, pp. 12–13).

Wooldridge hints, however, that acceptance at the lower level is the main threshold to cross: 'It has been conceded that if geography is to be taught in schools it must be learned in the universities' (David, 1973, pp. 12–13). The relevance of the school 'base' to university geography is well illustrated by St Catherine's College, Cambridge. The college has produced so many professors of geography for the country's universities that a conspiracy might be alleged. David Walker disagrees: 'In fact, to dispel the conspiracy, the reasons for this academic configuration are down to earth. St Catherine's was one of the first colleges to offer awards in geography: it established a network of contacts with sixth form teachers, many of whom later were its own graduates, and with particular schools like the Royal Grammar, Newcastle.' Walker points to the personal nature of subject induction. 'Since the Second World War, moreover, many of the St Catherine's geographers who went on to become professors, readers and lecturers who taught by one man, Mr A.A.L. Caeser, now the senior tutor' (Walker, 1975, p. 6).

The period following 1945 does seem to have been critical in geography's acceptance and consolidation within the university sector. Professor Alice Garnett explained in 1968 why this period was so important: 'Not until after the Second World War was it widely the case that departments were directed by geographers who had themselves received formal training in the discipline, by which time most of the initial marked differences and contrasts in subject personality had been blurred or obliterated' (Garnett, 1969, p. 387). At this point geography departments were established in most universities and the subject had a recognisable core of identity. By 1954, Honeybone could write a summary of the final acceptance and establishment of geography as a university discipline:

> In the universities, there has been an unparalleled advance in the number of staff and scope of the work in the departments of geography. In the University of London alone, there are now six chairs, four of them of relatively recent creation. Students, both graduates and undergraduates, are greater in number than ever before. Many of the training colleges and university departments of education are taking a full part in the progress; employers are realising the value of the breadth of a university training in geography; and the Civil Service has recently raised the status of geography in its higher examinations. In fact, on all sides, we can see signs that, at long last, geography is forcing its complete acceptance as a major discipline in the universities, and that geographers are welcomed into commerce, industry and the professions, because they are well educated men and women.
>
> (Honeybone, 1954)

So by the mid-1950s geography had achieved Layton's third stage in the acceptance of a subject. The selection of subject matter being 'determined in large measure by the judgements and practices of the specialist scholars who lead inquiries in the field'; the definition of the subject was increasingly in the hands of specialist scholars. The context in which these scholars operated was substantially divorced from schools; their activities and personal motivations, their status and career concerns were situated within the university context. The concerns of school pupils, thereby unrepresented, were of less and less account in the definition of this well-established academic discipline. The situation within the schools themselves soon became clear. In 1967 the report on *Society and the Young School Leaver* noted that its young subject felt 'at best apathetic, at worst resentful and rebellious to geography...which seems to him to have nothing to do with the adult world he is soon to join' (p. 3). The report adds:

> A frequent cause of failure seems to be that the course is often based on the traditional belief that there is a body of content for each separate subject which every school leaver should know. In the least successful courses this body of knowledge is written into the curriculum without any real consideration of the needs of the boys and girls and without any question of its relevance.
>
> (*Society and the Young School Leaver*, 1967)

The threat to geography began to be appreciated at the highest level. A member of the Executive and Honorary Secretary of the Geographical Association recalls: 'Things had gone too far and geography became a too locally based regional thing...at the same time the subject began to lose touch with reality...geography got a bad name' (Interview, 30 June 1976). A college lecturer, David Gowing, saw the same problem facing the subject and argued:

> One must recognise the need to take a fresh look at our objectives and to re-examine the role and nature of geography in school. It is not difficult to identify the causes of increasing dissatisfaction. Pupils feel that present curricula have little relevance to their needs and so their level of motivation and understanding is low. Teachers are concerned that the raising of the school leaving age and some forms of comprehensive reorganisation may exacerbate the problems.
>
> (Gowing, 1973, p. 153)

The increasing definition of geography by the university specialists plainly posed problems for the subject in schools. To recapture the sense of utility and relevance of earlier days the subject would have needed to focus more on the needs of the average and below average school student. However, geography still faced problems of academic status within some universities and also among the high status sections of the secondary sector.

The advances in university geography after the Second World War partly aided the acceptance of geography as a subject suitable for the most able children, but problems remained. In 1967 Marchant noted: 'Geography is at last attaining to intellectual respectability in the academic streams of our secondary schools. But the battle is not quite over.' He instanced the continuing problem: 'May I quote from just two reports written in 1964, one of a girls' grammar school and the other on a well-known boys' independent school.' First, 'geography is at present...an alternative to Latin, which means that a number of girls cease to take it at the end of the third year...there is no work available at "A" level'. Or second, perhaps a more intriguing situation: 'In the "O" level forms, the subject is taken only by those who are neither classicists, nor modern linguists, nor scientists. The sixth form is then drawn from this rather restricted group with the addition of a few scientists who failed to live up to expectations' (Marchant, 1965, p. 133).

To seal its acceptance by the universities and high status sixth forms, geography had to embrace new paradigms and associated rhetoric. The supreme paradox is that the crisis in school geography in the late 1960s led not to change which might have involved more school pupils but to changes in the opposite direction in pursuit of total academic acceptance. This push for university status centred around the 'new geography', which moved away from regional geography to more quantitative data and model building. The battle for new geography represented a major clash between those traditions in geography representing more pedagogic and utilitarian traditions (notably the fieldwork geographers and some regionalists) and those pushing for total academic acceptance.

'New geography' as an academic discipline

At the Madingley Lectures in 1963, which effectively launched the era of 'new geography', E.A. Wrigley contended: 'What we have seen is a concept overtaken by the course of historical change. "Regional" geography in the great mould has been as much a victim of the industrial revolution as the peasant, landed society, the horse and the village community, and for the same reason' (Wrigley, 1967, p. 13). To this problem Chorley and Haggett proposed an 'immediate solution' through 'building up the neglected geometrical side of the discipline'. They noted:

> Research is already swinging strongly into this field and the problem of implementation may be more acute in the schools than in the universities. Here we are continually impressed by the vigour and reforming zeal of 'ginger groups' like the School Mathematics Association which have shared in fundamental review of mathematics teaching in schools. There the inertia problems – established textbooks, syllabuses, examinations – are being successfully overcome and a new wave of interest is sweeping through the schools. The need in geography is just as great and we see no good reason why changes here should not yield results equally rewarding.
>
> (Chorley and Haggett, 1960, p. 377)

The messianic nature of their appeal is shown when they argue that it is:

> Better that geography should explode in an excess of reform than bask in the watery sunset of its former glories; for in an age of rising standards in school and university, to maintain the present standards is not enough – to stand still is to retreat, to move forward hesitantly is to fall back from the frontier. If we move with that frontier new horizons emerge in our view, and we find new territories to be explored as exciting and demanding as the dark continents that beckoned any earlier generation of geographers. This is the teaching frontier of geography.

The Madingley Lectures proved a watershed in the emergence of the subject. Two years before, E.E. Gilbert – in an article on 'The Idea of the Region' – had stated that he regarded new geography in the universities as an 'esoteric cult' (Gilbert, 1961). After Madingley, this was no longer the case, as a college lecturer who was secretary of his local Geographical Association recalled: 'After Madingley my ideas were turned upside down ... That's where the turn around in thinking in geography really started' (Personal interview, 5 January 1977). But as Walford later noted, Madingley was 'heady to some, undrinkable brew to others'

(Walford, 1973, p. 95). Following the second Madingley Conference in 1968, Chorley and Haggett sought to consolidate the changes they were advocating by a new book entitled *Models in Geography* (Chorley and Haggett, 1967). By this time opinions were becoming progressively polarised about the 'new geography'. Slaymaker wrote in support of the book:

> In retrospect, a turning point in the development of geographical methodology in Britain. After the exploratory and mildly iconoclastic contents of the first Madingley lectures, recorded in *Frontiers in Geographical Teaching*, a more substantial statement of the methodological basis and aims of the so-called 'new geography' was required...with the publication of this book [it is demonstrated that] the traditional classificatory paradigm is inadequate and that in the context of the 'new geography' an irreversible step has been taken to push us back into the mainstream of scientific activity by process of model building. The discussion of the relevance of new conceptual models in geographical research and teaching should serve as a stimulus to participation in methodological debate to which, with notable exceptions, British geographers have made a disproportionately small contribution. It is therefore a major publication, both in achievement and potential.
>
> (Slaymaker, 1960)

Teachers of the subject received less enthusiastic advice from their journal, *Geography* and its anonymous reviewer 'PRC':

> What...is its object, and to whom is it addressed? These questions are avoided with perverse skill and in the absence of guidance, the conviction gradually takes root that, in fact, the authors are writing for each other! This may explain, though it does not excuse, the use in some papers of a barbarous and repulsive jargon. Is it then a joint expression of faith on the part of the New Geographers? This would indeed have been welcome but a new faith is hardly likely to be attained by a frenzied search for gadgets which might conceivably be turned to geographical ends. The nature of those ends calls for solid thought, a task which cannot be delegated to computers.
>
> (Review in *Geography*, 1968)

A year later the president of the Geographical Association pursued a similar opposition with a more explicit statement of the fears which new geography engendered. The new systematic geography, she argued, was:

> creating a problem that will increase in acuteness over the decades ahead for it leads towards subject fragmentation as fringe specialisms in systematic fields proliferate and are pursued independently to the neglect of the very core of our discipline – a core that largely justified its existence. Geography in our universities is in fact becoming so sophisticated, and its numerous branches in diverse fields at times so narrowly specialised, that sooner or later, the question must arise as to how much longer the subject can effectively be held together.
>
> (Garnett, 1969, pp. 388–389)

The implications of this analysis are clear:

> So my first plea to the academic teachers who will be the leaders of tomorrow must be: let there never be question (other than at an advanced post-graduate

and research level) of the coexistence of two geographies, physical and social, regarded as one without reference to the other. University departments have a duty to ensure that, at least at the first degree level, the core of our subject is neither forgotten nor neglected, and that the synthesis of the specialist fields and their relevance to the core are clearly appreciated by our undergraduate students. In my mind, it is only on the foundation of a first degree course structure so designed that a geographer is basically qualified either to teach in our schools or to carry his studies further at a postgraduate research level.

(Garnett, 1969, p. 389)

The overwhelming worry reflected in this quote was that the myth of the discipline would be exposed. Geography was supposedly a unified academic discipline into which the schoolteacher initiated young pupils. If there was no obvious link between university and school geography this version of events – the Hirstian vision of school subjects – would stand exposed. Teachers themselves became very worried: 'Geography was in a state of ferment...it was moving too quickly...Let alone in the schools even many of the universities didn't have new geography'; and 'This new approach, however you felt about it, caused a sort of schism...both at university and at school level' (Interview, 30 June 1976).

Fears of this schism were expressed in a number of contemporary books. The gap between schools and universities, of which there is much evidence in previous periods, was thought particularly worrying:

Techniques of study are changing more rapidly in modern geography than at any previous time in the subject's history. As a result there is a great need for a dialogue between research workers and those being admitted to the mysteries of the subject. Teachers provide the necessary link; and it is dangerous for the vitality and future health of geography that some teachers find current developments either incomprehensible or unacceptable.

(Cooke and Johnson, 1969, p. 8)

Rex Walford made a similar diagnosis: 'The need for unity within the subject is more than a practical one of preparing sixth formers for their first lectures on campus; it is, I would assert, a basic requirement for the continued existence of the subject' (Walford, 1973, p. 97).

In spite of the opposition of teachers and academics, many of who saw regional geography as the 'real geography', there were strong pressures working in favour of the advocates of new geography. Beyond the problems in schools, the scholars in universities who controlled the new definitions of the subject were concerned to progress to the front rank of university academic disciplines. (Their concerns would of course be reflected in greater sixth form status.) New geography was conceived and promoted to achieve this end. The alliance between university status and school status ensured that ultimately the Geographical Association would embrace 'new geography'.

The perceived problems encountered by school geography were used as an argument for change. The change then moved in those directions most likely to satisfy geography's aspiration for the full acceptance as a first rank academic discipline in universities and sixth forms. The changes emanating from universities were partly mediated through the Geographical Association to the schools. At stages where the gap between the two widened, the Association was always on hand to warn against too rapid redefinition and to exhort teachers to change and to encourage their re-training. In recent years, fears about 'new geography' seem to have subsided and a period of consolidation has set in. Of the Cambridge base of Chorley and Haggett it was recently written, by David Walker, himself a protagonist: 'The academic revolution of quantification which has battered traditional scholarship in fields like economic history and linguistics has taken its toll in geography in recent years, but the Cambridge department which Professor Darby took over in 1966 remains on even keel. The tripos system continues to offer a fine balance of specialisation and liberal education' (Walker, 1975, p. 6).

Perceptions of the subject as being in crisis have considerably mellowed. A professor, who is on the Executive Committee and past holder of a number of positions in the Geographical Association stated: 'I see geography traditionally as a core to understand why places are as they are' but said of the present condition of geography: 'It isn't in flux...there is no end to the subject...of course the techniques by which you advance the subject will change...if the present emphasis on quantitative techniques helps our preciseness who could deny that it is an advance within the subject' (Interview, 14 December 1978).

Ultimately the reconciliation with new geography was closely linked with geography's long aspiration to be viewed as a scientific discipline. In a previous decade Professor Wooldridge had written a book on *The Geographer as Scientist* (1956), but in 1970 Fitzgerald, reviewing the implications of new geography for teaching wrote: 'The change which many think is at the heart of geography is that towards the use of the scientific method in approaching problems' (Walford, 1973, p. 85). Similarly, M. Yeates wrote: 'Geography can be regarded as a science concerned with the rational development and testing of theories that explain and predict the spatial distribution and location of various characteristics on the surface of the earth' (Yeates, 1968, p. 1).

At the 21st International Geographic Congress at New Delhi in 1968, Professor Norton Ginsburg identified *social* science as the 'fraternity' to aspire to. He saw: 'the beginnings of a new age for human geography as a fully-fledged member of the social science fraternity...the future of geography as a major research discipline will, I submit, be determined on the intellectual battlefields of the universities, where competition and conflict are intense; and where ideas are the hallmark of achievement' (Ginsburg, 1969, pp. 403–404). He considered that 'research has moved rapidly, albeit erratically, towards the formulation of general propositions and theories of organisation and behaviour and away from preoccupation with patterns *per se*. In this sense geography's internal organisation and intellectual apparatus have come to resemble those of the social sciences, whereas formerly they were markedly at variance with them'. Hence by 1970, geography had finished its 'long march' to acceptance as an academic discipline; from now on its future would indeed be determined not in the school classroom but on 'the intellectual battlefields of the universities'.

Conclusion

The establishment of geography – how geography was rendered a discipline – was a protracted, painstaking and fiercely contested process. The story is not of the translation of an academic discipline, devised by ('dominant') groups of scholars in universities, into pedagogic version to be used as a school subject. Rather the story unfolds in reverse order and can be seen as a drive on the part of low status groups at school level progressively to colonise areas within the university sector – thereby earning the right for scholars in the new field to define knowledge that could be viewed as a discipline. The process of development for school subjects can be seen not as a pattern of disciplines 'translated' *down* or of 'domination' *downwards* but very much as a process of 'aspiration' *upwards*.

To summarise the stages in the emergence of geography: in the earlier stages teaching was anything but 'messianic', for the subject was taught by non-specialists and comprised a 'dreary collection of geographical facts and figures'. The threshold for take-off on the route to academic establishment began with Mackinder's remarkably successful recipe for the subject's promotion drawn up in 1903. In the Mackinder manifesto the geography teacher is to set the exams and is to choose exams that are best for the 'common acceptation' of the subject, the teaching of geography is to be exclusively in the hands of trained geographers and the universities are to be encouraged to establish schools of geography 'where geographers can be made'.

The strategy offered solutions for the major problems geography faced in it development. Most notable of these was the idiosyncratic and information-based nature of school geography. Initially the subject stressed personal, pedagogic and vocational arguments for its inclusion in curricula: 'we seek to train future citizens' and moreover a citizen 'must have a topographical background if he is to keep order in the mass of information which accumulates in the course of this life' (1919). Later the subject was advocated because 'travel and correspondence have now become general' (1927). But the result of these utilitarian and pedagogic emphases was that comments arose as to the 'expansiveness' of the subject and the fact that it came 'more and more to be a "world citizenship" subject' (1930s).

The problem was that identified by Mackinder in 1903: geographers needed to be 'made' in the universities, then any piecemeal changes in pursuit of school relevance or utility could be controlled and directed. The growth of the subject in the schools provided an overwhelming argument for the subject to be taught in the universities. As Wooldridge noted later, 'it has been conceded that if geography is to be taught in schools it must be learned in universities'. Slowly therefore a uniformity in the subject was established to answer those who observed the chameleon nature of the subject's knowledge structure. Alice Garnett noted that it was not until after 1945 that most school departments of geography were directed by specialist-trained geographers but as a result of this training 'most of the initial marked differences and contrasts in subject personality had been blurred or obliterated' (one might say 'masked and mystified').

The definition of geography through the universities rapidly replaced any pedagogic or utilitarian promotional bias with arguments for academic rigour: and as early as 1927 Hadlow had contended that 'the main objective in good geographical teaching is to develop, as in the case of history, an attitude of mind and mode of thought characteristic of the subject'. However, for several decades university geography was plagued both by the image of the subject as essentially for school children, and by the idiosyncratic interpretations of the various university departments, especially in respect to fieldwork. Thus, while establishment in universities solved the status problems of the subject within schools, within universities themselves the subject's status still remained low. The launching of 'new geography' with aspirations to scientific or social scientific rigour is therefore partly to be understood as a strategy for finally establishing geography's status at the highest level. In this respect the current position of the subject in universities would seem to confirm the success of new geography's push for parity of esteem with other university disciplines.

The aspiration to become an academic subject and the successful promotion employed by geography teachers and educationists, particularly in the work of the

Geographical Association, has been clearly evidenced. We know what happened in the history of geography: less evidence has been presented as to why this should be so. A clue can be found in Garnett's presidential address to the Geography Association in 1968; a clear link is presented between 'the recognition of our subject's status among university disciplines' and 'the costly provision made available for its study'. Plainly the drive towards higher status is accompanied by opportunities to command larger finance and resources.

The close connection between academic status and resources is a fundamental feature of our educational system. The origin of this connection is the examination system created by universities from the late 1850s and culminating in the school certificate system founded in 1917. As a result the so-called 'academic' subjects provide examinations which are suitable for 'able' students whilst other subjects are not.

Byrne's work has provided data on resource allocation within schools. She discerned that: 'two assumptions which might be questioned have been seen consistently to underlay educational planning and the consequent resource allocation for the more able children. First, that these necessarily need longer in school than non-grammar pupils, and secondly, that they necessarily need more staff, more highly paid staff and more money for equipment and books' (Byrne, 1974, p. 29). The implications of the preferential treatment of academic subjects for the material self-interest of teachers are clear: better staffing ratios, higher salaries, higher capitation allowances, more graded posts, better careers prospects. The link between academic status and resource allocation provides the major explanatory framework for understanding the aspirational imperative to become an academic subject. Basically since more resources are given to the academic examination subject taught to able students the conflict over the status of examinable knowledge is above all a battle over the material resources and career prospects of each subject teacher or subject community.

The historical profile tentatively discerned for geography exposes certain omissions, in some cases misconceptions, within the main philosophical and sociological accounts. The philosophical perspective has provided support for the view that school subjects derive from forms or fields of knowledge or 'disciplines'. Of course once a school subject has brought about the establishment of an academic discipline base it is persuasively self-fulfilling to argue that the school subject receives intellectual direction and inputs from university scholars. This version of events simply celebrates a *fait accompli* in the history of the school subject and associated disciplines. What is left unexplained and unrecorded are the stages of evolution towards the culminating pattern and the forces which push aspiring academic subjects to follow similar routes. By starting with the final historical product philosophical studies forego the opportunity to examine school subjects fully.

In a way, sociological accounts also celebrate the *fait accompli* and assume that university control of school subjects reflects a continuing pattern of pervasive domination. As we have seen the major agencies actively involved in constructing this pattern were the teachers of school subjects themselves – not so much domination by dominant forces, more solicitous surrender by subordinate groups. The stress on domination leads to an emphasis on teachers 'being socialised within institutionalised structures' which legitimate high status patterns of academic subjects. Far from this socialisation in dominant institutions being the major factor creating the pattern we have examined, it was much more considerations of teachers' material self-interest in their working lives. Since the misconception is purveyed by sociologists, who often exhort us 'to understand the teachers' real world', they should really know better. High status academic knowledge gains its adherents and aspirants less through control of the curricula which socialise than through well-established connection with patterns of resource allocation and the associated work and career prospects these ensure. The historical study of school subjects directs our attention to the development of patterns of resource allocation and I think shows how generative this approach might be in replacing crude notions of domination with patterns of control in which subordinate groups can be seen actively at work.

References

Apple, M.W., 1978, Ideology, Reproduction and Educational Reform. *Comparative Education Review*, 22.

Bernstein, B., 1971, On the Classification and Framing of Educational Knowledge. In M. Young (ed.), *Knowledge and Control* (London: Collier, Macullan).

Bird, C., 1901, Limitations and Possibilities of Geographical Teaching in Day Schools. *The Geographical Teacher*, 1.

Board of Education, 1927, *Report of the Consultative Committee: The Education of the Adolescent*, Hadlow Report (London: HMSO).

Bourdieu, P., 1971, Systems of Education and Systems of Thought, and Intellectual Field and Creative Project. In M. Young (ed.), *Reproduction in Education, Society and Culture* (London: Sage).

Bourdieu, P. and Passeron, J.C., 1977, *Reproduction in Education, Society and Culture* (London: Sage).

Byrne, E.M., 1974, *Planning and Educational Inequality* (Slough: NFER).

Chorley, R. and Haggett, P., 1960, *Frontier Movements and The Geographical Tradition*.

Chorley, R. and Haggett, P., 1967, *Models in Geography* (London: Methuen).

Cooke, R. and Johnson, J.M., 1969, *Trends in Geography* (London: Methuen).

Council of the Geographical Association, 1919, The Position of Geography, *The Geographical Teacher*, 10.

David, T., 1973, Against Geography. In D. Bale, N. Graves and R. Walford (eds), *Perspectives in Geographical Education* (Edinburgh: Oliver and Boyd).

Esland, G.M. and Dale, R. (eds), 1972, *School and Society*, Course E282 Unit 2 (Open University, Milton Keynes).

Fitzgerald, B.P., 1970, Scientific Method, Quantitative Techniques and the Teaching of Geography. In Walford (ed.), 1973.

Garnett, A., 1969, Teaching Geography: Some Reflections, *Geography*, 54, November.

Gilbert, E.W., 1961, The Idea of the Region, *Geography*, 45(1).

Ginsburg, N., 1969, Tasks of Geography, *Geography*, 54.

Gowing, D., 1973, A Fresh Look at Objectives. In R. Watford (ed.), *New Directions in Geography Teaching* (London: Longmans).

Hirst, P., 1967, The Educational Implications of Social and Economic Change. In Schools Council Working Paper No. 12 (London: HMSO).

Honeybone, R.C., 1954, Balance in Geography and Education, *Geography*, 34(184).

Interview (30 June 1976).

Interview Geography Professor (14 December 1978).

Jenkins, D. and Shipman, M.P., 1976, *Curriculum: An Introduction* (London: Open Books).

Layton, D., 1972, Science as General Education, *Trends in Education*, January.

Mackinder, H.J., 1887, On the Scope and Methods of Geography. In *Proceedings of the Royal Geographical Society*, IX.

Mackinder, H.J., 1903, *Report of the Discussion on Geographical Education* at the British Association meeting, September 1903. In *Geographical Teacher*, 2, 1903, pp. 95–101.

Manifesto of Geographical Association printed on the inside cover of all copies of *Geography*.

Marchant, E.C., 1965, Some Responsibilities of the Teacher of Geography, *Geography*, 3.

Musgrove, F., 1968, The Contribution of Sociology to the Study of the Curriculum. In J.F. Kerr (ed.), *Changing the Curriculum* (London: University of London Press).

Personal Interview College of Education Lecturer (5 January 1977).

Phenix, P.M., 1964, *The Realms of Meaning* (New York: McGraw-Hill).

PRC, Review, 1968, *Geography*, 53, Part 4, November.

Slaymaker, O., 1960, Review, *Geographical Journal*, 134, Part 2, September.

Society and the Young School Leaver, 1967, In Working Paper No. 11 (London: HMSO).

The Norwood Report, 1943, *Curriculum and Examinations in Secondary Schools* (London: HMSO).

Walford, R., 1973, Models, Simulations and Games. In R. Walford (ed.).

Walker, D., 1975, The Well-rounded Geographers. *The Times Educational Supplement*, 28 November, p. 6.

Wooldridge, S.W., 1956, *The Geographer as Scientist* (London: Nelson).

Wrigley, E.A., 1967, Changes in the Philosophy of Geography. In R. Chorley and P. Haggett (eds), *Frontiers in Geographical Teaching* (London: Methuen).

Yeates, M.H., 1968, *An Introduction to Quantative Analysis in Economic Geography* (New York: McGraw-Hill).

Young, M., 1971, An Approach to the Study of Curricula as Socially Organised Knowledge. In M. Young (ed.).

Young, M., 1977, Curriculum Change: Limits and Possibilities. In M. Young and G. Whitty (eds), *Society State and Schooling* (Brighton: Falmer Press).

CHAPTER 6

ON CURRICULUM FORM

Sociology of Education, 1992, 65(1): 66–75

Sociologists of education interested in the school curriculum have long faced a paradox. The curriculum is avowedly and manifestly a social construction. Why then in so many of our studies of schooling is this central social construct treated as a timeless given? In particular why have social scientists, traditionally more attuned than most to the ideological and political struggles which underpin social life, themselves largely accepted the 'givenness' of the school curriculum? This was always a peculiar omission but as the curriculum wars rage in American higher education over the choice of 'canon' it would seem to be a good time to begin again to theorise the school curriculum.

At the moment, in many Western countries the school 'curriculum' is back on the political agenda. In the US following the Holmes Group and the Carnegie Task Force and publications such as a 'Nation at Risk', this is clearly evidenced; in Britain the givenness of curriculum is being literally enshrined by parliamentary legislation in the form of a 'National curriculum'; in Australia the provinces are 'mapping' their curriculum to discern commonalities, some scholars would argue, as a precursor to defining more 'national' curriculum guidelines.

In these circumstances it is important to review the state of sociological knowledge with regard to the curriculum. For our knowledge of the school curriculum remains severely under-theorised. Much of the work in this domain has been that carried out by sociologists of knowledge but pioneering work in this area remains partial and flawed if we are concerned to develop our theoretical understanding of curriculum. As Apple (1979, p. 17) has conceded, a good deal of the significant work in this field has been conducted in Europe: Emile Durkheim's and Karl Mannheim's early work remains important as does the work of the late Raymond Williams and in the 1960s and 1970s the work of Pierre Bourdieu and of Basil Bernstein. In the work of Williams, most of the theoretical focus was on the *content* of the curriculum, Bernstein meanwhile pointed to underlying principles for the classification and framing of curriculum but placed his emphasis on the relationship *between* subject content (Bernstein, 1971). Interestingly the obsession with subject content is continued in Lee Shulman's work on the knowledge base required for teaching. In his leading section on 'scholarship in content disciplines' we learn that 'the first source of the knowledge base is *content*' (Shulman, 1987, p. 8).

The issue of relationships *within* subject matter has remained unexplored and untheorised. In this chapter the question of the internal relations of curriculum – the form of curriculum – is analysed: as Apple has said, 'for methodological reasons one does not take for granted that curricular knowledge is neutral.

Instead, one looks for social interests embodied in the knowledge form itself' (Apple, 1979, p. 17). The social conflict within the subject is central to under-standing the subject itself (and hence relations between subjects). The subject is not a monolithic entity and hence analyses, which view subjects and relations between subjects in this manner, mystify a central and ongoing social conflict. On this analysis an understanding of the internal relations of curriculum would be an important precursor to the kind of work Bernstein has exemplified on the external relations and modalities of curriculum.

A less theoretical justification for analyses of curriculum form is the pervasive-ness of what Connell has called the 'competitive academic curriculum'. This form of curriculum sets the agenda and the discourse for schooling in many countries. The results are fairly generalisable:

> To say it is hegemonic is not to say it is the only curriculum in those schools. It is to say that this pattern has pride of place in those schools; it dominates most people's ideas of what real learning is about. Its logic has the most powerful influence on the organisation of the school and of the education system generally; and it is also to marginal or subordinate the other curricula that are present: Above all 'the competitive academic curriculum makes the sorting and the hardening of hearts a central reality of contemporary school life.
>
> (Connell, 1985, p. 87)

Yet the continuing dominance of the competitive academic curriculum is the result of a continuing contest within school subjects.

Conceptions of 'mentalities'

By way of exemplifying a broader conception for studying school subjects I will examine the emergence of certain conceptions of 'mentalities' as they provide antecedent assumptions for our contemporary social construction of school knowledge. In doing this I am building on the work of others and am not follow-ing a consistent line of development. I might therefore be justifiably accused of raiding history, of dipping into periods without full knowledge or portrayal of the complexity of context. But my objective is not so much a sustained historical explanation as to show how antecedent factors could be a factor in contemporary construction and consciousness. The aim is to show how we might pursue a longer time perspective on current events and how in doing this we might provide a reconceptualisation of the mode of curriculum study which will allow us to connect specific acts of social construction to wider social impulses.

The notion of 'mentality' owes a good deal to the work of the Annaliste School of historians. Following them, I take the view that in studying historical periods it is important to generate insights into the world views held by distinct cultural and sub-cultural groups. In this sense mentality is related to the micro-concept of 'habi-tus' as developed by Bourdieu and Passeron (1977) or 'resistance' as a distinctive view held by British working class 'lads' in the work of Paul Willis (1977).

In his work on Australian school reform, which derives from the Annaliste School, Pitman has argued that 'with a given civilisation, there are multiple cultures related to location, class, occupation, gender and any other relevant criterion':

> The dialectic relationships of the various groups with their material worlds and with each other permit the development of world views, or mentalities within these groups which are distinct from each other. For example, in the

division of labour and the class exchange of labour to organisers of labour and owners of the means of production, then the participants in the asymmetrical exchanges interact differently with their material worlds, at least in relation to the nature of work.

(Pitman, 1986, p. 60)

Shapin and Barnes have examined a selection of educational writings on pedagogy in Britain in the period 1770–1850. In examining the 'rhetoric' of pedagogy they found 'remarkable agreement upon the mentality of the subjects of those programmes' (Shapin and Barnes, 1976, p. 231). Different mentalities were ascribed depending on whether the persons in question came from 'the higher orders' or 'the lower ranks'.

Three dichotomies

Three central dichotomies were discerned. The first places the *sensual* and *concrete* character of the thought of the lower orders against the *intellectual, verbal* and *abstract* qualities of upper class thoughts. The second places the *simplicity* of the lower orders thought against the *complexity* and *sophistication* of their betters.

In *Wealth of Nations*, Adam Smith provided the crucial link between division of labour and division of mentalities (and, of course, curriculum). In patterns of exploitation and domination this is the crucial rationalisation to enshrine. Thus, Smith stated:

In the progress of the division of labour the employment of the far greater part of those who live by labour, comes to be confined to a few very simple operations; frequently to one or two. But the understandings of the greater part of men are necessarily formed by their ordinary employments. The man whose whole life is spent in performing a few simple operations, of which the effects too are, perhaps, always the same or very nearly the same, has no occasion to exert his understanding or to exercise his invention ... He naturally ... becomes as stupid and ignorant as it is possible for a human creature to become.

(Quote in Shapin and Barnes, 1976, p. 231)

For the elite Smith was similarly strident:

The employments, too, in which people of some rank or fortune spend their lives, are not, like those of the common people, simple or uniform. They are almost all of them extremely complicated, and such as exercise the head more than the hands.

(Quote in Shapin and Barnes, 1976, p. 231)

The third central dichotomy concerns the *passive* response of the lower orders to experience and knowledge compared with the *active* use of the upper ranks. This spectrum of passivity to activity is perhaps the most crucial part of the conundrum of mentalities when related to the evolution of school knowledge. Hence:

The sensually-based, superficial and simple thoughts of the lower orders did not allow them to produce mediated responses to experience, or to make deep connections between different pieces of information, such as would permit them to be generalised for use as resources in a wide range of contexts.

(Smith, Quote in Shapin and Barnes, 1976, p. 231)

From these early stages the link between the lower orders and specific, contextu-alised knowledge was forged. This need for immediate contextualised knowledge provided the diagnosis 'which justified the characterisation of their learning process as passive and mechanical' (Shapin and Barnes, 1976, p. 234). Knowledge was presented and accepted in a way that connections were not made between specific and contextualised facts, the lower orders did not act upon knowledge or generalise from data. A devil's bargain emerged: the lower order were taught specific, contextualised 'facts' mechanically – the capacity to generalise across contexts was not provided or encouraged. Decontextualised knowledge was for others then – for the lower orders it became a deeply alien and untouchable form of knowledge. In due course it too ensured passivity.

In contrast the upper orders could incorporate their perceptions, intuitions, information and knowledge into coherent systems of thought and inference:

> By so doing, they could, on the one hand, extend their range of applicability, and, on the other, bring a range of abstract principles and symbolic operations to bear upon them. Thus, they could, unlike the lower orders, make *active use* of knowledge and experience. Whatever it was, it served to extend the possibilities of their thought.

Hence:

> In society, as in the body, the head was reflective, manipulative and controlling; the hand, unreflective, mechanical, determined by instructions.
> (Smith, quote in Shapin and Barnes, 1976, p. 235)

Shapin and Barnes judge therefore that 'as one moved up into the higher ranks of society, one increasingly encountered more abstract, refined and complex modes of thought, and more extensive, finely structured and profound bodies of "knowl-edge"'. But alongside this was the requirement that knowledge should be 'properly distributed' not 'improperly graded' or taught 'out of place'. Thus:

> Properly distributed, it could operate as a symbolic display of social standing, enabling the various orders better to recognise the hierarchy and sectors to which deference was due. And it might also serve as a medium enabling communication between the top and the base of society, a vehicle through which head could control hand. Incorrectly distributed, knowledge could stimulate the masses to aspire upwards and give them the resources to use in doing so. Although, perhaps, their natural inferiority would doom these aspirations to ultimate failure, the temporary turbulence would be troublesome and inconvenient.
> (Shapin and Barnes, 1976, p. 236)

The two distinct mentalities defined for the upper and lower orders were essentially cultural resources employed in a whole range of debates and discourses:

> They are a tribute to man's skill and endless creativity in the construction of rationalisations and adaptation of cultural resources to the exigencies of concrete situations. And it is as situated responses to particular polemical requirements and not necessarily as the coherent philosophies of individuals that we must treat these individuals.
> (Shapin and Barnes, 1976, p. 237)

In the process of favouring the 'head more than the hands', new patterns of differentiation and examination were emerging in English secondary schooling in the mid-nineteenth century. By the 1850s, schooling was developing links with universities through the founding of the first examination boards. Here was a structural response to the privileges of the higher orders and their allied abstract knowledge of the head. The universities of course were for 'fine minds' and developed curricula to 'train the mind'. They were unequivocally for the 'head more than the hands', indeed 'training the mind' was their exclusive preserve.

The links with the social order were then clear and were often explicitly stated as the university examination boards were constructed. For instance, the University of Cambridge Local Examination Syndicate was founded in 1858: 'The establishment of these examinations was the universities' response to petitions that they should help in the development of "schools for the middle classes"' (University of Cambridge, 1958). As the university examination boards came into being, a hierarchy of social orders and associated curricula were, in effect, being established and linked to a system and structure of schooling. At the top, schools were for 'training the mind' and developed links at the level of examinations, and at times future destinations, with the universities and with their classical curriculum. As one descended the levels of schooling, on found that the curriculum became progressively more rudimentary, was taught mechanically, and had a practical 'orientation'.

The contest over science

In the decades that followed, there were, of course, challenges to this 'political settlement' on levels of curriculum that corresponded so well to the gradations of society. Most notable was the battle over the inclusion of science. The perceived social danger of science, particularly applied science, was partly that education could be related to the cultural experience of the lower orders. There was knowledge that could be contextualised – not abstract, not classical, not quintessentially decontextualised but the opposite knowledge whose relevance and interest might be secured for the lower orders. For the masses, a possible educational medium was at the hand. Here, then, was a litmus test of the interestedness or disinterestedness of school knowledge. In the early nineteenth century, opinions on science had been clear. Thus, a 'country gentleman' judged in 1825 that:

> if the working classes are to be taught the sciences, what are the middle and higher classes to learn, to preserve the due proportion? The answer is obvious enough. There is nothing they can be taught by which they can maintain their superiority.
>
> (Quote in Shapin and Barnes, 1976, p. 239)

In his early work, Mannheim thought science to be 'disinterested knowledge', but science as school knowledge was plainly entirely another matter, much more a case of 'interested knowledge'.

The problems raised by 'country gentleman' grew in the period following 1825, for some successful experiments were underway to teach science to the working classes in the elementary schools. For instance, the Reverand Richard Dawes opened a National Society School in King's Somborne in England in 1842. Here he proceeded to teach science as applied to 'the understanding of common things'. In short, he taught contextualised science, but with a view to develop the academic understanding of his pupils from the lower orders. Scientific knowledge, then, was contextualised within the culture and experience of the common people's children, but taught in a way that could open the door to understanding and the exercise of thought. This was schooling as education – and what is more, for the labouring poor. But the curriculum was limited to elementary schools with predominantly working class students. There is clear evidence in contemporary government reports, that the science of common things allowed considerable practical success in classrooms. One would be wrong, however, to assume therefore that the problem was solved and that the science of common things provided the basis for the definition of school science. Far from it. Other definitions of school science were being advocated by powerful interests. Lord Wrottesley chaired a Parliamentary Committee of the British Association for the Advancement of Science on the most appropriate type of science education for the upper classes. Hodson argues that the report:

> reflected a growing awareness of a serious problem: that science education at the elementary level was proving highly successful, particularly as far as the development of thinking skills was concerned, and the social hierarchy was under threat because there was not corresponding development for the higher order.
>
> (1987, p. 139)

Wrottesley gave an example that confirmed his worst fears:

> a poor boy hobbled forth to give a reply; he was lame and humpbacked, and his wan emaciated face told only too clearly the tale of poverty and its consequences... but he gave forthwith so lucid and intelligent a reply to the question put to him that there arose a feeling of admiration for the child's talents combined with a sense of shame that more information should be found in some of the lowest of our lower classes on matters of general interest than in those far above them in the world by station.

He concluded:

> It would be an unwholesome and vicious state of society in which those who are comparatively unblessed with nature's gifts should be generally superior in intellectual attainments to those above them in station.
>
> (Quote in Hodson, 1987, p. 139)

Soon after Wrottesley's comments in 1860, science was removed from the elementary curriculum. When it eventually reappeared in the curriculum of the elementary schools some 20 years later, it was in a very different form from the science of common things. A watered-down version of pure laboratory science had become accepted as the *correct* view of science, a view that has persisted, largely unchallenged, to the present day. Science, as a school subject, was powerfully redefined to become similar in form to so much else in the secondary curriculum – pure, abstract, a body of knowledge enshrined in syllabuses and textbooks (Goodson, 1988).

The fundamental insight is that even with a subject conceived of as a challenge to the traditional academic curriculum incorporation can take place. Hence, science, which was thought of a practical and pedagogical, ended up as 'pure laboratory science'.

Continuities and complexities

The early nineteenth century pattern of differing 'mentalities' and differing curricula that Shapin and Barnes noted has had considerable durability. Of course, the continuities that can be discerned must be fully related to the complexity of each historical period. In this sense, I am only pointing to an agenda for future historical work.

The apparent continuities are sufficiently clear, however, as to warrant substantial further historical study. For instance, almost a century later, the Norwood Report of 1943 advocated the notion of different mentalities and of different curricula and, indeed, different schools to serve these mentalities. This report led, in Britain, to the 1944 Education Act, which may be seen as institutionalising a social and political order for schooling, built upon a hierarchy of mentalities.

The Norwood Report argued that throughout Europe, 'the evolution of education' had 'thrown up certain groups, each of which can and must be treated in a way appropriate to itself'. In England three clear groups could be discerned. Firstly:

> the pupil who is interested in learning for its own sake, who can grasp an argument or follow a piece of connected reasoning, who is interested in causes, whether on the level of human volition or in the material world, who cares to know how things came to be as well as how they are, who is sensitive to language as expression of thought, to a proof as a precise demonstration, to a series of experiments justifying a principle; he is interested in the relatedness of related things, in development, in structure, in a coherent body of knowledge.
>
> (The Norwood Report, 1943, p. 2)

These pupils from the continuing clientele of the traditional subject-based curriculum for as Norwood states, 'such pupils, educated by the curriculum commonly associated with the Grammar School, have entered the learned professions or have taken up higher administrative or business posts' (p. 2). Secondly, the needs of the intermediate category, 'the pupil whose interests and abilities lie markedly in the field of applied science or applied art', were to be fulfilled by the technical schools. Thirdly, Norwood states with a very partial view of educational history, 'There has of late years been recognition, expressed in the framing of curricula and otherwise of still another grouping of occupations' (p. 4). This third group was to provide the clientele for the new secondary modern schools.

> The pupil in this group deals more easily with concrete things than with ideas. He may have much ability, but it will be in the realm of facts. He is interested in things as they are; he finds little attraction in the past or in the slow disentanglement of causes or movements. His mind must turn its knowledge or its curiosity to immediate test; and his test is essentially practical.
>
> (The Norwood Report, 1943, p. 4)

This curriculum, whilst ruling out certain occupational futures, certainly facilitated those destined for manual work. It 'would not be to prepare for a particular job or profession and its treatment would make a direct appeal to interests, which it would awaken by practical touch with affairs' (p. 4).

The Norwood Report summarises the patterns of curriculum differentiation that had emerged through 'the evolution of education' over the past century or so. The close alliance between patterns of curriculum differentiation and social structure was often conceded (as in the Taunton Report in 1868): different curricula are explicitly linked to different occupational categories. The academic tradition was for the grammar school pupil destined for the learned professions and higher administrative or business posts. The more utilitarian curriculum in the technical schools was for the pupil destined to work in 'applied science or applied art'. Whilst for the future manual worker in the secondary modern the emphasis was on utilitarian and pedagogic curricula; these studies were to 'make a direct appeal to interests which it would awaken by practical touch with affairs' (p. 4). The close identity between different curriculum traditions, occupational destinations (and social classes) and different educational sectors was confirmed in the 1944 Education Act which organised schools into grammar schools for the academic pupils, technical schools for the 'applied' pupils and secondary modern schools for the 'practical' pupils.

The 1944 act therefore produced an organisational pattern that was in close resonance with social configurations that were in the tradition established by the Taunton report. However in 1945, the election of a socialist Labour government initiated a period in which the entrenched and explicit class-based educational organisation came under substantial attack. In Britain the battle for the common school was fought late – a symptom of the entrenched class structure of the country. The comprehensive school was thus only 'won' in 1965. The 1965 circular had sought to 'eliminate separatism in secondary education' (Department of Education and Science (DES), 1965, p. 1). But a close reading of the circular implies that the major concern, perhaps understandably at the time, was with eliminating separatism in the form of different school types and buildings.

Indeed, there were clear indications that far from expecting a new synthesis of curricula, the main concern in 1965 was to defend and extend the grammar school education previously mostly confined to the professional and middle class. The House of Commons motion which led to Circular 10/65 was fairly specific:

> This House, conscious of the need to raise educational standards at all levels, and regretting that the realisation of this objective is impeded by the separation of children into different types of secondary schools, notes with approval the efforts of local authorities to reorganise secondary education on comprehensive lines which will preserve all that is valuable in grammar school education for those children who now receive it and make it available to more children.
>
> (DES, 1965, p. 1)

What was unclear and unspoken was whether the logic of providing a comprehensive education for all in the common school would be pursued into also providing a common curriculum.

Yet if it seems that the comprehensive school had thereby been achieved, a more systematic historical analysis of internal curriculum patterns tells another story. In a sense, the move to the common school represents a change only in the geometrical axis of differentiation. Thus, in Table 6.1, differentiation from 1944 is vertical, being based on separate school sectors.

Table 6.1 Tripartite schooling: educational system after 1944 Act

Grammar school	Technical school	Secondary modern
Academic: route to universities	Technical knowledge	Practical/manual

Table 6.2 Comprehensive school 'streams'

Academic subjects
Technical subjects
Manual/practical subjects

Comprehensive schooling limited all these separate types of schooling 'under one roof'. The class-based recruitment to the three types of school was thereby challenged by every child to have the same 'equal' opportunity to attend the same, comprehensive school (notwithstanding those 'children of rich' parents who continued to go to private schools). But the results of this reform were less substantial when internal patterns were established. For *inside* the comprehensive school the old tripartite system was re-established with a pattern of horizontal differentiation (see Table 6.2).

In many cases the bottom two categories effectively merged: the crucial distinction was between academic and non-academic subjects. Pupils were categorised quite clearly along these lines as 'academic' and 'non-academic' students. Close studies of the reform of schooling from tripartite to comprehensive, affords an opportunity for scholars of curriculum history to reconceptualise curriculum reform. Reform therefore provides a 'matrix of possibility' when the conflict over whether to redefine or simply re-negotiate differentiation takes place.

In this matrix a range of possible curriculum combinations can be discerned. For instance, Option A in Figure 6.1 represents a situation, which prevailed for a long time in Britain, in which the elite alone received schooling of an academic nature. Combining A with B provides recontextualised academic schooling for the higher orders and contextualised practical training for the lower orders – in effect a hierarchical and stratified 'caste curriculum'.

Attempts to reform curricula can be top-down (A to C) or bottom-up (B to D). In the top-down model, academic decontextualised knowledge is distilled and made available to a wider audience (many of the curriculum reforms in the 1960s were of this sort). In the bottom-up model, contextualised knowledge is used as a vehicle for more general theoretical education (as was the case with the Science of Common Things).

A pattern of structuration

The matrix of curricular forms illustrates a range of potential patterns for programming, developing and reforming curricula. But behind the apparent flexibility lie established patterns of finances and resources. In Britain these patterns were established mostly in the period 1904–17. Their establishment and continuance into the late twentieth century provide us with a historical instance of the social and political processes that underpin school subjects.

The 1904 *Secondary Regulation*, list and prioritise the subjects that are suitable for education in the secondary grammar schools. The subjects were largely those that have come to be seen as 'academic' subjects, a view confirmed and consolidated by their enshrinement in the School Certificate examinations launched in 1917.

From 1917 onwards, examination subjects, the 'academic' subjects, inherited the preferential treatment in finance and resources directed at the grammar schools. It should be noted that the examination system itself had developed for a comparable clientele. The foundation of these examinations in 1858

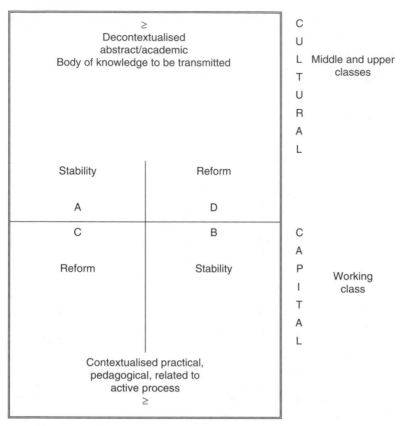

A – alone Elite curriculum.

A + B Caste curriculum. Hierarchical, stratified

AΔC Top-down reform. Exversion

BΔD Bottom-up reform. Inversion

Figure 6.1 Curriculum form.

'was the universities' response to petitions that they should help in the development of "schools for the middle classes"' (University of Cambridge, 1958, p. 1).
(The genesis of examinations and their subsequent centrality in the structure of
the educational systems are a particularly good example of the importance of
historical factors for those developing theories about curriculum and schooling.)

The structure of resources linked to examinations has effectively survived
the ensuing changes in the educational system (although currently these are now
subject to challenge). Byrne for instance has stated 'that more resources are given
to able students and hence to academic subjects', the two are still synonymous
'since it has been assumed that they necessarily need more staff, more highly paid
staff and more money for equipment and books' (Byrne, 1974, p. 29).

The material interests of teachers – their pay, promotion and conditions – are
intimately interlinked with the fate of their specialist subjects. In schools, school
subjects are organised in departments. The subject teacher's career is pursued
within such a department and the department's status depends on the subject's

status. The 'academic' subject is placed at the top of the hierarchy of subjects because resource allocation takes place on the basis of assumptions that such subjects are best suited for the 'able' students (and *vice versa* of course) who, it is further assumed, should receive favourable treatment.

Thus, in secondary schools, the material and self-interest of subject teachers is interlinked with the status of the subject, judged in terms of its examination status. Academic subjects provide the teacher with a career structure characterised by better promotion prospects and pay than less academic subjects.

The pattern of finances and resources that emerged in the period 1904–17 proved durable and has only very recently been subject to substantial challenge. As a result a common process of school subject promotion and development began to emerge in response to the 'rules of the game' defined in this manner for those pursuing finance, resources and status (Goodson, 1987, 1988).

Conclusion

This paper has noted that a polarised pattern of mentalities emerged in Britain in the period 1770–1850. For the 'higher order', mentalities were judged to be intellectual, abstract and active, for the 'lower orders', they were considered sensual, concrete and passive. In time, these polarised mentalities were built into the deep structures of curriculum – they were, so to speak, internalised. In this way, the process of mentality 'production' was extended, for school subjects themselves became, in turn, the makers of subjectivities. A self-confirming circle was drawn around different social groupings. Given the resonance with patterns of cultural capital, this was to prove a resilient settlement.

At the time that these constellations of mentalities, curriculum and cultural capital began to gather a state schooling system was emerging. In time therefore these patterns were institutionalised – initially into a system of separate schools for distinct mentalities and curriculum. Later, as common schooling was 'developed' (or 'conceded', depending on your location) the pattern of distinct mentalities and curriculum remained as a mechanism of differentiation *within* that which was ostensibly unified and common. It is as if the mental/manual 'division of labour' is institutionalised in a 'division of curriculum'. Certainly with regard to the current policy associated with the new 'National Curriculum' the emerging patterns of traditionalism demarcated from new vocationalism seem set to continue and strengthen this division (Bates, 1989).

In the historical period considered here, the deliberate structuration of a state schooling in which the head rather than the hands was preferred can be clearly discerned. The academic form of curriculum was deliberately and systematically favoured by the structure of resources and finances. Hence, a pattern of prioritising certain social groups was replaced by an ostensibly neutral process of prioritising certain forms of curricula. But though the name changed, the game was much the same. It is not surprising, therefore, that similar social groups continued to benefit and, likewise, that other social groups, as before, were disadvantaged. But the internalisation of differentiation effectively masked this social process of preferment and privilege.

Thus, the focus on conflicts *within* the curriculum responds to this internalisation of social differentiation. In short, to understand fully the process that is schooling, one must look *inside* curriculum. Part of the complex conundrum of schooling is to be understood by capturing the internal process of stability and change in the curriculum.

References

Apple, M., 1979, *Ideology and Curriculum* (London, Boston, MA and Henley: Routledge and Kegan Paul).

Bates, I., 1989, Versions of Vocationalism: An Analysis of some Social and Political Influences on Curriculum Policy and Practice. *British Journal of Sociology of Education*, 10(2), 215–231.

Bernstein, B., 1971, On the Classification and Framing of Educational Knowledge. In M.F.D. Young (ed.) *Knowledge and Control: New Directions for the Sociology of Education* (London: Collier-Macmillan), pp. 47–69.

Bourdieu, P. and Passeron, J.C., 1977, *Reproduction in Education, Society and Culture* (London and Beverly Hills: Sage).

Byrne, E.M., 1974, Planning and Inequality (Slough: NFER).

Connell, R.W., 1985, *Teachers Work* (Sydney, London and Boston, MA: George Allen and Unwin).

Department of Education and Science (DES), 1965, *Organisation of Secondary Education* (Circular 10/65) (London: HMSO).

Goodson, I.F., 1987, *School Subjects and Curriculum Change* (London, New York and Philadelphia, PA: Falmer Press).

Goodson, I.F., 1988, *The Making of Curriculum: Collected Essays* (London, New York and Philadelphia, PA: Falmer Press).

Hodson, D., 1987, Science Curriculum Change in Victorian England: A Case Study of the Science of Common Things. In Goodson, I.F. (ed.), *International Perspectives in Curriculum History* (London: Croom Helm), pp. 139–178.

Pitman, A.J., 1986, *A Study of School Reform from the Perspective of the Annaliste School of French Historiography: Restructuring Victorian Schooling*, Unpublished PhD dissertation, University of Wisconsin-Madison.

Shapin, S. and Barnes, B., 1976, Head and Hand: Rhetorical Resources in British Pedagogical Writing, 1770–1850, *Oxford Review of Education*, 2(3), 231–254.

Shulman, L., 1987, Knowledge and Teaching Foundations of the New Reform. *Harvard Educational Review*, 57(1), 1–22.

The Norwood Report, 1943, Curriculum and Examinations in Secondary Schools. Report of the Committee of the Secondary School Examinations Council, appointed by the President of the Board of Education in 1941 (London: HMSO).

University of Cambridge Local Examinations Syndicate, 1958, One Hundredth Annual Report to University, 29 May.

Willis, P., 1977, *Learning to Labour* (Westmead: Saxon House).

CHAPTER 7

THE MAKING OF CURRICULUM

The Making of Curriculum, 2nd edition, London: Falmer Press, 1995

C. Wright Mills argued that 'the production of historians may be thought of as a great file indispensable to all social science' and that 'every social science – or better, every well-considered social study – requires historical scope and a full use of historical materials' (Wright Mills, 1977, pp. 161–162). If we use these criteria it is plain that most of our studies of schools, certainly in relation to curriculum, are not 'well considered'; the great file indispensable to all social science has proved eminently dispensable.

In undertaking studies of curriculum production it has been contended that historical research should indeed be viewed as indispensable. Three levels of historical study have been discerned: (a) the individual life history; (b) the group or collective level: by professions, or the communities which make up subjects and disciplines; (c) the relational level: the various permutations of relations between groups and between individuals and groups.

Whilst much of curriculum study has either been prescriptive or ahistorical the work of some of the sociologists of knowledge has directed our attention to the curriculum as a socio-historical product. In this sense their work has sought to employ historical data and perspective to elucidate our understanding of curriculum and its relationship to schooling. But the use of historical data is some distance from the use of historical methods. There is a danger of 'raiding' history where studies span centuries of change at all levels of content and context. A more systematic *evolutionary* (although not in any Darwinian or uncontested sense) understanding of how the curriculum is negotiated is therefore needed. One is concerned to ensure that histories make evolutionary connections partly to secure against 'raiding' but more constructively to facilitate the use of such histories in developing theoretical frameworks. A continuity thesis cannot be assumed but has to be established (or disproven) over time. It is most decidedly at the centre of the sociological as well as historical enterprise to examine curriculum transformation and reproduction at work over time. But such complex undertakings cannot be fully elucidated by 'snapshots' of unique events, which may be entirely aberrant and without general significance.

By this view to seek to provide from the macro level theories of schooling and curriculum without related empirical studies of how the curriculum has been negotiated at mezzo and micro level over time is an unsatisfactory and thoroughly dangerous sequence through which to proceed. On the other hand developing studies of the complexity of curriculum action and negotiation over time is a meaningful sequence through which to approach theory. Besides acting as a 'seedbed' for theory such work is a vital complement to macro-level theorising.

Modes of historical study

In arguing for curriculum as a central source in the investigation of schooling and in juxtaposing history and curriculum study, there is an evident and basic problem. History is not first and foremost a theoretical mode of study. Above all the concern is with particular historical situations which are in their nature unique. The process of explanation, generalisation and theorising is of necessity secondary to the pursuit of understanding at this level. Ricoeur puts it this way: 'Explanation in history is not an end in itself: it serves to mediate historical understanding which is tied in turn to the narrativity of the historical text' (Ricoeur, 1981, p. 17).

Yet, accepting the primacy of the pursuit of understanding unique historical events and situations does not deny history explanatory potential. In this sense the Ricoeur quote is exact: there is a place for explanation, even if not pride of place. Moreover, the *recurrence* of factors and events in a range of unique locations can help in discerning explanatory frameworks, in testing and contributing to theory.

Curriculum historians need to ensure that their capacity to develop their 'great file indispensable to all social science' makes optimum connections with strategies for explanation and theory. The current debate over *realism* in the philosophy of science is an instructive example.

Roy Bhaskar states that realist explanations develop the distinction between observed regularities and those underlying 'mechanisms' which account for these regularities. Bhaskar discerns three levels of reality: firstly 'mechanisms', causally efficacious processes, secondly 'events', those consequences or effects of mechanisms and thirdly 'experiences', subjectively perceived aspects of events. Bhaskar argues that:

> once it is granted that mechanisms and structures may be said to be real, we can provide an interpretation of the independence of causal laws from the pattern of events, and *a fotiori* of the rationale of experimental activity. For the real basis of this independence lies in the independence of the generative mechanisms of nature from the events they generate. Such mechanisms endure when not acting...

Some of these mechanisms:

> act through the flux of conditions that determine whether they are active and co-determine the manifest outcome of their activity. That is to say, it entails that generative mechanisms endure when inactive and act even where, as in open systems, there is no one-to-one relationship between the causal law representing the characteristic mode of operation of the mechanism and the particular sequence of events that occurs.
>
> (Bhaskar, 1978)

Deriving from Bhaskar, Olin Wright sees a realist process of explanation proceeding in this manner:

1 Regularities are identified (within a conceptual field which makes such observational regularities possible).
2 A mechanism is postulated in the imagination: it is *invented* by the creative activity of the scientist acting on existing explanations and theories.
3 The reality of the entities and processes postulated in the mechanism is then checked through empirical investigation (experiment, quasi-experiment or some other procedure).

(Olin Wright)

Now clearly the sequence or posture to theory is starkly different for the historian. But at the same time it should be evident that historical study can be a useful mode for those investigations which may test or contribute to such theories. 'Regularities' or 'mechanisms' may then be identified or scrutinised as operant in particular historical locales: their status or existence may then be clarified, elaborated or modified.

Whilst historical studies may indeed discern 'regularities' these have to be consistently related to changing historical contexts. Regularities cannot be assumed as timeless and invariant. The historian starts, so to speak, from the other end. To give one example: in the next section certain explanatory frameworks are tentatively advanced, certain regularities if you will. But they are historically specific, they refer to a period of some stability in curriculum history when an integrated structure of examinations and associated resource allocations has been paramount. It has not always been so and given the current British Government's intentions will most decidedly not stay so. Educational 'systems' themselves are subject to historical flux. Yet as has been seen in previous instances we do tend to take the present system for granted, to assume that at least some of the salient features are pervasive and continuous.

Developing studies of context: an historical instance of English schooling in the twentieth century

The studies undertaken of life histories and curriculum histories point to the importance of aspects of the structure of the educational system in understanding the actions at individual, collective, and relational levels. These structures, which might be viewed from the actors' standpoint as the 'rules of the game', arise at a particular point in history, for particular reasons: until changed they act as a structural legacy constraining but also enabling contemporary actors. The pervasiveness of these structures and degree of similarity of response at all levels allows some explanatory frameworks or studies of context to be developed as the following instance I think indicates. This is not to argue that structures are timeless or invariant; it is strictly an instance relating to a particular period of curriculum history. There are many indications that this curriculum structure is currently coming under stress and new modes of control and operation can be discerned. So fundamental might the change be that groups currently 'outside' the educational system – such as the Manpower Service Commission – may be viewed as entering the terrain.

Above all the historical study of teachers' life histories and school subjects histories in recent decades directs our attention to the structuring of material interests – and to the associated structuring of the internal discourse on the school curriculum – in particular the manner in which resources and career chances are distributed and status attributed. We are here focussing on the political economy of the curriculum, in particular the 'convention' of the school subject. The main historical period for the emergence of this salient structure was 1904–17. The 1904 Secondary Regulations (in which Morant played such a central defining role), list and prioritise the subjects suitable for education in the secondary grammar schools. These were largely those that have come to be seen as 'academic' subjects, a view confirmed and consolidated by their enshrinement in the School Certificate examinations launched in 1917 (see Chapter 6). 'Academic' subjects are those which attract 'able' students, hence 'the need for a scholarly discipline' characterises the way in which the discourse on curriculum is structured and narrowed. Locating our studies at these points ensures that exploration will focus on relationships between aspects of structure and action.

Structure and mediation: internal and external factors

Studies of context with regard to subject teachers and communities provide us with a 'cognitive map of curriculum influence' (or, more basically, the 'rules of the game'). Essentially the 'rules of the game' discerned in the limited number of studies so far conducted are those 'internal' to the educational system. Since external factors are also of eminent importance broader theories of context will need to be elaborated if more general models of change are to be envisaged. In the section which follows therefore the 'internal affairs' of curriculum are linked with 'external relations'.

Internal affairs

1   'Invention'

   i   In one model of subject evolution the early stages focus on pedagogic and utilitarian functions but plainly there are stages which proceed the formation of subject groups. In this situation the 'ideas necessary for creation are normally available over a relatively prolonged period of time in several places' (Ben-David and Collins, 1966).

   ii Westbury has conceptualised this initial stage as 'invention'. These inventions may originate with educators themselves trying out new ideas or practices; or they may sometimes be a result of pupil demands or of pupil resistance to existing forms, or they may arise in response to new 'climates of opinion'. They may also come from 'inventions in the outside world' e.g. squared graph paper, books, micros (Westbury, 1984).

   iii Internally there is one overwhelming reason for the take-up of 'inventions' by subject groups. 'Inventions' normally exist in several places over a long period of time but 'only a few of these potential beginnings lead to further growth': 'such growth occurs where and when persons become interested in the new idea, not only as intellectual content but also as a potential means of establishing a new intellectual identity and particularly a new occupational role' (Ben-David and Collins, 1966).[1]

2   Subjects as 'coalitions'

i   The process model developed by Bucher and Strauss for the study of professions provides valuable guidelines for those studying school subjects. Within a profession, they argue, are varied identities, values and interests.

Hence professions are to be seen as 'loose amalgamation of segments pursuing different objectives in different manner and more or less delicately held together under a common name at particular periods in history' (Bucher and Strauss, 1976, p. 19). The most frequent conflicts arise over the gaining of institutional footholds, over recruitment and over external relations with clients and other institutions. At times when conflicts such as these become intense professional associations may be created or if already in existence become more strongly institutionalised.

ii   The Bucher and Strauss model of profession suggests that perhaps the 'subject community' should not be viewed as a homogeneous group whose members share similar values and definition of role, common interests and identity. Rather the subject community should be seen as comprising a range of conflicting groups, segments or factions (referred to as subject sub-groups). The importance of these groups might vary considerably over time. As with professions, school subject associations (e.g. the Geographical Association) often develop at particular points in time when there is an intensification of conflict over school curriculum and resources and over recruitment and training.

3   Establishment: coalitions in action

i   Initially a subject is often a very loose coalition of sub-groups and less coherent, even idiosyncratic versions often the focus is on pedagogic and utilitaraus concerns.

ii   A sub-group emerges arguing for the subject to become an 'academic discipline' so as to be able to claim resources and status.

iii   At the point of conflict between earlier sub-groups and the proselytising 'academic' sub-group, a subject association is often formed. The association increasingly act to unify sub-groups with a *dominant coalition* promoting academic. The dominant coalition promotes the subject as a 'scholarly discipline', or a 'real science', defined by university scholars.

iv   For the successful establishment of an 'academic' subject the culminating phase is the creation of the 'university discipline' base. The subject boundaries now increasingly defined by university scholars and it is to the structure of their material interests and resulting aspirations that we must look to explain curriculum change.

External relations

As we have noted some of the 'inventions' which initiate internal curriculum change begin externally. But 'external relations' are of more importance than as initiators of change at this level. There is considerable evidence that for many subjects, especially the more applicable' subjects, the influence of industrial and commercial interests can be substantial. This, it should be noted, is not to argue a direct 'correspondence' thesis nor for the existence of a 'selective tradition' where all content opposed to capitalism is ultimately 'purged' from aspiring curriculum categories.

Much of the latter work has focussed on textbooks. Anyone for example has persuasively show how US Social Studies texts do omit much of labour history (Anyon, 1979). Clearly textbooks are an important 'external' factor but they are dependent on internal take-up and can be supplemented internally. Ultimately we are back with which models of internal curriculum can be sustained: in this act of sustenance external relations are vital.

In sustaining internal models of curriculum the role of agencies external to the school is of central import. Herbert Blumer elaborated the concept of 'public' to characterise the groups who collectively use or view a particular service and therefore contribute to the 'public debate' about it (Blumer, 1986). But as C. Wright Mills pointed out:

> The problem of 'the public' in western societies arises out of the transformation of the traditional and conventional consensus of medieval society; it reaches its present-day climax in the idea of a mass society. What were called 'publics' in the eighteenth and nineteenth centuries are being transformed into a society of 'masses'. Moreover the structural relevance of publics is declining, as men at large become 'mass men' each trapped in quite powerless milieu.
>
> (Wright Mills, 1977, p. 62)

Because of the power of particular 'publics' the ideologies of dominant 'publics' relate to particular views of education and particular 'rhetoric of legitimation' or 'discourses'. Esland has begun to conceptualise a range of questions which surround this issue:

> The question one would be asking about these publics is, what characterises their thinking about education? How are changing conceptual thresholds for defining valid school experience communicated and made plausible to the teacher and to other publics? How is the dialogue between consumers of education and its professional exponents indicative of changing concepts of order and control? The institutional correlates of these processes will be manifested in the career flow of teacher and pupil and the definitions which are attached to particular mental states and experiences.

The rhetoric and ideologies of 'publics' are of course located in the socio-cultural processes which support and label particular kinds of enterprise as educationally worthwhile (Esland, 1971, p. 109).

The work of John Meyer is valuable in allowing us to conceptualise external relations (Meyer, 1980). His work, concerned with the US, has been modified by Reid with the UK system in mind. In this approach 'external forces and structures emerge not merely as sources of ideas, promptings, inducements and constraints, but as definers and carriers of the categories of content, role and activity to which the practice of schools must approximate in order to attract support and legitimation'. In short, these external constituencies are vital elements in the discursive formation, the way in which the debate on school curriculum is constructed and organised. External relations then are seen less in terms of formal or conventional groups such as parents, employers, trade unions and universities, but in terms of more broadly conceived '*publics*' or '*constituencies*' which include all these people but go more widely to include scholars, politicians, administrators and others:

> These interested publics which pay for and support education hand over its work to the professionals in only a limited and unexpected sense. For while it may appear that the professionals have power to determine what is taught (at school, district or national level, depending on the country in question) their scope is limited by the fact that only the forms and activities which have significance for external publics can, in the long run, survive.
>
> (Reid, 1984, p. 68)

In winning the support of the crucial 'publics' or 'constituencies' suitable categories or rhetoric need to be defined. Reid has painstakingly constructed the evolution of one such category, the 'sixth form', and the associated evolution of the supporting constituency. Reid claims that we have to take the logic of these categories seriously and accept that 'within the terms of such logic, success rhetoric *are* realities'. Though teachers and administrators

> have to be careful that dysfunctions between practice and belief do not escalate to the point where credibility collapses, nonetheless it remains true that what is most important for the success of school subjects is not the delivery of 'goods' which can be publicly evaluated, but the development and maintenance of legitimating rhetoric which provide automatic support for correctly labelled activity.

Hence Reid concludes:

> The choice of appropriate labels and the association of them in the public mind with plausible rhetoric of justification can be seen as the core mission of those who work to advance or defend the subjects of the curriculum.
>
> (Reid, 1984, p. 75)

Curriculum change as political process: an example of the process of academic establishment

The internal affairs and external relations of curriculum change point to a socio-historical or more specifically a political process at work. Placing the internal and external together leads to evolutionary or historical models of political action which mediates aspects of the structure of the educational system. Hence, in one such model of change, school subjects might be seen as progressing through a number of stages in pursuit of academic establishment (once established of course new ground rules may operate).

1   *Invention*   Invention may come about from the activities or ideas of educators; sometimes as a response to 'climates of opinion' or pupil demands or resistance or from inventions in the 'outside world':

> The ideas necessary for creation...are usually available over a relatively prolong period of time in several places. Only a few of these inventions will lead to further action
>
> (Ben-David and Collins, 1966)

2   *Promotion (or 'agit prop')*   Promotion by educator groups internal to the educational system. Inventions will be taken up 'where and when persons become interested in the new idea, not only as intellectual content but also as a means of establishing a new intellectual identity and particularly a new occupational role'.

Hence subjects with low status, poor career patterns and even with actual survival problems may readily embrace and promote new inventions such as environmental studies. Conversely high-status subjects may ignore quite major opportunities as they are already satisfactorily resourced and provide existing desirable careers. The response of science groups to 'technology' or (possibly) contemporary Maths groups to 'computer studies' are cases in point.

Promotion of invention arises from a perception of the possibility of basic improvements in occupational role and status.

3   *Legislation*   The promotion of new inventions if successful leads to the establishment of new categories or subjects. Whilst promotion is initially primarily internally generated it has to develop external relations with sustaining 'constituencies'. This will be a major stage in ensuring that new categories or subjects are fully accepted, established and institutionalised. And further that having been established they can be sustained and supported over time. Legislation is associated with the development and maintenance of those discourses or legitimating rhetoric that provides automatic support for correctly labelled activity.

4   *Mythologisation*   Once automatic support has been achieved for a subject or category a fairly wide range of activities can be undertaken. The limits are any activities that threaten the legitimating rhetoric and hence constituency support. The subject at this point is mythological. It represents essentially a licence that has been granted (or perhaps a 'patent' or 'monopoly rights'), with the full force of the law and establishment behind it. At this point the tradition has been successfully 'invented', the process of invention and of establishment is completed.

Curriculum histories point to the evolutionary nature of subjects as coalitions 'more or less delicately held together under a common name at particular periods'.

The nature of these coalitions responds to both the structuring of material interests and discourse and to the 'changing climates' for action. Because of the manner in which resources (and associated career prospects) are distributed, and status attributed, 'academic' subjects groups most often develop as 'dominant coalitions'. The conflict over the status of examinable knowledge therefore becomes the crucial conflict arena where the subject coalitions (and their representative associations) contest the right to material resources and career prospects. The dominance of 'academicism' can be shown over the last century or more. But historical studies pose question about in whose interests this dominance prevails: professional groups, culturally dominant groups or industrial or financial capital. Academicism may be the past cultural consequence of previous domination rather than a guarantee of future domination.

In fact the studies in this collection would lead us to re-conceptualise curriculum change and conflict. For instance in the United Kingdom the current Government's initiatives look like an attack on a system (and associated bureaucracy) that was conceived in response to middle class pressure and moulded by a Government bureaucracy steeped in public school values. Once it most definitely served dominant interest groups. But since then the system and bureaucracy have developed progressive autonomy and their one vested interest (or seen alternatively from the radical right grown flatulent, stale and obsolescent). The latest governmental strategies challenge this model arguing for more direct connections with economic and financial interests. At present it appears curriculum conflict resembles less a clash between dominant and subservient groups than a clash between *once* dominant and *currently* dominant bureaucracies.

Note

1   It is instructive to note that after this contention Ben-David and Collins speculate about 'the conditions under which such interest can be identified and used as a basis for eventually building a predictive theory'.

References

Anyon, J., 1979, Ideology and United States History Textbooks, *Harvard Educational Review*, 41, 361–386.

Ben-David, T. and Collins, R., 1966, Social Factors in the Origins of a New Science: The Case of Psychology, *American Sociological Review*, 31, (4) (August).

Bhaskar, R., 1978, *A Realist Theory of Science* (Brighton: Harvester Press).

Blumer, H., 1986, *Symbolic Interactionism – Perspective and Method* (Berkeley and Los Angeles, CA: University of California Press), 195–208.

Bucher, R. and Strauss, A., 1976, Professions in Process. In M. Hammersley and P. Woods (eds), *The Process of Schooling* (London: Routledge and Kegan Paul).

Esland, G.M., 1971, Teaching and Learning as the Organisation of Knowledge. In M.F.D. Young (ed.), *Knowledge and Control: New Directions for the Sociology of Education* (London: Collier Macmillan).

Meyer, J.W., 1977, The Structure of Educational Organisation. In J.W. Meyer and W. Marshall *et al.* (eds), *Environments and Organisations* (San Francisco, CA: Jossey Bass).

Meyer, J.W., 1980, Levels of the Educational System and Schooling Effects. In C.E. Bidwell and D.M. Windham (eds), *The Analysis of Educational Productivity*, 2 vols. (Cambridge, MA: Ballinger).

Olin Wright, E., unpublished papers.

Reid, W.A., 1984, Curriculum Topics as Institutional Categories: Implications for Theory and Research in the History and Sociology of School Subjects. In I.F. Goodson and S.J. Ball (eds), *Defining the Curriculum: Histories and Ethnographies* (Brighton: Falmer Press).

Ricoeur, P., 1981, *Hermeneutics and the Human Sciences* (Cambridge: Cambridge University Press).

Westbury, I., 1984, 'Invention' of Curricula, notes to open a theme for Discussion Paper at AERA (April, Mimeo: New Orleans).

Wright Mills, C., 1977, *The Sociological Imagination* (London: Pelican).

CHAPTER 8

NATIONS AT RISK AND NATIONAL CURRICULUM

Journal of Education Policy, 1991, section in *Handbook of the American Politics of Education Association*, pp. 219–232

Ideology and identity

Whilst a good deal of our curriculum study should be conducted, at the school and local level other historical work is required to examine wider initiatives of a national and even global scope. Here I focus on the phenomenon emergent in a number of countries of 'national curriculum'. My primary evidence is of the emergence of the national curriculum in the United Kingdom (UK)[1]: I focus on the antecedents to the national curriculum and the arguments and groups through which it has been promoted, the structures, rhetorical, financial and political, which have been established to support it, and finally the content, form, and pedagogical assumptions embedded within it.

As in other countries, the national curriculum debate in the UK has been precipitated by a widespread, and largely correct, perception that the nation is threatened by economic decline. Rhetorically then, the national curriculum is presented as a part of the project of economic regeneration. Behind this broad objective, however, two other projects can be discerned. Firstly, the reconstitution of older class-based British traditional subjects,[2] and secondly, a reassertion of the ideology and control of the nation-state.

A good deal of recent historical work has furthered our understanding of the origins of state schooling and curriculum. The common feature uniting the wide range of initiatives by states to fund and manage mass schooling was, these scholars argue, the endeavour of constructing a national polity; the power of the nation-state, it was judged, would be unified through the participation of the state's subjects in national projects. Central in this socialization into national identity was the project of mass state schooling. The sequence followed by those states, promoting this national project of mass schooling, were strikingly similar. Initially there was the promulgation of a national interest in mass education. Legislation to make schooling compulsory for all followed. To organize the system of mass schools, state departments or ministries of education were formed. State authority was then exercised over all schools – both those 'autonomous' schools already existing and newly proliferating schools specifically organized or opened by the state.

If the central project behind the initiation of state schooling and state-prescribed curriculum was nation-building, this may partly explain the response to certain moral panics which are currently evident. Above all is the new sense of panic over the '*Nation at Risk*', the title chosen for the major US report on education in 1983. The perception of national crisis is common among western nation-states. Often the matter is presented as essentially economic: certain nations (e.g. the USA) are falling behind certain other nations (e.g. Japan) in terms of economic prosperity. But behind this specific economic rationale lie a range of further more fundamental issues which render 'nations at risk' and develop general legitimation crises. The globalization of economic life, and more particularly of communications, information and technology, all pose enormous challenges to the existing modes of control and operation of nation-states. In this sense the pursuance of new centralized national curriculum might be seen as the response of the more economically endangered species among nations. Britain provides an interesting case of this kind of response.

Behind the myths projected by the current UK government and echoed by some of the more sympathetic newspapers and media, the UK economy remains under-capitalized and in many instances, hopelessly uncompetitive. So much for the economic basis of the 'nation at risk'. But perhaps even more significant are the tendencies towards globalization of economic and social life. In the UK case this is rendered particularly acute by the impending full-scale integration into the European Community. Symbolically the Channel Tunnel will connect UK life with that in Europe. The 'island nation' will quite literally be opened up to subterranean entry. The fear of the nation being at risk no doubt explains the hysteria behind so much of the Thatcher government's response to European integration.[3] Pervasive in this response is the sense of a loss of control, a loss of national destiny and identity. The school curriculum provides one arena for reasserting control and for re-establishing national identity.

The move towards a national curriculum in the UK can be traced back to the late 1970s. The key date in UK post-war educational history was Prime Minister James Callaghan's Ruskin College [Oxford] Speech in 1976. Here economic decline and an accelerating sense of national demise (the UK had joined the EEC in 1973) were attached to the decline in educational standards which it was argued had been fostered in comprehensive schools by the use of more 'progressive' methods. Callaghan's speech called for a 'Great Debate' on the UK's educational policies. Following this initiative, in 1977, a Green Paper, *Education in Schools: A Consultative Document*, was issued. The arguments for a common 'core' or a 'protected' element emerged. The principal points of concern appear to be:

1   the curriculum has become overcrowded; the timetable is overloaded, and the essentials are at risk;
2   variations in the approach to the curriculum in different schools can penalize a child simply because he or she has moved from one area to another;
3   even if the child does not move, variations from school to school may give rise to inequality of opportunities;
4   the curriculum in many schools is not sufficiently matched to life in a modern industrial society.

Not all these comments may be equally valid, but it is clear that the time has come to try to establish generally accepted principles for the composition of the secondary curriculum for all pupils. This does not presuppose uniform answers: schools, pupils, and their teachers are different, and the curriculum should be flexible enough to reflect these differences. But there is a need to investigate the part which might be played by a 'protected' or 'core' element of the curriculum common to all schools. There are various ways this may be defined. Properly worked out, it can offer reassurances to employers, parents, and the teachers themselves, as well as a very real equality of opportunity for pupils.

(Fowler, 1988, p. 38)

The emerging 'consensus' that there should be a 'core' curriculum was further promoted in the period after the election of a Conservative Government under Margaret Thatcher in 1979. The 1980 consultative paper, *A Framework for the School Curriculum*, argued that:

> In the course of the public and professional debate about the school curriculum a good deal of support has been found for the idea of identifying a 'core' or essential part of the curriculum which should be followed by all pupils according to their ability. Such a core, it is hoped, would ensure that all pupils, whatever else they do, at least get a sufficient grounding in the knowledge and skills which by common consent should form part of the equipment of the educated adult.
>
> Thus expressed, the idea may appear disarmingly simple; but as soon as it is critically examined a number of supplementary questions arise. For example, should the core be defined as narrowly as possible, or should it, for the period of compulsory schooling at least, cover a large part of the individual's curriculum? Should it be expressed in terms of the traditional school subjects, or in terms of educational objectives which may be attained through the medium of various subjects, appropriately taught? The difficulties and uncertainties attached to the application of the core concept do not mean, however, that it may not be a useful one in carrying forward the public debate about the curriculum to the point at which its results can be of practical benefit to the schools.
>
> (Fowler, 1988, pp. 59–60)

These difficulties not-with-standing from this point on there was a fairly consistent drive to establish a core curriculum. Following the Conservative Party's third election success in 1987, this curriculum was established as a new 'national curriculum', comprising the 'core subjects' of mathematics, English, and science, and the 'foundation subjects' of history, geography, technology, music, art and physical education.

Alongside this specification of subject titles was a panoply of major new central powers over the school curriculum. The Secretary of State for Education and Science now has responsibility for specifying attainment targets, programmes of study, and assessment procedures for each specified subject area. It should be noted that these are powers for very detailed prescription, indeed, these are not the powers of merely a general overview. Written into the parliamentary legislation is the obligation to assess pupils on the curriculum studied at the ages 7, 11, 14 and 16. In addition, a National Curriculum Council and a School Examinations and Assessment Council (subsequently these bodies were merged) have been set up to advise on the research, development, and monitoring procedures required.

The styling of the new curriculum specifications as 'national', the composition of subjects included, and the wide ranging new power for governmental agencies suggest three levels of inquiry in coming to understand this new initiative. First there is the need for further inquiry of the theme with which we began: the relationship of these curriculum initiatives to national economic regeneration and national identity. Second the focus on a small number of traditional subjects raises the question of the social antecedents of this choice: we need to analyse the social and cultural, as well as political, choices which underpin the new national curriculum. Third the initiative needs to be scrutinized in terms of the changing modalities of government control which are so clearly pronounced.

The national curriculum and national identity

The national curriculum has been initiated with pronouncements casting national regeneration in terms of links to the economy, industry and commerce, in particular the so-called 'wealth creating' sector. Yet in practice the balance of subjects in the national curriculum suggest that questions of national identity and control have been pre-eminent, rather than industrial or commercial requirements. For example, information technology has been largely omitted, whilst history has been embraced as a 'foundation subject', even though it is quite clearly a subject in decline within the schools.

The reasons for favouring history whilst omitting more commercially 'relevant' subjects are intriguing. On the face of it, this pattern of prioritizing might seem encouraging: sponsoring liberal education and humanist study over more narrow utilitarian concerns, favouring education over training. Regrettably this does not seem to be the case. History has, I believe, been chosen to revive and refocus national identity and ideology.

The recent National Curriculum History Group Interim Report provides information on the new curriculum proposals for school history. Firstly the report confirms that prior to the revival initiated by the incorporation in the national curriculum, history was a subject in decline: 'It now has a tenuous place in the primary curriculum and it is under threat in a growing number of secondary schools, both in terms of the number of pupils taking it, and as a coherent, rigorous and free-standing course of study' (DES, 1989, quoted in *Times Educational Supplement*, p. 4). One of the reasons for the progressive decline of history has been the growth of social studies and sociology. The latter subject is a very popular examination subject, but has been omitted in the national curriculum in favour of reviving history. The questions therefore remain as to why has history been so favoured.

The Interim Report provides some evidence on this issue for the national curriculum in history will have some distinctive features. At the core will be UK history which overall will take up 40% of the timetable. 'This figure, however, is slightly misleading because children at key stage one infant level will study UK history almost exclusively, while pupils in the early years of the secondary school will study it as a core subject for just one-third of the time earmarked for history' (*Times Educational Supplement*, p. 4). The focus of the national curriculum on British history in the formative early years of schooling indicates a wish to inculcate at an early stage a sense of national identity. This desire for a major and increased UK dimension in history has plainly come from within the Government. We are told for instance that:

> The issue which has hitherto aroused the most controversy is the Minister's insistence that the group should increase the proportion of British history for secondary pupils. At the moment, the group is planning to devote only one-third of the syllabus to British history as a compulsory subject for 11 to 14-year-olds. This figure rises slightly to two-fifths for 14 to 16-year-olds. Mr. MacGregor wants British history to be taught for at least 50% of the time devoted to history in secondary schools.
>
> (*Times Educational Supplement*, p. 4)

John MacGregor, appointed by Prime Minister Thatcher as the Secretary of State for Education and Science, was clear therefore where the Government's priorities lay. Certainly the revival of UK history seems unrelated to any strong desires among history teachers themselves, where many disagreements have been voiced. These disagreements have even been voiced inside the select curriculum working group: 'At the heart of these disagreements on historical knowledge, British history and chronology, is the lingering fear among some numbers of the group particularly those who are teachers or educationists that the history curriculum will be dominated by rigid external testing and rote learning of famous dates in British history' (*Times Educational Supplement*, p. 4).

National curriculum and social prioritizing

The styling of the curriculum as 'national' begs a number of questions about which nation is being referred to, for the UK is a nation sharply divided by social class, by race, by gender, by region and by country. One of the short hands for Conservative criticism of what the French Prime Minister has called the UK government's 'social cruelty' has been a reference to the danger of creating 'two nations'. This refers to the UK phenomenon of there being two recognizably different constituencies or nations inside the UK's borders: one nation which is richer and more secure and often resides in the so-called 'Home Counties' of southern England, and the other nation which is less well-endowed, primarily working class, and lives in that 'other country' beyond southern England. In truth, of course, the UK comprises a range of communities, segmented by class, race, gender, region and country; there are in fact far more than two nations.

Hence, in examining the national curriculum as a social construction, it is important to establish whether the different groups which comprise 'the nation' are being treated equally, or whether processes of social prioritizing can be discerned. In this section, by way of exemplification, I focus mainly on the issue of social class but work urgently needs to be undertaken around issues of race, gender, region and country. In each of these cases the construction of particular priorities and the simultaneous silencing of multiple other claims needs to be painstakingly examined.

The pattern of secondary schooling has a long history but a crucial watershed was the 1902 Education Act and the subsequent issue of the Secondary Regulations in 1904. At the turn of the century a number of alternative versions of secondary schooling were vying with each other. The well-established public schools and grammar schools carried the highest status and catered for the more elite social groups through a traditional classical curriculum, but increasingly the school boards administering local schools were providing education for secondary age pupils. In these schools a more vocational curriculum, covering commercial, technical and scientific subjects, were provided for a predominantly working class clientele.

The 1902 Education Act and the Secondary Regulations therefore arbitrated between these two traditions. Ryder and Silver have judged that the 1902 Act ensured that 'whatever developments in secondary education might occur, it should be within a single system in which the dominant values should resemble those of the traditional grammar school and its curriculum' (Ryder and Silver, 1970). Likewise, Eaglesham judged that:

> These regulations were the work of a number of officials and inspectors of the Board. It may be argued that they gave a balanced curriculum. They certainly effectively checked any tendencies to technical or vocational bias in the secondary schools. They made them schools fit only for a selected few.

Moreover they proclaimed for all to see the Board's interest in the literary and classical sides of secondary education. For the future the pattern of English culture must come not from Leeds and West Ham but from Eton and Winchester.

(Eaglesham, 1967, p. 59)

Whilst these two quotes present grammar and public curricula in too monolithic a manner the general point can be summarized in this way: 'Secondary education was in 1904 given so academic a curriculum that it suited only a few' (Eaglesham, 1967, pp. 59–60). In this manner the settlement of 1902–04 chose the historical legacy and curriculum aimed at certain groups over that aimed at other groups and legislated that this model should constitute the secondary school curriculum. The 1904 Secondary Regulations outline clear guidelines; we see then curriculum as social prioritizing.

The division of post primary schooling between public schools, grammar schools and other schools pre-eminently for the working class, the elementary schools, and subsequently secondary modern schools, survived into the period following the Second World War. Opposition to the selective examination for deciding who went to grammar school, the so-called 11-plus, grew, and some experiments in comprehensive or multilateral schooling began in the 1940s. In 1964, a Labour Government was returned, and began dismantling the existing divisive system and introducing comprehensive schools.

The implications of this change for the curriculum were substantial, and a range of curriculum reform projects were initiated through the Schools Council for Curriculum and Examinations founded in 1964. Whilst the comprehensive schools initially derived their main curriculum areas from the grammar schools, these reform projects sought to seriously apply the logic of comprehensive school reform to curriculum reform. For plainly without curriculum reform organizational reform was of severely limited significance.

Rubinstein and Simon summarize the climate of educational reform in 1972 following the raising of the school learning age to 16, and the rapid growth of the comprehensive system:

The content of the curriculum is now under much discussion, and comprehensive schools are participating actively in the many curriculum reform schemes launched by the Schools Council and Nuffield. The tendency is towards the development of the interdisciplinary curricula, together with the use of the resources approach to learning, involving the substitution of much group and individual work for the more traditional forms of class teaching. For these new forms of organising and stimulating learning mixed ability grouping often provides the most appropriate method; and partly for this reason the tendency is towards the reduction of streaming and class teaching. This movement in itself promotes new relations between teachers and pupils, particularly insofar as the teacher's role is changing from that of ultimate authority to that of motivating, facilitating and structuring the pupils' own discovery and search for knowledge.

(Rubinstein and Simon, 1973, p. 123)

The belief that rapid curriculum reform, with a range of associated political and pedagogical implications, was well under way was commonly held at this time. Kerr asserted in 1968 that 'at the practical and organisational levels, the new curricula promise to revolutionise English education' (Kerr, 1971).

But at precisely the time Kerr was talking new forces were seeking to defend, and if possible re-invigorate, the old grammar school subjects. These were presented as the 'traditional' subjects. This campaign culminated in the National Curriculum but it is important to grasp that this re-assertion of a subject-based curriculum is part of a broader strategy of reconstitution. Moreover, the re-establishment of traditional subjects is taking place at the expense of many of those new subject areas devised specifically to sponsor and promote learning across the full range of the comprehensive school: Social Studies, Environmental Studies, General Science, Urban Studies, Community Studies and so on. These subjects had sought to develop new forms of connectedness to the interests and experiences of the pupils of the comprehensive school. The national curriculum pronounces that the approach can now only take place at the margins and that the core curriculum will once again be those subjects 'traditionally' taught since their 'establishment' in 1904.

The comparison with the Secondary Regulations in 1904 shows the extent to which a patterning of schooling has been reconstituted in this new political settlement called the national curriculum.

1904	1988
English	English
Maths	Maths
Science	Science
History	History
Geography	Geography
Physical exercise	Physical education
Drawing	Art
Foreign language	Modern foreign language
Manual work	
Domestic subjects	Technology
(Music added soon afterwards)	Music

The similarity between 1904 and 1988 questions the rhetoric of 'a major new initiative' employed by the government, and points to some historical continuities in social and political purpose and priorities. The 1904 Regulations embodied that curriculum historically offered to the grammar school clientele as opposed to the curriculum being developed in the Board Schools and aimed primarily at the working classes: one segment or vision of the nation was being favoured at the expense of another. In the intervening period more equalitarian impulses brought about the creation of comprehensive schools where children of all classes came together under one roof. This in turn led to a range of curriculum reforms which sought to redefine and challenge the hegemony of the grammar school curriculum.

Seeking in turn to challenge and redirect these reforms and intentions the political right has argued for the rehabilitation of the 'traditional' (i.e. grammar school) subjects. The national curriculum can be seen as a political statement of the victory of the forces and intentions representing these political groups. A particular vision, a preferred segment of the nation has therefore been reinstated and prioritized, and legislated as 'national'.

The historical continuities evident in the national curriculum have been commented on in a number of places. For instance, the *Times Educational Supplement* stated that 'the first thing to say about this whole exercise is that it unwinds 80 years of English (and Welsh) educational history. It is a case of go back to Go' (*Times Educational Supplement*, 1989). In writing of the National Curriculum Project, Moon and Mortimore commented:

> The legislation, and the much-criticized consultative document that preceded it, present the curriculum in needlessly rather restricted terms. Thus the primary curriculum was put forward as if it were no more than a pre-secondary preparation (like the worst sort of 'prep school'). All the positive aspects of British primary schooling so valued by HMI and the Select Committee of the House of Commons and so praised by many foreign commentators were ignored.
>
> The secondary curriculum, in turn, appears to be based on the curriculum of a typical 1960s grammar school. We would not take issue with the subjects included, but we believe that such a curriculum misses out a great deal. Information technology, electronics, statistics, personal, social and careers education have all been omitted. Yet, surely, these are just the areas that are likely to be of importance for the future lives of many pupils?
>
> (Moon and Mortimore, 1989, p. 9)

The national curriculum then can be seen as a response to a 'nation at risk' at two levels. Firstly there is the general sense of the nation-state being in economic decline and subject to globalization and to amalgamation in the wider European Community. There the response is paradoxical. Nation-building curricula are often favoured over commercially 'relevant' curricula. The solution therefore may exacerbate the problem. Further economic 'decline' may follow leading to even more desperate attempts to reassert national identity.

Secondly, given that the UK is clearly a divided nation, investigation of the national curriculum allows insights into precisely *which* nation is at risk. It would seem it is the elite and middle class groups which were perceived of as 'at risk'. For it is this group that have the greatest historical connections to the 'traditional subjects': these subjects have been revived and reinstated in the national curriculum.

The perception of nations at risk and social groups at risk has further provided one source of support for developing the powers of central state over the school curriculum. This is the third level at which the national curriculum is significant. In the central project of rebuilding the nation-state, the issue of re-establishing national identity and ideology has been dealt with but there remains the issue of rebuilding the power of the nation-state itself.

National curriculum and national power

In post-war Britain the national state's powers over education were increasingly devolved to local education authorities (LEAs). This made the schools more responsive to the local 'communities' than to 'the nation'. In addition the teachers' unions were able to assert a growing influence over issues of curriculum and assessment reform. As we have noted, this led some comprehensive schools to develop more comprehensive curricula which moved beyond the 1904-style academic curriculum 'suited to only a few'. The national state's loss of control, specifically loss of control over curriculum, therefore led to patterns of prioritizing which went a long way from the political settlement enshrined in the 1904 Regulations: the so-called traditional subjects. This loss of control therefore threatened those groups which had benefited from this political settlement. The social prioritization so well-established in the early twentieth century was plainly under attack. In short, the 'nation' as represented in these privileged groups was 'at risk'.

Of course reasserting the primacy of curriculum as a vehicle for the education of the elite and custodial classes entirely fits a version of nation-building. These leadership and professional groups are precisely those who will rule and administer the nation – it is consistent to remake the curriculum in their image and reconstruct schools as mechanisms for the selection of this national meritocracy.

But the form of this national reconstruction at the level of curriculum, of course, reflects the existing perception and situation of the 'nation'. Plainly at this point in its history the UK nation-state reflects the post-war period of precipitous decline. Since 1945 the large aspirations of the nation-state as a major imperial power, a major player on the world stage, have had to be severely redefined. A particularly problematic aspect of this imperial angst had been how to deal with the plurality of other cultures. This concern is often wished off into the field of 'multicultural studies' but is of course integral to notions of identity and democracy in general. Alongside ideological decline has been a savage experience of economic decline. In both of these aspects of decline the British establishment, the elite and the professions, have been implicated. As a result any campaign to reconstruct and revive the nation would have to respond to this experience of precipitous decline. The particular version of nation-building through curriculum is therefore likely to reflect this perception.

The definition of a central curriculum could in fact take a number of forms, but there are two major directions. One version would specify a common set of goals and objectives and certain amount of common content. In this version the teachers and students are allowed some flexibility and a degree of accommodation with local conditions and concerns is both expected and encouraged. This version of central curriculum would have resonated well with the experience of the UK educational system in the twentieth century.

A second version of central curriculum would prescribe in detail what is to be taught, learned and tested. There would be little allowance for choice on the part of teachers and students. One caricature of this version would be the mythical French Minister of Education who could look at his watch and say what every child in France was studying at any given time. This version of common curricula would go against the grain of twentieth century UK experience.

That the 1988 UK national curriculum in fact represents the second model of central curriculum says a good deal. It reflects the response of a political establishment that has experienced more than four decades of precipitous and accelerating political and economic decline. In such circumstances the replay of paranoid fears within the domain of the school curriculum seems an understandable, if indirect, response.

The unprecedented expansion of powers over the school curriculum has not gone unnoticed or unchallenged. The Cabinet's intention in the report on history has led the Historical Association, an august and conservative body representing history teachers, to question whether the government has any 'constitutional right' for such detailed intervention.

The major expansion of state power over the curriculum and over assessment leads to a parallel diminution in the teachers' power and therefore has associated implications for pedagogy. At one level the new power over curriculum and the battery of tests represent a substantial push to make the details of teachers' work accountable to the state. The experience of the 1960s where teachers were judged to have superior expertise in assessing the educational needs of their pupils has been rapidly dismantled.

Much of the commentary on the new national curriculum has been sympathetic and optimistic about the results of the expansion of state power. For instance, *The Times* carried an editorial on the passing of the 'True Education Bill', which argued 'most important, a national curriculum, accompanied by attainment targets and tests at key ages, will ensure that a large proportion of young people leave school literate, numerate, and more broadly educated than they are now'. Standards in short, will rise. That is because 'teachers will have a clearer idea of what is expected of them' (*Times Educational Supplement*, 1989). In short, greater accountability (and less power over definition) leads to clearer objectives and better work habits. This is a crude simplification employing an almost-Taylorist optimism about a strategy for tackling a most complex enterprise.

Lessons from previous historical episodes must be treated with considerable caution for we are not comparing like with like. Yet so clear have been the experiences of teachers and taught in the face of previous nineteenth century government interventions in matters of curriculum and assessment that the pious simplifications behind *The Times*'s viewpoint should be severely scrutinized. For it may not be the case that 'standards in short, will rise' rather 'morale, in short, will fall'.

A major experiment in state control of school curricula was conducted in the years 1862–95. The teachers were made subject to a system of 'payment by results': the teachers' pay was linked to pupils' results in school examinations. E.G.A. Holmes, a school inspector at the time, has left a detailed commentary on the results of this experiment. He notes that from 1862 to 1895 'a considerable part of the grant received by each school was paid on the results of a yearly examination held by H.M. (Her Majesty's) Inspector on an elaborate syllabus, formulated by the Department and binding on all schools alike'. The results of this mechanism were clear. 'On the official report which followed this examination depended the reputation and financial prosperity of the school, and the reputation and financial prosperity of the teacher' (Holmes, 1928, p. 103). The Government therefore had established deliberate and detail control over curriculum and assessment and thereby over the teacher and student. Power was thus established, but what of the 'side-effects' on education? On this Holmes was adamant:

> The consequent pressure on the teacher to exert himself was well nigh irresistible; and he had no choice but to transmit that pressure to his subordinates and his pupils. The result was that in those days the average school was a hive of industry.
>
> But it was also a hive of misdirected energy. The State, in prescribing a syllabus which was to be followed, in all the subjects of instruction, by all the schools in the country, without regard to local or personal considerations, was guilty of one capital offence. It did all his thinking for the teacher. It told him in precise detail what he was to do each year in each 'Standard', how he was to handle each subject, and how far he was to go in it; what width of ground he was to cover; what amount of knowledge, what degree of accuracy was required for a 'pass'. In other words, it provided him with his ideals, his general conceptions, his more immediate aims, his schemes of work; and if it did not control his methods in all their details, it gave him (by implication) hints and suggestions with regard to these on which he was not slow to

act; for it told him that the work done in each class and each subject would be tested at the end of each year by a careful examination of each individual child; and it was inevitable that in his endeavour to adapt his teaching to the type of question which his experience of the yearly examination led him to expect, he should gradually deliver himself, mind and soul, into the hands of the officials of the Department, the officials at Whitehall who framed the yearly syllabus, and the officials in the various districts who examined on it.

What the Department did to the teacher, it compelled him to do to the child. The teacher who is the slave of another's will, cannot carry out his instructions except by making his pupils the slaves of his own will. The teacher who has been deprived by his superiors of freedom, initiative, and responsibility, cannot carry out his instructions except by depriving his pupils of the same vital qualities. The teacher who, in response to the deadly pressure of a cast-iron system, has become a creature of habit and routine, cannot carry out his instructions except by making his pupils as helpless and as puppet-like as himself.

But it is not only because mechanical obedience is fatal, in the long run, to mental and spiritual growth, that the regulation of elementary or any other grade of education by a uniform syllabus is to be deprecated. It is also because a uniform syllabus is, in the nature of things, a bad syllabus, and because the degree of its badness varies directly with the arc of the sphere of educational activity that comes under its control.

(Holmes, 1928, pp. 103–105)

Holmes provided more details of the working of a system of state prescription of syllabus and control of examinations:

It was preordained, then, that the syllabuses which the Department issued, year by year, in the days of payment by results should have few merits and many defects. Yet even if, by an unimaginable miracle, they had all been educationally sound, the mere fact that all the teachers in England had to work by them would have made them potent agencies for evil. To be in bondage to a syllabus is a misfortune for a teacher, and a misfortune for the school that he teaches. To be in bondage to a syllabus which is binding on all schools alike is of all misfortunes the gravest. Or if there is a graver, it is the fate that befell the teachers of England under the old regime – the fate of being in bondage to a syllabus which was bad both because it had to come down to the level of the least fortunate school and the least capable teacher, and also because it was the outcome of ignorance, inexperience, and bureaucratic self-satisfaction.

Of the evils that are inherent in the examination system as such of its tendency to arrest growth, to deaden life, to paralyse the higher faculties, to externalize what is inward, to materialize what is spiritual, to involve education in an atmosphere of unreality and self-deception I have already spoken at some length. In the days of payment by results various circumstances conspired to raise those evil tendencies to the highest imaginable 'power'. When inspectors ceased to examine (in the stricter sense of the word), they realised what infinite mischief the yearly examination had done. The children, the majority of whom were examined in reading and dictation out of their own reading-books (two or three in number, as the case might be), were drilled in the contents of those books until they knew them almost by heart. In arithmetic they worked abstract sums, in obedience to formal rules, day after day, and month after month; and they were put up to various tricks and dodges which would, it was hoped, enable them to know by what precise rules the various questions on the arithmetic cards were to be answered. They learned a few lines of poetry by heart and committed all the 'meanings and allusions' to memory, with the probable result – so sickening must the process have been – that they hated poetry for the rest of their lives. In geography, history, and grammar they were the victims of unintelligent oral cram, which they were compelled, under pains and penalties, to take in and retain till the examination day was over, their ability to disgorge it on occasion being periodically tested by the teacher. And so with the other subjects. Not a thought was given, except in a small minority of the schools, to the real training of the child, to the fostering of his mental (and other) growth. To get him through the yearly examination by hook or by crook was the one concern of the teacher. As profound distrust of the teacher was the basis of the policy of the Department, so profound distrust of the child was the basis of the policy of the teacher. To leave the child to find out anything for himself, to work out anything for himself, to think out anything for himself, would have been regarded as a proof of incapacity, not to say insanity, on the part of the teacher, and would have led to results which, from the 'percentage' point of view, would probably have been disastrous.

(Holmes, 1928, pp. 106–108)

In fact the experience of this episode of state intervention had long-lasting effects. In 1944 when the Government was drawing up the influential Education Act of that year James Chuter Ede, parliamentary secretary to the Minister, said in a speech to the House:

there is not one curriculum for every child, but every child must be a separate problem for the teacher. The teacher is the servant of the State, and I hope that no one will say that the State should lay down the curriculum of the schools. Some of us were brought up under the old payment-by-results system, and were the time earlier, I could amuse the House with descriptions that some of my Hon. friends know would be no caricature of the way in which State control of the curriculum prevented the development of a wise and sound system of education.

(Chitty, 1988)

Holmes and Chuter Ede then warn us of some of the dangers that attended a 'national curriculum and assessment' strategy. But the implications for teachers and particularly pupils are of profound concern. The development of attitudes of 'mechanical obedience' strike at the very heart of the 'democratic' system of governance. This matter assumes great importance at a time when there is widespread comment in the UK about the absence of constitutional rights and the consequent possibility of substantial erosion of 'traditional' rights by more authoritarian government whether of the right (as at the moment) or of the left. The link between the national curriculum and mechanical obedience therefore highlights a major problem with regard to the education of pupils with the capacity to be functioning citizens in a democracy. I find the following statement about 'the erosion of British liberty' particularly chilling in this light: 'Britons have been schooled to think of themselves as subjects, not citizens; as people with freedoms granted by government, not with rights guaranteed against government interference' (Broder, 1989, p. 7). The traditional school subject based National Curriculum plays a key role in constructing the particular subjectivities of subjects in this sense (Corrigan, 1990).

Seen in this light the political project underpinning the national curriculum assumes a further dimension, for the hidden curriculum of the national curriculum is a reassertion of the power of the state in nation-building. This project is diametrically opposed to the alternative project of educating pupils, from a plurality of cultures, for active citizenship in a democracy. The history of mass mechanical obedience as a bedrock for nation-building is well known, but it leads not to democracy but to totalitarianism.

Conclusion

The introduction of the national curriculum in the UK has been linked to the problems of national economic decline and a belief that curriculum co-ordination will aid a project of national economic regeneration. Behind the rhetorical priority given to economic revival, two other agendas have been discerned.

First, the reconstitution of a traditional subjects-based curriculum. These traditional subjects evoke a past 'golden age' when schooling was selective and people 'knew their station'. A number of empirical studies have pointed up the links between traditional subjects and social class.[4] The obsessive presentism of many of the current government initiatives has successfully obscured this deeply-embedded connectedness which is of course relevant to the present and future of the UK as a class society.

In developing this commentary for a global audience, it is important to note the distinctiveness and strength of UK class politics. For instance, in the USA at the moment a debate is underway about defining a national curriculum comprising traditional subjects. However, the intention, at least one important intention, is to provide rigorous academic subject-based courses of study covering curriculum content and form which will appeal to *all* children. Hence, the pattern of state and class-formation in the USA mean that a national curriculum initiative will have sharply different resonances to those in a somewhat obsolescent class-based society like the UK. (This is not, of course, to say that an initiative in the USA will not have powerful implications for matters of class, race and gender.) Moreover, the patterns of civic culture, citizenship education and constitutional rights are sharply different in the UK from the USA: so that once again a national curriculum will be likely to affect the two societies differently.

The second agenda in the UK is one of establishing new modalities of control over schooling on behalf of the nation-state. These new modalities will allow detailed control to be exercised over the school curriculum, both in terms of content, form and assessment. In the UK case this would seem a late and somewhat desperate attempt at nation-building, both in terms of nation-state governance and the partial propagation through curriculum of national ideologies, selective memories and images. It would seem possible that declining nations in their post-imperial phase have nowhere to go but to retreat into the bunker of the school curriculum. In this case, in particular, there may well be some lessons for the USA.

Notes

1   I have employed the term 'United Kingdom' as a statement of a particular governmental aspiration towards national identity. In many ways it links with a broader project of

privileging a particular form of 'Englishness' (a form with which I personally have no empathy or sympathy). In the event as the National Curriculum proceeds it is leading to a fragmented response in the different 'kingdoms' – Scotland for instance has managed to modify the testing requirements for the 'National' Curriculum.

2   Subjects here might be read in both senses, as we shall see, the institutionalised school subject and the subjectivities that those institutionalised subjects seek to implant and patrol.

3   This section was written before the withdrawal of the UK pound from the European Exchange Rate mechanism and the effective devaluation of the pound and of course before the replacement of Thatcher by Major.

4   See Goodson (1988, 1993). North American readers unfamiliar with the shorthand way in which I have dealt with issues of social structure may need to refer to these books to examine the argument in greater detail.

References

Broder, D.S., 1989, Mrs Thatcher and the Erosion of British Liberty. *Manchester Guardian Weekly*, 141(5).

Chitty, C., 1988, Central Control of the School Curriculum, 1944–87. *History of Education*, 17(4), 321–334.

Corrigan, P., 1990, *Social Forms of Human Capacities* (London and New York: Routledge).

Department of Education and Science, 1989, *National Curriculum History Group Interim Report* quoted *Times Educational Supplement*, 18 August (London), p. 4.

Eaglesham, E.J.R., 1967, *The Foundations of Twentieth-Century Education in England* (London: Routledge and Kegan Paul).

Fowler, W.S., 1988, *Towards the National Curriculum* (London: Kogan Page Ltd).

Goodson, I.F., 1988, *The Making of Curriculum* (London: Falmer Press).

Goodson, I.F., 1993, *Subjects and Schooling: The Social Construction of Curriculum* (London: Routledge).

Holmes, E.G.A., 1928, *What Is and What Might Be* (London: Constable and Co. Ltd).

Kerr, J., 1971, The Problem of Curriculum Reform. In R. Hooper (ed.), *The Curriculum Context, Design and Development* (Edinburgh: Oliver and Boyd), pp. 178–200.

Moon, B. and Mortimore, P., 1989, *The National Curriculum: Straitjacket or Safety Net?* (London: Colophon Press).

Rubinstein, D. and Simon, B., 1973, *The Evolution of the Comprehensive School 1926–1972* (London: Routledge and Kegan Paul).

Ryder, J. and Silver, H., 1970, *Modern English Society, History and Structure 1850–1970* (London: Methuen).

CHAPTER 9

LONG WAVES OF EDUCATIONAL REFORM

Extract from 'Report to the Spencer Foundation'

Submitted September 2003

Introduction

Restating the problem: the salience and invisibility of 'time'

This chapter grows out of work on the 'Change Over Time' project conducted in the USA and Canada between 1998 and 2004 and funded by the Spencer Foundation. In naming our project 'Change Over Time', we were hoping to highlight an aspect of our study which we judged to be worthy of wider concern and interest. It is a recurrent mystery to those with historical training that so many of our social studies, particularly one might argue our educational studies, take time for granted. We might seek to explain this by the current obsession with contemporary change, by the 'velocity of change' itself, or by the progressive erosion of foundational disciplines, such as 'history of education'. But such assertions would themselves be a-historical; ignoring time, for the taken-for-grantedness of time is one of the great continuities.

Yet we live our lives by the clock; we are in fact regulated by time everyday. This is the paradox – that which is all-pervasive becomes invisible to us. As Young and Schuller (1988) noted in their pioneering study, *The Rhythms of Society*, 'if we are not only obsessed with clock-time but getting more so, it is all the more strange that social scientists should have done so little to make time one of their special apprehensions' (p. 2). This mysterious omission is common in studies of education and schooling. In this sense, the scholar of education reflects the consciousness of his or her subjects – the teachers, administrators and students, who take time for granted:

> The everyday authority of time is, even in a permissive society, so complete that it rarely appears as problematic, and if it is not problematic to the people who are the subjects, it will not be all that problematic – to the other people . . .
>
> (op. cit., p. 3)

There is, however, a particular and peculiar irony in the fact that studies of social 'change' – herein educational and school 'change' – should ignore time. It seems *prima facia*, a major omission. After all, if change is about anything, it is about time. Yet a cursory examination of the literature will, we think, confirm that this is the case. Many of the most eminent contemporary change theorists ignore time.

They should be reminded that to ignore time is to ignore history, and to ignore history is to ignore human agency in its fullest application.

A wide range of contemporary studies of school change, including cross-site studies, work primarily with snapshot notions of social context and time (e.g. Fullan, 1999, 2000; Lieberman, 1995). This predominant category of school change study does not allow the change and reform efforts to be 'grounded' in trajectories of influence and causation which are linked to the past, or indeed pursued longitudinally from the past into the present and from there into the future. This a-historical feature of the dominant change literature is pervasive and endemic. Indeed it enters the very rhetoric of 'change', which is somehow seen as uniquely powerful at this time of global restructuring. (As we shall see later, this is a contention with some virtue, but it must be painstakingly established historically, not polemically assumed and asserted.) Again history alerts us to continuities:

> Once time is recognized as a continuous flow – with the essential continuity being the flow itself – what is being observed cannot be anything other than change, continuous change. This is not to say there is no pattern, no structure in the welter. But whatever has pattern, structure, an appearance of the static, is made up of change, change wrapped within change.
>
> (Young and Schuller, 1988, p. 5)

These continuities have, of course, been systematically observed by some historians of education. The focus has tended to be on broad patterns of organizational persistence and evolution (e.g. Cuban, 1984); on the 'persistence of the recitation' (Westbury, 1973); on the fate of specific reform policies (Tyack and Hansot, 1992; Tyack and Tobin, 1994); or on reforms in particular areas – such as curriculum (e.g. Goodson, 1994). A range of work has studied the links between cycles of economic growth and educational expenditure. For instance the British *History of Education Journal* published a special issue derived from a conference on Education and Economic Performance (Special issue on Education and Economic Performance, 1998). French historians have been studying long waves of economic performance and education for some time particularly those located at the University of Montpelier (Fontvieille, 1990). Following our Spencer study and the discerning of long waves within the data, Carpentier produced a very interesting version of his doctoral thesis that looks at long cycles of change related to educational expenditure in the nineteenth and twentieth centuries with a particularly interesting analysis of the period 1945–73 (Carpentier, 2001).

As noted in this chapter the work of historians David Tyack and Larry Cuban at Stanford has been particularly insightful on cycles of reform as has the work of their colleague in sociology, John Meyer. Work by Murphy on waves of reform within US educational policy add further to our cognitive map of cycles of school change (Murphy, 1990, 1991).

The work of historians then has patiently sought to elucidate the deep contextual inertia within patterns of change and continuity whether cycles of reform are long or short. In the world of change initiatives and indeed a good deal of change theory such complexity and contradiction has too often been ignored or denied. Moreover our longitudinal sweep needs to search beyond internalistic patterns of organizational persistence and evolution to study the interaction between these internal patterns and external movements. External movements that are within economic and social structures, and in the 'external consistencies' (Meyer and Rowan, 1978), which impose limits upon the possibilities for educational change and reform. Change theory, which focuses only on internal movements in each school, ignores the broad changes in external and economic context, which set parameters and possibilities for internal change.

The dominant educational change theory of the moment then works with two inter-linked lacunae. Firstly, questions of time and historical periodization are ignored or glossed over in favour of a belief in unique, contemporary possibility. Secondly, the broad sweep of changes in economic and external context are subordinated to a belief in more internalistic, institutional change patterns.

For these reasons, above all, because change must be viewed historically, our study will adopt a focus on change located in historical periods.[1] This approach is derived from the *annaliste* methodology for understanding social and historical change. In a real sense, the *Annaliste School* develops a combination of history and sociology. In England, this approach has been developed by the late Philip Abrahams and by Peter Burke in his book *History and Social Theory* (1993). More recently, the *Journal of Historical Sociology* has pursued the same themes of enquiry.

Historians and social scientists following the *Annaliste School* see change operating at three levels of time – long, medium and short – which interpenetrate in a complex manner. Here theorists provide an allegory of the ocean to capture the main characteristics of these three categories or levels and their interdependent mode of operation.

Looking at the ocean, at the bottom, representing long-term time, are deep currents which, although apparently quite stable, are moving all the time. Such long-term time covers major structural factors: worldviews, forms of the state, etc. The movement from pre-modern to modern, or modern to postmodern forms can be understood in terms of these broad epochal shifts (Bell, 1973; Denzin, 1991; Lyotard, 1984; Wright Mills, 1959). The effects of the emerging social, economic and political conditions of the postmodern era upon the organization and practices of schooling might be understood in these terms (e.g. Aronowitz and Giroux, 1991; Hargreaves, 1994).

Above this level are the swells and tides of particular cycles representing medium time. Such medium-term time has been conceived in boom-bust like spans of 50 years or so – although, with the compression of time and space in the post-modern age, these cycles may themselves undergo compression (Giddens, 1991). It is within these medium-term cycles that one might explain the establishment of the current 'grammar of schooling', for example, as classroom-based, graded and subject-specialized schooling in the latter years of the nineteenth and early years of the twentieth centuries. As Tyack and Tobin (1994) admonish, unless reformers begin to talk the historical 'grammar of schooling', their attempts to initiate educational change will be forever thwarted.

At the top of the ocean, representing the waves and froth, is short-term, everyday time: the everyday events and human actions of ordinary daily life. Proponents of this view of history often celebrate its empirical specifics against the grander theo-retical claims of epochal shifts between different historical periods (e.g. McCulloch, 1995). These theorizations of history should not be treated as competitive, though. Fine-grained empirical detail and broad-based theoretical sensibility are comple-mentary forces in history and complementary resources for interpreting such history. Much of contemporary change positions itself here 'at the top of the ocean' in the waves and froth: the legacy is therefore unlikely to be enduring.

The most interesting points for inquiry and investigation are when the different layers of historical time coincide; for it is at such points that inclinations towards and capacity for change and reform are strongest. Such co-incidences or conjunctures can be seen in key moments of educational history and change.

Long waves of historical change

The *annaliste* historians saw time as occurring in waves as the oceanic allegory they use indicates. Febvre (1925) was clear about the vital importance of time in social research. He says history 'does not think merely in human terms. Its natural setting is duration' (Ibid., p. 32).

But as we saw, duration can be divided into different segments: short-term change – what the *annalistes* call *eventements* – focus on individual events that happen in a regular way and are of short duration. Medium-term change, they call *conjonctures*. These happenings have a continuous and hard to reverse rhythm, and represent changes of substantial duration. Long-term stabilities and continuities, they call the *longue duree* periods, like the reformation or first Industrial Revolution.

In searching for the long waves of educational change in our Spencer case study schools, we are focusing at the level of *conjonctures*. Here our study derives a good deal, not only from *annaliste* history but also from major work in economic history, particularly the work of Nikolai Kondratiev, who had founded the Institute of Conjuncture in Moscow in 1920. In 1922, Kondratiev published a book which defined long waves or 'cycles' of economic growth, what he called 'major cycles of the conjuncture' (Kondratiev, 1923, p. 524).

Kondratiev had worked out that, over and above the short-term waves of economic cycles of boom and bust, of upswing and downswing, were longer waves. Freeman and Louçã (2001) summarize these in Figure 9.1.

In general, Kondratiev was pointing to long wave conjunctures of 30 to 40 years' duration. These long waves were superimposed on the short-term economic cycles that we are more familiar with in the everyday parlance as periods of 'growth' and 'recession'. Kondratiev's explanatory framework for these long-wave cycles (resembling the medium-term *conjoncture* of the *annalistes*) focused upon the life cycle of technology systems. Freeman and Louçã characterize this technology life cycle in the following way.

Thus, in a simplified and schematic way, the following phases in the life cycle of a technology system may be distinguished:

1   The laboratory-invention phase, with early prototypes, patents, small-scale demonstrations and early applications.
2   Decisive demonstrations of technical and commercial feasibility, with widespread potential applications.
3   Explosive take-off and growth during a turbulent phase of structural crisis in the economy and a political crisis of coordination as a new regime of regulation is established.
4   Continued high growth, with the system now accepted as commonsense and as the dominant technological regime in the leading countries of the world economy; application in a still wider range of industries and services.
5   Slow-down and erosion of profitability as the system matures and is challenged by newer technologies, leading to a new crisis of structural adjustment.
6   Maturity, with some 'renaissance' effects possible from fruitful co-existence with newer technologies, but also the possibility of slow disappearance.

(Freeman and Louçã, 2001, p. 146)

Approx. timing of the 'upswing' (boom)
'Downswing' (crisis of adjustment)
1780–1815
1815–48
1848–73
1873–95
1895–1918
1918–40
1941–73
1973–

Figure 9.1 Waves of economic cycles (Freeman and Louçã, 2001, p. 141).

After this stage model, they state:

> we shall try to show that it is phases 2–5 that are associated with those wavelike movements in the economic and social system that have been designated since Schumpeter as 'Kondratiev waves' or cycles.
>
> (Ibid., p. 146)

The work of Freeman and Louçã is vitally important for those examining the long waves of educational change. This is because they link the technological and economic life cycle they describe to institutional and social changes. The Venezuelan economist, Carlota Perez, has extended this argument, judging that each long wave has a specific technological style, a model or paradigm for organizing production in the most efficient manner. For the upswings, this model and the social and institutional framework are broadly harmonized; conversely in the downswing, a new technological pattern brings a dysfunctional relationship with the existing socio-institutional system. In the upswings, we have conjuncture, in the downswings disjuncture (Perez, 1983; Young, 1988).

From the point of view of educational changes, the period of conjuncture provides maximum harmonization with new technological and economic regimes. As a result, the flow of resources to the educational system is maximized as the economic cycle produces better and better profit margins for funding the socio-institutional frameworks that accompany and facilitate the economic upswing. We would expect them to find rapid changes to schooling in periods of accelerated upswing, such as the late 1960s and early 1970s.

Whilst the link between economy and education is indirect, there are few who would not accept that economic cycles affect educational patterns. Hence, if Kondratiev is right, we would expect to see long waves of educational change which, in a general way, follow the long waves of economic change.

Long waves of educational change

Now most commonly, our educational study focuses on individual events and reform initiatives (*eventementes*). Our study is concerned with short spans and snapshots because education is understandably concerned with immediate delivery of educational services in the here and now of the present. In general, our focus is short-term and action focused.

Our Spencer study was a bountiful opportunity to explore a longer view of educational change. We employed a range of data to explore change in schools from our earliest school which began in 1916 through to the millennium. Two major sources of data helped our analyses of the history of school change. Firstly we sought where possible to develop detailed historical archives of each school: school records of curriculum and timetables, school year books, journals, reports, departmental records and so on. Our initial worry was that so much of this would have been destroyed but in fact we were surprised how much had been retained: a veritable treasure trove for the reconstruction of school change. Besides this textual database, we conducted a wide range of interviews with teachers across the lifespan of each school, there were often full life history interviews. As noted on p. 8, the teacher interviews covered the 1950s and 1960s teacher (cohort one); the 1970s and 1980s (cohort two) and the teachers from the 1990s onwards (cohort three). In addition we collected a range of choreographic data from school visits to meetings and lessons.

Our schools were chosen to cover a spectrum of secondary schools in our two locations in the US and Canada. The site in the US we called Bradford School district located in New York State in a medium sized industrial town. Bradford was similar to many US cities in the changes to its urban population. There had been successive waves of 'white flight' to the suburbs leaving the urban core mainly populated by poor families of ten minorities, particularly Afro-American. According to the district statistics in 1985, 40 per cent of Bradford pupils lived in poverty rising five years later to nearly 70 per cent. By 1989 of the districts pupil population 62 per cent were African-American and 18 per cent Hispanic. In fact it was partly as a response to these demographic shifts that the school district began creating 'Magnet schools' in 1980. Such magnet schools were created by the federal government in the mid-1970s in order to encourage voluntary desegregation.

One of our chosen schools, Barrett was therefore a magnet school created in 1989 from one of the original high schools; a second school was chosen to reflect the tradition of alternative education, Durant School set up in 1971 at a time when 'schools within walls' were fashionable aimed to provide flexible individualized programmes for students who favoured a style of education beyond the main-stream high school programmes; our third school reflected the white flight noted earlier. Set up in the 1950s, Sheldon had once been a showpiece comprehensive high school. But the urban catchment was transformed by the increasing poverty of the local families while the minority representation in the school sky-rocketed. These three schools were chosen to represent some of the major developments in secondary education in the Bradford District in the second half of the twentieth century.

The second site for our schools was the province of Ontario in Canada, Ontario. In New York State a range of restructuring had gained impetus in the second half of the 1990s. The introduction of Regents examinations transformed the landscape of secondary schooling. In Ontario a similar wave began in 1995 with the election of a market fundamentalist progressive conservative government. In the next five years more legislation was passed initiating educational reform than in the provinces preceding history. The financing of schools was transformed with government grants to school districts severely cut back. A range of draconian curricula and assessment reforms were rapidly brought in which aimed at central-ization of curricular development and design with the Ministry of Education. The schools were made to stream between academic and practical routes whilst a range of new tests and assessment systems were introduced. Our four schools covered a spectrum of historical profiles. Eastside School is in a medium sized town in the south west of Ontario, was founded early in the century as a landmark technical school. It continued to innovate across a broad front from Art through to Computer Studies. The school was located in the working class downtown area. Lord Byron School in a large metropolis was one of Canada's most innovative schools in the 1960s and rather like Durant School focused on progressive, often individualized methods and curriculum. Talisman Park in the suburbs of a metro-polis was a fairly traditional academic high school where cultural migration was bringing greater diversity to the school student body. Stewart Heights also broad-ens its cultural base having been when it was established a primarily middle class institution in a village-like location. Blue Mountain was a technological beacon school that was run innovatively as a learning organization at the cutting edge of developments from its inception in 1992.

When we had analysed our historical archives in each school, conducted our visits and undertaken our ambitious programme of interviews, our portrayals of each school provided a broad historical profile. These profiles were broken down by each of the school report writers according to periods of time that echoed the changes in the organization and internal character of each school.

Deliberately, we did not set out with detailed historical hypotheses beyond a general belief that historical scrutiny would aid elucidation. Our concern was also ethnographic and inter-actionist and, since it focuses on change over time, historical patterns only emerged out of a set of specific school studies conducted by different researchers. We judged that if a pattern of conjunctures emerged from such differentiated studies by different researchers, then truly a pattern might be established. The periods discerned for each school site are summarized in Figure 9.2.

The chart (see Figure 9.2) indicates that a pattern of conjunctures can be discerned for all schools in the late 1990s, and for five of the schools for the period 1967–79. The exceptions to the latter conjunctures are Blue Mountain (which was not founded until 1992), and Barrett School (which ran counter to the trend by becoming a 'Magnet School' in 1980) and Stewart Heights.

The features of the 1967–79 conjuncture (see Figure 9.3) can be generally discerned in all of the case study schools, even though they are very different types of schools with different clienteles and objectives in different districts and coun-tries. It would seem that at this time, there was a shift in the ethos of schooling is

	1916	1920	1955–59	1960–64	1965–69	1970–74	1975–79	1980–84	1985–89	1990–94	1995–99
Sheldon			Jewel of the district				Holding its own	Fall from grace		Troubled period	
Barrett						Begins as junior high		Camelot days	Increasing competition		
Durant			Early development		Educational alternative			Screw tightens	New beginning/end		Fight for survival
Eastside					Relaxing the rules: defining a new system			Lighthouse school		Change is constant	
Talisman			Formative years		Optimism and innovation		Insecurity and uncertainty			Retrenchment/intransigence	
Lord Byron						Creativity/experimental	Overreaching entropy		Survival and continuity		Creativity is gone
Blue Mountain										Formative years	Attrition years (Surviving)

Figure 9.2 Periods discerned for each school site.

1916–99

	1916	1920	1955–59	1960–64	1965–69	1970–74	1975–79	1980–84	1985–89	1990–94	1995–99

Sheldon — Jewel of the district

Durant — Educational alternative

Eastside — Relaxing the rules: defining a new system

Talisman — Optimism and innovation

Lord Byron — Creativity/Experimental

Figure 9.3 Conjuncture.

part of a generalized economic upswing throughout the western world. Studies in the United Kingdom and Europe, in Australia and New Zealand, point to similar characteristics emerging in schools in this period.

In the Canadian case study schools, a clear link can be made with the changing climate of opinion among educational policy-makers in the economically buoyant period of the mid-1960s. In the United States at this time, Lyndon Johnson was busy laying down the foundations for the 'Great Society', with a wide range of inclusive educational policies typified by project Headstart.

In Canada, in June 1968, the Committee on Aims and Objectives of Education in the Schools of Ontario (the Hall-Dennis committee) published its report, recommending wholesale reform of the provincial system to establish 'a child-centered learning continuum that invites learning by individual discovery and inquiry' (1968, p. 179). In the opinion of the standard history of twentieth century Ontario schools, *Living and Learning* was 'the most radical and bold document ever to originate from the bureaucratic labyrinth of the provincial Department of Education' (Stamp, 1982, p. 217).

Hall-Dennis created an atmosphere conducive to curriculum change at Eastside School. Teachers were taking the freedom implied by Hall-Dennis and trying new curriculum and new teaching methods, although many of them had no direct relationship to the recommendations of the committee. One teacher recalled:

> It was a time, when I got there; there was a lot of experimentation going on. Hall-Dennis had just come in. And it was a very interesting situation because I don't think people really understood what Hall-Dennis was all about. And as a result, everybody was experimenting trying to find out what worked.
>
> (Interview, 2 May 1993)

Unusually, this was especially true in academic subjects, where a typical time-intensive project saw one class making a film remake of *Easy Rider* on the city's streets (Interview, 2 May 1993).

In the spring of 1969 came what was perhaps the most important direct result of Hall-Dennis – the introduction of a credit system, to which all high schools had to convert by September 1972. The credit system marked Ontario's turn to a subject promotion approach, applied not only to academic areas but also, for the first time, to vocational subjects. Under the new regulations, students needed to take a minimum of 27 credits (each equivalent to 110–120 hours' class time) to receive a Grade 12 graduation diploma. Of these 27, 12 had to come from particular areas (though students had some choice within the areas), and 15 were totally elective (Gilbert, 1972, pp. 10–11 and 54–59). The credit system – made feasible by the ability of computers to do the timetabling – gave students a new degree of freedom in managing their secondary school career. According to proponents, it was intended to also give teachers greater autonomy in course design, while allowing students to contribute to curriculum development through their choice of subject (Stamp, 1982, pp. 220–222).

All of our case study schools were influenced by the ethos of Hall-Dennis: in Lord Byron School, the founding philosophy of the school stressed the progressive intentions of this government policy. In Talisman Park, a new period of innovation set in at this time, and in Eastside School, the established rules and procedures were dramatically changed in this period.

At Eastside School, the new approach had major repercussions on the school ethos. For one thing, it marked the end of the system where a whole class moved together. In academic subjects, this had led teachers to specialize the content of each class to accommodate students' practical interest. With the new system, each class had what older teachers thought a 'peculiar mixture' of students from a variety of courses (Interview, January 1994).

The credit system also proved the end of the central concept of concentration in a specific technical area at the high school level. Under the old regime, technical students had taken a core specialty, supplemented with strictly related areas – a route intended to lead straight to employment. Now students tended to pick a variety of subjects. As one teacher said, 'it monkeyed around with a system that I thought was working quite well, and it's pretty well destroyed it' (Interview, October 1994).

At the same time, the Ministry of Education – under the influence of the Teachers' Federation – tightened the rules for teacher qualification. Suddenly schools could only get letters of permission allowing them to hire uncertified teachers if absolutely no certified teacher in the province had applied for the job in question. Even when there was a pool of certified teachers, department heads lost their right to choose from them; they had to take whoever had the certificate and was next on the Board's list (Interview, January 1995).

The effects of these new rules were magnified by a series of trends which caused substantial drainage of existing teachers from Eastside and their replacement by a large new cohort of younger teachers. Many of these teachers went to new schools: in 1960 the Federal Technical and Vocational Training Assistance Act had inaugurated a boom in secondary school building and resulted in the construction of 335 new high schools in the province as well as funding 83 expansions. To meet the requirements of the Act, all of these schools and additions had to feature vocational education (Stamp, 1982, pp. 203–204). The job market for vocational teachers expanded widely and prospects for advancement opened throughout the provincial system. Lots of young new teachers flooded into the system.

Other veteran teachers from Eastside moved to administrative positions. In the 1960s, the city's Board of Education went through a tremendous evolution; in this period of growth, it needed many more people at supervisory positions. At the same time, the idea that people who stayed too long in one place became biased, and thus poor candidates for higher administrative positions came into general acceptance. For prospective supervisors, it became a good career move to go through different schools (Interview, January 1995).

Finally, some Eastside teachers left the employ of the Board to work in two new city institutions. The city's new teacher training institution, needed people to instruct the next generation of technical, commercial and academic teachers, while the nearby Vocational Centre offered post-secondary education in many of the subjects taught at Eastside.

Alongside a new younger school staff cohort, one additional trend reaching a peak at this time appears under a variety of names, including the youth revolt. By the last years of the 1960s, 'there were a lot of hippie types at Eastside. I mean, if you didn't have hair to your shoulders, then you know, you weren't part of the crowd so to speak. It attracted that type' (Interview, February 1994). Long hair and beards for men and 'frizzy hair' and miniskirts for girls were becoming the rule. The new youth culture celebrated feeling over thought and sought ways to enhance the emotional experience – including drugs. The use of marijuana and LSD became common within school walls: 'the first floor was the entrance and the staircase. You could smell the marijuana sifting up...Nobody seemed to care about it; the teachers didn't do anything to stop it' (Interview, February 1994).

Students also turned to alcohol. The lowering of the legal drinking age to 18 (during the summer of 1971) made this more prevalent – lunchtime and afternoon drinking sessions became institutionalized in the student culture.

More than just dress and recreational habits changed. This was a time of change in substance as well as style, of serious challenge, as well as superficial change. Student challenges to more fundamental school rules in this period reflected the larger assault being mounted by Western youth culture against the hegemony of those over 30. In secondary schools, this vocal movement reached its provincial peak in late 1968 and early 1969, with a large-scale protest over the date chosen for the end of the school year and a three-week student sit-in at a Toronto high school (Stamp, 1982, pp. 225–228).

At Eastside, the school's student newspaper, *The Word*, reflected the radical side of the youth movement. The issue for May 1969, for instance, opened with a satiric front page featuring a look at the school's latest 'torture machines' under the slogan, 'If you can't beat a student, kill him.' Inside, an editorial called on the student body to protest loudly and frequently against any perceived injustice, stating that a recent protest 'showed the Department of Education that the Universities were not the only ones capable of raising a bit of trouble if pushed too far'. The issue also included a full-page futuristic comic strip titled, 'The Revolution passed this way.' In that episode, the hero – a city revolutionary named Alex – kills an evil 'brain policeman' and heads for the life of a fugitive in the city's slums (*The Word*, 1969).

This new attitude also generated less dramatic, but more effective, agendas within the school walls. Students took an active role in determining the microstructures of their schooling experience. They sought to modify curriculum and pedagogy in the classroom. As one teacher put it, 'they were testing, testing, testing all the time' (Interview, January 1995).

Like Eastside School, Lord Byron School was a center of innovation in the spirit of the Hall-Dennis report from its foundation in 1970. For the first five years, until 1975, this was a period of 'creativity and experimentation'. Again, the school was largely staffed by a young and experimental new cohort of teachers. As a former teacher recalled: 'we were largely very young and single – not everybody. Many were beginning their careers and not only brought youth and idealism, but also a particular philosophy because they had come through the universities of the 1960s. The times were significant for the things we did.'

As a confirmation of the conjuncture of change in this period, the assertion that 'the times were significant for the things we did' provides evidence for the belief in the distinctiveness of this period. In some senses, the wider cultural and social ethos of these times pervaded the school as they did at Eastside. 'The flower children of the 1960s – that was the perception. They had this beautiful school that the Board had pumped all kinds of money into, selected the very best of the best to go there, and they were free floaters, free thinkers. They were literally likened to the flower children and some of that never went away.'

With a youthful and idealistic staff, the first principal, Ward Bond, was able to experiment with the organization of the school following the Hall-Dennis objectives and the flexibility this report facilitated. Ward Bond took full advantage of this flexibility to create an organization that was intended to alter conventional use of time and space to achieve his vision of a school that was sufficiently flexible to meet diverse student needs.

In terms of time, his answer was to semester the school, design a 32-credit diploma and one-hour teaching periods. Students had an individualized timetable that required they take eight subjects per year and four per semester. In terms of space, Bond followed an 'open plan' concept, backed up by a resource centre as the hub and a large comfortable staff room. Bond also introduced differentiated staffing; augmented guidance resources to help students make choices; reduced the number of formal leaders compared to other high schools; hired a community relations coordinator, and structured interdisciplinary departments. To many among the educational and community representatives this was, not, however, the 'grammar' of a 'real school'.

For Lord Byron then, this was a substantial conjuncture of change, where many of the established rules and practices of schooling were challenged, problemized and replaced.

The major quality of teaching at this time, as compared with the periods before and after, appears to have been the way teachers thought about their work mission. At this time, it seems to have represented far more than just any ordinary job undertaken for the salary that it bought in. Teachers came to the job with a sense of inspired vocation, a feeling that they were involved in a mission over and above normal everyday schooling. 'The early years were inspiring. There was a lot of altruism. People came to work because they were doing something for humanity – "more than a job, it was a mission" '.

This kind of vision came with a sense of commitment that often affected the work/life balance in deleterious ways. Conjunctures of innovation and change make heavy demands – a full-tilt mission brings heavy-time commitments. The comments of teachers involved in the school at the time reflect the onerous aspects of teaching as a mission. As one said: 'I was working long hours and barely saw my family'; and another: 'the kind of relationships you build in that kind of pressure cooker situation were very difficult to repeat – a pressure cooker in that you shared so many things and the hours we were putting in and so on. There was very little time outside schools.'

Talisman Park Collegiate, unlike Lord Byron, but in common with Eastside, was a school with a history dating back to the early twentieth century. It was established in the small rural community of Kohler's Landing outside Toronto in 1920. This period set up the basic grammar of schooling in Talisman Park as a firmly defined academic collegiate so, from the beginning and throughout, Talisman Park remained committed to a subject-centered pattern of teaching and learning. Changes in the 1960s built upon this solid base and the period 1967–74 was an age of hope and optimism, a time of synergy when a youthful teacher cohort, innovative curriculum policy and humanistic principal leadership came together in an unparalleled burst of creativity.

The impact of many new teachers coming to the school in this period at the beginning of their careers led to a sense of transformation. These teachers describe the period as one of 'massive change' in education. They characterized Talisman Park as pedagogically 'innovative', professionally 'challenging' and personally 'exciting'. The transformative reinvigoration of this demographic change with many new teachers, built upon the affluent economic climate and contemporary cultural belief in social progress and social justice. This was an era in the life of Talisman Park when cohort one teachers were brimming with optimism, clout and faith in education, proud and happy to be teachers, and confidant that they could achieve their life projects and missions. Their idealism, vigour and energy permeated the school's culture.

These teachers wanted to make a difference in young people's lives, and saw a public system as a 'huge leveler' and 'liberator' from social and economic disadvantage. One teacher spoke of the feelings at this time:

> One of the greatest purposes of schooling is to build community and some common experiences. So it's a cultural experience.... Community in the sense of the sort of cultural community that we speak the same language on a variety of levels. And I don't mean the English language. I mean we understand that the history, the traditions, the culture, the norms. The values of this society are learned through the education system. So it's that collective experience.

Alongside the young and innovative new staff, the leadership of the school worked to nurture and develop professional expertise. Rowan was the Principal for the period of hope and optimism and, when he left in 1974, so close were his bonds with the staff, that some of those most devoted and loyal went with him to open a new school. When he left, the management of the school changed direction. Rowan embodied the idealism, collegiality and empowerment of cohort one teachers just beginning their careers. Arness took them in the opposite direction of formality, top-down control and paternalism – representing a gradual decline in faculty mission and morale and optimism.

This disjuncture between the two leadership periods makes a very clear dividing line at the end of the conjunctural period. The unparalleled burst of creativity was now at an end and a new era, which was to culminate in standardization and a wave of early retirements, was beginning.

In the United States, the 1960s were a decade of social ferment and of questioning and challenging established traditions and procedures. This was the time when President Lyndon Johnson announced he was building the 'Great Society', a society inclusive of race and of all social classes, a society that would tackle inequality and pursue social justice. Tyack and Tobin provide a valuable summary of these times:

> In the 1960s, years of innovation when rebels were questioning the conventional wisdom in education, reformers proposed another rethinking of time, subjects, space, and class size. They believed that because humans had created institutional forms, they could and should change them when they no longer served humane goals. Typically, they regarded the old grammar of schooling as rigid, hierarchical, and based on a negative view of human nature. Students, the old system implicitly announced, were young workers who needed to be compelled to learn by their supervisors – teachers – in classes standardized in size, time, space, and subjects. Instead, the young should be seen as active, intellectually curious, and capable of taking charge of their own learning. If one started from that premise, the existing grammar of schooling was hardly 'functional'.
>
> Reinventing the Rousseauian notion that people are born free but are everywhere in chains, some radical reformers rejected the institutional form of the public school outright, advocating 'free schools' and 'schools without walls' to take the place of conventional classrooms, preset curricula, and traditional teacher roles.
>
> (Tyack and Tobin, 1994, p. 471)

In the decade of the 1960s, a wide range of more liberal organizations and groups sought to replace the isolated classroom with the pattern of teacher recitation and student passivity. Students were to become active learners in partnership with facilitating teachers who often formed into teams. These teams operated in open plan buildings following J. Lloyd Trump's ideas in his 'images of the future' blueprint (Lloyd Trump, 1959).

Bradford is a medium-sized industrial city located in the northeast United States. Like much of North America, the 1960s saw a range of new social policies and initiatives, which sought to broaden social class and racial inclusion. The pattern of racial composition changed drastically in these years. Bradford School District records indicate the percentage of 'minority' students as follows: 10.4 per cent in 1966, 14 per cent in 1968, 23.7 per cent in 1969. By 1989, the district's pupil population was 62 per cent Afro-American and 18 per cent Hispanic. Social class patterns reflected a growing pattern of poverty in the urban core of the district. By 1985, 40 per cent of Bradford pupils lived in poverty.

In Bradford, a range of educational reforms was under way in the 1960s. In 1969, a small group of teachers at Livingston High School started to meet to discuss the deleterious impact of traditional grammars of schooling on teaching and learning. These teachers, witness to violent school riots at Livingston, believed that many of the problems of the school could be traced to the traditional structure of schooling with its isolated teachers and classrooms. Inspired by such leaders of the alternative school movement as Ivan Illich and John Holt, these teachers wanted to break down the artificial walls of classroom life and develop new learning patterns and environments so that students would learn how to become independent learners, by pursuing issues and topics of their own interest in real-life settings throughout the community, and by making decisions with staff on how to develop and run their school.

Therefore, a plan for an alternative school, Durant School, was developed and submitted as a proposal to the Bradford Board of Education in January 1971. The Board voted its approval and appointed David Henry, a charismatic and gifted teacher, at Livingston and instigator of the plan, as Principal. Henry assembled a staff of ten teachers – all young and innovative, keen to experiment and pioneer – virtually all in their 20s and 30s. The school was 'without walls': an office for Henry and his secretary, a couple of rooms, and a central meeting place for the whole school community in a converted warehouse. Classes – not organized in grade level – took place throughout the city, including 'architecture', with a local architect at his office; 'education redesign', with an assistant superintendent for the Bradford Schools at his office, and 'anatomy of a business', with a vice-president of a local company. Staff, who went by their first names, held their classes in any available space – church basements, community centres, students' homes, even their own homes – and frequently took their students to different parts of the city as befit a particular topic.

Alongside this pattern of urban education in real-life situations, each staff member also met with a small group of students four mornings a week to discuss program issues and provide guidance. The fifth morning, the entire school community gathered together at the 'warehouse' headquarters for a full school meeting to discuss policy and vote on a 'one person one vote' basis.

These early experiments lasted for the first years, but by September 1973, Durant had moved into a former college building with classrooms for all the staff. However, the goal of developing independent learners connected to the community at large remained paramount, and the staff encouraged students to take classes at local colleges and pursue independent studies and community internships under teacher supervision. In this sense, in many ways, the school still therefore existed 'without walls', and the 1970s saw much of the original innovative spirit carried forward. The 1970s was a stable period, with David Henry working to keep the School's unique goals at the forefront of staff meetings and school discussions, Durant's mission permeated the day-to-day life of the school.

Sheldon School moved into a new building in 1959. Whilst it enjoyed a period as the 'Jewel in the Crown' of the district, it certainly did not in any way challenge the grammar of schooling in the same way as Durant. Because Sheldon was a neighborhood school, it had a strong feeder pattern – if you lived in the neighborhood you went to the high school in that area. The feeder pattern helped to instill a sense of pride for one's school both among teachers and among students. According to one teacher, 'the feeder pattern developed a feeling towards the school of an attraction, connectivity if you will. You know, "I went to that school, my old man went to that school." A lot of families, a lot of children who went here [Sheldon], their parents went here. And that's good. There was a feeling, a sense of pride.' As a result of the new facility and the comprehensive school set-up, Sheldon became known as the best school in the district. Another teacher recalled being interviewed by the Bradford City School District in the late 1960s and being told by the citywide director of English to 'Go to Sheldon, it's the best!' Sheldon was a school that was known to have many high academic achievers and subsequently became a school with a great pride in its academic reputation.

The newness of the building, and the development of new activities and curriculum to fit this new milieu, gave Sheldon a fresh and innovative feel, even though its academic program was more conventional than Durant's. In both schools, however, the sense of innovation and change began to ebb in the seventies, first at Sheldon, where racial strife began to break out, and later at Durant, where in 1981 it was re-designated as a magnet school. In both cases, changes in the matrix of schooling in Bradford and in overall broad policy began to transform the missions of the two schools.

In the case, particularly of Durant, it began to regress towards a more conventional school with less external control over its clientele or its goals. One is reminded of Tyack and Tobin's epitaph for the attempts to define alternatives to traditional schools in the period of the late 1960s and 1970s: 'a bold yet fragile challenge to the grammar of schooling, the rebellion of the 1960s and early 1970s ebbed. Policy talk on flexible scheduling rose and fell rapidly. The experiment left behind here and there some new forms of flexibility, but the older institutional patterns were still dominant' (Tyack and Tobin, 1994, pp. 475–476).

What our case studies of schools in the 1960s and 1970s show is a complex response to the economic conjuncture of this period. Some schools, such as Talisman and Sheldon, were sites of reform and innovation with new young cohorts of teachers or new buildings. But reform was within the existing grammar of schooling, stressing academic subjects, teacher initiation and hierarchical management. Alongside these schools were a cluster of sites – Durant, Lord Byron and Eastside – where a sustained attempt was made to reform the school. This was attempted in a 'root and branch' manner at Durant and Lord Byron, a full-tilt innovation at almost all levels from classroom to school management. Eastside embodied all of the demographic and youth culture changes, but with some continuing genuflection to established grammars of school.

The conjuncture of the 1960s and 1970s then, provide growth, innovation and change in all school sites, with some schools going further and attempting truly revolutionary changes in the patterns of schooling and the associated patterns of social and racial reproduction.

In some ways, this commentary provides the footnote to the conjuncture of the sixties and seventies: Herculean efforts to transform schools, break down walls, connect subjects to life, make learning active and teaching facilitatory, ended with the economic downturn following the oil crisis of 1973. From this point on, social programs were less well funded; there were no longer so many new buildings or new initiatives. The huge influx of post-war baby boomers had worked their way through school and the school staff themselves began to 'grey' as contraction and consolidation set in. From the late 1970s through to the early 1990s, we encounter a kind of interregnum of regression and decline in some schools. 'The screw tightens' (Durant); 'fall from Grace' (Sheldon); 'insecurity and uncertainty' (Talisman), alongside consolidation and improvement in others: 'Camelot days' (Barrett) and 'Lighthouse School' (Eastside). In all cases, however, a more traditional grammar of schooling reasserted itself, alongside a vigorous new pattern of stratification and standardization. This new conjuncture begins to emerge in the 1990s.

In Eric Hobsbawm's phrase, the conjuncture of the 1960s and 1970s was a 'golden age' for social justice and social inclusion (Hobsbawm, 1994). Caught in a cold war to prove they could offer more social and political opportunities than the competing communist bloc, Western countries followed policies of social welfare and inclusion. In 1989, with the collapse of the communist bloc, this suddenly changed. From now on the mantra of 'free markets' became the triumphalist slogan and public education was restructured with the procedures and principles of the new business orthodoxy as the engine of 'change forces'. Hence, since 1989, curricula control passed to central and provincial governments with closely prescribed content and detailed targets and standards for performance, accountability and assessment procedures. These standardized reforms became a 'world movement', vigorously promoted by a range of agencies aligned to the globalizing free market.

From the late 1980s, a new 'world movement' focusing on standards-based reform began to spread especially in the vanguard Western countries. The new reforms focused on standardized tests and guidelines. New curricula were centrally prescribed and linked to detailed targets and accountability, and assessment procedures.

Politically, the reforms aimed to satisfy voters' concerns about educational standards and about public education in general. Politicians and bureaucrats were seen to be acting and responding and, although many of the reforms were hastily implemented and rapidly conceived, they achieved widespread currency.

As we can see in Figure 9.4, by the mid-1990s, these reforms, and the changing patterns of stratification in schools associated with them, had begun to impact on all our case study schools. This new conjuncture of change begins then in the mid-1990s and was in 'full swing' as we conducted our research. Hence, any findings about this conjuncture will be by their nature tentative and provisional.

In our United States case study schools, the growing demographic shifts, noted earlier in the article, confirmed a concentration of poverty in the downtown center of Bradford. By 1989, 69 per cent were Afro-American and 18 per cent Hispanic.

The Bradford School district, partly in response to these demographic patterns, began the creation of magnet schools in 1981. Federally magnet schools were created from the middle of the 1980s onwards in order to help sponsor desegregation. Under the market fundamentalism of the governments, beginning with Reagan in 1980 and continued by Bush Senior, Clinton and Bush Junior, magnet schools pursued market competition through promoting 'school choice'.

One of our case study schools, Barrett, became a Magnet School in 1980. Initially, the result was that the school attracted resources, highly qualified teachers and motivated students, but the effects on Sheldon School were the opposite. High performers left for the magnet school and poverty concentrated more and more, obscenely with 70 per cent of pupils living in poverty as the new millennium dawned. At Durant School, the student clientele also began to change, to be more diverse and to be organized in larger classes, which threatened the 'alternative' style of schooling that had been developed.

1916–99

	1916	1920	1955–59	1960–64	1965–69	1970–74	1975–79	1980–84	1985–89	1990–94	1995–99
Sheldon								Troubled period			
Barrett							Increasing competition				
Durant											Fight for survival
Eastside							Change is constant				
Talisman										Retrenchment/ intransigence	
Lord Byron											Creativity is gone
Blue Mountain										Attrition years	Surviving

Figure 9.4 Conjectural conjuncture.

But if the matrix of schooling that began to change radically after 1981 was a part of the picture preceding the new conjuncture of the mid-1990s, the major catalyst was the launching of standards-based reforms. As we saw, this movement emerged in the late 1980s as part of a growing world movement to transform schooling in new ways. In Bradford, the school district had to respond to new state initiatives. In the late 1980s, the state extended its mandated competence tests from three to five subjects, and in 1990 to six. In 1990, they also extended required credits for graduates from 20.5 in 1986 to 23.5 for pupils entering in 1991.

In the period following 1995, a new testing regime was put in place, tied to the State's new standards-based reforms. Student graduation was thereby linked to passing standardized tests in the assessed subjects. In Bradford, school students who entered Year 9 in 1998 will have to pass four out of five examinations with a minimum score of 55 in order to graduate. Pupils entering a year later must pass all five examinations at the same standard. For Year 9 students entering in 2000, the standard was increased to 65 in three of the exams, and by 2001 to all five-subject exams. These are truly 'high stakes' assessments because schools and districts are being ranked across the state by their test scores, with public report cards of the results.

In Sheldon, the 'fall from grace' began in 1980 as we saw. With the restructuring of secondary schools and the new magnet program, 'school spirit' and the student body changed as Sheldon became a 'dumping ground' for those who failed to get into the magnet school. When this happened, not only were teachers sent to Sheldon against their will, so were the students. The results were less school pride and less academic achievement.

By 1994, as standards-based reform began to bite, Superintendent Vega seriously considered naming Sheldon a 'priority school' because of its academic failures and high dropout rate. By the end of the decade, Sheldon was a school named on a state list as in need of 'improvement'. One teacher commented: 'we used to have some really bright kids that went through this building; we had some excellent students. But things are not what they used to be.' This teacher attributed the change in academic ability of his students to the 'dumbing down' of the curriculum because of the new high-stakes tests and because the magnet schools continued to attract the better students in the district. One Sheldon teacher summarized the effects of standards-based tests by saying 'so much emphasis [was] put on the amount of material you're supposed to cover that [all] you're really doing is a skim job and it's a question of quality versus quantity.' Another commented: 'in terms of change...we no longer have a real strong nucleus...a real strong contingent of students who are at the upper levels. Now I'd say 75 per cent of our population are academically in trouble' (Sheldon High School Report).

The new standards and testing regimes act to underline the residential patterns of segregation with new patterns of academic 'segregation'. Overall patterns of inequality are thereby underwritten by the new regimes of schooling. What was once a 'Jewel in the Crown' comprehensive high school for all, becomes a dumping ground for the socially disadvantaged, a transformation underwritten by, and accompanied by, a rhetoric of standards.

At Durant School, the commitment to developing alternatives to the traditional patterns, which failed to educate the disadvantaged, also unraveled in the face of standards-based reform. So, if Sheldon was facing its most 'troubled period' in the conjuncture, Durant faced a 'fight for survival'. The fight for survival focused on defending the school as a learner-centred environment. The new testing regime demanded exacting compliance with the state's definition of curriculum and content standards in five areas of subject knowledge. This deprived the school of space to follow a learner-centred policy, focusing on project-based multi-disciplinary study.

The students who wanted to graduate had to pass the state tests. This meant that the focus on learner-centred curriculum had to be replaced by preparation for the externally delivered test. Durant's teachers were caught between defending their learner-centred beliefs and fulfilling the students' requirement to pass the state subject tests.

One teacher described the effect of the high-stakes state tests on his professional self:

> So the [state tests] are coming and I think it's a damn shame that that sense of autonomy, that ability to create your curriculum with high standards has to be thrown out every place by something that I think is artificial. It takes out the creativity of teaching and you're teaching to the test. Just the thought that I'm doing this is totally counter to what I believe, it really is, but you know I'm a captive... You're selling your soul to the devil.

Another staff member also described the effects on his professional self:

> What it is, is it's a taking away of my professional judgment and autonomy as a teacher. I was trained at good colleges for both my bachelor's and my master's degrees. I was interned by a brilliant teacher at my old high school as a matter of fact. I spent years learning how to teach, learning why kids learn how they learn, what I can do to help that happen. And suddenly the state says no, none of that means anything. None of that means anything at all. We're going to tell you what to teach. Essentially tell you how to teach it, although they would deny that. They are telling us how to teach it. And then they're telling me what the outcomes need to be. And to me that's saying all right, why don't we just get a videotape in here of somebody and they can do it, because it ignores so much about kids.

Another echoed those sentiments:

> We're trying to do two things at once with graduation by demonstration and still cover all our bases for the possibility that the kids will have to take the [state exams] and it's killing everybody. Like it's just too confusing and too much work. And it makes it really hard for the kids to use this school as it was intended, to explore things that they're interested in because they're spending so much time focusing on other things.

The troubled period at Sheldon, and the fight for survival at Durant, show how a standards-based and standardizing reform initiative has marked a severe new conjuncture for the schools in question. In both cases, the sense of mission and meaning has been severely depleted, and morale and motivation undermined. In the new conjuncture, teachers' hearts and minds are moving away from their schoolwork and the search for meaning and mission is moving elsewhere, most commonly into the personal domain. As one teacher summarized his withdrawal, 'I can't deal with the system it has absolutely torn me apart and I'm tired of fighting it.'

This disillusionment can be read against the growing demographic change in Bradford. From a young vigorous innovative teaching cohort in the conjuncture of the 1960s and 1970s, Bradford's teaching force is aging, with a third of the teachers expecting to retire in the next five years. Likewise, patterns of leadership have been transformed, from the period of charismatic and heroic principals in the 1960s and 1970s, to a period of 'faceless managers' who move flexibly from post to post in the late 1990s.

In Ontario, the new conjuncture of change can be clearly marked with the election of the Progressive Conservative Government in 1995. The policies proved to be deeply conservative and profoundly unprogressive. Honesty would require its renaming as the 'Regressive' Conservative Government, for the era initiated massive cuts in educational spending, alongside a new regime of curriculum and assessment reforms. Gidney has judged that, from 1995, the next five years were the most extensive and extended period of reform ever seen in Ontario. In the period 1995–2000, more legislation was passed on education than in the whole of the provinces preceding history (Gidney, 1999). Gidney's historical overview alerts us to the truly epoch-making nature of the Harris Government. This was a starkly marked conjuncture of change: the new curriculum and assessment reforms were centrally designed, new testing regimes were instigated, and report cards and computerized reporting introduced.

The teachers' response to the blitzkrieg of reforms was to go for early retirement in unprecedented numbers – demoralization among teaches was rife. In fact, this flocking towards early retirement was exacerbated by the demographic profile of the teaching force. An aging teaching force reacted to a flurry of reforms at the later stages of their careers by deciding to leave rather than undergo such drastic professional surgery. If this was the case with classroom teachers, it was a similar pattern with school principals. They too chose early retirement in large numbers and the resulting instability was compounded by school district policies which insisted on rotating principals between schools.

Against this conjuncture of change, with financial retrenchment, staff demoralization and turnover linked to standards-based reforms, the case study schools in Ontario echo many of the experiences of the Bradford schools. One of the starkest reminders of the discontinuities between our early conjuncture in the 1960s and 1970s, and the post-1995 conjuncture, is provided by Lord Byron School. One teacher there defines the post 1995 period as one where 'the creativity is gone'. Byron's 'break the mould' ethos of earlier days has been lost to time. The new staff wrestles with daily survival of preparing three different classes, finding materials and establishing student discipline. The experienced staff juggles an increased workload with demands for curriculum change in a climate of negativity and confusion. This has an overall effect of the reforms on teachers' sense of mission and meaning. What has changed is how teachers first became part of the Byron staff. Through much of the 1970s and into the 1980s, teachers chose Byron because of its reputation as a creative, innovative place. A few saw it as a 1960s kind of school where you 'could do your own thing'. Most people in the late 1980s, however, came to Byron because it had a job that fitted their qualifications. In a number of cases they had been in a few schools beforehand and the system had force transferred them to comply with regional seniority rules. Loyalty to the school and its historical image has all but disappeared. Most of the younger people know they will probably be displaced – some are actively looking for different opportunities. These attitudes are strikingly different from the teachers in cohorts one and two who spoke proudly of being a teacher and how Byron had enriched and, in some cases, helped them to refocus their careers and lives.

At Eastside School, a bastion of innovation and cultural change in the 1960s and 1970s, the same transformations noted at Lord Byron are at work, although there is some residual loyalty to the Eastside legacy. While many of the older teachers have retired into second careers, the thousands of new teachers have willingly and enthusiastically entered a tired, battle-scarred environment with larger classes, more preparation, a new rigorous curriculum. The teachers left behind are those who look forward to retirement in the next few years and those who find themselves crushed between the massive exodus of their senior, embittered colleagues and the exuberance and naiveté of the young teachers on staff. This forgotten or ignored middle group of teachers has suddenly aged and finds itself the leaders and mentors of a 'new' secondary school system, a role imposed on them by those who have hastily left the profession and those youngsters in their twenties looking to them for support and guidance.

Likewise, the socio-political revolution of the Harris' Government, with its new centralized reforms of curriculum and assessment, has changed things. The socio-political renovation and renewal, including the political turmoil and the economic recession/resurgence of the 1990s has not left Eastside unaffected. While the teachers have remained committed – even sentimentally attached – to the school, its programs and students throughout this decade, the personal and emotional costs have been significant. Teachers, in general and by nature, represent a segment of the population that are rewarded in this chosen vocation by educating, which means the enlightenment, nurturing and caring of students. This seems even more visible in a school where the population is needy in all ways and the teachers are committed to supporting every student to be successful regardless of their background, race, gender, class, sexual orientation, intelligence and so on. Thus, while the political problems have been evident among teachers across the province, they have impacted deeply on the teachers who teach at Eastside. They are ill at ease with the standardized reforms and want a different kind of change altogether. Their unhappiness with the changes is starkly at odds with the support for change in the 1960s and 1970s.

At Talisman Park, an 'age of retrenchment and intransigence' begins in 1995. Following the massive reforms introduced by the Progressive Conservative Government, the range and rapidity of the reform initiatives were deeply disconcerting for the Talisman teachers. The older cohort of teachers, as with other case study schools, found the new reforms collided with their sense of mission and meaning. As the reforms grew in intensity and speed, these teachers experienced a collapsing sense of both commitment and indeed competence.

The new conjuncture contrasts starkly with the earlier period of optimism and change. The market fundamentalist orientations of Secondary School Reform in Ontario (Hargreaves, 2003), with its elements of imposed prescription, breakneck speed of implementation, denigration of resource levels and working conditions, and denial of professional involvement and recognition – coupled with a more cumulative experience of reform as being inconsistent or even capricious – have led Talisman Park's teachers to feel so disenfranchised politically, alienated intellectually, depressed emotionally and drained physically, that many just want to escape the system that they originally entered with confidence, hope and enthusiasm as new teachers in the 1970s.

In the conjuncture following 1995, Talisman Park began to lose more and more of its early cohorts of teachers to retirement – normally in their 50s, but sometimes in their 40s. As a result, a young cohort of teachers began to replace them, and with it a new acceptance of market fundamentalist reform became instantiated in the school. A vision of the school as a caring inclusive community, autonomous and academically insulated, was replaced by a school driven by market imperatives and occupying a stratified position in the new market matrix of schooling.

Whilst Blue Mountain cannot provide a comparison with the early conjuncture of the 1960s and 1970s since it was founded in 1992, its evolutionary profile is instructive. From optimistic and committed beginnings in 1992, the period since 1995 echoes many of the earlier findings about the second conjuncture. In the early years from 1992, Blue Mountain sustained high levels of commitment and competence from teachers and from students. But with the waves of reforms following 1995, all this changed. Some of the original teachers left; the leadership of the school became over stretched and uncertain in the face of change driven from outside, and a general climate of demoralization and professional disorientation grew up. As one informant noted: 'I think we're on a track to mediocrity, whereas we were on a track to stardom before.' Such an epitaph marks an incisive indictment of so much of the standardized reform of the conjuncture following 1995.

Conclusion

Our studies of eight schools in the United States and Canada, during the post-war period, point up clear patterns in the periodization of educational change and reform. Our data shows how employing an *annaliste* methodology, and a Kondratievian conception of conjuncture and long waves, helps conceptualize periodization. The most distinctive conjunctures of change are the periods from the mid-1960s to the late 1970s, and the period beginning in 1996, which is currently underway (see Goodson, 2003).

The conjuncture of the 1960s and 1970s aligns with the economic long wave upswing, which ended with the oil crisis of 1973. There all schools were sites of reform and innovation with large new cohorts of teachers, and often new, purpose-built facilities. Some schools organized their changes around teacher initiation and student culture, but within the existing 'grammar of schooling'. Whilst other schools attempted 'root and branch' revolutionary change at all levels, from classroom through to school management. All schools were affected by the progressive desire to build a 'Great Society', characterized by social inclusion and social justice. In Hobsbawm's words, this was in general a 'golden age' of social progress, although one littered with contradictions and contestations.

The later conjuncture, beginning in the mid-1990s, is starkly different. In many ways, instead of a progressive purpose, this is a social experiment with strong regressive tendencies. We have cohorts of teachers who are disenfranchised politically, alienated intellectually, depressed emotionally and drained physically.

It seems that over-prescribed targets and objectives, and the market fundamentalist ethos, do little to 'inspire sound vision' and vocational commitment. Whilst the new change forces have sought to plan schools on a more coherent vision, than the 'free spirit' of the 1960s/1970s conjuncture, this has come with a substantial downside. A more systematic pattern of governance and accountability there may be, but when linked to regressive and prescriptive policies, this seems to have been a source of irritation, rather than inspiration to the teachers at the delivery end of the process. We suspect that the new conjuncture of change is running towards the end of its provenance and that new conceptions of improvement will begin to work their way on to center stage in our classrooms and schools.

Acknowledgements

Besides the valuable work undertaken by Martha Foote and Michael Baker previously noted, this chapter draws on other work from the Spencer team notably reports written by Dear Fink, Corrie Giles, Andy Hargreaves, Carol Beynon and finally the invaluable Shawn Moore. The sections on schools and systems draw extensively on these studies.

Note

1   This chapter works with a notion of historical periods because these patterns emerge so consistently from the data. Whilst aware of Fischers work or the 'fallacy of periodization', here the data seems to override any concerns about historical over interpretation (see Fischer, 1970).

References

Aronowitz, S. and Giroux, H., 1991, *Postmodern Education: Politics, Culture and Social Criticism* (Minneapolis, MN: University of Minnesota Press).

Bell, D., 1973, *The Coming of Post-Industrial Society* (New York: Basic Books).

Board of Education for the City of London, 1960–70, *Minutes of the Board of Education for the City of London* (London: Board of Education).

Board of Education for the City of London, 1963, *Annual Report of the Board of Education for the City of London* (London: Board of Education).

Burke, P., 1993, *History and Social Theory* (New York: Cornell University Press).

Carpentier, V., 2001, Developpement educatif et performances economiques au Royaume-Uni: 19th et 20th siecles (Paris: L'Harmattan).

Committee on Aims and Objectives of Education in the Schools of Ontario, 1968, *Living and Learning: The Report of the Committee on Aims and Objectives of Education in the Schools of Ontario* (Toronto: Newton).

Cuban, L., 1984, *How Teachers Taught: Constancy and Change in American Classrooms, 1890–1980* (New York: Longman).

Denzin, N., 1991, *Images of Postmodern Society: Social Theory and Contemporary Cinema* (London: Sage).

Febvre, L., 1925, *A Geographical Introduction to History* (New York: Alfred Knopf).

Fischer, David Hackett, 1970, *Historians' Fallacies: Toward a Logic of Historical Thought* (New York: Harper and Row).

Fontvieille, L., 1990, Education, Growth and Long Cycles: The Case of France in the 19th & 20th Centuries. In G. Tortella (ed.), *Education and Economic Development Since the Industrial Revolution* (Valencia: Generalitat valenciana), pp. 317–335.

Freeman, C. and Louçã, F., 2001, *As Time Goes By: From the Industrial Revolutions to the Information Revolution* (Oxford and New York: Oxford University Press).

Fullan, M., 1999, *Change Forces: The Sequel* (London: Falmer Press).

Fullan, M., 2000, The Return of Large-Scale Reform. *The Journal of Educational Change,* 1(1), 5–28.

Giddens, A., 1991, *Modernity and Self-Identity: Self and Society in the Late Modern Age* (Stanford, CA: Stanford University Press).

Gidney, R.D., 1999, *From Hope to Harris: The Reshaping of Ontario's Schools* (Toronto: University of Toronto Press).

Gilbert, V.K., 1972, *Let Each Become: An Account of the Implementation of the Credit Diploma in the Secondary Schools of Ontario* (Toronto: Faculty of Education, University of Toronto).

Goodson, I., 1994, *Studying Curriculum: Cases and Methods* (Buckingham: Open University Press).

Goodson, I., 2003, *Professional Knowledge/Professional Lives* (Maidenhead and Philadelphia, PA: Open University Press).

Hargreaves, A., 1994, *Changing Teachers, Changing Times: Teachers' Work and Culture in the Postmodern Age* (New York: Teachers' College Press).

Hargreaves, A., 2003, *Teaching in the Knowledge Society* (New York: Teachers' College Press).

Hobsbawm, E., 1994, *The Age of Extremes. The Short Twentieth Century 1914–1991* (London: Michael Joseph).

Journal of Historical Sociology (1988 to present) (Oxford and Malden, MA: Blackwell Publishing).

Kondratiev, N., 1923, Some Controversial Questions Concerning the World Economy and Crisis (Answer to Our Critiques). In L.F. Fontvieille's edition of Kondratiev's works (1992) (Paris: Economica), pp. 493–543.

Lieberman, A. (ed.), 1995, *The Work of Restructuring Schools* (New York: Teachers College Press).

Lloyd Trump, J., 1959, *Images of the Future* (Urbana–Illinois: Committee on the Experimental Study of the Utilization of Staff in the Secondary School).

Lyotard, J. (ed.), 1984, *The Postmodern Condition: A Report on Knowledge* (Minneapolis, MN: University of Minnesota Press).

McCulloch, G., 1995, Essay review of *Changing Teachers, Changing Times*, by A. Hargreaves, *British Journal of Sociology of Education*, 16(1), 113–117.

Meyer, J. and Rowan, B., 1978, The Structure of Educational Organizations. In J. Meyer and W. Marshall *et al.* (eds), *Environments and Organizations: Theoretical and Empirical Perspectives* (San Francisco, CA: Jossey-Bass), pp. 78–109.

Murphy, J., 1990, The Educational Reform Movement of the 1980s: A Comprehensive Analysis. In J. Murphy (ed.), *The Reform of American Public Education in the 1980s: Perspectives and Cases* (Berkeley, CA: McCutchan).

Murphy, J., 1991, *Restructuring Schools: Capturing and Assessing the Phenomena* (New York: Teachers College Press).

Perez, C., 1983, Structural Change and the Assimilation of New Technologies in the Economic and Social System, *Futures*, 15, 357–375.

Special issue on Education and Economic Performance, 1998, *History of Education Journal*, 27(3).

Stamp, R., 1982, *The Schools of Ontario, 1876–1976* (Toronto: University of Toronto Press).

The Word, 1969, 28 May.

Tyack, D. and Hansot, E., 1992, *Learning Together: A History of Coeducation in American Public Schools* (New York: Russell Sage).

Tyack, D. and Tobin, W., 1994, The 'Grammar' of Schooling: Why Has it Been so Hard to Change? *American Educational Research Journal*, 31(3), 453–479 (Fall).

Westbury, I., 1973, Conventional Classrooms, 'Open' Classrooms and the Technology of Teaching. *Journal of Curriculum Studies*, 5(2), 99–121.

Wright Mills, C., 1959, *The Sociological Imagination* (London: Oxford University Press).

Young, M., 1988, *The Metronomic Society: Natural Rhythms and Human Timetables* (London: Thames and Hudson).

Young, M. and Schuller, T. (eds), 1988, *The Rhythms of Society* (London and New York: Routledge).

PART 2

METHODS

CHAPTER 10

TOWARDS A SOCIAL CONSTRUCTIONIST PERSPECTIVE

Journal of Curriculum Studies, 1990, 299–312

One of the perennial problems of studying curriculum is that it is a multi-faceted concept constructed, negotiated and re-negotiated at a variety of levels and in a variety of arenas. This elusiveness has no doubt contributed to the rise of theoretical and overarching perspectives – psychological, philosophical and sociological – as well as more technical or scientific paradigms. But these perspectives and paradigms have been criticized recurrently because they do violence to the practical essentials of curriculum as conceived of and realized.

In this chapter, I shall argue that we need to move firmly and sharply away from de-contextualized and disembodied modes of analysis whether they be philosophical, psychological or sociological; away from technical, rational or scientific management models – away from the 'objectives game'. Above all, we need to move away from a singular focus on curriculum as prescription. This means that we must embrace fully the notion of *curriculum as social construction* firstly at the level of prescription itself, but also at the levels of process and practice.

Curriculum as prescription

The primacy of the ideology of curriculum as prescription (CAP) can be evidenced in even a cursory glimpse at curriculum literature. This view of curriculum develops from a belief, that we can dispassionately define the main ingredients of the course of study, and then proceed to teach the various segments and sequences in systematic turn. Despite the obvious simplicity, not to say crudity of this view the 'objectives game' is still, if 'not the only game in town', certainly the main game. There may be many reasons for this continuing predominance, but explanatory potential is not, I think, one of the factors.

Curriculum as prescription supports important mystiques about state schooling and society. Most notably CAP supports the mystique that expertise and control reside within central government, educational bureaucracies or the university community. Providing nobody exposes this mystique, the two worlds of 'prescription rhetoric' and 'schooling as practice' can co-exist. Both sides benefit from such peaceful co-existence. The agencies of CAP are seen to be 'in control' and the schools are seen to be 'delivering' (and can carve out a good degree of autonomy if they accept the rules). Curriculum prescriptions thereby set certain parameters but with transgression and occasional transcendence being permissible as long as the rhetoric of prescription and management is not challenged.

Of course there are 'costs of complicity' in accepting the myth of prescription: above all these involve, in various ways, acceptance of established modes of power relations. Perhaps most importantly the people intimately connected with the day-to-day social construction of curriculum and schooling, the teachers are thereby effectively disenfranchised in the 'discourse of schooling'. To continue to exist their day-to-day power must basically remain unspoken and unrecorded. This then is the price of complicity. The vestiges of day-to-day power and autonomy for schools and for teachers are dependent on continuing to accept the fundamental lie.

With regard to curriculum study the 'costs of complicity' are ultimately catastrophic. For the historic compromise we have described has led to the displacement of a whole field of study. It has led to the directing of scholarship into fields which service the mystique of central and/or bureaucratic control. For scholars who benefit from maintaining this mystique – in the universities particularly – this complicity is, to say the least, self-serving.

The devil's bargain: critiques and counters

I do not wish however to mount a substantial critique of CAP in this paper. That has already been attempted, in my view with conclusive success, in many other places. My intention is rather to briefly repeat that critique and then explore the new directions in which we might progress if we are to provide a valid counter-culture for curriculum research.

In terms of the diagnosis of the problem they are at one with Schwab. Let me briefly repeat:

> The field of curriculum is moribund. It is unable, by its present methods and principles, to continue its work and contribute significantly to the advancement of education. It requires new principles which will generate a new view of the character and variety of its problems. It requires new methods appropriate to the new budget of problems.
>
> (Schwab, 1978, p. 287)

Schwab was absolutely clear why the curriculum field was moribund; his indictment is plain and powerful:

> The curriculum field has reached this unhappy state by inveterate, unexamined, and mistaken reliance on theory. On the one hand it has adopted theories (from outside the field of education) concerning ethics, knowledge, political and social structure, learning, mind, and personality, and has used these borrowed theories theoretically, i.e. as principles from which to 'deduce' right aims and procedures for schools and classrooms. On the other hand, it has attempted construction of educational theories, particularly theories of curriculum and instruction.

Schwab then lists the 'grave difficulties (incoherence of the curriculum, failure and discontinuity in actual schooling)' to which theoretic activities have led. This is because:

> theoretical constructions are, in the main, ill-fitted and inappropriate to problems of actual teaching and learning. Theory, by its very character, does not and cannot take account of all the matters which are crucial to questions of

what, who, and how to teach: that is, theories cannot be applied as principles to the solution of problems concerning what to do with or for real individuals, small groups, or real institutions located in time and space – the subjects and clients of schooling and schools.

(Schwab, 1978, p. 289)

Above all then Schwab wishes us to move away from the theoretic and embrace the practical. In terms of subject matter he juxtaposes the two options in this way: the theoretic is always something taken to be universal or pervasive and is investigated as if it were constant from instance to instance and impervious to changing circumstance. The practical on the other hand is always something taken as concrete and particular and treated as infinitely susceptible to circumstance, and therefore highly liable to unexpected change: 'this students, in that school, on the South side of Columbus, with Principal Jones during the present mayoralty of Ed Tweed and in view of the probability of his re-election'.

Schwab's diagnosis should be read alongside Veblen's and Clifford and Guthries' strictures about the relationships between University Schools of Education and state schooling. Veblen said the difference between the modern university and the lower schools is broad and simple; not so much a difference of degree as of kind (Veblen, 1962, p. 15).

This distinctiveness of purpose and mission:

unavoidably leads them to court a specious appearance of scholarship and so to invest their technological discipline with a degree of pedantry and sophistication whereby it is hoped to give these schools and their work some scientific and scholarly prestige.

(Veblen, 1962, p. 23)

The resonance of Veblen's strictures has been confirmed in Clifford and Guthries' recent work:

Our thesis is that schools of education, particularly those located on the campuses of prestigious research universities, have become ensnared improvidently in the academic and political cultures of their institutions and have neglected their professional allegiances. They are like marginal men, aliens in their own worlds. They have seldom succeeded in satisfying the scholarly norms of their campus betters and science colleagues, and they are simultaneously estranged from their practicing professional peers. The more forcefully they have rowed toward the shores of scholarly research, the more distant they have become from the public schools they are duty bound to serve. Conversely, systematic efforts at addressing the applied problems of public schools have placed schools of education at risk on their own campuses.

(Clifford and Guthrie, 1988, pp. 3–4)

In short the Schools of Education entered into a 'Devil's Bargain' when they entered the university milieu. The result was their mission changed from being primarily concerned with matters central to the practice of schooling towards issues of status passage through more conventional university scholarship. The resulting dominance of conventional 'disciplinary' modes has had disastrous impact on educational theory in general and curriculum study in particular.

The Devil's Bargain over education was an especially pernicious form of the displacement of discourse and debate which surrounded the evolution of university knowledge production. University knowledge evolved as separate and distinct from public knowledge for as Mills noted:

> Men of knowledge do not orient themselves exclusively toward the total society, but to special segments of that society with special demands, criteria of validity, of significant knowledge, of pertinent problems, etc. It is through integration of these demands and expectations of particular audiences which can be effectively located in the social structure, that men of knowledge organize their own work, define their data, seize upon their problems.

This new structural location of 'men of knowledge' in the university could have profound implications for public discourse and debate. Mills believed this would happen if the knowledge produced in this way did not have public relevance, particularly if it was not related to public and practical concerns.

> Only where publics and leaders are responsive and responsible, are human affairs in democratic order, and only when knowledge has public relevance is this order possible. Only when mind has an autonomous basis, independent of power, but powerfully related to it, can it exert its force in the shaping of human affairs. Such a position is democratically possible only when there exists a free and knowledgeable public, to which men of knowledge may address themselves, and to which men of power are truly responsible. Such a public and such men – either of power or of knowledge, do not now prevail, and accordingly, knowledge does not now have democratic relevance in America.
>
> (Wright Mills, 1979, p. 613)

Of course the dilemma facing 'men of knowledge' (sic), which Mills describes is of acute importance when that knowledge relates to schooling. For in the schools knowledge is transmitted to future generations – hence if our knowledge of such knowledge transmission is flawed we are doubly imperiled. But schooling is so intimately related to the social order that if our knowledge of schooling is inadequate or has no public relevance then major aspects of social and political life are obscured.

Hence the question of 'whither educational or curriculum research' is one of great importance. Mills, I think, come close to the nature of our dilemma and spells out the implications of the Devil's Bargain when he talks of the way 'men of knowledge' orient themselves to 'special segments of society'. This has been the fate of much educational and curriculum theory and the effect has been that as Mills put it different groups 'talk past each other'. With few exceptions I would argue this is precisely the relationship between curriculum scholars and school practitioners: they comprise a model exercise in how to 'talk past each other'. It is to the resolution of this problem that I now turn. Again partly in the spirit of Mills who once said in a letter to a 'white collar wife' in a weekly mass publication journal: 'It is one thing to talk about general problems on a national level and quite another to tell an individual what to do. Most "experts" dodge that question. I do not want to' (Wright Mills, 1970, p. 3).

Recent reactions to CAP

As a result of the perceived moribund nature of curriculum scholarship and its peculiarly displaced location in University Schools of Education in the 1960s and 1970s the distinction between theory and practice often led to a reaction against theory *per se* not to a reformulation of theory. Theory as it had been constituted merely collided with curriculum reality. The collision left the theorists fairly overtly at a loss – 'we'd better leave this to others'. But the 'others' who were more immersed in the reality of curriculum production and operation drew their own conclusions about theory. If it had so little to say about the reality of practice, if in fact it grievously misrepresented or even 'threatened to replace' practice was it not best to do without theory altogether or at least leave theorizing until later?

The response in the curriculum field strongly echoes the pendulum swings in sociology at about the same time. The preeminent positivist enterprise employed a scientific hypothetical-deductive model. The aim was to discover the social laws that underpinned everyday reality. Above all they followed a model related to the philosophy of science, which had as its major objective the seeking of objective facts about the social world. The scientist seeks a knowledge of the social system separate and beyond the perceptions of the people who inhabit that system, pursuing wide-ranging laws and truth.

The reaction to this pursuit of scientific and universalistic laws came from symbolic inter-actionists, ethno-methodologists and sociologists of knowledge arguing for the rehabilitation of man himself and his subjective perceptions and 'constructions' of reality. Drawing on Weber and Mead we had the work of Schutz, Goffman, and Berger and Luckman. The latter were characteristic in arguing that 'common sense knowledge rather than ideas must be the central focus for the sociology of knowledge. It is precisely this knowledge that constitutes the fabric of meanings without which no society can exist' (Berger and Luckman, 1967).

The stress on subjective perceptions in sociology engendered substantial responses in the curriculum field. Here more than ever the ambivalence about theory, the manifest lack of fit with practice caused the pendulum to fly wildly to the other side when the reaction began.

In the United Kingdom the rehabilitation of the practice and process of schooling followed similar lines echoing the new trends in sociology and certain tendencies, not only Schwabian, within American curriculum studies. A wide new range of ethnographic and inter-actionist studies emerged focusing on the process of schooling and most particularly on the classroom. The Manchester School, in particular Hargreaves, Lacey and Lambart, adopted an approach with antecedents in anthropology. The commitment was to trying to understand how teachers and pupils 'constructed' the world of the school. Without detailed study of the school progress was impossible. Their academic leadership often led to a more applied approach in curriculum research and, as curriculum reforms got under way in the wake of comprehensivization, in curriculum development.

One centre which took a lead in applied work was The Centre for Applied Research in Education (CARE) at the University of East Anglia. CARE was founded in 1970 and embraced commitment to the teacher and his/her perceptions and constructions. The wide range of publications produced allows us to analyse the intentions and positions of those working at CARE. Whilst claims can be made for the uniqueness of CARE there is much that is symptomatic and typical of beliefs at the time. By looking in some detail at CARE it may then be possible to understand some of the reasons for the posture adopted by leading curriculum developers during this period.

In his influential book *An Introduction to Curriculum Research and Development*, Lawrence Stenhouse stated that it is the thesis of this book that:

> curriculum development must rest on teacher development and that it should promote it and hence the professionalism of the teacher. Curriculum development

translates ideas into classroom practicalities and thereby helps the teacher to strengthen his practice by systematically and thoughtfully testing ideas.

(Stenhouse, 1975, pp. 24–25)

The stress on classroom practicalities echoes Schwab and became a strongly held value position at CARE. Working as a teacher at the time in contact with a number of CARE personnel including Stenhouse, MacDonald and Walker, I was a beneficiary of their commitment and quite literally, care. Walker, with whom I have worked especially closely on projects and articles, and to whom my debt is substantial, put the posture with regard to curriculum studies in this way. The work he argued, would start with, and remain close to, the common-sense knowledge of the practitioner, and the constraints within which he works. It would aim to systematize and to build on practitioners' lore rather than supplant it (Walker, 1974, p. 22).

Barton and Lawn have commented that:

in separating 'pure' from 'applied' research, Walker feels he has successfully rid himself of a theoretical stance and, moreover, reduced the isolation of the researcher. What now counts for him is not a theoretical understanding of any particular situation but the understanding and self-recognition he can give his subjects.

On the latter point I can certainly testify but the points on the aversion to theory are I think substantial and the authors go on to claim that 'CARE's aversion to theory and to theorising is consistent throughout its membership...the question often appears to be a choice between theory and truth' (Barton and Lawn, 1980/81, p. 4).

Of course from the critique presented herein of curriculum theory the latter point is well taken. The danger however is that the reaction to prescriptive theory had led to a full flight from theory *per se*. There is substantial evidence of this happening at CARE.

The significance of the CARE position, in articulating this strong 'action' and practice position, is that it was symptomatic of a major counter-tendency in the curriculum field at the time – spreading throughout the new 'applied research' to 'action-research' and pervading case study, ethnography, inter-actionist studies, of classrooms and evaluation. MacDonald the *eminence grise* of British evaluation once broke cover to explain why his view of evaluation was thus, above all it was in reaction to controlling theories of 'cost benefit' and 'management by objectives': 'The tendency of language like this is to suggest that the production of educated people is much like the production of anything else, a technological problem of specification and manufacture' (MacDonald, 1976, p. 89).

The reasons for the reaction to theory are then clear but it was, one must remember, a reaction to a particular kind of prescriptive theory suiting the ideological and economic context in which it was produced. The pendulum swing produced a full-scale flight to the arena of action, of practice, the classroom, the practitioner, the practical. We stand witness to a celebration of the practical, a revolt against the abstract. We are back with Rousseau and Emile but with the same problems if progress is ever to be pursued.

The problem of the hasty embrace of action and practice was compounded by the kind of action embraced. To the problems of the methodology of action and practical specificity must be added the problem of *focus*. Not surprisingly those with a strong belief in practice and action sought ways of becoming involved.

Curriculum projects offered a way into curriculum action: the ethos of CARE developed from the involvement of the key personnel in the preceding Humanities Curriculum Project. The particular view of professionalism and politics developed on HEP was later transferred over to become a total position about curriculum research in general.

In the 1960s and the early part of the 1970s a wide range of curriculum research studies and papers discussed the issue of curriculum change. It was always dealt with as synonymous with *innovation*. Eric Hoyle's 'How Does the Curriculum Change: A Proposal for Inquiries' is a good example (Hoyle, 1969). In addition innovation and curriculum projects were viewed as synonymous. To confirm the point it is worth re-reading Parlett and Hamilton's important paper on *Evaluation as Illumination*. The specificity of focus for those seeking to change the school curriculum is clear. The illuminative evaluator was characteristically concerned with 'what is happening'. They wanted therefore to:

> study the innovatory project: how it operates, how it is influenced by the various school situations in which it is applied; what those directly concerned regard as it's advantages and disadvantages and how students' intellectual tasks and academic experiences are more affected.

The illuminative evaluator then:

> aims to discover and document what it is like to be participating in the scheme, whether as a teacher of pupil; and in addition, to discern and discuss the innovation's most significant features, recurring concomitants and critical processes.
>
> (Parlett and Hamilton, 1972)

So a major milieu for those reacting to the rational/scientific school of prescriptive theorizing, given the terrain of the 1960s and 1970s curriculum field, was the innovative curriculum project. Those projects in a sense offered a perfect milieu for those with an ambivalence or antipathy to theory and a wish to be immersed in the day-to-day realities of practice and action. The problem however was not that it offered immersion in the milieu of action but that it was immersion in very *specific* milieu of action. This allowed project staff to initially have it both ways. There was no need for the generalizability of theories or programmes for the project normally centred on a limited number of chosen 'pilot' schools. The need for theory could be easily and justifiably suspended.

The problems began when projects sought to generalize their work: the move if you like from the pilot stage towards new mainstream structures. Here though beginning from the opposite starting point, the projects often responded with the very prescriptions and programmes they had reacted against. There were prescriptions of idealized practice like the 'neutral chairman'; modules and courses, like 'Man a Course of Study'; and new materials and curriculum packages. The prescriptions were buttressed with more theoretical pronouncements again with stark similarity to the prescriptive theories they had reacted against. There were now RDD models (research, development, dissemination) or KPU models (knowledge, production and utilization).

The sad truth was that starting from utterly different points prescriptive theory and immersion in practice led to the same collision point: everyday classroom life and existing syllabuses, exams, subject structures, subject communities, government guidelines, and new educational policies. Again the posture ended up as exhortation, or 'we must leave this to others'.

A further paradox emerges through recent changes in education: once again the argument against the theoretical and the sponsorship of the practical is being pursued. This time however the vision of the practical owes little to Schwab and involves a decidedly undeliberative modality. The emergent pattern may well involve a dismantling of the ineffective existing disciplinary structure for studying education. In its place however will not be a reformist embrace of the practical but a starkly utilitarian embrace. Trainee students will now learn by 'sitting with Nellie' observing and ultimately replacing for short periods established teachers who will act as their main tutors. The redundancy of existing theory will earn the ultimate reward: occupational extinction for the scholars who practice the moribund habits. As it emerges this prospect might prove a major spur to a paradigmatic overthrow in educational research.

Towards a social constructionist perspective: from diagnosis to solution

CAP and major tendencies in the reaction to CAP both share one characteristic: namely a concern to develop models of 'idealised practice' (Reid, 1978, p. 17). Both models are concerned with what *ought* to be happening in schools, 'our commitment to what should be', as Westbury argues, this can lead to 'Meliorism':

> A vision can so easily slide into Meliorism and, unfortunately, the consequences of such a Meliorist perspective have long beset our field: too often and for too much of our history we have not been able, because of our commitment to what should be, to look at what is. To look at what is betrays, our emphases suggest, too little passion, even perhaps a conservative willingness to accept schools as they are. Indeed, all too often our stances imply a condemnation of what schools do.
>
> (Westbury, 1973, p. 99)

For those reacting to the often conservative prescriptions of CAP theorists the full embrace of practice faced the somewhat comparable possibility of conservatively accepting existing practice. In doing this, the reaction to CAP threw the baby out with the bathwater. Neither model therefore came to terms with understanding practice, with why matters work the way they do in schools.

It is therefore important to restate the problems of CAP. The problem with CAP is not only that the focus is solely on prescription but that the kind of focus is disembodied and de-contextualized. A solution would therefore be closer if we had systematic inquiries of how curriculum prescriptions are in fact socially constructed for use in schools. Studies of the actual development of courses of study, of national curriculum plans, of subject syllabuses and so on.

The problem therefore as we restate it is not the fact of the focus on prescription but the *singular* nature of that focus and the *kind* of focus. In short what we require is a combined approach to social construction – a focus on the construction of prescriptive curricula and policy coupled with an analysis of the negotiations and realization of that prescribed curriculum. The approach therefore is to broaden the deliberative mode with studies of practice *and* prescription, focusing on the essentially dialectical relationship of the two.

We want, in short, 'the story of action within a theory of context'. This then is to move a step back towards the centre following the moves of Schwab and some curriculum reformers to fully embrace the practical terrain. This I have argued was too extreme a reaction albeit understandable at the time. Since prescription continues (and given the current centralist thrust will in fact strengthen) we need to understand social construction of curricula at the levels of prescription *and* process *and* practice. In short, the diagnosis of Schwab and some of the curriculum reformers who saw the curriculum field as moribund is broadly accepted; their solution, however, is seen as too extreme. What is required is indeed to understand the practical but to locate this understanding within a further exploration of the contextual parameters of practice.

In curriculum research there are a range of foci that are amenable to social constructionist study, for instance:

- The individual: life history and career.
- The group or collective: professions, categories, subjects and disciplines, for instance, evolve rather as social movements over time. Likewise schools and classrooms develop patterns of stability and change.
- The relational: the various permutations of relations between individuals, between groups and collectivities and between individuals, groups and collectivities; and the way these relations change over time.

Of course the relationship between individual and collective (as between action and structure) is perennially elusive. But our studies may, as has largely been the case in the past, accept or exacerbate fragmentation or alternatively, as should be our intention in the future, seek integration.

In examining individual teachers' lives the life history method might be usefully rehabilitated. The genesis of life histories can be located in anthropological work at the beginning of this century; the main take-up by sociologists occurred later in a series of urban and social studies at the University of Chicago.

For a number of reasons, which I have analysed elsewhere (Goodson and Sikes, 2001), this work became less and less of a priority in the Chicago studies of the city and as a result the method fell into neglect until recently. In its more contemporary usage life history work has focused mainly on studies of deviance, crime and urban ethnography. The methodology of life history is therefore still relatively undeveloped and its use in the study of schooling only just beginning. This omission in the study of schooling is regrettable and moving from programmatic exhortation to empirical investigation have employed life history data to explore the intersection between biography, history and structure with specific regard to the secondary school curriculum.

The exhortation to re-embrace life history methods was first detailed in an article in 1981 (Goodson, 1981). This was taken up in a study of Teachers' Careers undertaken by Sikes *et al.* (1985). They were from the beginning aware of the substantial problems and commented that 'life histories do not present themselves to as a fully-fledged method ready to use. There is, as yet, no substantial body of methodological literature to support life history studies' (Sikes *et al.*, 1985, p.14). Nevertheless their work in *Teachers' Careers: Crises and Continuities* does provide us with important insights on teachers' lives and careers. Other work such as Bertaux's collection *Biography and Society* (1981), and Ken Plummer's excellent *Documents of Life* (1983), begin the rehabilitation of life history method and the exploration of the substantial methodological and ethical problems that such work entails. In *Life History in Educational Settings* (2001), Pat Sikes and I extend the arguments for life history into the area of educational study.

Yet beyond problems intrinsic to the life history methods are problems of relationship to other foci and modes of analysis and investigation. As Mannheim warned in 1936 'Preoccupation with the purely individual life-history and its analysis is not sufficient' (Mannheim, 1972). Above all, and rightly, I suspect, Mannheim is railing against individualism. What he calls 'The fiction of the isolated and self-sufficient individual'. Plainly given the powerful legacy of individualism and of individualist assumptions present in so many epistemologies this danger must be continually scrutinized with regard to life history work. As Mannheim says: 'The genetic method of explanation, if it goes deep enough, cannot in the long run limit itself to the individual life history and the more inclusive group situation. For the individual life history is only a component in a series of mutually intertwined life histories...it was the merit of the sociological point of view that it set alongside the individual genesis of meaning the genesis from the context of group life' (Mannheim, 1972, p. 25).

Life history study pursued alongside the study of more collective groupings and milieu might promote better integration in a study of differing foci. The problem of integration is of course partly a problem of dealing with modes and levels of consciousness. The life history penetrates the individual subject's consciousness and attempts also to map the changes in that consciousness over the life cycle. But at the individual level as at other levels we must note that change is structured, but that structures change. The relationship between the individual and wider structures is central to our investigations but again it is through historical studies that such investigations can be profitably pursued:

> Our chance to understand how smaller milieu and larger structures interact, and our chance to understand the larger causes at work in these limited milieu, thus require us to deal with historical materials.
>
> (Wright Mills, 1970, p. 165)

Ultimately we are back with the integrative focus suggested by C. Wright Mills as essential for all good social science:

> Social science deals with problems of biography of history and of their intersections within social structures. That these three – biography, history, society, are the coordinate points of the proper study of man has been a major platform on which I have stood when criticizing several current schools of sociology whose practitioners have abandoned this classic tradition.
>
> (Wright Mills, 1970, p. 159)

In curriculum study the relationship between the individual teacher's life and the pre-active and interactive curriculum will allow insights into structuration as well as action. For as Esland has argued:

> Trying to focus the individual biography in its socio historical context is in a very real sense attempting to penetrate the symbolic drift of school knowledge, and the consequences for the individuals who are caught up in it and attempting to construct their reality through it.
>
> (Esland, 1971, p. 111)

What is needed is to build on studies of participants immersed in immediate process, to build on studies of historical events and periods but to develop a cumulative understanding of the historical contexts in which the contemporary curriculum is embedded. The experience of the past decades has shown the painful limitations of a-historical or transcendent approaches both at the level of curriculum reform and study. By developing our analysis from further back we should be able to throw more light on the present and afford insights into the constraints immanent in transmitted circumstance.

Those studies with an action-orientation have most often been confined to the view of participants at a moment in time, to the here and now of events. Their essential omission was data on the *constraints beyond* the event, the school, the classroom and the participant. What above all is needed, therefore, is a method that stays with the participants, stays with the complexity of the social process but catches some understanding of the constraints beyond. Although the human process by which men make their own history does not take place in circumstances of their own choosing as both men and women and circumstances do vary over time so too do the potentialities for negotiating reality. Historical study seeks to understand how thought and action have developed in past social circumstances. Following this development though time to the present affords insights into how those circumstances we experience as contemporary 'reality' have been negotiated, constructed and reconstructed over time. Stenhouse saw this need for history to provide an authenticated context for hypothetical actions'. His concern was also with: 'What might be termed the contextual inertia within which events are embedded. It is here that history generalizes and becomes theoretical. It is, as it were, the story of action within a theory of context' (Stenhouse, 1977, p. 7).

The historical context of course reflects previous patterns of conflict and power. It is not sufficient to develop a static notion of the historical contexts and constraints inherited *in tacto* from the past. These contexts and constraints need to be examined in relationship to contemporary action. Moreover we need a dynamic model of how syllabuses, pedagogy, finance, resources, selection, the economy all interrelate. We cannot, in short, view the curriculum (and its associated historical contexts and constraints) as a bounded system. Williamson has reflected on the fact 'that it is not sufficient to be aware only on the fact that the principles governing the selection of transmittable knowledge reflect structures of power. It is essential to move beyond such suspicions to work out the precise connections' (Williamson, 1974). This he argues predicates historical study of curriculum 'if the aim is to understand power in education'. Above all we need to develop cognitive maps of curriculum influence and curriculum constraints for as he says: 'What is provided in schools and what is taught in those schools can only be understood historically. Earlier educational attitudes of dominant groups in society still carry historical weight' (Williamson, 1974, pp. 10–11).

Social constructionist perspectives therefore seek a re-integrated focus for studies of curriculum. Moving away from singular focus whether on idealized practice or actual practice towards developing data on social construction at both pre-active and interactive levels. At this point in time, as I have argued elsewhere, the most significant lacuna for such a reconceptualized programme of study are historical studies of the social construction of school curricula. We really know very little about how the subjects and themes prescribed in schools originate, are promoted and re-defined, and metamorphose.

Hence work on the history of the social construction of school curricula is a vital pre-requisite for reconceptualized curriculum study. Fortunately however, a good deal of work has been undertaken in the last decade which is coming to fruition. The series *Studies in Curriculum History* now comprises volumes which provide a wide range of different studies of the social construction of school curricula (Goodson). New studies are now being commissioned for this series and in time we hope to have a fairly comprehensive set of studies of the origins and promotion of curricula in a range of settings and at a range of levels. Other work, especially in North America, complements this initiative and develops our understanding of the contestation which has surrounded the development of prescriptive curricula (Kliebard, 1975).

In *The Making of Curriculum* I have worked with and across the range of foci listed (Goodson, 1988) from the individual to the group and collective. In particular I have sought to examine individual life histories and how these allow us to develop themes and frameworks for viewing structures and organizations. Some of the individual testimonies provided in this book show how teachers come to understand and reflect upon the broader contexts in which their professional lives are embedded. In the next chapter we see how 'in the life of Patrick Johnson we gain insights into him wrestling with imperatives in the social structure' (p. 112). Likewise in *School Subjects and Curriculum Change* I have tried to develop the group or collective focus by studying school subjects in historical evolution. Here I contended that:

> historical case studies of school subjects provide the 'local detail' of curriculum change and conflict. The identification of individuals and sub-groups actively at work within curriculum interest groups allows some examination and assessment of intention and motivation. Thereby sociological theories which attribute power over the curriculum to dominant interest groups can be scrutinized for their empirical potential.
>
> To concentrate attention at the micro level of individual school subject groups is not to deny the crucial importance of macro level economic changes or changes in intellectual ideas, dominant values or educational systems. But it is asserted that such macro level changes may be actively reinterpreted at the micro level. Changes at macro level are viewed as presenting a range of new choices to subject factions, associations and communities. To understand how subjects change over time, as well as histories of intellectual ideas, we need to understand how subject groups are all-powerful in engineering curriculum change but that their responses are a very important, and as yet somewhat neglected, part of the overall picture.
>
> (Goodson, 1987, pp. 3–4)

In *Biography, Identity and Schooling* (Goodson and Walker, 1990), *Studying Curriculum* (Goodson, 1994) and *Subject Knowledge*...(Goodson, 1998), I looked at ways to integrate different foci and levels of analysis. In developing an integrated social constructionist perspective this pursues the promise that the theoretic and the practical, or seen another way that structure and agency might be reconnected in our vision of curriculum scholarship. Were this to come about we might be saved from the recurrent 'flight to theory' followed by the counterbalancing 'flight to practice' (and the occasional intervening 'flight to the personal'). Our scholarship would thereby be encompassing in integrated manner the complexity of levels of analysis which reflects the reality of curriculum.

To begin any analysis of schooling by accepting without question a form and content of curriculum that was fought for and achieved at a particular historical point on the basis of certain social and political priorities, to take that curriculum as a given, is to forego a whole range of understandings and insights into features of the control and operation of the school and the classroom. It is to take over the mystifications of previous episodes of governance as unchallengeable givens. We are, let us be clear, talking about the systematic 'invention of tradition' in an arena of social production and reproduction, the school curriculum, where political and social priorities are paramount. Histories of other aspects of social life have begun to systematically scrutinize this process. Hobsbawm argues that the term 'invented tradition':

> includes both traditions actually invented, constructed and formally instituted and those emerging in a less traceable manner within a brief and dateable period – a matter of a few years perhaps – and establishing themselves with great rapidity.

Hobsbawm defines the matter this way:

> Invented tradition is taken to mean a set of practices, normally governed by overtly or tacitly accepted rules and of a ritual or symbolic nature which seek to circulate certain values and norms of behaviour by repetition, which auto-matically implies continuity with the past. In fact, where possible, they nor-mally attempt to establish continuity with a suitable historic past.
>
> (Hobsbawm and Ranger, 1985, p. 1)

In this sense the making of curriculum can be seen as a process of inventing tradi-tion. In fact this language is often used when the 'traditional disciplines' or 'tradi-tional subjects' are juxtaposed against some new fangled innovation of integrated or child-centred topics. The point, however, is that the written curriculum whether as courses of study, syllabuses, guidelines, or textbooks is a supreme example of the invention of tradition: but as with all tradition it is not a once and for all given, it is a given which has to be defended, where the mystifications have to be con-structed and reconstructed over time. Plainly, if curriculum theorists substantially ignore the history and social construction of curriculum, such mystification and reproduction of 'traditional' curriculum form and content becomes easier.

An important stage then in the development of a social constructionist perspective is the production of a wide series of studies on the social construction of the pre-scriptive curriculum. But this is only a part of the story as the advocates of 'prac-tice' have long and correctly maintained. For what is prescribed is not necessarily what is undertaken, and what is planned is not necessarily what happens. But, as we have argued, this should not imply that we abandon our studies of prescription as social construction and embrace, in singular form, the practical. We should instead seek to study the social construction of curriculum as both the levels of prescription and interaction.

The challenge is to develop new substantive and methodological foci which integrate studies at the pre-active and the interactive levels. The linkage and inte-gration of these studies is the major problem for we are dealing with different lev-els and arenas of social construction. This difference of levels and arenas has often led to the argument that there is a complete break between pre-active and interac-tive and that the latter is to all and intents and purposes autonomous. This of course leads us back to the argument that 'practice is all that matters' and hence that we should focus our studies solely on practice.

The focus of recent curriculum study on projects and innovation (noted earlier) is partly responsible for this belief in autonomy. Two quotes from an unpublished curriculum report illustrate this tendency: 'The project team had to explain what it was going to do before it could do it. The teachers started by doing it and only then looked for an explanation of why they were doing it that way.'

But what was the 'it' the teachers were doing and how and where was it socially constructed. Likewise 'the end product of the project was determined in the field, in contract with the school, not on the drawing board...in the end it was what worked that survived'.

Both these quotes celebrate the autonomy of the school and of practice. But both of them are likely to lead to our missing the point. For only what is prepared on the drawing board goes in to the school and therefore *has a chance* to be interpreted and to survive. Of course if this is so for the notoriously unloved curriculum project it is even more the case for the traditional (and less scrutinized and contested) school subject. With the latter clear parameters to practice are socially constructed at the pre-active level. Practice in short is socially constructed at the pre-active *and* interactive level: it is a combination of both and our curriculum study should acknowledge this combination.

And if the questions of the form and scale of 'parameters' remain elusive and it is above all for this reason that we need to link our work on social construction at the pre-active and interactive levels. At one level this will mean urging a closer connection between studies of school process and practice as currently constituted and studies of social construction at the pre-active level. A culminating stage in developing a social constructionist perspective would be to develop studies which themselves integrate studies of social construction at *both* pre-active and interactive levels. We shall need to explore and develop integrative foci for social constructionist study and in this respect exploring the relational level would provide a strategy for strengthening and bringing together studies of action and of context in meaningful ways. Above all social constructionist perspectives would improve our understanding of the politics of curriculum and in doing so would provide valuable 'cognitive maps' for teachers seeking to understand and locate the parameters to their practice.

References

Barton, L. and Lawn, M., 1980/81, Back Inside the Whale: A Curriculum Case Study. *Interchange,* 11(4).

Berger, P.L. and Luckman, T., 1967, *The Social Construction of Reality* (Harmondsworth: Allen Lane).

Bertaux, D. (ed.), 1981, *Biography and Society: The Life History Approach in the Social Sciences* (London: Sage).

Clifford, G.J. and Guthrie, J.W., 1988, *Ed School: A Brief for Professional Education* (Chicago, IL: The University of Chicago Press).

Esland, G.M., 1971, Teaching and Learning as the Organisation of Knowledge. In M.F.D. Young (ed.), *Knowledge and Control New Directions for the Sociology of Education* (London: Collier Macmillan).

Goodson, I.F., 1981, Life Histories and the Study of Schooling. *Interchange,* 11(4), 62–76.

Goodson, I.F., 1987, *School Subjects and Curriculum Change* (London, New York, Philadelphia, PA: Falmer Press), See also, *School Subjects and Curriculum Change,* 3rd edition, 1993, for very interesting introduction by Peter MaClaren.

Goodson, I.F., 1988, *The Making of Curriculum: Collected Essays* (London, New York, Philadelphia, PA: Falmer Press).

Goodson, I.F. (ed.), 1985–1988, *Studies in Curriculum History* (London, New York, Philadelphia, PA: Falmer Press). Book series covering the years 1985–1998.

Goodson, I.F., 1994, *Studying Curriculum – Cases and Methods* (Philadelphia, PA and London: Open University Press).

Goodson, I.F., 1998, *Subject Knowledge: Readings for The Study of School Subjects,* with C. Anstead and J.M. Mangan (London and Washington, DC: Falmer Press).

Goodson, I.F. and Sikes, P., 2001, *Life History Research in Educational Settings: Learning from Lives* (Buckingham and Philadelphia, PA: Open University Press).

Goodson, I.F. and Walker, R., 1990, *Biography, Identity and Schooling* (London: Falmer Press).

Hobsbawm, E. and Ranger, T., (eds), 1985, *The Invention of Tradition* (Cambridge: Cambridge University Press).

Hoyle, E., 1969, How Does the Curriculum Change? A Proposal for Inquiries. *Journal of Curriculum Studies,* 1(2).

Kliebard, H.M., 1975, Persistent Curriculum Issues in Historical Perspective. In W. Pinar (ed.), *Curriculum Theorising* (Berkeley, CA: McCutchan).

MacDonald, B., 1976, Who's Afraid of Evaluation. *Education,* 4(2), 3–13.

Mannheim, K., 1972, *Ideology and Utopia: An Introduction to the Sociology of Knowledge* (London: Routledge and Kegan Paul).

Parlett, M. and Hamilton, D., 1972, *Evaluation as Illumination.* Occasional Paper 9 (Edinburgh: Centre for Research in Educational Sciences).

Plummer, K., 1983, *Documents of Life: An Introduction to the Problems and Literature of a Humanistic Method* (London: George Allen and Unwin).

Reid, W.A., 1978, *Thinking about the Curriculum* (London: Routledge and Kegan Paul).

Schwab, J.L., 1978, The Practical: A Language for Curriculum. In I. Westbury and N. Wilkof (eds), *Science, Curriculum and Liberal Education* (Chicago, IL: University of Chicago Press).

Sikes, P.J., Measor, L. and Woods, P., 1985, *Teacher Careers: Crises and Continuities* (Lewes: Falmer).

Stenhouse, L., 1975, *An Introduction to Curriculum Research and Development* (London: Heinemann).

Stenhouse, L., 1977, *Case Study as a Basis for Research in a Theoretical Contemporary History of Education* (Centre for Applied Research in Education, University of East Anglia, Norwich).

Veblen, T., 1962, *The Higher Learning in America.* Reprint of 1918 edition (New York City: Hill and Wang).

Walker, R., 1974, *Classroom Research: A View of SAFARI. Innovation, Evaluation, Research and the Problem of Control* (CARE, University of East Anglia, Norwich).

Westbury, I., 1973, Conventional Classrooms, 'Open' Classrooms and the Technology of Teaching. *Journal of Curriculum Studies,* 5(2) (November).

Williamson, B., 1974, Continuities and Discontinuities in the Sociology of Education. In M. Flude and J. Ahier (eds), *Educability, Schools and Ideology* (London: Croom Helm).

Wright Mills, C., 1970, *The Sociological Imagination* (London: Penguin).

Wright Mills, C., 1979, *Power, Politics and People* (London, Oxford, New York: Oxford University Press).

Additional sources

Cooper, B., 1985, *Renegotiating Secondary School Mathematics: A Study of Curriculum Change and Stability.*

Cunningham, P., 1988, *Curriculum Change in the Primary School since 1945: Dissemination of the Progressive Ideal.*

Finkelstein, B., 1989, *Governing the Young: Teacher Behavior in Popular Primary Schools in Nineteenth Century United States.*

Franklin, B., 1986, *Building the American Community: Social Control and Curriculum.*

Goodson, I.F. (ed.), 1985, *Social Histories of the Secondary Curriculum: Subjects for Study.*

Goodson, I.F., 1987, *School Subjects and Curriculum Change.*

Goodson, I.F., 1988, *The Making of Curriculum: Collected Essays.*

McCulloch, G., 1990, *The Secondary Technical School: A Usable Past?*

McCulloch, G., Jenkins, E. and Layton, D., 1985, *Technological Revolution? The Politics of School Science and Technology in England and Wales since 1945.*

Moon, B., 1986, *The 'New Maths' Curriculum Controversy: An International Story.*

Musgrave, P.W., 1988, *Whose Knowledge? A Case Study of the Victorian Universities Schools Examinations Board, 1964–1979.*

Popkewitz, T.S. (ed.), 1987, *The Formation of School Subjects: The Struggle for Creating an American Institution.*

Woolnough, B.E., 1988, *Physics Teaching in Schools 1960–85: Of People, Policy and Power.*

CHAPTER 11

HISTORY, CONTEXT AND QUALITATIVE METHODS

R.G. Burgess (ed.), *Strategies for Education Research,*
London: Falmer Press, 1985

In this chapter I argue for methods that rehabilitate life histories and integrate studies of historical context. In the introductory section the reasons for concentrating on life history and curriculum history data are explored by analysing some of the inadequacies of research methods as perceived in the mid 1970s when my own work began (Goodson, 1983).

It should be noted that since then other studies have emerged which have also sought to address these inadequacies. Studies of teacher socialisation have focussed on teacher culture and careers (Lacey, 1977), whilst a range of 'strategies' studies have pointed to the importance of background and biography (Pollard, 1982). This work has considerably extended the range and theoretical aspiration of qualitative studies but I shall stay with the original intention of exploring the role of historical studies in redressing certain emergent tendencies within qualitative methods.

In retrospect several reasons would seem to have led to a predilection for historical and biographical work when devising a research programme:

1   Grew out of my teaching experience. Certainly after teaching at Countesthorpe (recently described as an 'unemulated educational maverick') I was susceptible to Nisbet's arguments in *Social Change and History*. Here he argues that we are often deluded into thinking fundamental social change is taking place because we do not take account of a vital distinction between:

> re-adjustment or individual deviance within a social structure (whose effects, although possibly cumulative are never sufficient to alter the structure or the basic postulates of a society or institution) and the more fundamental though enigmatic change of structure, type, pattern or paradigm.
>
> (Nisbet, 1969, pp. 204–205)

To pursue this distinction demands, I think, that we undertake historical work. This holds whether we seek to understand how change is contained, as readjustment or individual deviance in particular schools like Countesthorpe or within curriculum reforms in general.

2   The documents and statements of the curriculum reform movement inaugurated in the 1960s reveal a widespread belief that there could be a more or less complete break with past tradition. A belief, in short, that history in general and

curriculum history in particular could somehow be *transcended*. For instance it was asserted that the new curricula then being devised promised to 'revolution-alise' English schooling (Kerr, 1971, p. 180). Retrospectively there still seems something admirable, however misconceived, about such belief in contemporary possibility that history seemed of little relevance. At a time when traditional curriculum practice was thought to be on the point of being overthrown it was perhaps unsurprising that so many reforms paid scant attention to the evolution and establishment of traditional practice. In the event radical change did not occur. By 1975 when my research programme began one was in a position of needing to re-examine the emergence and survival of the 'traditional' as well as the failure to generalise, institutionalise and sustain the 'innovative'.

3   But if this was a view from the curriculum chalk face, it later became clear that the *transcendent* view of curriculum change had infected many of those involved in researching schools and curriculum. The irony is supreme but for the best of reasons. Once again it is partly explained by an historical climate of opinion where curriculum change was thought the order of the day. Parlett and Hamilton's influential paper on illuminative styles of evaluation, though claiming general application, focussed on the evaluation of *innovation*. They wanted 'to study the innovatory project; how it operates, how it is influenced by the various school situations in which it is applied; what those directly concerned regard as its advantages and disadvantages' (Parlett and Hamilton, 1972). Preoccupation with 'those directly concerned', with 'what it is like to be participating' were to characterise a major school of evaluators and case study workers. Indeed this posture characterised those researchers both most sympathetic and sensitive to the aspirations of the innovators. Above all they wanted to 'capture and portray the world as it appears to the people in it'. Some went even further 'in a sense for the case study worker what *seems* true is more important than what is true' (Walker, 1974).

Writing later, with a strong sense of my own delusions on curriculum reform, I saw the evaluators who had studied my school as merely confirming the partici-pants' myopia:

> Focussing the evaluators' work on the charting of the subjective perceptions of participants is to deny much of its potential – particularly to those evaluators aspiring to 'strong action – implications'. The analysis of subjective percep-tions is incomplete without analysis of the historical context in which they occur. To deprive the subject of such knowledge would be to condemn new evaluation to the level of social control – a bizarre fate for a model aspiring to 'democratic' intentions.
>
> (Goodson, 1977, p. 24)

4   Yet if many of those employing qualitative methods in evaluation and case study took a transcendent view of history they were not alone. Many contempo-rary inter-actionist and ethnographic studies were similarly a-historical.

Life histories and curriculum history

At the time of planning my original research the blending of individual history and curriculum history had been recently explored in Mary Waring's study of Nuffield

Science. For Waring the understanding of curriculum innovation is simply not possible without a history of context:

> If we are to understand events, whether of thought or of action, knowledge of the background is essential. Knowledge of events is merely the raw material of history: to be an intelligible reconstruction of the past, events must be related to other events, and to the assumptions and practices of the milieu. Hence they must be made the subject of inquiry, their origins as products of particular social and historical circumstance...
>
> (Waring, 1975, p. 12)

Waring's focus on individual background as well as curriculum history grew from an awareness of how the Nuffield innovations were implemented:

> Organisers of individual Nuffield projects were given considerable autonomy with regard to the interpretation and carrying out of their brief, and to the selection and deployment of their teams. As a result, these aspects reflect very clearly the background and personality of the men and women chosen.
>
> (Waring, 1979, p. 12)

This belief in the importance of individual history and personality is confirmed in the study (although the role of ideological bias is conceded):

> The evidence in this study supports the view that, while differences of degree no doubt existed between individuals, the sincerity, the commitment and the dedicated work over a long time on the part of the principal characters at least, and probably of many others, dwarf and transcend whatever vested interest may have been operating.
>
> (Waring, 1979, p. 15)

Whilst I am unsure about the primacy of individual will over vested interests (hardly a lesson of history!) the contention does add force to the need to explore curriculum at both the individual and collective level. Combining life histories with contextual history seems therefore a strategy for building on the wide range of case study, evaluative and inter-actionist work.

In this way a methodology is established which stays with the focus on participation and eventfulness but which allows examination of the constraints beyond, which in fact allows us to see how *over time* individual will and fundamental vested interests interrelate.

School subjects and curriculum history

Symptomatic of the focus on participants and events has been the absence of work on school subjects. Young has, as we have noted, spoken of these as 'no more than socio-cultural constructs of a particular time' (Young, 1971, p. 23), but a historical view of curriculum would attribute considerably more significance than this. In choosing to research school subjects I was cognisant that in studies of schooling the subject provides *par excellence* a context where antecedent structures collide with contemporary action; the school subject provides one obvious manifestation of historical legacies or as Waring puts it 'monumental accretions' with which contemporary actors have to work.

Williams made the case for studying the content of education over 20 years ago. He argued that:

> The cultural choices involved in the selection of content have an organic relation to the social choices involved in the practical organisation. If we are to discuss education adequately, we must examine, in historical and analytic terms, this organic relation, for to be conscious of a choice made is to be conscious of further and alternative choices.
>
> (Williams, 1965, pp. 145–146)

Developing this notion of school subjects being dependent on previous choices the concern in my work was to begin with the histories of those teachers who had played a central role in defining a school subject over the last half century: a period spanning the change-over from the tri-partite system where the subject was taught largely in secondary moderns to a subject taught in most comprehensive schools. The school subject in question, Rural Studies, changed from being a deeply utilitarian subject based on gardening in the 1920s to a subject offering 'O' and 'A' levels in Environmental Studies in the 1970s. By collecting the life stories of key participant teachers spanning this generation it was hoped that insights might be provided not only of how the curriculum changes but of how structural constraints are evidenced in such a process. Understanding a curriculum innovation such as the launching of Environmental Studies required a detailed understanding of historical context and life histories provided a valuable access point to this context.

In talking to the key participants understandably a range of personal values and idiosyncrasies emerged but on certain points their life histories substantially concurred. At this point, however, a number of doubts surfaced. The most significant was that I was clearly, in talking to the main innovators, following one of the tactics for which I had indicted earlier research. The innovators did represent a group who had been able to 'hijack' the subject association and thereby change the direction and definition of the subject. In this sense they did not formally represent the range of traditions and 'alternative visions' among the teachers of the subject. In fact the fascinating aspect of the testimonies of the key participants was their cognisance of 'other voices in other rooms', of the alternative traditions and choices, which were closed off in pursuit of the status and resources that would promote the subject.

At this point the research might have progressed in a number of directions. I was aware of three that seemed sustainable.

1   Was to fill out the initial life histories of the key participants into fully-fledged life histories which would be of sufficient depth to capture and portray the main issues within this curriculum area.
2   Was to collect a wider range of life histories, to try and cover the main 'traditions' and sub-groups within the subject.
3   Was to develop a detailed documentary history of the subject, of the conflicts that were generated, during a period of over half a century.

In retrospect all three of these strategies seem to offer both problems and possibilities but in the event strategy (1) was rejected. The main reason was that the focus on the innovative in-group seemed unrepresentative and in a strong sense 'against the grain' of much of the history of the subject. To be too focussed on this group opened up the problem mentioned in the introduction where historical perspective is lost by a focus on 'innovation' which might in the longer span turn out to be merely 'aberration'.

To seek a way of overcoming the problems of uniqueness and idiosyncrasy which combine with substantial methodological problems in the life history method a combination of strategies (2) and (3) were adopted. A number of additional life histories of non-innovators were collected whilst the main focus of the study turned towards documentary research of the history of the subject. Combining a group of life histories with subject history resembles the methods adopted in a range of recent 'oral histories'. Certainly the combination offered a strategy to 'triangulate' the data and thereby partially assess the reliability of the findings (Denzin, 1970).

The problem here is how to characterise the blend of curriculum history and life history data without involving a substantive and recapitulative account. The major intention in the next section is therefore to fill out the argument with some data which gives a 'feel' of combining life histories with historical context. Of course the account has all the normal problems of trying to evidence the general category with one very specific case. In addition, it should be remembered that in assembling final accounts not just one but a range of life histories would be presented in combination with studies of historical context.

The following section deals with certain critical episodes in one teacher's life. They are chosen because they represent a common viewpoint in the life history data collected: namely a conviction that the embrace of specialist examination subject identity was a watershed in the original educational visions of a generation of rural studies teachers. But above all the concern in the section is to provide an account of certain critical decision points in one teacher's life: critical in the sense that the teacher, who is now retired, regards these episodes as the main turning point in his professional life.

The work began with a long series of interviews with the subject teacher – covering a period of eight years up until his retirement and after. Again and again, in the interviews the teacher returned to the episodes when in his terms 'the dream began to fade', 'the alternative vision died'.

Critical episodes in a teacher's life

1947–54 The innovative secondary modern

The 1944 Education Act foreshadowed the tripartite system of State schooling in Grammar, Technical and Secondary Modern Schools in England and Wales. The compulsory school leaving age was raised to fifteen in 1947. The Act marks the beginning of the modern era of curriculum conflict not so much because of its details but because from this date onwards curriculum conflict becomes more visible, public and national. Glass has noted that in this respect there was no 'pre-war parallel', for there was now:

> a recognition that Secondary education is a proper subject for discussion and study . . . in striking contrast to the pre-war position when attempts to investigate access to the various stages of education tended to be looked at by the Government as attacks on the class structure.
>
> (Glass, 1971, p. 35)

In the emerging secondary modern schools the curriculum was initially free from the consideration of external examinations. This freedom allowed some schools, always a minority, to experiment with their curricula and to pursue vocational and child-centred objectives. Social Studies and Civics courses, for instance, were rapidly established in a number of the schools. Kathleen Gibberd has argued that the secondary modern school as conceived in 1944 was never intended to work to any universal syllabus to take any external examination: 'it was to be a field for experiment.' She considered that:

> Behind the official words and regulations there was a call to the teacher who believed in education for its own sake and longed for a free hand with children who were not natural learners. Many of those who responded gave an individual character to their schools.

> (Gibberd, 1962, p. 103)

However, the period during which certain secondary moderns were a 'field for experiment' with vocational, child-centred and integrated curricula was to prove very limited. This can be evidenced by following the changes in rural education in the secondary state sector.

Entering the profession – secondary modern innovations

At the time the new secondary moderns, a few embracing the integrated concept of rural education, were being launched, Patrick Johnson was completing his training at Wandsworth Emergency College. His choice of subject was initially somewhat fortuitous:

> Well, I didn't really know what subject I wanted to do. In fact I really wanted to do English. But when I got home after the war I didn't feel I could be cooped up inside. I moved into Kent where all my wife Jean's people were farm workers on the fruit farms...I heard there was a thing called rural studies.

First Job: Snodland (age 27–34)

In November 1947 he got a Teacher's Certificate and then had to do a probationary year. His first year was spent teaching general subjects at a school called Snodland...

> Gardening it was really, but I taught everything. It was a secondary modern, a very early one, illiterate kids – their standard was terrible, just after the war. It was a big elementary school at a place called Snodland, with a big cement works on the Medway estuary, Rochester direction. Terrible place, the kids were very backward. I always remember the first day I arrived. The Head said, 'Good God! a teacher!' and grabbed me, shoved me inside a classroom saying 'this is your lot' and shut the door! Then I was faced by this mob who hadn't had a teacher for some years during the war. I fought a running battle with them:
>
> IG: What had they been doing, then?
> PJ: Well, they had been going into the classroom occasionally. They literally could not read or write. They were desperate kids, nice kids but they were absolutely, completely illiterate at 12 years of age. And undisciplined too.

IG: So did you just have a class?

PJ: Yes, I did everything – PE, music, everything.

IG: So you weren't a rural studies teacher in your first post.

PJ: No, there was a lesson called gardening, and I did some of that as well.

Wrotham secondary modern

Patrick's next job for his second probationary year was a new secondary modern at Wrotham. The head, 'one of the very exceptional headmasters', had run the village school where his wife and son had attended. The head was very enthusiastic about school gardens and invited Patrick to come and teach rural science:

> So I said 'yes', I could see the opportunities...I'd often talked with him of things I'd like to do. When he started the new school I went along to teach rural science. The new school consisted of three Nissen huts in a field. Literally, that was all. The type made of clay bricks with cinders, half way between Wrotham and Borough Green. That was the school. There wasn't a classroom. One of them, the largest, doubled for assembly and art room. One half was elementarily equipped as a lab. The others were ordinary classrooms. I had an ordinary classroom and I had fourth year class, which was then the top leaving class of the school. There were three streams and the 3rd and 4th year classes were called 4F (farming) and 4P (practical) with extra needle-work and cooking, and 4A (academic) where the kids did extra English and so on. But of course there were no examinations, so in fact A wasn't the top class, but they probably did turn out a few who could read and write. They were really equivalent and we used to sit down once a year and think out who would we get into each class. Well, 4F class, which I had...we established a school farm. We built this up from nothing. We had one and a half acres of land along the playing fields as it was too steep for football pitches. I got that fenced off, got bits of wire and so on...as things developed I had my class for practically everything – not quite every subject, but a good deal and I developed my ideas on this form. We built bits and pieces gradually. We built a pigsty, and the 4 Practical did the actual building of that. We built a rabbit house which we built up. Eventually we kept about two calves, about six goats, a pig and a litter; we had a poultry run and hens of course, a dairy which we fitted out, and I managed to get from Gascoynes because my father was a friend of the chairman or something, dairy equipment.

Johnson taught 4F for about two thirds of their timetable, other teachers taught science and woodwork. He was much influenced by the idea of rural education as the 'curriculum hub' which his headmaster actively encouraged:

> I taught them maths, English, history etc., all tied in completely, because, for example, maths I based as much as possible on the farm activities. In fact, I used a series of books that were popular then, called *Rural Arithmetic* – the other I can't quite remember the title of. They were all about problems of the land: e.g. if you were mixing things for the pigs, you didn't buy ready-made meal for the pigs. You calculated by the weight what meal they require, you broke this down, the various ingredients of the meal, you get them all out separately, weighted them up, mixed them up and it had to work out right to

14 rations, one for every morning and evening of the week. That was a piece of arithmetic it could take two people most of the day to do.

We were fairly poorly off for books in those days, frankly, so we read a lot of literature associated with the countryside. We didn't over do this to the extent of doing nothing else. They wrote compositions. We had an English textbook, which I at any rate, kept an eye on to make sure some sort of progression of spelling was maintained. But a lot of English was straightforwardly connected with the farm. For example, they each had to write a diary every day and they had to write a summary at the end of the week. It was passed on to the next students who took on the animals. That was a good piece of English, and I had said that must be perfect – no spelling mistakes, no blots – nothing!

Johnson reckons that these were some of the happiest days of his teaching career. His own enthusiasm (and that of his wife) coupled with the interest of the children seem to have generated considerable motivation to learn:

IG: Did they respond pretty well?
PJ: They absolutely lapped it up, loved it. You'd never get absences unless the kid was really ill. You'd get kids... often at the weekends... We had to feed them at the weekends – there was no-one else to. I can't remember any occasion when the kids didn't turn up at the weekend. It may have happened but I can't remember.
IG: So you had to spend a lot of time at weekends?
PJ: Lived up there. But Joan helped a lot too. Frankly we hadn't any money to be doing anything else in those days. Until it reached a stage when my kids were getting a bit older and I took a job during the holidays because I needed the money – pay was poor. But I still did that as well.

Johnson attributed the main influences on his developing concept of rural education to his contacts with the Kent farm workers' family which he had married into and which he lived among.

I did a lot of walking about the orchards in Kent and talking to farm workers and I can remember lots of occasions when the attitude of these people struck me very much. I had a strong feeling that education wasn't just book-learning – that's an old phrase – it involved in fact skills in the field and commonsense applied to a problem.

Johnson felt that he dealt with many very able pupils in 4F; partly a reflection of the social structure in Kent in the early 1950s. The pupils were, with one exception (for whom he could not find a job), boys, the most able of whom today would be in the sixth forms, who went as agricultural apprentices to farms who were glad to get them. 'Good farms, good employers!' I asked at this point if he felt any resentment that they were forced to go on to the land:

PJ: No, first of all because I didn't know anything about 'A' levels at my level of teaching. Grammar schools were a separate world and while I knew them throughout my own background, I never associated these kids with it. It never occurred to me at the time that these kids could have got into the sixth form. It didn't occur to me at that time that they were bright.

IG: Why didn't it occur to you that these children were bright?

PJ: They were bright to me but it didn't occur to me that that meant they should have an academic education. Because I was meeting people throughout the war – meeting people then whose field of work was similar to farm workers and every bit as bright. I don't think this is true today. One of the effects of the introduction of the 11 + was to cream the working class of its bright people who went into academic jobs. You constantly hear it's happened in places like India – all being bank clerks or professionals. There were a lot of intelligent people in the working class then, who by and large are not there today. They have all been creamed off into sixth forms and professional jobs. At that time I know there were people as simple farm workers who were highly educated – not educated – but highly cultured intelligent people. I didn't find it a problem at the time, nor did the kids, it was never raised.

Secondary modern examinations

From the early 1950s more and more secondary modern schools began to focus on external examinations. This posed insuperable problems for those heads and teachers in secondary moderns who were exploring new modes of curricula such as rural education.

Towards rural studies examinations

As the tripartite system of education gradually emerged in the form of new school buildings and modified curricula, it became clear that rural studies and gardening were only developing in the secondary modern schools. In a questionnaire survey of gardening and rural studies teachers in Kent produced, with three exceptions, the reply from grammar and technical schools of 'subject not taught', whilst in 63 of the 65 secondary modern schools the subject was given an important position in the curriculum (Pritchard, 1957, p. 4).

Rural education having been decimated as a concept within the increasingly exam-conscious secondary moderns it now became clear that the successor subject of rural studies faced major problems. Writing in 1957, Mervyn Pritchard described the situation in this way:

There appears to be two extremes of thought in secondary modern schools:

1   a concentration on external examinations;
2   those who won't have them at any price.

In those schools where the brighter pupils are examined it is unusual to find Rural Science as one of the subjects taken and as the pupils concentrate more and more narrowly on their examination subjects it is unusual to find Rural Science used as a social subject such as craft, art or music may be. 'Even where pupils are not examined there appears to be a concentration of the teaching of the subject in streams of classes of duller children' (HATGRS survey in 1957).

The concern of rural studies teachers at the deteriorating status and position of their subject led to a variety of responses in the latter part of the 1950s. Mervyn Pritchard exhorted: 'as often as possible the Rural Studies Teacher should mix with his colleagues, even if he has to kick off muddy gum boots to drink his cup of tea. Much useful interchange of knowledge and information is carried out among the staffroom gossip. Informal discussion of school policy can be helped along judiciously by the Rural Science Teacher. Frequent contact can convince our colleagues of one's normality and value' (Pritchard, 1957, p. 5). Apart from such exhortations some teachers were concerned to develop a 'Philosophy of Rural Studies'. In 1954 Carson and Colton produced a paper which appeared in the Kent Association Journal. And later in 1957, in the Lincolnshire 'Rural Science News'. It was a systematic attempt to think through a subject philosophy, a first, embryonic attempt to define a subject, and one equipped with a contemporary rationale. They argued:

> For this study to justify its inclusion in the school curriculum it must be shown to play a vital part in developing a fully educated citizen who is aware in his heart of his kinship with the rest of life and yet realised the unique qualities of the human spirit.
>
> (*Rural Science News*, 1957)

Carson and Colton were editors of the Kent Association of Teachers of Gardening and Rural Science Journal. The 'Rural Science' appendage was added at Carson's insistence when the Association was formed in 1949. The Association was pre-dated by an ephemeral association of rural science teachers in 1925, and by a small association in Nottingham founded in 1940, and the Manchester Teachers' Gardening Circle founded in 1941.

By 1954 the Kent Journal was beginning to define a philosophy for rural studies and soon after claimed, 'this Association has constantly sought parity of esteem with the rest of the curriculum for all rural studies' (*Kent Journal*, 1954).

At the same time new rural studies associations were forming in other counties, normally to pursue the aims expressed in the Kent Journal. By now rural studies was a specialised subject of very low status, literally fighting for its existence in the exam-conscious secondary modern schools. In 1960 the County subject association banded together to form a National Rural Studies Association with its own journal. The 1961 Journal stated in 'The Constitution':

> The aim of this association shall be 'to develop and co-ordinate Rural Studies'. Rural Studies includes Nature Study, Natural History pursuits of all kinds, the study of farming and the activities of the countryside, as taught in primary and secondary schools. Rural Studies should be regarded as an art, a science and a craft; a subject as well as a method of teaching.
>
> (*National Rural Studies Association Journal*, 1961)

The Association soon became involved in promoting examinations in rural studies. They initiated a pilot CSE (Certificate of Secondary Education an examination aimed at Secondary modern schools) project and although many practising teachers complained at the inappropriateness of written examinations a range of new CSE's in Rural Studies were duly promoted.

1954–58 Secondary modern certification (age 34–38)

In 1953 the headmaster at Wrotham who had so strongly promoted rural education left; his successor was more examination conscious. Johnson began to look for a new job and in the Spring term of 1954 noticed a post at Royston in Hertfordshire where a teacher was required to start an ambitious rural studies programme. On the interviewing panel was a rural studies adviser, Geoff Whitby (he was, in fact, the first rural studies adviser and was steeped in the concept of rural education in which Herfordshire had long been a pioneer):

> Whitby asked me about rural education and I described what I'd been doing in Kent, and I could see at once that I'd got the job. I should guess he's never met anyone else who had done this sort of thing. The Head saw it differently. This was very interesting. He didn't see it as rural education in that sense because he was already thinking ahead to raising the standards of this school to what could eventually be CSE. None of this existed but he was thinking in terms of this. Although I understood when I got there I could have the same set up as in Kent, with three top classes and I could have anyone who wanted to volunteer for the subject, it never in fact worked out. The classes were streamed; I only ever got the lower of the three streams. While at first I could do what I liked with that bottom stream, and I did the same sort of thing as in Kent, over the next few years this was whittled away from me, and more spe-cialism invaded the curriculum and these kids eventually spent practically no time in running the farm. Whereas in Kent they did the whole operation of running the farm in lesson time, in Herts they had to do it before school. So it never really got going.
>   The problems were in fact both internal and external to the school. Inside the school there was streaming and a belief that it was vocational training for agriculture. Outside the school the community remained hostile to the whole concept, partly a result of the very different social structure of Hertfordshire compared with Kent. In Kent farm workers were better paid and treated and respected because their job was skilled.
>   In Hertfordshire there was a long history of poverty on the land going back to Arthur Young's travels. If you meet any of the farm workers in this area there are tales of great poverty even in this day. So there was a feeling that going on the land here was nothing but condemnation...nothing but plough-ing and sowing, no other skills, very little mixed farming, no orchards.

But beyond the different social structure of the new locality Johnson had moved towards an awareness that 'society was changing'.

> The concern was that selection was important, children were getting into grammar schools and other people were beginning to see what was happening to them. Therefore they wanted their children to do as well academically as possible in order to get better jobs...certainly the atmosphere was different.

Johnson's disillusionment with his new school grew as he realised he would only ever be given the problem children and those stigmatised as less able. In 1956, his third year, he had a series of interviews with the head:

> I had arguments with Young. I made my case and he was adamant that this was not what was required today. They gave a school-leaving certificate, and they required qualifications in other things. In my opinion he never really saw what I was up to.

At the time he felt a deep sense of professional betrayal. After all in Kent he had seen a working model of rural education as an integrated 'eminently satisfactory situation of mixed ability type'. Again and again in his retirement interviews he returns to this critical point when as he puts it 'my dream faded', 'my vision of educating children faltered'. However, at the time, although disappointed there were other goals:

> My ambition was to be a head, and I had long talks with Young about how I could get to be a head. It became increasingly obvious to me that as a Rural Studies man I wasn't going to get a look in.

1958–79 Rural studies and environmental studies advisor (age 39–59)

In 1958 Johnson was asked by the Rural Studies adviser who had brought him to Hertfordshire if he would like to take over his job:

> I didn't think twice when Whitby asked. I thought an opening like this, I'll do something good in this. I started off in 1958 with part-time, half my time, and he worked the other half for a year and then he retired, and I got his job. By this time I'd really given up hope of getting rural studies seen in the way I'd taught it in Kent. Then I saw it as a specialist subject which had certain weak links. For the first 2–3 years I did two things; I read all about the rural education tradition in the papers Whitby gave me on his background, etc. At the same time I was visiting the secondary school teachers and stimulated them to get themselves organised to try and get any kids other than the least able, to get them better facilities in their schools. I spent the first 3–4 years with this aim.

At this stage in his life Johnson was enthused by the prospect of using his influence as an adviser to change things. Initially this enthusiasm carried him over the loss of 'hope of getting real rural education' for by now it was clear that, whatever his preference, the specialist subject was taking over:

> IG: What kind of people were they, as you travelled round in 1958–60?
>
> PJ: They were pre-war teachers of gardening who'd come back, and there were people of my own generation living through the war who came into teaching. Gradually then we began to get the post-war younger teacher coming in and the colleges who specialised in rural studies from the 60s onwards. Before that they were the older chaps generally.
>
> IG: So what did you decide would be your strategy? By then you were involved in the national association?
>
> PJ: No, we started the national association in 1960. I called the first meeting in the name of the Herts Association. We knew there were various other groups around the country. I have no idea how we found that out.
>
> IG: What was the thinking behind calling this meeting?
>
> PJ: It was quite definitely to raise the standard of rural studies as a subject and the status of it because we decide that until it was raised nationally we wouldn't be able to do much in Herts. 'If you're not given a proper classroom refuse to teach this subject in any old place, and as adviser call me in', was what I told my teachers, and I will say 'this chap is entitled to a classroom just the same as anyone else'. To some heads this was a bit of a shock. They'd never been faced with this problem. If it rained

they all just sat in the bicycle shed. We had Broad who was sympathetic to ideas...we produced that report, and as a result every school from 1960 onwards where I was adviser, we got minimal provisions called the rural studies unit in Herts.

From this point on Johnson became a leading campaigner for rural studies as a subject – self-promotion and subject promotion became finally and inextricably linked. This pursuit of subject promotion over time was reflected upon in an article he wrote in 1963 for the Rural Studies Association Journal. It begins with the polarity that teachers actually have two duties 'one to their classes and one the educational climate in which they worked'. It was argued that the subject had to respond to these 'changing climates' to ensure influence and resources:

> During the next few years considerable changes are likely both in the framework of our school system and in the curricula within school if rural studies is to retain its influence, then those teachers who believe in the subject must be clear about their aims and ready to adapt their methods to new conditions.

He concluded:

> Thus the climate is changing continually, now perhaps more rapidly than ever before. But rural studies teachers are used to British weather. Have we not all got a lesson up our sleeves for the sudden downpour or the unexpected fine day? Within the educational climate too, we are ready with new ideas to meet whatever the weather has in store!
> (*National Rural Studies Association Journal*, 1963)

In fact what the weather had in store at this time was the new Beloe CSE examinations for secondary moderns. Rural Studies became one of the pilot studies for the new examination and despite a range of evidence that it was ill-suited to written examination, subject opportunism demanded a positive response to the changing climate. As a result CSE's in Rural Studies were promoted wherever possible. This embracing of examinations was pursued obsessively when the comprehensive system was launched. Rural Studies then, Johnson thought, had to 'adapt or perish'. Again the response was opportunistic. Rural Studies was changed into Environmental Studies, and a new 'A' level in the subject was launched for as Johnson says 'this way, you got more money, better kids, better careers'.

The alternative vision: a retrospect

Although during the period when he was building his career Johnson embraced the notion of his subject as an examinable specialism, in later years doubts surfaced. On his retirement he stated quite clearly that it was the embrace of the specialist curriculum and subject examination that killed his educational vision. 'This was when my dream began to fade, I was not aware of it at the time.' For him now his alternative vision, his dream, is all-powerful:

> My alternative vision was that in more general terms and I'm still convinced this is true, a lot of kids don't learn through paper and pencil and that we do far too much of this. A lot of kids could achieve success and use all the mental skills that we talk about in the classroom such as analysing and comparing through

physical activities. Through such things as building the school farm, looking after animals. I used to talk about the fact that the real reason for keeping the farm wasn't to teach farm work. With the farm it was a completely renewing set of problems and the fact it was a farm was incidental. You were thinking in educational terms of process with these kids. That's the sort of dream I was well aware of giving up, and talked about it a number of times. I always felt dissatisfied since and I've met many teachers who have come across the same realisation, not in quite such explicit terms as they'd never had the chance of doing it, whereas I had. I meet them now in schools...a teacher whom I met today knew that the teaching she was doing with these less able girls was not the right way to educate the girls, but what was the right way she couldn't think. Well, I know what is the right way. The right way is the sort of thing we were doing in '47 whether it's using the farm or whatever. The attitude is that you use your hands. You don't always sit at a desk necessarily. You are facing problems of a three-dimensional kind at an adult level. You use terms like man's problems; and this is no longer feasible in a school situation. I couldn't tell that girl today to do that sort of thing; she wouldn't succeed at all.

To my mind one of the tragedies of education in my life, and I would call this the secondary modern ethos, maybe it's one of many, but I don't know, was that the best thing that secondary moderns did was to promote this idea that it's just as good to be a skilled craftsman as, say, a white collar worker, and that you get as much satisfaction and challenge from it at your own level. This was what was really behind what we were doing in Kent. The fact that this is no longer recognised in schools at all is I think responsible for the problems we have in school today, both academically with the less able and with the anti-school group and the apathetic group.

Conclusion

This episode in a subject teacher's life illustrates the way that the collection of life histories and elucidation of the historical context can combine.

Above all the strength of beginning curriculum research from life history data is that *from the outset* the work is firmly focussed on the working lives of practitioners. Other researchers have commented in similar manner on the peculiar force of this kind of data as the initial strategy in a research programme:

> When one conducts a life history interview the findings become alive in terms of historical processes and structural constraints. People do not wander round the world in a timeless, structureless limbo. They themselves acknowledge the importance of historical factors and structural constraints (although of course, they would not use such pompous language). The analysis of life histories actually pushes one first of all to the problems of constraints bearing down upon the construction of any one life...
>
> (Faraday and Plummer, 1979, p. 780)

In articulating their response to historical factors and structural constraints life story tellers provide us with sensitising devices for the analysis of these constraints and the manner in which they are experienced. We are alerted to historical legacies and structural constraints and can pursue understanding of aspects such as, in the instance given, strategies for self and subject promotion and career construction.

Certainly in the life of Patrick Johnson we gain insights into him wrestling with imperatives in the social structure. From his early professional life he develops a vision of how schools might be, this vision is challenged and defeated as subject specialism and examinations invade the early secondary modern schools; we see how self-promotion and subject promotion interrelate; and we see now one educational ideology is initially replaced by another as the teacher's career is constructed; the ideological renunciation only follows his retirement at the end of his career. Our attention is therefore left on the link between the structuring of material interests, strategies for career aggrandisement and the acceptance of particular educational ideologies.

A combination of life histories and curriculum histories should then offer an antidote to the depersonalised, historical accounts of schooling to which we are only too accustomed. Above all we gain insights into individuals coming to terms with imperatives in the social structure. From the collection of a range of life stories located in historical context we can discern what is general within a range of individual studies. We can thereby develop our understanding from a base that is clearly grounded within personal biography and perception.

Critical questions

Here I have taken the view that a combination of life history and curriculum history data can both broaden and deepen our accounts of schooling and curriculum. But, a range of critical questions remain. Certain problems are specific to life history data, others specific to curriculum history and a further set of questions arise from the relationship between the two.

The first range of problems turns on the relationship between life stories as told by the subjects themselves, retrospectively recounting episodes in their life, and life histories where those stories are supplemented by other data and placed in their historical context. If we seek a full retrospective life story then we come at the stage Vonnegut has described so well in his most recent novel. He argues that sociologists have ignored the fact that:

> We all see our lives as stories... If a person survives an ordinary span of sixty years or more, there is every chance that his or her life as a shapely story has ended; and all that is to be experienced is epilogue. Life is not over, but the story is.
>
> (Glendening, 1983, p. 47)

But John Mortimer has summarised the problems of writing an autobiography at this stage. In the last paragraph he says: 'That is how it was, a part of life seen from a point of view. Much more happened that I cannot tell or remember. To others it would be, I am quite sure, a different story' (Mortimer, 1983, p. 256).

At root the problem is to retain and defend the authenticity of the participant's account. But to do this, such problems of lapsed memory or partial or selective recall must be faced. We only get a part of the picture, to be sure a vital part, but we need to push for more of the picture, more bits of the jigsaw.

In part the problem is addressed by triangulation through collecting a range of life stories, and by developing an associated documentary history of the context. But the development of research which moves across a range from life stories through to curriculum history concentrates the focus of the work; arguably in a way which challenges the authenticity of the accounts and certainly in ways which effect the relationship between the life story teller and the researcher. By moving from life story to curriculum history control is passing irrevocably to the researcher. In addition the life story data is being concentrated onto particular issues and themes. In this case the linkage with the history of a subject could well have led, in spite of the range of life stories gathered, to an over-concentration on the career conscious, upwardly mobile teachers. Once again there is the danger of an over-emphasis on the unrepresentative.

I explore later the relationship of the work to theory. But in this respect it must be noted that as with life histories, so with curriculum histories, the specificity of their focus can act against their capacity for generalisation.

A further question is the nature of interpretation, the role of the commentary. As Bertaux has reminded us moving from the personal life story to wider histories involves considerable questions of methodological reliability: 'What is really at stake is the relationship between the sociologist and the people who make his work possible by accepting to be interviewed on their life experiences' (Bertaux, 1981, p. 9). This question if deeply significant both at the ethical and procedural level.

The ethical and procedural questions relate closely to the relationship between life storyteller and researcher and the potential for mutuality. This is further related to the question of 'audience'. If the earlier contention that life story data placed in a historical context offers the opportunity for research which 'engages' teachers is correct then the prospects for mutuality are enhanced. In developing life histories teachers could be involved in work which would illuminate and feed back into the conditions and understandings of their working lives.

References

Bertaux, D., 1981, *Biography and Society: The Life History Approach in the Social Sciences* (Beverley Hills, CA: Sage).

Denzin, N.K., 1970, *The Research Act* (Chicago, IL: Aldine).

Faraday, A. and Plummer, K., 1979, Doing Life Histories. *Sociological Review*, 27(4).

Gibberd, K., 1962, *No Place Like School* (London: Michael Joseph).

Glass, D.V., 1971, Education and Social Change in Modern England. In R. Hooper (ed.), *The Curriculum: Context, Design and Development* (Edinburgh: Oliver and Boyd).

Glendening, Victoria, 1983, Slaughterhouse Epilogue. *Sunday Times*, 20 February.

Goodson, I., 1977, Evaluation and Evolution. In Nigel Norris (ed.), *Theory in Practice* (Safari Project, Centre for Applied Research in Education, University of East Anglia, Norwich).

Goodson, I., 1983, *Curriculum Conflict 1895–1975*. Unpublished, D.Phil. Sussex 1980 and *School Subjects and Curriculum Change – Case Studies in the Social History of Curriculum* (London: Croom Helm).

Hammersley, M. and Woods, P., 1976, Blumer, H., quoted in *The Process of Schooling* (London: Routledge and Kegan Paul), p. 3.

Herfordshire Association of Teachers of Gardening and Rural Subjects. A survey in 1957. *Kent Journal*, (4)1954.

Kerr, J., 1971, The Problem of Curriculum Reform. In R. Hooper (ed.), *The Curriculum: Context, Design and Development* (Edinburgh: Oliver and Boyd).

Lacey, C., 1977, *The Socialization of Teachers* (London: Methuen).

Mortimer, John, 1983, *Clinging to the Wreckage* (London: Penguin).

National Rural Studies Association Journal, 1961, 5.

National Rural Studies Association Journal, 1963, The Changing Climate, 14–15.

Nisbet, Robert A., 1971, Social Change and History (1969). In J.R. Wesker (ed.), Curriculum Change and Crisis. *British Journal of Educational Studies*, 3 (October).

Parlett, M. and Hamilton, D., 1972, *Evaluation as Illumination: A New Approach to the Study of Innovatory Programs*. Occasional paper 9, Edinburgh Centre for Research in Educational Sciences.

Pritchard, M., 1957, The Rural Science Teacher in the School Society. *Journal of the Hertfordshire Association of Gardening and Rural Subjects*, (2) September 4.

Rural Science News, 1957, 10(1) (January).

Walker, R., 1974, The Conduct of Educational Case Study. In Nigel Norris (ed.), *Innovation, Evolution, Research and the Problem of Control: Some Interim Papers* (Safari Project, Centre for Applied Research in Education, University of East Anglia, Norwich).

Waring, M., 1975, *Aspects of the Dynamics of Curriculum Reform in Secondary School Science*, PhD, University of London.

Waring, M., 1979, *Social Pressures and Curriculum Innovation: A Study of the Nuffield Foundation Science Teaching Project* (London: Methuen).

Williams, R., 1965, *The Long Revolution* (London: Pelican).

Woods, Peter or Pollard, Andrew, 1982, A Model of Coping Strategies. *British Journal of Sociology of Education*, 3(1).

Young, M.F.D., 1971, Curriculum as Socially Organised Knowledge. In M.F.D. Young (ed.), *Knowledge and Control: New Directions for the Sociology of Education* (London: Collier MacMillan).

CHAPTER 12

THE STORY OF LIFE HISTORY

Identity: An International Journal of Theory and Research,
2001, 1(2): 129–142

Searching for the origins of the life history method, we found that the first life histories, in the form of autobiographies of Native American chiefs, were collected by anthropologists at the beginning of the century (e.g. Barrett, 1906; Radin, 1920). Since then, sociologists and other scholars working in the humanities have increasingly adopted the approach, although its popularity and acceptance as a research strategy has tended to wax and wane. Life history and other biographical and narrative approaches are now widely seen as having a great deal to offer, and we argue that they should be employed in identity research. In examining their scholarly fate, however, it is necessary to scrutinize their use to date within sociology, which has been a major battleground in their evolution.

For sociologists, the main landmark in the development of life history methods came in the 1920s, following the publication of Thomas and Znaniecki's (1918–20) mammoth study, *The Polish Peasant in Europe and America*. In exploring the experience of Polish peasants migrating to the United States, Thomas and Znaniecki relied mainly on migrants' autobiographical accounts, alongside extant diaries and letters. For these authors, life histories were the data par excellence of the social scientist, and they presented a strident case for using life histories above all other methods:

> In analyzing the experiences and attitudes of an individual, we always reach data and elementary facts which are exclusively limited to this individual's personality, but can be treated as mere incidences of more or less general classes of data or facts, and can thus be used for the determination of laws of social becoming. Whether we draw our materials for sociological analysis from detailed life records of concrete individuals or from the observation of mass phenomena, the problems of sociological analysis are the same. But even when we are searching for abstract laws, life records, as complete as possible, constitute the perfect type of sociological material, and if social science has to use other materials at all it is only because of the practical difficulty of obtaining at the moment a sufficient number of such records to cover the totality of sociological problems, and of the enormous amount of work demanded for an adequate analysis of all the personal materials necessary to characterize the life of a social group. If we are forced to use mass phenomena as material, or any kind of happenings taken without regard to the life histories of the individuals who participated, it is a defect, not an advantage, of our present sociological method.
>
> (pp. 1831–1833)

Thomas and Znaniecki's (1918–20) pioneering work established the life history as a bona fide research device. (Although as Miller (2000), pointed out, its foundations can be seen in the notion of historicism as expressed by Wilhelm Dilthey.) The prominent position of the life history was further consolidated by the flourishing tradition of sociological research stimulated at Chicago, particularly by Robert Park.

In the range of studies of city life completed under Park, the life history method was strongly in evidence: *The Gang* (Thrasher, 1928), *The Gold Coast and the Slum* (Zorbaugh, 1929), *The Hobo* (Anderson, 1923), and *The Ghetto* (Wirth, 1928). However, perhaps the zenith was reached in the 1930s with publications such as Shaw's (1930) account of a mugger, *The Jack-Roller*, and Sutherland's *The Professional Thief* (Cornwell and Sutherland, 1937). Becker's (1970) comments on Shaw's study underline one of the major strengths of the life history method:

> By providing this kind of voice from a culture and situation that are ordinarily not known to intellectuals generally and to sociologists in particular, The Jack Roller enables us to improve our theories at the most profound level: by putting ourselves in Stanley's skin, we can feel and become aware of the deep biases about such people that ordinarily permeate our thinking and shape the kinds of problems we investigate. By truly entering into Stanley's life, we can begin to see what we take for granted (and ought not to) in designing our research – what kinds of assumptions about delinquents, slums and Poles are embedded in the way we set the questions we study.
>
> (p. 71)

Becker's (1970) argument went to the heart of the appeal of life history methods at their best, for life history data disrupt the normal assumptions of what is known by intellectuals in general and sociologists in particular. Conducted successfully, the life history forces a confrontation with other people's subjective perceptions. This confrontation can be avoided, and so often is avoided in many other social scientific methods: one only has to think of the common rush to the quantitative indicator or theoretical construct, to the statistical table or the ideal type. This sidesteps the messy confrontation with human subjectivity, which we believe should comprise the heartland of the sociological enterprise. Behind or coterminous with this methodological sidestep, there is often a profound substantive and political sidestep. In the avoidance of human subjectivity, quantitative assessment and theoretical commentaries can so easily service powerful constituencies within the social and economic order. This tendency to favour and support existing power structures is always a potential problem in social science.

From the statement about "putting ourselves in Stanley's skin," Becker (1970) went on to assert that Stanley's story offered the possibility "to begin to ask questions about delinquency from the point of view of the delinquent" (p. 71). From this it followed that questions will be asked, not from the point of view of the powerful actors but rather from the perspective of those who are acted on in professional transactions. These are some important reasons why, beyond the issues of methodological debate, life history methods might be unpopular in some quarters. Life history, by its nature, asserts and insists that power should listen to the people it claims to serve, as Becker (1970) noted:

> If we take Stanley seriously, as his story must impel us to do, we might well raise a series of questions that have been relatively little studied – questions about

the people who deal with delinquents, the tactics they use, their suppositions about the world, and the constraints and pressures they are subject to.

(p. 71)

However, this contention should be read in the light of Shaw's (1930) own "early warning" in his preface, where he cautioned the reader against drawing conclusions about general causes of delinquency on the basis of a single case record. One of the best early attempts to analyze the methodological base of the life history method was Dollard's (1949) *Criteria for the Life History*. Foreshadowing Becker, he argued that "detailed studies of the lives of individuals will reveal new perspectives on the culture as a whole which are not accessible when one remains on the formal cross sectional plane of observation" (p. 4). Dollard's arguments have a somewhat familiar ring, perhaps reflecting the influence of George Herbert Mead. He noted that:

> as soon as we take the post of observer on the cultural level the individual is lost in the crowd and our concepts never lead us back to him. After we have 'gone cultural' we experience the person as a fragment of a (derived) culture pattern, as a marionette dancing on the strings of (reified) culture forms.

(p. 5)

In contrast to this, the life historian "can see his [*sic*] life history subject as a link in a chain of social transmission" (Dollard, 1949, p. 5). This linkage should ensure that life history methods will ameliorate the 'presentism' that exists in so much sociological theory and a good deal of symbolic inter-actionism. Dollard described this linkage between historical past, present, and future:

> There were links before him from which he acquired his present culture. Other links will follow him to which he will pass on the current of tradition. The life history attempts to describe a unit in that process: it is a study of one of the strands of a complicated collective life which has historical continuity.

(p. 15)

Dollard (1949) was especially good, although perhaps unfashionably polemical, in his discussion of the tension between what might be called the cultural legacy, the weight of collective tradition and expectation, and the individual's unique history and capacity for interpretation and action. By focusing on this tension, Dollard argued, the life history offers a way of exploring the relationship between the culture, the social structure, and individual lives. Thus, Dollard believed that in the best life history work:

> we must constantly keep in mind the situation both as defined by others and by the subject, such a history will not only define both versions but let us see clearly the pressure of the formal situation and the force of the inner private definition of the situation.

(p. 32)

Dollard (1949) saw this resolution, or the attempt to address a common tension, as valuable because "whenever we encounter difference between our official or average or cultural expectation of action in a 'situation' and the actual conduct of the person this indicates the presence of a private interpretation" (p. 32).

In fact, Dollard (1949) was writing sometime after a decline set in for life history methods (an unfortunate side effect of which is that Dollard's work is not as well known as it should be). After reaching its peak in the 1930s, the life history approach fell from grace and was largely abandoned by social scientists. At first this was because the increasingly powerful advocacy of statistical methods gained a growing number of adherents among sociologists but perhaps also because, among ethnographically inclined sociologists, more emphasis came to be placed on situation than on biography as the basis for understanding human behavior.

In the 1970s, something of a "minor resurgence" (Plummer, 1990) was observed, particularly and significantly, at first, among deviancy sociologists. Thus, there were studies of a transsexual (Bogdan, 1974), a professional fence (Klockars, 1975), and once again, with a fine sense of history following Shaw's 1930 study, a professional thief (Chambliss, 1972).

Although life history methods have long been popular with journalists-cum-sociologists like Studs Terkel in the United States, Jeremy Seabrook and Ronald Blythe in the United Kingdom, and a growing band of 'oral historians' (Thompson, 1978, 1988), Bertaux's (1981) collection, *Biography and Society*, marked a significant step in the academic rehabilitation of the approach. This book was closely followed by Plummer's (1983, revised in 2000) important *Documents of Life*. Tierney's (1998) special issue of *Qualitative Inquiry* is also of interest.

Feminist researchers have been particularly vocal in their support of the approach, mainly due to the way in which it can be used to give expression to, and in celebration of, hidden or 'silenced' lives (cf. McLaughlin and Tierney, 1993) – lives lived privately and without public accomplishment, the sorts of lives most women (and, it has to be said, most men) live (cf. Gluck and Patai, 1991; Middleton, 1997; Munro, 1998; Personal Narratives Group, 1989; Sorrell and Montgomery, 2001; Stanley, 1990, 1992; Weiler and Middleton, 1999). Similarly, those who research issues and aspects of sexuality, notably Plummer (1995) and Sparkes (1994), also have made considerable use of the approach.

Within the field of educational studies, working with teachers and pupils who are, again, arguably marginal in terms of social power, life history has been seen as particularly useful and appropriate because, as Bullough (1998) pointed out, "public and private cannot be separated in teaching. The person comes through when teaching" (pp. 20–21). Life history does not ask for such separation: Indeed, it demands holism. The growing number of life history studies dealing with educational topics is testimony to this (e.g. Ball and Goodson, 1985; Casey, 1993; Erben, 1998; Goodson, 1992; Goodson and Hargreaves, 1996; Kridel, 1998; Middleton, 1993; Osler, 1997; Sikes, 1997; Sikes *et al.*, 1985).

Among these scholars, albeit in marginal or fragmented groups, a debate is underway that promises a thorough re-examination of the potential of life history methods. Before considering the contemporary appeal of the life history method, however, it is important to discover why it was eclipsed for so long by social theory, social survey, and participant observation. In this examination, we distinguish fundamental methodological stumbling blocks from professional, micro-political, and personal reasons for the decline of life history work. Often the latter are far more important than participants in the methodological 'paradigm wars' acknowledge.

Reasons for the decline of the life history in early sociological study

By 1966, Becker (1970) was able to summarize the fate of the life history method among American sociologists, stating that "given the variety of scientific uses to which the life history may be put, one must wonder at the relative neglect into which it has fallen" (pp. 71–72).

Becker (1970) noted that sociologists have never given up life histories altogether, but they have not made it one of their standard research tools. The general pattern was, and by and large continues to be, that "they know of life history studies and assign them for their students to read. But they do not ordinarily think of gathering life history documents or of making the technique part of their research approach" (pp. 71–72).

The reasons for the decline of life history methods are partly specific to the Chicago School. From the late 1920s, life histories came increasingly under fire as the debate within the department between the virtues of case study (and life histories) and statistical techniques intensified. Faris (1967), in his study of the Chicago School, recorded a landmark within this debate:

> To test this issue, Stouffer had hundreds of students write autobiographies instructing them to include everything in their life experiences relating to school usage and the prohibition law. Each of these autobiographies was read by a panel of persons presumed to be qualified in life history research, and for each subject the reader indicated on a scaled line the position of the subject's attitude regarding prohibition. Inter reader agreement was found to be satisfactory. Each of the same subjects had also filled out a questionnaire that formed a scale of the Thurstone type. The close agreement of the scale measurement of each subject's attitude with the reader's estimate of the life history indicated that, as far as the scale score was concerned, nothing was gained by the far more lengthy and laborious process of writing and judging a life history.
>
> (pp. 114–115)[1]

Even within Chicago School case study work, use of the life history declined against other ethnographic devices, notably participant observation. One element of the explanation of this may lie in the orientations of Blumer and Hughes. These two sociologists provide a bridge between the Chicago School of the 1920s and 1930s and those Matza has termed the neo-Chicagoans, such as Becker (1970).

Blumer's symbolic inter-actionism placed primary emphasis on process and situation, whereas explanations in terms of biography, like those in terms of social structural forces, were regarded with considerable suspicion. Hughes's comparative approach to the study of occupations may have tended to limit interest in biography in favor of a concern with the typical problems faced by occupational practitioners and the strategies they adopt for dealing with them. An additional factor that hastened the decline of the methodological eclecticism of Chicago sociology in which the life history played a central role was the decline of Chicago itself as a dominant centre for sociological studies.

The fate of life history methods has been inextricably linked to the historical emergence of sociology as a discipline. Hence, the methodological weaknesses of the approach were set against the need to develop abstract theory. When sociology was highly concerned with providing detailed accounts of specific communities, institutions, or organizations, such weaknesses were clearly of less account. However, in the life history of sociology, the pervasive drift of academic disciplines toward abstract theory has been irresistible; in this evolutionary imperative it is not difficult to discern the desire of sociologists to gain parity of esteem with other academic disciplines. The resulting pattern of mainstream sociology meant that sociologists came to pursue "data formulated in the abstract categories of their own theories rather than in the categories that seemed most relevant to the people they studied" (Becker, 1970, p. 72).

Along with the move toward abstract academic theory, sociological method became more professional. Essentially, this led toward a model of single study research, defined by Becker (1970) in this way:

> I use the term to refer to research projects that are conceived of as self-sufficient and self-contained, which provide all the evidence one needs to accept or reject the conclusions they proffer. The single study is integrated with the main body of knowledge in the following way: it derives its hypotheses from an inspection of what is already known: then, after the research is completed, if those hypotheses have been demonstrated, they are added to the wall of what is already scientifically known and used as the basis for further studies. The important point is that the researcher's hypothesis is either proved or disproved on the basis of what he has discovered in doing that one piece of research.
>
> (p. 72)

The imperative toward this pattern of sociological research can be clearly evidenced in the traditions and organizational format of emergent professional sociology. The PhD student must define and test a hypothesis; the journal article must test the author's own or other academics' hypotheses; the research project or programme must state the generalizable aims and locate the burden of what has to be proved. However, this dominant experimental model, so fruitful in analogies with other sciences and, hence, so crucial in legitimating sociology as a full-fledged academic discipline, led to the neglect of sociology's full range of methodology and data sources.

It has led people to ignore the other functions of research and particularly to ignore the contribution made by one study to an overall research enterprise even when the study, considered in isolation, produced no definitive results of its own. Because, by these criteria, the life history did not produce definitive results, people have been at a loss to make anything of it and by and large have declined to invest the time and effort necessary to acquire life history documents (Becker, 1970, p. 73).

Becker (1970) ended by holding out the hope that sociologists would, in the future, develop a "further understanding of the complexity of the scientific enterprise" (p. 73); that this would rehabilitate the life history method and lead to a new range of life history documents as generative as those produced by the Chicago sociologists in the 1920s and 1930s.

In the period following Becker's strictures in 1970, sociology was subject to a number of new directions that sought to re-embrace some of the elements lost in the positivist, theory-testing models (Cuff and Payne, 1979; Morris, 1977). One new direction that clearly stressed biography, the phenomenological sociology of Berger and Luckmann (Berger, 1963; Berger and Luckmann, 1967), actually resulted in little empirical work.

Hence, research in interpretive sociology has displayed a heavy emphasis on situation under the influence of inter-actionism and ethno-methodology. The paradox is that these new directions in sociology moved away from the positivist model directly to situation and occasion; as a result, life history and biography have tended to remain at the sidelines of the sociological enterprise. For instance, inter-actionist studies have focused on the perspectives and definitions emerging among groups of actors in particular situations, the backdrop to this presented as a somewhat monolithic structural or cultural legacy that constrains, in a rather disconnected manner, the actors' potentialities. In overreacting to more deterministic models, this situational emphasis most commonly fails to make any connection with historical process. Thus, inter-actionists retained their interest in the meaning objects had for actors, but these meanings increasingly came to be seen as collectively generated to deal with specific situations, rather than as the product of individual or even collective biography.

Viewing sociology's evolution over half a century or so provides a number of insights into the life history method. First, as sociologists began to take seriously their social scientific pursuit of generalizable facts and the development of abstract theory, life history work came to be seen as having serious methodological flaws. In addition, because life history studies often appeared to be only "telling tales," these methodological reservations were enhanced by the generally low status of this as an academic or scientific exercise. Paradoxically, even when antidotes to the experimental model of sociology developed, these took the form of inter-actionism and ethno-methodology, both of which stressed situation and occasion rather than biography and background. Moreover, because these new directions had status problems of their own, life history work was unattractive on this count as well. At the conference where Goodson's (1983) early work on life history was originally delivered as a seminar paper, a classroom inter-actionist rejected the exhortation to consider life history work by saying "we should not suggest new methodologies of this sort because of the problem of our academic careers. Christ! Ethnography is low status enough as it is."

Set against the life history of the aspirant academic, keen to make a career in the academy as it is or as it has been shaped and ordered, we clearly see the unattractiveness of the life history method at particular stages in the evolution of sociology. However, by the 1980s, matters were beginning to change markedly in ways that have led to a re-embracing of life history methods.

From modernism to postmodernism

Under modernism, life history languished because it persistently failed the "objectivity tests": numbers were not collected and statistical aggregation was not produced and because studies were not judged to be representative or exemplary, contributions to theory remained parsimonious. In the historical aspiration to be a social science, life history failed its membership test.

However, as Harvey (1989) and others documented, the "condition of postmodernity" provides both new dilemmas and new directions. In some ways, the new possibilities invert the previous deficits that were perceived in life history work. In moving from objectivities to subjectivities, the way is open for new prospects for life history work and, as a result, a range of new studies have begun to appear (cf. Denzin and Lincoln, 1994, 2000). As is often the case, educational studies have been slow to follow new directions, but recently new work has begun to emerge.

Life history work has accompanied the turn to post-modernism and post-structuralism, particularly as evidenced in sociological studies, gender studies, cultural studies, literacy theory, and even psychology. Such work facilitates the move away from modernist master narratives, which are viewed as social productions of the Enlightenment Project. Alongside this move, the notion of a singular, knowable, essential self is judged as part of the social production of individualism, linked to argentic selves in pursuit of progress, knowingness, and emancipation.

Assumptions of linearity of chronological time lines and story lines are challenged in favour of more multiple, disrupted notions of subjectivity.

Foucault's work, for instance, focused sociological attention on the way in which institutions such as hospitals and prisons regulate and constitute our subjectivities. Likewise, discourse studies have focused on the role of language in constructing identities in producing textual representations that purport to capture the essential selves of others (Shotter and Gergen, 1989).

These new syntagmas in sociological work have led to a revival in the use of life history work:

> The current focus on acknowledging the subjective, multiple and partial nature of human experience has resulted in a revival of life history methodology. What were previously criticisms of life history, its lack of representativeness and its subjective nature, are now its greatest strength.
>
> (Munro, 1998, p. 8)

Yet, the post-modern concern with disrupting constructed selves and stories is itself not without difficulty, as Munro (1998) reflectively noted:

> In collecting the life histories of women teachers I find myself situated in a paradoxical position. I know that I cannot "collect" a life. Narrative does not provide a better way to locate truth, but in fact reminds us that all good stories are predicated on the quality of the fiction. We live many lives. Consequently, the life histories in this book do not present neat, chronological accounts of women's lives. This would be an act of betrayal, a distortion, a continued form of "fitting" women's lives into the fictions, categories and cultural norms of patriarchy. Instead, my understanding of a life history suggests that we need to attend to the silences as well as what is said, that we need to attend to how the story is told as well as what is told or not told, and to attend to the tensions and contradictions rather than succumb to the temptations to gloss over these in our desire for "the" story.
>
> (pp. 12–13)

Here, Munro (1998) began to confront the methodological and, indeed, ethical minefield that potentially confronts, confuses, and confounds the researcher and the researched. Fine (1994) wrote of some issues to be confronted:

> Self and Other are knottily entangled. This relationship, as lived between researchers and informants, is typically obscured in social science texts, protecting privilege, securing distance, and laminating the contradictions. Slipping into a contradictory discourse of individualism, persona-logic theorizing, and de-contextualization, we inscribe the Other, strain to white out Self, and refuse to engage the contradictions that litter our texts.
>
> (p. 72)

Fine's (1994) warnings are of inestimable value in approaching life history work. However, in the end we do face the inevitable closure of the text that is produced, or are forever caught in the politics of infinite regress where every closure must be re-opened. For Fine warned that the search for the complete and coherent is a delusion; we produce a snapshot of transgressions in process when we write up life history work. Furthermore, the relationship of the researcher and informant is much concerned in the postmodern predilection for "rejection of the unitary subject for a more complex, multiple and contradictory notion of subjectivity" (Munro, 1998, p. 35).

What does such researcher rejection mean in the face of an informant who narrates his or her life as a search for coherence? For it remains the case that many people narrate their lives according to an aspiration for coherence, for a unitary self. Should we, in Munro's (1998) word, "reject" this social construction of self? Rejection is not the issue here, for life history work should, where possible, refuse to play post-modern God. Life history work is interested in the way people actually do narrate their lives, not in the way they should. Here it seeks to avoid the fate of some post-modern fundamentalists.

Life stories then are the starting point for our work. Such stories are, in their nature, already removed from life experiences – they are lives interpreted and made textual. They represent a partial, selective commentary on lived experience. Freeman (1993) explored some of the issues that are raised here:

> For what we will have before us are not lives themselves, but rather texts of lives, literary artifacts that generally seek to recount in some fashion what these lives were like. In this respect, we will be – we must be – at least one step removed from the lives that we will be exploring: we can only proceed with our interpretive efforts on the basis of what has been written, [or related] by those whose lives they are. The basic situation, I hasten to emphasize, obtains not only in the case of literary texts of the sort we will be examining here, but in the case of interviews and the like along with the observation of human action more generally. Interviews, of the sort that social scientists often gather, are themselves texts, and while they may not have quite as much literary flourish as those we buy in bookstores, they are in their own right literary artifacts, taking the form of words, designed to give shape to some feature of experience. As for the observation of human action, the story is actually much the same: human action, which occurs in time and yields consequences the significance of which frequently extend beyond the immediate situation in which it takes place, is itself a kind of text; it is a constellation of meanings which, not unlike literary texts or interviews, calls forth the process of interpretation (see especially Ricoeur (1981)). In any case, the long and short of this brief excursion into "textuality" is that our primary interpretive takeoff point will not be lives as such but the words used to speak them.
>
> (p. 7)

The rendering of lived experience into a life story is one interpretive layer, but the move to life history adds a second layer and a further interpretation. Goodson (1992) wrote about the distinction between Stage 1, in which the informant relates her or his life story, and Stage 2, in which a life history is constructed employing a new range of interviews and documentary data. The move from life story to life history involves the range of methodologies and ethical issues noted earlier. Moving from personal life stories to life histories involves issues of process and power. As Bertaux (1981) noted, "What is really at stake is the relationship between the sociologist and the people who make his [*sic*] work possible by accepting to be interviewed on their life experiences" (p. 9).

Moving from life story to life history involves a move to account for historical context – a dangerous move, for it offers the researcher considerable colonizing power to locate the life story, with all its inevitable selections, shifts, and silences. Nonetheless, we hold to the need for providing historical contexts for reading life stories.

Dannefer (1992) wrote of the various meanings of context in studying developmental discourse. Here, the concern is to provide communications that cover the social histories and, indeed, social geographies in which life stories are embedded; without contextual commentary on issues of time and space, life stories remain uncoupled from the conditions of their social construction. This, above all, is the argument for life histories rather than life stories.

Although rightly concerned about the colonizing dangers of contextual commentary, even post-structuralist accounts often end up moving from life stories to life histories, and they confront issues surrounding the changing contexts of time and space. For instance, Middleton's early work (1992) on women teachers' lives related a substantive account of one feminist teacher's pedagogy within the specific socio-cultural setting of post-Second World War New Zealand. Likewise, Munro (1998), an avowed feminist post-structuralist, argued that:

> Since this study is concerned with placing the lives of women teachers within a broader historical context, historical data regarding the communities and the time period in which they taught were also collected. Although I am not an educational historian an attempt was made to understand both the local history and broader historical context in which these women lived.
>
> (p. 11)

The distinction between life stories or narratives and life histories is then a crucial one. By providing contextual data, the life stories can be seen in the light of changing patterns of time and space in testimony and action as social constructions.

Conclusions

The move from modernism to postmodernism presages a concern with objectivity moving toward a primary concern with the way subjectivities are constructed. Echoing this move, life history, whose methods failed the objectivity tests under modernism, has once again come into its own. The way is open for exploring new prospects for life history work. Already this exploration is under way in a range of fields from cultural studies to sociology and education, but it is hoped that the rehabilitation will broaden into the major arenas of the humanities such as history itself and psychology.

Note

1   Although the experiment does raise the question of why one would use the life history method simply to measure attitude. No doubt the autobiographies did contain explanations of why the informants' attitudes were of a particular degree. Such information could be valuable for other purposes than attitude measurement and would, moreover, not be accessible by means of a questionnaire.

References

Anderson, N., 1923, *The Hobo* (Chicago, IL: University of Chicago Press).
Ball, S. and Goodson, I. (eds), 1985, *Teachers' Lives and Careers* (New York: Falmer).
Barrett, S., 1906, *Geronimo's Story of his Life: Taken Down and Edited by S.M. Barrett* (New York: Duffield).
Becker, H., 1970, *Sociological Work: Method and Substance* (Chicago, IL: Aldine).
Berger, P., 1963, *Invitation to Sociology* (Garden City, NY: Doubleday).
Berger, P. and Luckmann, T., 1967, *The Social Construction of Reality* (Garden City, NY: Anchor).

Bertaux, D., 1981, *Biography and Society: The Life History Approach in the Social Sciences* (London: Sage).

Bogdan, R., 1974, *Being Different: The Autobiography of Jane Fry* (New York: Wiley).

Bullough, R., 1998, Musings on Life Writings: Biography and Case Study in Teacher Education. In C. Kridel (ed.), *Writing Educational Biography: Explorations in Qualitative Research* (New York: Garland), pp. 19–32.

Casey, K., 1993, *I Answer with my Life: Life Histories of Women Teachers Working for Social Change* (New York: Routledge).

Chambliss, W., 1972, *Boxman: A Professional Thief* (New York: Harper and Row).

Cornwell, C. and Sutherland, E., 1937, *The Professional Thief* (Chicago, IL: University of Chicago Press).

Cuff, E. and Payne, G., 1979, *Perspectives in Sociology* (Boston, MA: Allen and Unwin).

Dannefer, D., 1992, On the Conceptualization of Context in Developmental Discourse: Four Meanings of Context and Their Implications. In D. Featherman, R. Lerner, and M. Perlmutter (eds), *Life-span Development and Behavior*, Vol. 11 (Hillsdale, NJ: Lawrence Erlbaum Associates, Inc), pp. 84–110.

Denzin, N. and Lincoln, Y. (eds), 1994, *Handbook of Qualitative Research* (London: Sage).

Denzin, N. and Lincoln, Y. (eds), 2000, *Handbook of Qualitative Research*, 2nd edn. (Thousand Oaks, CA: Sage).

Dollard, J., 1949, *Criteria for the Life History* (Magnolia, MA: Peter Smith).

Erben, M., 1998, Biography and Research Methods. In M. Erben (ed.), *Biography and Education: A Reader* (London: Falmer), pp. 4–17.

Faris, R., 1967, *Chicago Sociology* (San Francisco, CA: Chandler).

Fine, M., 1994, Working the Hyphens: Reinventing Self and Other in Qualitative Research. In N. Denzin and Y. Lincoln (eds), *Handbook of Qualitative Research* (London: Sage), pp. 70–82.

Freeman, M., 1993, *Rewriting the Self: History, Memory, Narrative* (New York: Routledge).

Gluck, S. and Patai, D. (eds), 1991, *Women's Words: The Feminist Practice of Oral History* (New York: Routledge).

Goodson, I., 1983, Life Histories and Teaching. In M. Hammersley (ed.), *The Ethnography of Schooling* (Driffield, England: Nafferton).

Goodson, I. (ed.), 1992, *Studying Teachers' Lives* (New York: Routledge).

Goodson, I. and Hargreaves, A., 1996, *Teachers' Professional Lives* (London: Falmer).

Harvey, D., 1989, *The Condition of Postmodernity* (London: Blackwell).

Klockars, C., 1975, *The Professional Fence* (London: Tavistock).

Kridel, C. (ed.), 1998, *Writing Educational Biography: Explorations in Qualitative Research* (New York: Garland).

McLaughlin, D. and Tierney, W. (eds), 1993, *Naming Silent Lives: Personal Narratives and Processes of Educational Change* (New York: Routledge).

Middleton, S., 1992, Developing a Radical Pedagogy: Autobiography of a New Zealand Sociologist of Women's Education. In I. Goodson (ed.), *Studying Teachers' Lives* (New York: Routledge), pp. 18–50.

Middleton, S., 1993, *Educating Feminists: Life Histories and Pedagogy* (New York: Teachers College Press and Sage).

Middleton, S., 1997, *Disciplining Sexuality: Foucault Life Histories and Education* (New York: Teachers College Press).

Miller, R., 2000, *Researching Life Stories and Family Histories* (London: Sage).

Morris, M., 1977, *An Excursion into Creative Sociology* (New York: Columbia University Press).

Munro, P., 1998, *Subject to Fiction: Women Teachers' Life History Narratives and the Cultural Politics of Resistance* (Buckingham: Open University Press).

Osler, A., 1997, *The Education and Careers of Black Teachers: Changing Identities, Changing Lives* (Buckingham: Open University Press).

Personal Narratives Group (eds), 1989, *Interpreting Women's Lives: Feminist Theory and Personal Narratives* (Bloomington, IN: Indiana University Press).

Plummer, K., 1983, *Documents of Life* (London: Allen and Unwin).

Plummer, K., 1990, Herbert Blumer and the Life History Tradition. *Symbolic Inter-actionism*, 13, 125–144.

Plummer, K., 1995, *Telling Sexual Stories: Power, Change and Social Worlds* (London: Routledge).

Plummer, K., 2000, *Documents of Life 2*, Rev. edn (London: Sage).

Radin, I., 1920, Crashing Thunder. *Publications in Archaeology and Ethnology*, 26, 381–473.

Ricoeur, P., 1981, *Hermeneutics and the Human Sciences* (Cambridge: Cambridge University Press).

Shaw, C., 1930, *The Jack-Roller* (Chicago, IL: University of Chicago Press).

Shotter, J. and Gergen, K., 1989, *Inquiries in Social Construction Series: Vol. 2. Texts of Identity* (London: Sage).

Sikes, P., 1997, *Parents who Teach: Stories from School and from Home* (London: Cassell).

Sikes, P., Measor, L., and Woods, P., 1985, *Teachers' Careers: Crises and Continuities* (Lewes: Falmer).

Sorrell, G. T. and Montgomery, M. J., 2001, Feminist Perspectives on Erikson's Theory: Its Relevance for Contemporary Identity Development Research. *Identity: An International Journal of Theory and Research*, 1.

Sparkes, A., 1994, Self, Silence and Invisibility as a Beginning Teacher: A Life History of Lesbian Experience. *British Journal of Sociology of Education*, 15(1), 93–118.

Stanley, L., 1990, *Feminist Praxis, Research Theory and Epistemology in Feminist Sociology* (London: Routledge).

Stanley, L., 1992, *The Auto/Biographical: The Theory and Practice of Feminist Auto/Biography* (Manchester: Manchester University Press).

Thomas, W. and Znaniecki, F., 1918–20, *The Polish Peasant in Europe and America*, 2nd edn (Chicago, IL: University of Chicago Press).

Thompson, P., 1978, *The Voices of the Past: Oral History* (Oxford: Oxford University Press).

Thompson, P., 1988, *The Voices of the Past: Oral History*, 2nd edn (Oxford: Oxford University Press).

Thrasher, F., 1928, *The Gang: A Study of 1313 Gangs in Chicago* (Chicago, IL: University of Chicago Press).

Tierney, W., 1998, Life History's History: Subjects Foretold. *Qualitative Inquiry*, 4(1), 49–70.

Weiler, K. and Middleton, S. (eds), 1999, *Telling Women's Lives: Narrative Inquiries in the History of Women's Education* (Buckingham: Open University Press).

Wirth, L., 1928, *The Ghetto* (Chicago, IL: University of Chicago Press).

Zorbaugh, H., 1929, *The Gold Coast and the Slum: A Sociological Study of Chicago's North Side* (Chicago, IL: University of Chicago Press).

PART 3

LIFE POLITICS

CHAPTER 13

PREPARING FOR POST-MODERNITY
Storying the self

Educational Practice and Theory, 1998, 20(1): 25–31

Preparing for post-modernity: the peril and promise

The current changes in the economy and superstructure associated with post-modernity pose particular perils and promises for the world of education. As Wolf has argued, it is quite conceivable that it will not just be the welfare state which is dismantled in the new epoch but also aspects of the superstructure (Wolfe, 1989). In particular, some of the median associations such as universities and schools may well be diminished and decoupled in significant ways. This means that institutional sites may not be any longer the only significant sites of struggle, and it also means that methodological genres that focus on institutional analysis and institutional theorizing, may be similarly diminished.

Associated with this restructuring of institutional life is an associated change in the form of knowledge, particularly the forms of workplace knowledge that will be promoted. Significantly, much of the workplace knowledge currently being promoted is context specific and personal (Goodson, 1993, pp. 1–3). Putting these two things together means that there will be two different sites for struggle in the postmodernist period. Firstly, there will be the continuing struggle for the theoretical and critical mission inside surviving but conceivable diminished institutional sites.

Secondly, and probably progressively more important for the future will be the site of personal life and identity. It is here that perhaps the most interesting project, what Giddens calls 'the reflexive project of the self'; will be contested in the next epoch. Life politics, the politics of identity construction and ongoing identity maintenance will become a major and growing site of ideological and intellectual contestation. The agenda standing before us is one where identity and lived experience can themselves be used as the sites wherein and whereby we interrogate, theoretically and critically, the social world. If that sounds a bit pompous which it does, what it really means, as far as I am concerned, is that we should be investigating and promoting the life history genre. Here the important distinction is between life story and life history. The life story is the initial selected account that people give of their lives: the life history is the triangulated account, one point of the tripod being the life story but the other two points being other people's testimony, documentary testimony and the transcripts and archives that appertain to the life in question.

Storying the self

The use of personal stories and narratives in teacher education has to respond meaningfully to the new conditions of work and being in the post-modern world.

As a number of social scientists have recently argued, this means we should reformulate our conceptions of identity and self-hood. The global forces that are undermining traditional forms of life and work are likewise transforming notions of identity and self. Identity is no longer an ascribed status or place in an established order rather identity is an ongoing project, most commonly an ongoing narrative project. In the new order, we 'story the self' as a means of making sense of new conditions of working and being. The self becomes a reflexive project, an ongoing narrative project. To capture this emergent process requires a modality close to social history and social geography – modes which capture the self in time and space.

For Giddens, the reflective project of the self:

> consists in the sustaining of coherent, yet continuously revised, biographical narratives, takes place in the context of multiple choice as filtered through abstract systems. In modern social life, the notion of lifestyle takes on a particular significance. The more tradition loses its hold, and the more daily life is reconstituted in terms of the dialectical interplay of the local and the global, the more individuals are forced to negotiate lifestyle choices among a diversity of options.
>
> (Giddens, 1991, p. 5, quoted in Coupland and Nussbaum, 1993, p. xv)

he adds:

> Self-identity for us [in the late modern age] forms a *trajectory* across different institutional settings of modernity over the *duree* of what used to be called the 'life cycle', a term which applies more accurately to non-modern contexts than the modern ones. Each of us not only 'has', but *lives* a biography reflexively organised in terms of flows of social and psychological information about possible ways of life. Modernity is a post-traditional order, in which the question, 'How shall I live?' has to be answered in day-to-day decisions about how to behave, what to wear and what to eat – and many other things – as well as interpreted within the temporal unfolding of self-identity.
>
> (Giddens, 1991, p. 14)

> The idea of the 'life cycle'...makes very little sense once the connections between the individual life and the interchange of the generations have been broken...Generational differences are essentially a mode of time-reckoning in pre-modern societies.... In traditional contexts, the life cycle carries strong connotations of renewal, since each generation in some substantial part rediscovers and relives modes of life of its forerunners. Renewal loses most of its meaning in the settings of high modernity where practices are repeated only in so far as they are reflexively justifiable.
>
> (Giddens, 1991, p. 146)

Above all Giddens is arguing that the 'situational geography' (p. 84) of modern social life and modern social selves has been drastically repositioned by the electronic media to the extent that the experience of social life and self is more fluid, uncertain and complicated than in previous epos. In the global market place, we are allowed to choose between a series of decontextualized self-identities rather in the manner of the commodified market place generally. Hence, the local and traditional elements of self are less constitutive. This leads to the self as an ongoing reflexive and narrative project for as Giddens writes 'at each moment, or at least at regular intervals, the individual is asked to conduct a self interrogation in terms of what is happening' (p. 76).

The self then becomes an ongoing process of self-building and self-negotiation and in this sense, it is possible to see the self as an ongoing narrative project.

This conceptionization of self-building is not unlike the conclusions arrived at by Leinberger and Tucker in their book *The New Individualists* (1991). Here they are concerned with the offspring cohort from the 'organization men' of William White's study in 1950. They argue that the whole epistomogical basis of individual life has shifted because of the economic and social changes of the last decade. This economic and social change plays itself out in what they call a different 'self ethic'.

> As the organization men's off springs came of age in the 60s and 70s, they were exhorted to find themselves or create themselves. They undertook the task with fervor, as self-expression, self-fulfilment, self-assertion, self-actualization, self-understanding, self-acceptance, and any number of other *self* compounds found their way into everyday language and life. Eventually, all these experiences solidified into what can only be called the self-ethic, which has ruled the lives of the organization offspring as thoroughly as the social ethic ruled the lives of their parents. Many people mistakenly regarded this development as narcissism, egoism, or pure selfishness. But the self-ethic, like the social ethic it displaced, was based on a genuine moral imperative – the *duty* to express the authentic self.
> (Leinberger and Tucker, 1991, pp. 11–12)

Leinberger and Tucker push the argument about self to the point where they argue that the authentic self is being replaced with by an artificial self.

> In pursuing the ideal of the authentic self, the offspring produced the most radical version of the American individual in history – totally psychologized and isolated, who has difficulty 'communicating' and 'making commitments', never mind achieving community. But by clinging to the artist ideal, the organization offspring try to escape the authentic self and simultaneously to maintain it as the ultimate value. It is a delicate balancing act to which many of them have been brought by the search for self-fulfilment, but it is a position that they are finding increasingly hard to maintain.

As our story will show, there are signs that the search for self-fulfilment is drawing to a close and with it, the era of the authentic self and its accompanying self-ethic. The ideal of the authentic self is everywhere in retreat. It has been undermined from within; it has been attacked from all sides; and, in many ways, it simply has been rendered obsolete by history:

- Self-fulfilment has proved to be unfulfilling, since the exclusive focus on the self has left many people feeling anxious and alone.
- The inevitable economic problems experienced by large generations, coupled with the long-term souring of the American economy, have introduced many members of the generation, even the most privileged among them, to limits in all areas of life, including limits on the self.
- Alternative and more inclusive conceptions of the self, especially those introduced into organizations by the influx of women, now challenge almost daily the more traditionally male conception of unfettered self-sufficiency.

- The macroeconomic issues of takeovers, buyouts, and restructurings that have dominated organizations for the past five years have left little room for psychological concerns in the workplace.
- The rise of a genuinely competitive global marketplace linked by instantaneous communications has accelerated the diffusive processes of modernity, further destabilizing the self.
- The centuries-old philosophical bedrock on which all our conceptions of individualism have rested, including the highly psychologized individualism embodied in the authentic self, is being swept away.
- Similarly, the most important developments in contemporary art *and popular entertainment* are subverting the conception of the artist on which the integrity of personalities who use the artist ideal to solve problems of identity depends.
- The rise of post-metropolitan suburbs, which are neither centre nor periphery, and the emergence of organizational networks, which replace older hierarchical structures, have thrust the new generation into concrete ways of life to which the authentic self is increasingly extrinsic (Leinberger and Tucker, 1991, pp. 15–17).

They argue that the authentic self is being replaced by what they call 'the artificial person'. Whilst this would seem to polarize authenticity and artifice too greatly, it is an interesting distinction to pursue and the authors make clear the ambiguities implicate its structure.

> Out of this slow and agonizing death of the authentic self, there is arising a new social character: the artificial person. This new social character is already discernible among a vanguard of the organization offspring and is now emerging among the remainder; it is likely to spread eventually throughout the middle class and, as often happens, attract the lower class and surround the upper.
>
> It cannot be emphasized enough that the designation *artificial person* does not mean these people are becoming phoney or insincere. Rather, it refers to a changing conception of what constitutes an individual and indeed *makes* someone individual. In the recent past, the organization offspring believed that individuality consists of a pristine, transcendent, authentic self-residing below or beyond all the particular accidents of history, culture, language, and society and all the other 'artificial' systems of collective life. But for all the reasons we have cited and many more besides, that proposition and the way of life it has entailed have become untenable. More and more the organization offspring are coming to see that the attributes they previously dismissed as *merely* artificial are what make people individuals – artificial, to be sure, but nonetheless persons, characterized by their particular mix of these ever-shifting combinations of social artificiality of every variety. Starting from this fundamental, and often unconscious, shift of perspective, they are evolving an individualism that is 'artificial' but particular, as opposed to one that is authentic but empty. It is an individualism predicated not on the *self*, but the *person*: while *self* connotes a phenomenon that is inner, non-physical, and isolated, *person* suggests an entity that is external, physically present, and already connected to the world. In effect, it is the realization that *authentic self* is more of an oxymoron than is *artificial person*.
>
> (Leinberger and Tucker, 1991, pp. 15–17)

The process of self-definition or as Leinberger and Tucker would have it, person building, is increasingly recognized as an emergent process, an ongoing narrative project. In this emergent process, stories and narrative change and metamorphose over time. The life story changes and so does its meaning for both the person and the listener. The story or narrative then provides a contemporary snapshot of an ongoing process – every picture tells a story but as the picture changes so do the stories. To establish a broader picture we need to locate the stories and collaborate the discussion and understanding of stories and narratives.

> A life, it is assumed, is cut of whole cloth, and its many pieces, with careful scrutiny, can be fitted into proper place. But this writing of a life...is constantly being created as it is written. Hence the meanings of the pieces change as new patterns are found.
>
> (Denzin, 1989, p. 20)

> the beginning coincides with the end and the end with the beginning – which is the end – for autobiography (like fiction) is an act of ceaseless renewal: the story is never 'told' finally, exhaustively, completely.
>
> (Elbaz, 1987, p. 13)

Narratives or life stories are a vital source for our studies of the social world in general and teaching in particular. But they are singular, selective and specific (both in time and context). In these senses unless they are complemented by other sources they are of limited value in understanding the patterns of social relations and interactions which comprise the social world. Indeed a primary reliance on narratives or life stories is likely to limit our capacity to understand social context and relationships as well as social and political purposes. Sole reliance on narrative becomes a convenient form of political quietism – we can continue telling our stories (whether as life 'stories' or research 'stories') and our searchlight never shines on the social and political construction of lives and life circumstances. No wonder the narrative and life story have been so successfully sponsored at the height of New Right triumphalism in the west. As we witness the claim that we are at 'the end of history' it's perhaps unsurprising that life stories are being divorced from any sense of history, any sense of the politically and socially constructed nature of the 'circumstances' in which lives are lived and meanings made. Truly 'men make their own history' but also more than ever 'not in circumstances of their own choosing'. We need to capture 'agency' but also 'structure': life stories but also life histories.

In this sense the distinction between life stories/narratives and life histories become central. The life story comprises the person's account of her/his life (most often delivered orally) at a particular point in time. The life history supplements the life story with data drawn from other peoples' accounts, official records and transcripts and a range of historical documentation.

The data then is distinctive but so too are the aspirations of life story and life history. In the first case the intention is to understand the person's view and account of their life, the story they tell about their life. As W.I. Thomas said 'if men define situations as real, they are real in their consequences'. In the life history, the intention is to understand the patterns of social relations, interactions and constructions in which lives are embedded. The life history pushes the question whether private issues are also public matters, the life story individualizes and personalizes, the life history contextualizes and politicizes.

In moving from life stories towards life histories we move from singular narration to include other documentary sources and oral testimonies. It is important to view the self as an emergent and changing 'project' not a stable and fixed entity. Over time our view of our self-changes and so therefore do the stories we tell about ourselves. In this sense, it is useful to view self-definition as an ongoing narrative project.

As the self is an ongoing narrative project, we should think more of multiple selves located in time and space. To link with this ongoing narrative project, we have to *locate* as well as narrate since the latter is a snapshot, a contemporary pin-point. To locate our ongoing narrative requires sources which develop our social history and social geography of circumstances and in many instances collaboration with others to provide contextual and inter-textual commentary. Along side *narration*, therefore, we need *location* and *collaboration*.

The reasons for location and collaboration arise from two particular features of life stories. First, the life story reflects partial and selective consciousness of subjective story building and self-building; and secondly, it is a contemporary pinpoint, a snapshot at a particular time. Collaboration and location allow us to get a finer sense of the emergent process of self-building and story telling and allow us to provide a social context of the time and space in which the story is located.

References

Coupland, Nikolas and Nussbaum, Jon F., 1993, Discourse and Lifespan Identity. In *Language and Language Behaviors Series*, Vol. 4 (Newbury Park, CA, London and New Delhi: Sage Publications).

Denzin, Norman, K., 1989, Interpretive Biography. In *Qualitative Research Methods Series 17* (Newbury Park, CA, London and New Delhi: Sage Publications).

Elbaz, Robert, 1987, *The Changing Nature of the Self: A Critical Study of the Autobiographical Discourse* (Iowa City: University of Iowa Press).

Giddens, A., 1991, *Modernity and Self-identity: Self and Society in the Late Modern Age.* (Cambridge: Polity Press, in association with Basil Blackwell).

Goodson, I.F., 1993, Forms of Knowledge and Teacher Education. *Journal of Education for Teaching, JET Papers*, 1.

Leinberger, Paul and Tucker, Bruce, 1991, *The New Individualists: The Generation After the Organization Man* (New York: HarperCollins).

Wolfe, A., 1989, *Whose Keeper? Social Science and Moral Obligation* (Berkeley, CA: University of California Press).

CHAPTER 14

THE STORY SO FAR

The International Journal of Qualitative Studies in Education, 1995, 8(1): 89–98

Personal knowledge and the political

In this paper I conduct an exploration of some forms of inquiry that are becoming influential within teacher education. In particular, I want to focus on forms of inquiry variously called 'stories', 'narratives', 'personal knowledge', 'practical knowledge' or in one particular genre 'personal practical knowledge'.

I find myself highly sympathetic to the urge to generate new ways of producing, collaborating, representing and knowing. They offer a serious opportunity to question many of the in-built biases of race, class or gender, which existing modes of inquiry mystify whilst reproducing (see Giroux, 1991). Storying and narratology are genres which allow us to move beyond (or to the side) of the main paradigms of inquiry – with their numbers, their variables, their psychometrics, their psychologisms, their decontextualized theories. Potentially then, the new genres offer the chance for a large step forward in representing the lived experience of schooling.

Because of this substantial potential the new genres require very close scrutiny. For whilst they have some obvious strengths, there are I think some weaknesses, which may prove incapacitating. If so, we may be sponsoring genres of inquiry in the name of empowerment, whilst at the same time, effectively disempowering the very people and causes we seek to work with.

Personal knowledge and the cultural logic of post-modernity

Before embracing personal knowledge in the form of narratives and story it is important to locate this genre within the emergent cultural patterns of contemporary societies and economies. Whilst the pace of change at the moment is rapid, a good deal of evidence points to an increasingly aggrandizing centre or state acting to sponsor 'voices' at the level of interest groups, localities and peripheries. From the perspective of these groups this may look like empowerment for oppressed aboriginals, physically and mentally challenged, gays and lesbians and other deserving groups. This is all long overdue. But we need to be aware of the overall social matrix. Specific empowerment can go hand in hand with overall social control.

Hence, alongside these new voices a systematic attack on median or secondary associations is underway – schools, universities, libraries, welfare agencies and the like. An attack, in fact, on many of the existing agencies of cultural mediation and production. Economic restructuring is being closely allied to cultural redefinition – a reduction of contextual and theoretical discourses and an overall sponsorship of personal and practical forms of discourse and cultural production. The overall effect will be to substantially redraw existing modes of political and cultural analysis. In its place we may end up with what Harvey (1989) calls the 'tyranny of the local' alongside what we might call the specificity of the personal. General patterns, social contexts, critical theories will be replaced by local stories and personal anecdotes.

Denzin (1991) has commented on this in his critique of the rehabilitated 'life story movement'.

> The cultural logics of late capitalism valorize the life story, autobiographical document because they keep the myth of the autonomous, free individual alive. This logic finds its modern roots on Rousseau's *Confessions*, a text perfectly fitted to the cultural logics of the new capitalist societies where a division between public and private had to be maintained, and where the belief in a pure, natural self was cherished. The logic of the confession reifies the concept of the self and turns it into a cultural commodity. The rise to power of the social sciences in the twentieth century corresponded to the rise of the modern surveillance state. That state required information on its citizens. Social scientists, of both qualitative and quantitative commitments, gathered information for this society. The recent return to the life story celebrates the importance of the individual under the conservative politics of late postmodernism.
>
> (p. 2)

Hence, in the cultural logic of late capital the life story represents a form of cultural apparatus to accompany a newly aggrandising state and market system. In the situation that is being 'worked for' the subject/state, consumer/market confrontation will be immediate. The range of secondary associations and bureaucracies which currently 'buffer' or mediate this pattern of social relations will be progressively reduced. The cultural buffer of theory, critique and political commentary will likewise wither. It will not be the state that withers (as in fond Marxist theory) but the critical theory and cultural critique that stand against the state. In the 'end of history' we shall indeed see the closure of cultural contestation as evidenced in theoretical and critical discourse. In its place will stand a learned discourse comprising stories and practices – specific local and located but divorced from understandings of social context and social process.

In the next section I review how this cultural redefinition is emerging in some aspects of the media.

The media context of personal knowledge

This section briefly examines the promotion of more personal stories at the level of the media. The promotional strategies at these levels pose questions about in whose interests the move to more personal knowledge is being undertaken. There is after all an 'opportunity cost' to the time being spent on personal stories – in a finite world of time, less time is thereby spent on other aspects, most notably on more wider ranging political and social analysis.

The move towards story-telling is becoming pronounced in the media. This can be seen most clearly in the media of those countries which have retained until recently, a strong tradition of political and cultural analysis. Michael Ignatieff, a Canadian working in Britain and one of the most elegant of cultural analysts recently wrote in *The Observer*, 'Whatever we hacks may piously profess, the media is not in the information business. It is in the story-telling business' (Ignatieff, 1992, p. 21). He then details a range of new developments in the British media which evidence this trend. Story-telling and personal anecdotes are the powerful new fashion he writes:

> As if to make this plain, ITN's *News at Ten* is reintroducing its 'And finally' end piece, 'traditionally devoted to animals, children and royalty'. After footage from Sarajevo, we'll be treated, for example, to the sight of some lovable ducks on a surfboard. The ducks are there not just to cheer us up but to reach those subliminal zones of ourselves which long to believe that the horror of Sarajevo is just so much nasty make-believe.
>
> The audience's longing for stories about ducks on surfboards is only one of the trends which is taking the media away from even notional attention to the real world. The other is the media's growing fascination with itself. The last few weeks have seen this obsession inflate to baroque extremes of narcissism. When Trevor McDonald gets the *News at Ten* job and Julia Somerville does not: when Sir David English vacates one editor's chair and Simon Jenkins vacates another; when Andrew Neil snarls at the 'saintly' Andreas Whittam-Smith and the saint snarls back, I ask myself: does anybody care but us hacks?
>
> (Ignatieff, 1992, p. 21)

He notes that, 'there's a price to pay when the media systematically concentrates on itself and ignores the world outside'. The opportunity cost of story-telling is that personal minutiae and anecdote replace cultural analysis. Above all, the 'story' is the other side of a closure on broad analysis, a failure for imagination. He writes:

> In this failure and in the media's amazing self-absorption, I see a shrinking in journalism's social imagination. What I know about the 1980's I owe to a journalism which believed that the challenge was to report Britain as if it was an unknown country: Bea Campbell's *Road to Wigan Pier*, for example, or Ian Jack's *Before the Oil Ran Out*. In place of genuine social curiosity, we have the killer interview, the media profile, the latest stale gossip. It's so fashionable we can't even see what a capitulation it represents.
>
> (Ignatieff, 1992, p. 21)

The reasons for the promotion of the anecdote and personal story, are both broadly cultural and political but also specifically economic. They relate to emerging patterns of globalisation and corporatisation. Broadly speaking, the British media is following American patterns in pursuit of American sponsorship. American capital is thereby reproducing the American pattern of decontextualized story-telling.

We find that with the British *News at Ten* the new initiatives in broadcasting style.

> [I]s part of a new-look bulletin, which will, in the words of one ITN executive, become 'more formulaic with a more distinctive human interest approach'. Viewers, it seems, like certainty both in the format of a bulletin and the person who presents it. Lessons have been learnt from American TV news by senior

ITN managers such as chief executive Bob Phillis, editor-in-chief Stewart Purvis and *News at Ten* producer Nigel Dacre (brother of Paul, the new editor of the *Daily Mail*).

(Brooks, 1992, p. 69)

The reason for the convergence which American styles of story-telling are addressed later.

By 1994, ITV companies must become minority shareholders in ITN. American TV companies, CNN, CBS and NBC, have already cast their eyes over ITN, though only one of them is likely to take a stake. It is no coincidence that *News at Ten* will have a more of an American look – the single anchor, like Dan Rather or Peter Jennings, for example.

In short, ITN and *News at Ten* are being dressed up to be more attractive not just to viewers, but also to prospective buyers.

(Brooks, 1992, p. 69)

In America it is obvious that the 'story' is being employed specifically to close off sustained political and cultural analysis. John Simpson (1992) recently wrote about 'the closing of the American media'. In this closure, the 'story' took pride of place in cutting America off from international news and political analysis. Simpson analyzed the CBS news.

After reports on drought in the western United States and the day's domestic political news, the rest of CBS's news broadcast was devoted to a regular feature, 'Eye on America'. This evening's item was about a man who was cycling across America with his son, a sufferer from cerebral palsy. It was designed to leave you with a warm feeling, and lasted for 3 minutes, 58 seconds; longer than the time devoted that night to the whole of the rest of the world.

It is no surprise that soon there will almost certainly be no American television network correspondent based anywhere in the southern hemisphere. Goodbye Africa; goodbye most of Asia; goodbye Latin America.

(Simpson, 1992, p. 9)

As you would expect from a Briton, Simpson concludes that the only repository of serious cultural analysis is on British television which as we have seen, is being re-structured according to American imperatives. The circle in short, is closed:

The sound of an Englishman being superior about America is rarely uplifting; but in this case the complaints come most fiercely from the people who work for American television themselves. They know how steep the decline has been, and why it has happened. All three networks have been brought up by giant corporations which appear to regard news and current affairs as branches of the entertainment industry, and insist they have to pay their way with advertisers just as chat-shows and sit coms do. Advertisers are not good people for a news organization to rely on: during the Gulf war NBC lost $25 million in revenue because companies which had bought space in the news bulletins cancelled their advertisements – they were afraid their products would appear alongside reports of American casualties.

The decline of the networks is depressing. CBS is one of the grandest names in journalism, the high-minded organisation which broadcast Ed Murrow's wartime despatches from London and Walter Cronkite's influential verdicts on the Vietnam war and Watergate. NBC's record is a proud one too. Recently it announced it was back in the news business and would stop broadcasting stories that were simply features. But NBC News seems very close to the rocks nowadays, and it does not have the money to send its teams abroad in the way it did until a couple of years ago. The foreign coverage will mostly be based on pictures from the British television news agency Visnews, and from the BBC.

(Simpson, 1992, p. 9)

We have entered the period of 'authoritarian capital', and Simpson argues that the 'story' is the indicator of this denouement. If this is so, the promoters of storying have strange bed fellows.

Earl and Irma, meanwhile, are still there in front of their television sets, serenely unaware of what is happening around them. Decisions which affect their lives are being taken every day in Frankfurt, Tokyo and London, but no one tells them about it. Most of the companies which advertise on television just want them to feel good so, therefore, do the people in charge of providing them with news. The freest society in the world has achieved the kind of news blackout which totalitarian régimes can only dream about.

(Simpson, 1992, p. 9)

In one sense the enshrinement of the personal story as a central motif for knowledge transmission links up with another theme in current restructuring. Namely: the reconstruction of the middle ground in the social and economic system. By sponsoring voices at the periphery, the centre may well be strengthening its hand. Hence, empowerment of personal and peripheral voices can go hand in hand with aggrandizement and a further concentration of power at the centre. As Alan Wolfe has pointed out in his new book *Whose Keeper?*: 'a debate that casts government and the marketplace as the main mechanisms of social organization leaves out all those intermediate institutions that are, in fact, the most important in people's lives: family, church, neighbourhood associations, workplace ties, unions and a variety of informal organizations' (quoted in Dionne, 1992, p. 18).

The current appeal to personal and 'family values' in the U.S. election undoubtedly is driven by a realisation of this kind of dissolution of mediating social structures. 'The appeal of this vague phrase is that fundamentally it reminds people that good society depends not only, or even primarily, on their economic well-being, but also on this web of personal-social relationships that transcend the marketplace and transcend government' (Rosenthal, 1992, section 4, p. 1).

This focus on storytelling emerged early in the movies. By 1914, William and Cecil DeMille had developed a technique of storytelling that would 'follow the old dramatic principles, but adapt itself to a new medium', 'find its own compensations for its lack of words…to make a train of thought visible enough to be photographed' (Berg, 1989, p. 48). By 1916, this had evolved to the point where a ghost-writer for Samuel Goldwyn could write, 'by the time I started the Goldwyn Company it was the player, not the play which was the thing' (p. 68).

Likewise in the world of fantasy, promoted by the movies, stories are the central motif for colonising and re-directing lived experience. This has been so since very early on as the Goldwyn quotes indicate.

A painless way to make sense of this new world was suggested by one of the modernizing forces itself: the movies. The movies offered many forms of guidance to confused Americans, particularly to immigrant urban dwellers; they became a virtual manual for acculturation. But one of the most important and most subtle services the movies offered was to serve as a popular model of narrative coherence. If reality was overwhelming, one could always carve it into a story, as the movies did. One could bend life to the familiar and comforting formulas one saw in the theatre.

(*The New York Times*, 1991, p. 32)

From the beginning, then, movies began to explore new terrains for formularizing and domesticating reality.

In American life, beginning in the 1920s, a number of media began to exploit the storying theme, first initiated in the movies. The tabloid press and then magazines and television began to provide a range of real life plots from kidnappings and murder to political scandals, to crimes in executive suites, to election campaigns, to Second World War, to the Cold War, to Watergate, to the recent Soviet coup attempt, to Operation Restore Hope.

Today, virtually all the news assumes a narrative configuration with cause and effect, villain and hero, beginning, middle and provisional end, and frequently a moral. Events that don't readily conform, the savings and loan scandal, for example, seem to drift in foggy limbo like a European art film rather than a sleek commercial American hit.

(*The New York Times*, 1991, p. 32)

It might be judged that the savings and loan scandal could have been made to conform to a very exciting storyline but it was in fact pushed off into foggy limbo. This raises the key question of the power of storying to make vivid and realistic certain storylines whilst suppressing others, hence, it is clear that murders and fires and kidnappings are exciting material for storylines but that many of the things that go on in American society somehow or other do not form a reasonable storyline. It is interesting, therefore, that so influential a newspaper as *The New York Times* should see the savings and loan scandal as not worthy of a storyline. They are, in short, accepting the assumptions which underpin the genre.

Let me return once more to *The New York Times* for one extended quote on the importance of storying in the news:

That is why reading the news is just like watching a series of movies: a hostage crisis is a thriller, the Milwaukee serial murders a morbidly fascinating real-life *Silence of the Lambs*, the Kennedy Palm Beach case a soap opera, a fire or hurricane a disaster picture.

One even suspects that Americans were riveted by the Clarence Thomas-Anita Hill hearings last week not because of any sense of civic duty but because it was a spellbinding show – part *Rashomon*, part *Thelma and Louise*, part *Witness for the Prosecution*.

But as with movies, if 'formularizing' reality is a way of domesticating it, it is also a means of escaping it. Michael Wood in his book *America in the Movies*, described our films as a 'rearrangement of our problems into shapes which tame them, which disperse them to the margins of our attention' where we can forget about them. By extending this function to life itself, we convert everything from the kidnapping of the Lindbergh baby to the marital misadventures of Elizabeth Taylor into distractions, cheap entertainments that transport us from our problems.

But before disapproving too quickly, one is almost compelled to admit that turning life into escapist entertainment has both a perverse logic and a peculiar genius. Why worry about the seemingly intractable problems of society when you can simply declare, 'It's morning in America' and have yourself a long-running Frank Capra movie right down to an aw-shucks President? Why fret over America's declining economic might when you can have an honest-to-goodness war movie that proves your superiority? Movies have always been a form of wish fulfilment. Why not life?

When life is a movie, it poses serious questions for those things that were not traditionally entertainment and now must accommodate themselves. Politics, for instance. Much has already been made of the fact that Ronald Reagan came to the White House after a lifetime as a professional actor. Lou Cannon, in his biography of Mr. Reagan, *President Reagan: The Role of a Lifetime*, details just how central this was to Mr. Reagan's concept of the Presidency and what it suggests about the political landscape.

(*The New York Times*, 1991, p. 32)

The important point to grasp about this quote and other quotes is that the storying genre is far from socially and politically neutral. As we saw in an earlier quotation, the savings and loan scandal was somehow not a valid storyline. Likewise, the great exploiters of storylines, the John Waynes, the Ronald Reagans, tend to be of a particular political persuasion and of a particular sensitivity to the dominant interest groups within American society. Storying, therefore, rapidly becomes a form of social and political prioritizing, a particular way of telling stories which in its way privileges some storylines and silences others. Once the focus shifts not to real events but 'what makes a good story', it is a short distance to making an argument that certain political realities 'would not make a good story', whilst others would. By displacing its focus from real life events into storying potential, it is possible also to displace some unwanted social and political realities. Even when unwanted realities do intrude in deafening ways, such as the LA riots, it is possible to story them in ways that create a distance of sorts. In Umberto Eco's words, it is possible to move from a situation where realities are scrutinized and analysed to the world of American life where 'hyper realities' are constructed.

Storytelling and educational study

Now because the media often employs stories to close off political and cultural analysis does not itself disprove the value of storying and narrative in educational study. I would however urge that it is cause for pause in two ways. Firstly, if stories are so easily used in this manner in the media it is plainly possible that they might act in this way as educational study. Secondly, as is made clear in some of the foregoing quotes, the way we 'story' our lives (and therefore the way we present ourselves for educational study, among other things) are deeply connected to storylines derived from elsewhere. In American life especially, but increasingly elsewhere, forms of narrative and storying, the classic 'storylines', are often derived from television and newspapers. In this sense Ronald Reagan is not alone; he made such a representative President because of his capacity to catch and dispatch the central storylines of American life. 'It's morning in America' sounded right and true. It was a powerful storyline and it was not seriously contested by political or cultural analysis. But with the power of hindsight wasn't it a gigantic lie which inaugurated a new economic depression?

Stories then need to be closely interrogated and analysed in their social context. Stories in short are most often carriers of dominant messages, themselves agencies of domination. Of course oppositional stories can be captured but they are very much a minority form and are often themselves overlaid or reactive to dominant storylines. As Gordon Wells (1986) has warned us a previous expression of reality is largely 'a distillation of the stories that we have shared: not only the narratives that we have heard and told, read, or seen enacted in drama or news on television, but also the anecdotes, explanations, and conjectures that are drawn upon in everyday conversation (p. 196)' or as Passerini (1987) has noted 'when someone is asked for his life-story, his memory draws on pre-existing story-lines and ways of telling stories, even if these are in part modified by the circumstances (p. 28)'. Put in another way this means that we often narrate our lives according to a 'prior script', a script written elsewhere, by others, for other purposes.

Seen in this way the use of stories in educational study needs to become part of a broader project of re-appropriation. It is not sufficient to say we wanted 'to listen to people', 'to capture their voices' 'to let them tell their stories'. A far more active collaboration is required. Luisa Passerini's work on the Turin's working class and on women's personal narratives is exemplary in this regard (Passerini, 1987, 1989). As Weiler (1991) has summarized:

> Passerini's emphasis on recurrent narrative forms begins to uncover the way people reconcile contradictions, the ways they create meaning from their lives, and create a coherent sense of themselves through available forms of discourse. At the same time, she is concerned with the 'bad fit' or 'gap' between 'pre-existing story lines' and individual constructions of the self through memory. As individuals construct their past, they leave unresolved contradictions at precisely those points at which authoritative discourse conflicts with collective cultural meanings.
>
> (pp. 6–7)

At the centre of any move to aid people, teachers in particular, to reappropriate their individual lived experiences as stories is the need for active collaboration. In the case of teachers, this will sometimes be in association with educators located in the academy, especially in faculties of education.

The relationship of studies of teachers' stories to the academy sits, I believe, at the centre of one of the major ethical and methodological issues involved in any move to develop collaborative use of stories. Of course, views of the academy cover a wide spectrum from a belief in its role in the 'disinterested pursuit of knowledge' through to the assertion of the Situationist International that 'The intelligentsia is power's hall of mirrors.' In general, I would take a position which stresses the *interestedness* rather than disinterestedness of the academy. I see a good deal of empirical evidence that David Tripp's (1987) contention in this matter may be correct for he argues that: 'When a research method gains currency and academic legitimacy, it tends to be transformed to served the interests of the academy' (p. 2).

Becker (1970) has commented on the 'hierarchy of credibility regarding those to whom we tend to listen'. This has general relevance to our research on schooling and school systems and specifically to our desire to listen to the teacher's voice.

> In any system of ranked groups, participants take it as given that members of the highest group have the right to define the way things really are. In any organization, no matter what the rest of the organization chart shows, the arrows indicate the flow of information point up, thus demonstrating (at least formally) that those at the top have access to a more complete picture of what is going on than anyone else. Members of lower groups will have incomplete information and their view of reality will be partial and distorted in consequence. Therefore, from the point of view of a well socialized participant in the system, any tale told by those at the top intrinsically deserves to be regarded as the most credible account obtainable of the organizations' workings.
>
> (Becker, 1970, p. 126)

He provides a particular reason why accounts 'from below' may be unwelcome:

> [O]fficials usually have to lie. That is a gross way of putting it, but not inaccurate. Officials must lie because things are seldom as they ought to be. For a great variety of reasons, well-known to sociologists, institutions are refractory. They do not perform as society would like them to. Hospitals do not cure people; prisons do not rehabilitate prisoners; schools do not educate students. Since they are supposed to, officials develop ways both of denying the failure of the institution to perform as it should and explaining those failures which cannot be hidden. An account of an institution's operation from the point of view of subordinates therefore casts doubt on the official line and may possibly expose it as a lie.
>
> (Becker, 1970, p. 128)

For these reasons the academy normally accepts the 'hierarchy of credibility': 'we join officials and the man in the street in an unthinking acceptance of the hierarchy of credibility. We do not realize that there are sides to be taken and that we are taking one of them'. Hence Becker argues that for the academic researcher:

> The hierarchy of credibility is a feature of society whose existence we cannot deny, even if we disagree with its injunction to believe the man at the top. When we acquire sufficient sympathy with subordinates to see things from their perspective, we know that we are flying in the face of what 'everyone knows'. The knowledge gives us pause and cause us to share, however briefly, the doubt of our colleagues.
>
> (Becker, 1970, p. 129)

Research work, then, is seldom disinterested and prime interests at work are the powerful, Becker's 'man at the top', and the academy itself. Acknowledgement of these interests becomes crucial when we conduct studies of teachers' stories; for the data generated and accounts rendered can easily be misused and abused by both powerful interest groups and by the academy. Middleton (1992, p. 20) notes that 'in schools people are constantly regulated and classified' but this surveillance extends to teachers themselves. Plainly studies of teachers' stories can be implicated in this process unless we are deeply watchful about who 'owns' the data and who controls the accounts. If Becker is right that 'officials lie' it is also plain that they might appropriate and misuse data about teachers' lives. Likewise, those in the academy might take information on teachers' lives and use it entirely for their own purposes.

Yet Becker reminds us that the terrain of research involves not only differentiated voices but stratified voices. It is important to remember that the politicians and bureaucrats who control schools are part of a stratified system where 'those at the top have a more complete picture of what is going on than anyone else.' It would be unfortunate if in studying teachers' stories, we ignored these contextual parameters which so substantially impinge upon and constantly restrict the teacher's life. It is, therefore, I think a crucial part of our ethical position as researchers that we do not 'valorize the subjectivity of the powerless' in the name of telling 'their story'. This would be to merely record constrained consciousness – a profoundly conservative posture and one, as Denzin has noted, which no doubt explains the popularity of such work during the recent conservative political renaissance. In my view teachers' stories should, where possible, provide not only a '*narrative of action*', but also a history or *genealogy of context*. I say this in full knowledge that this opens up substantial dangers of changing the relationship between 'story giver' and 'research taker' and of tilting the balance of the relationship further towards the academy.

I think, however, that these dangers must be faced if a genuine collaboration between the life story giver and the research taker is to be achieved. In a real sense 'it cannot be all give and no take'. In what sense is the 'research taker' in a position to give and provide the basis for a reasonably equitable collaboration. I have argued elsewhere that what we are searching for in developing genuine collaboration in studying teachers' stories is a viable '*trading point*' between life story giver and research taker. The key to this trading point is, I believe, the differential structural location of the research taker. The academic has the time and the resources to collaborate with teachers in developing 'genealogies of context'. These genealogies can provide teachers as a group with aspects of 'the complete picture' which those that control their lives have (or at least aspire to have).

> Much of the work that is emerging on teachers' lives throws up structural insights which locate the teacher's life within the deeply structured and embedded environment of schooling. This provides a prime 'trading point' for the external researcher. For one of the valuable characteristics of a collaboration between teachers as researchers and external researchers is that it is a collaboration between two parties that are differentially located in structural terms. Each see the world through a different prism of practice and thought. This valuable difference may provide the external researcher with a possibility to offer back goods in 'the trade'. The teacher/researcher offers data and insights. The terms of trade, in short, look favourable. In such conditions collaboration may at last begin.
>
> (Goodson and Walker, 1990, pp. 148–149)

In arguing for the provision of histories or genealogies of context, I am reminded of V.S. Naipaul's comments. Naipaul has the ultimate sensitivity to the 'stories' that people tell about their lives, for him subjective perceptions are priority data (Naipaul, 1987). Buruma (1991) has judged:

> What makes Naipaul one of the worlds most civilized writers is his refusal to be engaged by the People, and his insistence on listening to people, individuals, with their own language and their own stories. To this extent he is right when

he claims to have no view; he is impatient with abstractions. He is interested in how individual people see themselves and the world in which they live. He has recorded their histories, their dreams, their stories, their words.

(p. 3)

So far then Naipaul echoes the concern of those educational researchers who have sought to capture teachers' stories and narratives, told in their own words and in their own terms. But I am interested by the more recent shifts in Naipaul's position; he has begun to provide far more historical background, he seems to me to be moving towards providing the stories but also genealogies of context. He is clear that he sees this as empowering those whose stories which he once told more passively: 'to awaken to history was to cease to live instinctively. It was to begin to see oneself and one's group the way the outside world saw one; and it was to know a kind of rage' (Buruma, 1991, p. 4).

MacIntyre (1981) has followed a similar line in arguing that man is 'essentially a story-telling animal'. He argues that, 'the story of my life is always embedded in the story of those communities from which I derive my identity'.

> What I am, therefore, is in key part what I inherit, a specific past that is present to some degree in my present. I find myself part of a history and that is generally to say, whether I like it or not, whether I recognise it or not, one of the bearers of a tradition. It was important when I characterised the concept of a practice to notice that practices always have histories and that at any given moment what a practice is depends on a mode of understanding it which has been transmitted often through many generations. And thus, in so far as the virtues sustain the relationships required for practices, they have to sustain relationships to the past – and to the future – as well as in the present. But the traditions through which particular practices are transmitted and reshaped never exist in isolation for larger social traditions.

He continues:

> Within a tradition the pursuit of goods extends through generations, sometimes through many generations. Hence the individual's search for his or her good is generally and characteristically conducted within a context defined by those traditions of which the individual's life is a part, and this is true both of those goods which are internal to practices and of the goods of a single life. Once again the narrative phenomenon of embedding is crucial: the history of a practice in our time is generally and characteristically embedded in and made intelligible in terms of the larger and longer history of the tradition through which the practice in its present form was conveyed to us; the history of each of our own lives is generally and characteristically embedded in and made intelligible in terms of the larger and longer histories of a number of traditions.
>
> (MacIntyre, 1981, pp. 206–207)

In many ways Middleton (1992) summarizes the aspirations when she says:

> Teachers, as well as their students, should analyse the relationship between their individual biographies, historical events, and the constraints imposed on their personal choices by broader power relations, such as those of class, race and gender.

(p. 19)

In providing such inter-contextual analysis, the different methodologies highlighted in this volume all provide important avenues. They all combine a concern with telling teachers' stories with an equal concern to provide a broader context for the location, understanding and grounding of those stories.

In awakening to history in our studies of teachers' stories, I have felt for some time that life history work is a most valuable avenue for collaborative, inter-contextual work (Goodson, 1992). The distinction between life stories and life histories is an important one to restate. The life story is a personal reconstruction of experience, in this case by the teacher. 'Life story givers' provide data for the researcher often in loosely structured interviews. The researcher seeks to elicit the teacher's perceptions and stories but is generally rather passive rather than actively interrogative.

The life history also begins with the life story that the teacher tells but seeks to build on the information provided. Hence other people's accounts might be elicited, documentary evidence and a range of historical data amassed. The concern is to develop a wide inter-textual and inter-contextual mode of analysis. This provision of a wider range of data allows a contextual background to be constructed.

Crucial to the move to life history is a change in the nature of collaboration. The teacher becomes more than a teller of stories and becomes a more general investigator; the external researcher is more than a listener and elicitor of stories and is actively involved in textual and contextual construction. In terms of give and take, I would argue a more viable trading point can be established. This trading point, by focussing on stories *in context*, provides a new focus to develop our joint understandings of schooling. By providing this dialogue of a 'story of action within a theory of context' a new context is provided for collaboration. In the end, the teacher researcher can collaborate in investigating not only the stories of lives but the contexts of lives. Such collaboration should provide new understandings for all of us concerned with the world of schooling.

Personal knowledge and educational research

As we have seen, story telling has been a sign in the media of a move away from cultural and political analysis. Why then might we assume that it would be any different in educational and social research. After all, educational research has tended to be behind mainstream cultural and political analysis in its cogency and vitality rather than ahead of it.

Let us go back a step. Storytelling came in because the modes of cultural and political analysis were biased, white, male and middle class. Other ways of knowing and representing grew at the periphery to challenge the biased centre. However, these oppositional discourses, having achieved some success in representing 'silenced voices' have remained ensconced in the particular and the specific. They have, in short, not developed their own linkages to cultural, political analysis.

The assumption of so much postmodernist optimism is that by empowering new voices and discourses, by telling you stories in short, we will rewrite and re-inscribe the old white male bourgeois rhetoric, so it may be. But, so what?

New stories do not of themselves analyse or address the structures of power. Is it not the commonsensical level, worthy of pause, to set the new stories and new voices against a sense of the centre's continuing power? The Western version of high modernity is everywhere ascendant – we have an unparalleled 'end of history triumphalism' with most of the historical challenges vanquished. Is this new ascendant authoritarian capital a likely vehicle for the empowerment of the silenced and the oppressed? This seems unlikely, particularly as capital has historically been the vehicle for the very construction and silencing of the same oppressed groups. Is it not more likely then that new discourses and voices that empower the periphery actually at one and the same time fortify, enhance and solidify the old centres of power. In short, are we not witnessing the old game of divide and rule?

Acknowledgements

This paper was presented at two sessions at AERA, Atlanta April 1993, *Living Lives, Studying Lives, Writing Lives: An Educational Potpourri or Pot-au-Feu?* Invitational Session and *Living Lives, Studying Lives, Writing Lives* A Roundtable Discussion Session.

References

Becker, H.S., 1970, *Sociological Work: Method and Substance* (Chicago, IL: Aldine).
Berg, A.S., 1989, *Goldwyn. A Biography* (New York: Knopf).
Brooks, R., 1992, And Finally... News at Ten Goes Tabloid. *The Observer* (July 19).
Buruma, I., 1991, Signs of Life. *New York Review of Books*, 38(4), 3.
Denzin, N.K., 1991, Deconstructing the Biographical Method. Paper presented at the 1991 AERA Annual Meeting, Chicago, IL, April.
Dionne, E.J. Jr., 1992, The Disillusion with Politics could be Dangerous. *Guardian Weekly* (July 19).
Giroux, H., 1991, *Border Crossings* (London and New York: Routledge and Kegan Paul).
Goodson, I.F. (ed.), 1992, *Studying Teachers' Lives* (London and New York: Routledge).
Goodson, I.F. and Walker, R., 1990, *Biography, Identity and Schooling* (London, New York and Philadelphia, PA: Falmer Press).
Harvey, D., 1989, *The Condition of Postmodernity* (Oxford: Basil Blackwell).
Ignatieff, M., 1992, The Media Admires Itself in the Mirror. *The Observer* (July 19).
MacIntyre, A., 1981, *After Virtue: A Study in Moral Theory* (London: Duckworth).
Middleton, S., 1992, Developing a Radical Pedagogy. In I.F. Goodson (ed.), *Studying Teachers' Lives* (London and New York: Routledge).
Naipaul, V.S., 1987, *The Enigma of Arrival* (London: Viking).
Passerini, L., 1987, *Fascism in Popular Memory: The Cultural Experience of the Turin Working Class* (Cambridge: Cambridge University Press).
Passerini, L., 1989, Women's Personal Narratives: Myths, Experiences, and Emotions. In Personal Narratives Group (eds), *Interpreting Women's Lives* (Bloomington, IN: Indiana University Press).
Rosenthal, A., 1992, What's Meant and What's Mean in the 'Family Values' Battle. *The New York Times* (July 26).
Simpson, John., 1992, The Closing of the American Media. *The Spectator* (July 18).
The New York Times, 1991, Now Playing Across America: Real Life, the Movie. *The New York Times* (October 20).
Tripp, D., 1987, Teacher Autobiography and Classroom Practice (Western Australia: Murdoch University, Mimeo).
Weiler, K., 1991, Remembering and Representing Life Choices: A Critical Perspective on Teachers' Oral History Narratives. Mimeo.
Wells, G., 1986, *The Meaning Makers* (London: Hodder and Stoughton).

CHAPTER 15

ACTION RESEARCH AND THE REFLEXIVE PROJECT OF SELVES

'International Action Research: A Casebook for Education Reform',
in S. Hollingsworth (ed.), *Action Research Reader*,
London: Falmer Press, 1997

> Here we have a poem which is holding Eliot together as much as he is holding the poem together.
>
> (Peter Ackroyd on *The Wasteland*)

In this chapter, I look at the field of action research through the life histories of some of the key protagonists. This provides a way of investigating the personal missions which underpin social movements life action research.

A common way of proceeding in exploring a project's impact and dissemination might be textual analysis. Following this mode, it is assumed that a project is disseminated through the textual production of the key players. Here it is tacitly asserted that new recruits to action research would be persuaded by reading the texts and hearing the interpretations of the main advocates of the movement. Hence, by inter-textual exchange and inter-subjective negotiation, new recruits join the movement and the movement develops and expands.

A countervailing view to this rational/textual view would be that here we are more, or at least as much, concerned with issues of personal knowledge and construction; we might argue that new recruits are less than concerned with textual justification than with issues of lifestyle and identity. Hence, counterpoised against textual conversion would be a possibility that new recruits to social movements such as action research are actually involved in identity or lifestyle shopping. What they would be more concerned with by this view would be the kind of lifestyles or identities which are carried in suspension within new social movements. Hence, rather than a view of action research as dissemination, as proceeding through rational adoption after textual conversion, here we would be looking for a more personal set of rationales. These would be closely meshed with issues of identity and lifestyle and hence, the best mode for enquiring into this countervailing view would be the collection of a number of life histories.

The Teachers as Researchers project at the University of East Anglia allowed us to test this view of social action as identity politics. In the fieldwork stage of the project a range of life history interviews have been conducted with teachers who employed action research modalities and/or were members of action research projects and groups. The group included a number of the 'key players' in action research.

This move towards the analysis of identity politics, whilst partially no doubt a response to post-modern discourses, is related to changes in the economy and superstructure. As Wolf has argued, it is probable that it will not be the welfare state which is dismantled in the new epoch 'following the end of history' but also aspects of the superstructure (Wolf, 1989). In particular, he argues, some of the median associations such as universities and schools may well be diminished and coupled in significant ways. This means that institutional sites, institutional missions, institutional objectives and institutional movements may not any longer be the most significant sites of struggle and analysis. It further means that methodological genres, which focus on institutional analysis and institutional theorizing, may be similarly diminished and hence, the need to develop new genres becomes pressing.

One of the new arenas for struggle and definition will undoubtedly be personal life and identity. It is here that perhaps one of the most interesting projects, what Giddens (1991) calls 'the reflexive project of the self' will be contested in the new epoch. Life politics, the politics of identity construction and ongoing identity maintenance will become a major growing cite of ideological and intellectual contestation.

Of course the link between identity politics, the reflexive project of the self and broader social and institutional movements and missions has always been there. In analyzing that interrelationship, we need to develop broader patterns of data and data analysis which focus on the reflexive project of the self. Indeed, we need to broaden and deepen the conception of self away from a singular, unitary, linear notion of narrative of self towards a multiple and more fluid notion of self. Hence, the focus in this work is on the reflexive project of selves which is meant to refer to the multi faceted aspect of the project. It is argued that whilst singularly embodied and embedded the self has multiple facets and prospects.

Before dealing with some of the themes and topics which emerge in interviews and in subsequent data analysis, let me by way of exemplification provide an extended quote from a leading action research proponent which shows the close relationship between the reflexive project of the self and the development of action research. There has been little attempt to keep 'theories' hidden until the interviews are completed. In this model which has not been employed, the theorist can emerge from the undergrowth of the interview and provide the pristine theory that has been hatching unbeknown to the interviewee. We have tried instead in this report to carry as much of the 'voice' of the interviewees as is possible, whilst noting that their voice is in fact a 'third voice' – the voice constructed by the interviewee and interviewer in interactive negotiations. There has certainly been no attempt for the interviewer to play 'neutral chairman in these interviews'. Emerging themes and ideas are paraded, tested and often times rejected. So we see a third voice being negotiated, contested and constructed in these interviews.

Int: Well I don't know I grew up with a lot of aggression that I turned towards myself and then gradually learned how to externalise that aggression. And I've always had this tension between being in many ways an extreme extrovert, I mean the life and the soul of the party, very articulate, verbal and er do you know what I mean?

IG: That's just performance though.

Int: That's just performance, that's act. And then there's been this rather sort of neurotic introverted character as well. Most people don't see that now...

IG: Mm. You just mentioned there –

Int: Er that macho thing and then this sort of rather shy sensitive retiring recluse.

IG: Mm. Which is the real you, the latter?

Int:　No I think they're both me, hence action-research and the theory practice problem. I think they're both me and I try to keep them together in some way interactive with one another. Um so why would *Sailing* be my favourite song? Rod Stewart right? – a) because it's a –

IG:　It's transcendent...

Int:　Yes, because you see the sea. The sea and sailing, I mean the navy was another vision I had of a vocation which didn't come to fruition. Um but I've always seen myself as a man of action and as an intellectual.

IG:　Why do you think that? I mean just go back to this thing about, early on you said something about this aggression that you were able to internalise, where did the aggression come from? What was that about?

Int:　Well I always thought it was aggression against my father that I daren't express otherwise I got clobbered.

IG:　I bet it was the other way.

Int:　What?

IG:　It was more your mother wasn't it?

Int:　Yeah, I think it was now, aggression towards my mother, and so I've had a tremendous problem that I live with to this day aggression towards women.

IG:　And was it aggression that she wasn't, although she was there she wasn't really interested? I mean what –

Int:　No, no not at all. My mother doted on her sons, I was a spoilt mother's boy in some ways.

IG:　Smothered?

Int:　Definitely smothered so I've had a great fear of getting tied down by women, which is a fear most men have to some extent.

IG:　Mm, so it was the smothering that lead to the aggression?

Int:　Yeah, it took me until I was about 45 to be able to relate to an emotional woman. All the women I was attracted to before then were the kind of cool, ice-cool Grace Kelly types, who I saw as a profound challenge breaking down the barrier, of course I never did and never wanting to get into the emotional stuff because my mother was emotional but I always associated emotionality with manipulation.

IG:　So that action-research is a way of taking back that sense of autonomy is it?

Int:　Yeah, yeah.

IG:　Taking back power.

Int:　Oh yeah, that's why I'm talking about power. Autonomy, control over your life. And developing a distinction between, taking control and being in control. I mean I do have a concept that you cant in fact control your circumstances, the behaviour of everyone in the world, what you can do is you can always be in control over your own self, the construction of your own self in relationship to the situation.

The elements covered in this interview provide a useful backcloth for the thematic analysis of the range of interviews conducted with action research proponents. A number of the themes touched upon in this interview can be discerned more generally in the interview material. Three themes seem particularly salient. Firstly, the issue of the teacher as intellectual, the teacher as scientist, the teacher as researcher. These positional statements run in similar form across all of the interviews conducted. It is as if the interviewees are at pains to point out that they renounce a narrow definition of the teacher as technician, as deliverer, as implementer of other people's objectives. There is a strong stress on the autonomy of teacher's work and this seems clearly related to a definition of self as intellectual or scientist or researcher. A number of the interviewees speak eloquently of the sense of self and autonomy that is expressed through the spaces and locations associated with intellectual visions and work.

This issue which deals with the autonomous space to undertake the 'reflective project of the self' relates to two other themes. These may be seen as different routes of movement or escape. So as a second theme, there is what may be described as the 'escape from the self'. The attempt to transcend initial social definitions and locations through movement to another locational place and psyche. Thirdly, there is the movement beyond the classroom towards a more purist notion of intellectual location. The themes of escape from the classroom and escape from the original self seem common within the interviews conducted. But before we examine notion of escape, we need to define starting points.

Origins and destinations

Before exploring the main themes discerned in the interviews, it is important to provide some contextual background of the origins and destinations of the main interviewees. Some of the interviewees spoke frankly of some of the trails and traumas of their early years. These experiences may go some way to explaining the appeal of a social movement like action research in terms of its general missionary posture but also in terms of its potential for 'playing out' more broader psychic struggles. This relates specifically to its core belief – its psychic promise if you will – that action can be 'researched', intellectualized, rationalized as a guide to behaviour and as a means of asserting control in a precarious and sometimes hostile psychic and, later, workaday world.

One of the interviewees spoke of her mother before analyzing some of her early experiences. The interview makes clear some of the links between early experiences and the appeal of the 'action research movement' in which she has now become a key player.

> *Int:* She was a very independent spirit. I mean she learnt to drive in India. She insisted upon driving as much as my father drove. She insisted on having her own bank account, which she saw as a matter of pride that they didn't have a joint account. So when she got left money by some of her old aunts and things she had control over that. I mean it cost her very hard that she couldn't work. But her father was so ashamed that his wife, (so my grandmother), my grandmother had actually been a nurse. She was the vicar's daughter and they had to work because they weren't really very wealthy, but when she married a doctor nobody knew any more that she'd been a nurse, they didn't discover that she'd been a nurse until after she died and they found documents in her possession which showed that she had this qualification and she had worked as a nurse before her marriage. So he saw it as a matter of real pride that he supported his family, even though he never had any money, they were always incredibly hard up. So this, this was a very, this was no doubt a very, very powerful influence in me, it still is. I find the hardest thing to understand about my, one of my children is that she has absolutely no desire to have a career, she lives in a bus, she's a, a new age traveller or

whatever. And that's fine, I understand it intellectually but it was so important to me to actually, what I saw at the time was doing something with my life. To me just spending it on bringing up the next generation of children was a kind of, I wasn't making any mark, you know, I felt that life would be purposeless, that my own statement would have been lost if I would simply then become the person who produced the next generation. And I felt that really strongly.

IG: Tell me what it was.

Int: Because I felt so trapped.

The feeling of being 'trapped' or 'smothered' or encased in a very circumscribed class or regional environment was a common theme. This often led to a desire for forms of 'escape' or 'transcendence'.

The scholarship route to grammar school as 'an area of self transcendence' was commented on by most of the interviewees. Clear gender differences emerge in the telling of these tales of scholarship success.

I was the first person to go to university in my family – you know, the usual story. I was an only child – there was my mother and me, my father had died when I was very small. There was no-one in the family to offer any kind of advice about higher education. Going to university was really quite a big step and we were also very poor so it was also quite a strain. I was growing up in south-east London – I'd always live in London.

My mother was a Harris and there was a rich end of the family who owned Harris's Break and Cakes. I don't think the firm exists any longer. The family was committed to educating the boys. They paid for the boys to go to grammar schools but the girls left school early – presumably with the expectation that they would marry. So my mother left school at 14 and went into a variety of jobs, but she also spent a long time then going to evening sessions at Morley College. It offered a range of music. She didn't win any qualifications because she was always in and out of things. There was a lot of music in the family. The men drank a bit and gambled a bit and I was brought up in a female setting – with none of the females having any qualifications. The pattern was that the women saved and the men spent – and I had to learn to break out of the female habit!

But they knew it was important to go to university. I remember going for interviews in Nottingham and various places but chose to go to London because my mother was ill and wanted me to see her at weekends. I went to Westfield College in Hampstead.

My father had trained as a chemist but he died when I was very small. I don't know much about my father's side of the family.

The 'scholarship boys' and 'scholarship girls' who went to Grammar Schools in the 1950s and 1960s experienced considerable uncertainty at their cultural marginality. This has been closely documented by Hoggart (1958), Steedman (1986) and perhaps most influentially in Jackson and Marsden (1962).

The salience of scholarship boy and girl stories in the accounts collected is of considerable significance and in all probability provides a natural seedbed for transition to stories of 'the teacher as intellectual'. It would seem that the arena of schooling provided the location for the acts of transcendence and rational engagement recounted by the interviewees. In this sense, it is probable that schools have a mythic place in the stories and dreams for these people. It is almost as if, therefore, they were socialized into modernism because of the close link with the reflexive project of the self. Not surprisingly then, later in life, their work turned to using action research to seek to improve (sometimes in transcendent ways) public schooling. In this sense, the relationship between individual reflexive projects of selves and their collective outcome in the social movement of action research is an important locus for our social analysis.

Teachers as intellectuals

The possibility of a conception of 'teachers as intellectuals' or 'teachers as researchers' depends very much on the social and political conditions of particular historical periods. It is significant that much of the exploration and operationalization of the 'teacher as researcher' and 'teacher as intellectual' conception were undertaken in the 1960s. In the United Kingdom, this was a time when the Labour government was sponsoring the search for a number of solutions through schooling as part of the broad implementation of comprehensive schooling. This is the period Eric Hobsbawm (1994) has characterized as the 'golden age' – an age of social democratic capitalism where patterns of profit and accumulation allowed degrees of looseness in social reproduction and construction which would be entirely unthinkable in current times. Hence, the encouragement of teachers as researchers and intellectuals as part of a broader, albeit partial, social and political project was specific to the late 1950s and 1960s.

> Ivor: But would it be fair to say just going back through the biography there and sifting through, what you're really saying in terms of why the teacher as researcher thing began for you in a school that you were trying in teaching to carve out the biographical space that you'd always wanted?
>
> Int: Yes.
>
> Ivor: You'd wanted to be a researcher?
>
> Int: Yes, absolutely right.
>
> Ivor: You'd wanted to be a scientific researcher but this was a say of parleying that in to where you ended up which was teaching?
>
> Int: Yes, but don't forget my research was always action-research in one sense. I mean as a nuclear physicist I wanted to –
>
> Ivor: Yeah, sure.
>
> Int: Split the atom and get bombs going off [laughs]
>
> Ivor: Yeah, that's pretty active.

For this reason, it is of considerable interest that many of the interviewees express opinions that are similar to Henry Giroux's notion of 'teachers as intellectuals' a conception that derives a considerable amount, possibly unknowingly, from the earlier conceptions of the teacher as researcher – that were pioneered in Europe. Giroux writes:

> As intellectuals, they will combine reflection and action in the interest of empowering students with the skills and knowledge needed to address injustices and to be critical actors committed to developing a world free of oppression and exploitation.
>
> (Giroux, 1988, p. xxxiv)

He goes on to define the transformation and transcendent aspects of this conceptualization of self and work.

> The material conditions under which teachers work constitutes the basis for either delimiting or empowering their practices as intellectuals. Therefore teachers and intellectuals will need to reconsider and, possibly, transform the fundamental nature of the conditions under which they work. That is teachers must be able to shake the way in which time, space, activity, and knowledge organise everyday life in schools. More specifically, in order to function as intellectuals, teachers must create the ideology and structural conditions necessary for them to write, research, and work with each other in producing curricula and sharing power. In the final analysis, teachers need to develop a discourse and set of assumptions that allow them to function more specifically as transformative intellectuals.
>
> (Giroux, 1988, p. xxiv)

One of the interviewees talked about the salience of this conception of being 'an intellectual' and the way that it dawned upon her in the months she spent in Ireland recovering from a divorce. Planning the conception of self as intellectual plays a crucial role in the reflexive project of self-building that has been undertaken and what is described in the interview.

Ivor: You've just used the phrase there 'taking control with all the ideas put together', interestingly I have noted just before rational/intellectual taking control, is that notion of being an academic, being an intellectual linked with this idea of how one takes control of one's life and one's biography from what has been a fairly rootless and fragmented childhood, do you think that issue of how one takes control through books and the imagination is very much part of the motif for you?

Int: Yes, I do. Yes, I think that's quite perceptive. Yes.

Ivor: So when you talk about becoming academic, becoming intellectual it must have a kind of biographical meaning about how one takes control of a life?

Int: Yes. I'm sure it does. I'm sure its easy to see the roots in my childhood, but I think also if you are a lonely child you turn to books very strongly. One of the few things I remember telling the psychoanalyst in Dublin for the short time I lay on the couch was that I had really lived in books for part of my childhood, and then suddenly found that people were interesting. I suppose this was when I made some very good friends in the last two or three years I was at that school in Dublin. I've always thought it was a very odd idea, and actually this does relate to the way I feel about action-research, the idea that you cant learn from books is very peculiar to me actually. I do see what the problems are, but I think one of the major problems about a lot of action-research work is that it hasn't been sufficiently rooted in knowledge of other peoples ideas. I'm impatient of people who ridicule something called propositional knowledge. I think one wants to have every kind of experience and reading is a hell of an interesting experience. And I include vicarious experience, I mean a lot of my childhood was locked up in pretty boring places but you could get tremendous vicarious experience through reading. So a big image for me was lying in that boarding school in Malvern which was in the old railway hotel and hearing the trains go past by night. It was so bloody wonderful to hear these trains whistling and to think of them going out there through the night, and free. I think I had practically no freedom during my entire childhood so when I finally got myself to Trinity, I was booked into one of the women's halls of residence, but I basically never ate a single meal there the whole term because it was something like a four mile bicycle ride out there, and it just wasn't worth going home because it would have meant that I couldn't do anything in the evening. So I just took off, I mean my memory of being a student was just riding around Dublin on a bicycle, luxuriously, thinking I can go anywhere I bloody like and do anything I bloody want. I'm completely free.

Patterns of transcendence

Later on, in discussing a period of secondment following years of teaching, the interviewee in the foregoing section referred to the 'absolutely transformative event in my entire career' certainly an absolutely crucial transition in the continuing project of self-building, of which the trajectory was emerging with increasing clarity: it happened while she was at the Cambridge Institute on a full time secondment from her teaching job.

> *Int:*   So over coffee somebody said to me that the big thing was curriculum studies and that he was going to do curriculum studies with this person called John Elliott, and I said, 'Well, I'll come along'. So I went to John's first session although I wasn't enrolled as his student and said to him, 'Would it be alright if I sat in because I was interested?' At the end of the session I went straight out thinking that this was the most mind-blowing thing, you know, because suddenly instead of it being just a great relief year there was a chance of something that would be absolutely riveting, i.e., going to schools to carry out research on behalf of teachers. This is what he told us in the first session, this is what he lined up for us, he'd got these schools where teachers were coming up with problems. They wanted his students to go in, work with them on something and carry out research on their behalf and help them to improve their practice. And I thought –
> *Ivor:*   And why did that appeal to you so much?
> *Int:*   I just thought it sounded the most exciting and interesting possibility of – why. [laughs]. Oh I think, I don't know, Ivor, really. I think, I suppose the word 'research' meant a lot, you know, I still, you see I never thought I was doing something called, I did call it action-research but I didn't differentiate it from research. I felt it was just as valuable as, I didn't really have any hang-ups that what I was doing wasn't proper research. I felt affronted when I found out that other people didn't necessarily feel it was, you know.

One of the recurrent themes in the interviews of people's backgrounds and life stories is the notice of what one interviewee actually calls 'transcendence', the move from one vision of self to a wider range of alternatives or multiple selves.

One of the interviewees spoke specifically of how notions of multiple selves began to emerge in her work as an action researcher.

> So I wrote a thing about my multiple selves and constructing my self for personnel managers. And the self-positioning, and the way in which what you are as a self has to act politically. Therefore, you cant have this notion of the one true self because you have to be a political actor, otherwise you're powerless. So you have to be conscious of the different selves you can employ.

The development of these reflexive project of selves often could be retrospectively, yet partially and selectively, reconstructed in the interviews. One episode for instance spoke of a 'breathtaking moment' where the person realized that there were a range of alternative futures which would make possible a different conceptualization of self. The episode took place when the teacher who, as we have seen earlier, aspired to a vision of himself as a scientific and ornithological researcher, was involved in catching birds.

> *Int:*   I mean I remember one night, just while we're talking about Kenneth Allsopp and stuff, catching these wagtails, which we did in huge numbers, and er a little falcon twigged on to what was happening and it just hovered around for a while for this big pile of wagtails to come in and just took the weakest one out and I mean it was just a breathtaking moment so there were those sort of moments but that's aside. Yeah, it gave me, it gave a connection with that, that world, that is was tangential to it and not part of it and, at the same time, there were beginning to be pressures like, oughtn't I, you know I was a scale 4 Head of Science, oughtn't I to be getting on to be deputy-head? Er which I could never visualise myself as. So what that gave, and I don't think I knew it at the time, but what it gave was an alternative vision of the future, and that's a Stenhousian phrase as you probably know recognise, you know –
> *Ivor:*   Mm, yes.
> *Int:*   Sort of dreams of, of possible futures and, not having read Stenhouse at that point, that's how I would characterise it.

The visions of alternative futures and alternative selves often arose from a recognition that the original social location and pattern of socialization was unacceptable. As one interviewee put it, she came to, 'understand that certain aspects of the way I was brought up stank'. Because of this background, she continued:

> It was difficult for me to be the kind of person I wanted to be. To have the kind of democratic values I wanted to aspire to wasn't something that I could automatically do. You know, 'every time I opened my mouth I made some other Englishman despise me.' It was not only the way I sounded but the sort of phrases I used, my discourse. It was terribly difficult to unpick an entire discourse system you've been brought up in, even if rationally you've come to understand you don't want to be part of it.

This seems as articulate and concise a statement of the desire to escape from the original social location and socially constructed self as it is possible to imagine.

Leaving teaching

Alongside the desire to escape from the original social location and pattern of socialization, was a subsequent desire to escape from the classroom, a similarly embedded site of self definition and socialization as systematic and penetrative as anything experienced in family life.

> *Ivor:* So you didn't really think hard about leaving teaching, it was an easy decision?
>
> *Int:* Mm, I didn't want to go back. I, I knew it was risky but, I felt confident and just went ahead with it.
>
> *Ivor:* When you say you didn't want to go back had you at that stage had enough of teaching and if so why?
>
> *Int:* Yes, I think I had. Well, because I felt like somebody who had gradually peeled off more and more protective layers as a result of trying to get away from the routines, the protective techniques that teachers had wrapped around themselves. You know that sense originally when I started that my personality was under attack, which I used to feel because I had to discipline people and force people to do things they didn't want to do. It was very good for me because I was actually very lacking in confidence in many ways when I first became a teacher. It was a curious mixture but there was a part of me which was very lacking in confidence and it toughened me up no end that I had to take this role all the time. But then when I started doing action-research the investigation into the interaction between myself and students and the examination of my own motives and tacit assumptions and all that stuff, and also looking carefully at what learning tasks I was setting meant that I was setting more and more challenging work really, so I was losing out on some of the, you know, reciprocal negotiation that people would get on comfortably because I wasn't challenging them too much. So the job was quite demanding and the more that you peel off these protective layers and try to engage with every individual student, and then people just say, 'Bugger off' because they're teenagers and they don't want to be there, its crushing. I began losing my temper sometimes. My big dilemma was always, how do you engage in one to one conversation with people sufficiently to actually take them forward intellectually. You know, how do you listen to what they've said, come back with a response which will enable them to take their thinking forward. In other words how do you have some kind of Socratic dialogue when you've got twenty-nine other people in the room? Well, the only way you do it is by changing the whole responsibility for learning and creating a new ambience where they take responsibility for their own learning. And I tried to achieve that and I achieved it in a lot of my classes but I didn't achieve it with, you know, groups who were in a sense –
>
> *Ivor:* I mean how were the other staff of the school responding to your Socratic interventions?
>
> *Int:* I don't think they much about it, I think that I had to keep quiet about what I was doing. Although interestingly my dissertation for my MA, in fact all of my research for my MA made me a lot more popular in the school in the end, because I interviewed people and I interviewed

them having divested myself from my role as Head of English. And I listened to them and wrote down what they said and they liked that enormously.

Ivor: But in terms of what you're saying, I mean here you are, you're going through this very reflective practitioner mode, but somehow it's lead you to the conclusion that you'd be best to move onto something else rather than going on in teaching, hasn't it?

Int: Well, yes, I know but that is the rub and that is the guilt. That's why, you know, when you first get your first job outside teaching you don't feel good about being in a town during a school day. You actually feel bad about going down to buy a pair of shoes or – you know, for a long time after you give up teaching you know precisely what people are doing at this moment if you were still at school. So you go past the school gate, to drive from Thatcham to Redmond, and instead of thinking shit how awful I've got an hour and a quarter to drive before I get to work, you think this is a wonderful trade-off for marking all those exercise books which I used to have to do all day on Sunday. And gone is the feeling of dread on Sundays about Monday morning. And I don't know why that's an integral part of teaching, but I've never yet, – you'll probably tell me you're the exception, but I've never yet met a teacher who didn't own up to feeling a sense of dread on Sunday afternoon.

The problems of the escape from the classroom are made very clear in the experience of one of the interviewees. After a sustained period on action research projects based in the university, she spoke of the problems of re-entering teaching.

Int: So, I had to fall backwards on the authority and they said, 'OK, you can go onto supply here'. And I went to a school in Cambridgeshire on supply and all of the cues that I thought I knew how to handle about kids just came unstuck. So I mean in a school that I had taught at for nine years I could cough and the whole school would come quiet, you know that? You know that they knew me, I knew them, they knew when I was serious and stuff, and yet in this other school I did that and a small kid came from the front and gave me a cough sweet, you know. Er, cheeky little sod. And all, all my practical skills had gone, and it was a nightmare actually, the whole summer term there, trying to stay with your head above water in a situation that formerly you could have wellied with your arm behind your back, you know, it was just a nightmare.

Ivor: It's very paradoxical, isn't it? As I mean after a long immersion in practitioner based action-research what you ended up being was deskilled.

Int: Totally so, totally so.

Ivor: And that is the paradox isn't it?

Int: Yes

Ivor: How do you explain it?

Int: I think, I mean there's numerous ways that you could explain it, I think it's a bit like this thing that people say horses can smell fear. It wasn't fear the kids could smell but they knew my lack of motivation, that I was being where I didn't want to be, in a world I didn't want to be in.

Ivor: Had you view of yourself changed then really during the years?

Int: Oh yes.

Ivor: From what to what? From practitioner –

Int: To researcher, I think would be the, the [pause] – and in the end I'd got a Masters in the process and so I'd begun to see myself in that metier. And that's where I wanted to be and to be elsewhere was if you like a failure in that project. Um –

Ivor: What do you mean?

Int: Well in the project to be within the research world. To have to dump yourself back in school. I mean I was doing the kids no service, not where I wanted to be and they knew it. I knew it.

What is so clear about this interview is the way that a new sense of self had emerged whilst on the action research project within universities. And it was, as it were, impossible to take that sense of self back into the classroom. As he says 'I'd begun to see myself in that metier'. And it was difficult, therefore, to re-enter the world of classrooms.

Conclusion

The range of themes which emerge in the interviews are compelling but also in their nature, selective. We chose to interview a number of the 'key players' from the action research movement and as a result we have a cohort of people who moved into elite positions inside the university sector. What is made clear, however, is that taking the notion of the teacher as intellectual and the teacher as researcher seriously, often led to the logical conclusion of moving from being a teacher to being, in a pure sense, a researcher or intellectual. This logic was built into the paradigm from the beginning and it is perhaps not surprising that some of the key players in the movement followed this metier to its conclusion.

The selective nature of the sample provokes other questions. Most notably, what about the large army of teachers who do not leave the classroom but continue to practice notions of the teacher as researcher or teacher as intellectual within their classrooms. Associated with this is perhaps the most critical question of all. Is action research institutionalized in university courses in ways that foster notions of escape and transcendence? Does action research as realized and institutionalized in universities take a particular form which encourages patterns of abstraction and intellectualization which are convenient for the university milieu and the careers pursued therein but inappropriate and decontextualized for those wishing to take action research back into the classroom.

This links to questions of the relationship between private lives (and self projects) and professional trajectories (and careers). The patterns of status and resources which structure professional careers influence the patterns, even of countervailing traditions such as action research, in ways that penetrate both private and public projects. They warn us that as C. Wright Mills argued: 'No social study that does not come back to the problems of biography, of history and of their intersections within a society has completed its intellectual journey' (Wright Mills, 1959, p. 6).

References

Giddens, A., 1991, *Modernity and Self-identity: Self and Society in the Late Modern Age* (Cambridge: Polity Press, in association with Basil Blackwell).

Giroux, H.A., 1988, *Teachers and Intellectuals: Towards a Critical Pedagogy of Learning?* (South Hadley, MA: Bergen and Garvey).

Hobsbawm, E., 1994, *Age of Extremes: The Short Twentieth Century, 1914–1991* (London: Michael Joseph).

Hoggart, R., 1958, *The Uses of Literacy* (Harmondsworth, Middlesex: Penguin Books, in association with Chatto and Windus).

Jackson, B. and Marsden, D., 1962, *Education and the Working Class* (London: Routledge and Kegan Paul).

Steedman, C., 1986, *Landscape for a Good Woman* (London: Virago Press).

Stenhouse, L., 1975, *An Introduction to Curriculum Research and Development* (London: Heinemann).

Wolf, A., 1989, *Whose Keeper? Social Science and Moral Obligation* (Berkeley, CA: University of California Press).

Wright Mills, C., 1959, *The Sociological Imagination* (London: Oxford University Press).

CHAPTER 16

SCRUTINIZING LIFE STORIES

N. Bascia, D. Thiessen and I. Goodson (eds), *Making a Difference about Difference*, Canada: Garamond Press, 1996, pp. 123–138

The use of life stories, life histories and narrative is currently a strongly emerging field of enquiry and one with exciting possibilities for reformulating some of the existing paradigms of educational study. There are, however, a number of question marks that immediately arise in scrutinizing stories such as those reported in the last few chapters. One of the issues I want to focus on in this chapter is the question of the 'prior script' on which such stories are based. For stories do not free themselves of the prior script and predilections which are a feature of all our social enquiries and accounts.

It should be noted that this prior script works in both chronological directions. A script, as we know, defines and gives meanings to our future actions, but social story-lines work backwards, too. As Schachtel has noted, we tend to recall and remember what the social order signifies as important 'perception and experience themselves develop increasingly into the rubber stamps of conventional clichés' (Schachtel, 1959, p. 288).

The power of the prior script is most clearly evident, of course, in the work of actors. But sometimes actors themselves take over as the authors of 'reality'. Take the B-picture actor called Ronald Reagan who went on to become President of the United States. In reviewing Reagan's capacity to suspend reality, as Shultz puts it, he 'did not believe that what happened had, in fact, happened'. Reagan, in short, developed a script to live and work from. Shultz says, 'he would go over the "script" of an event, past or present, in his mind, once that script was mastered, that was the truth – no fact, nor argument, no plea for reconsideration would change his mind'. For Reagan, the script was reality, and given his power, reality was the script. Draper notes: 'In effect, the grade-B pictures actor was still a grade-B pictures actor as president. He followed a script, because that was what he had learned to do' (Draper, 1993, p. 59).

In general, although most people are not actors and although people tell their stories in personal idiosyncratic ways, they employ prior scripts derived from the general cultural milieu. In this way, they tell their own story, but also narrate it according to wider stories. It is, in short, the relationship between agency and structure as it impinges on the world of storying and narrative.

To explain this interface, let me begin with an example. In much of North American life, the life story as told, if not as lived, follows a series of clear stages. As any Budweiser commercial will tell you, the adult life story opens with a period of feverish enjoyment during our youthful years which begins around 14 and goes on as long as it can be sustained. The collision between this view of life as exuberant and youthful and the indisputable (but heavily contested) acceptance that we die, normally comes with the invented episode of the midlife crisis. Levinson's (1978) *Seasons of a Man's Life* (which focuses very narrowly on professional men) narrates the life story, moving from youth to the articulation of a 'central dream'. Men strive to achieve this dream and the point of culmination, collision, or collapse is somewhere around forty. This is followed, whether you succeed in your dream or not, by the notion of midlife crisis.

What follows this period in most narratives is the beginning of a period of decline and deterioration, culminating in the end of life. Now, in many ways, this narrative of youth followed by a central professional dream followed by decline has at least represented, in a reasonable way, the life span which was to be expected up until the 1950s or 1960s. With the transformation of medical science and the lengthening of life expectancy, these prior scripts, these story lines, have become anachronistic, as a cultural story, it retains its power to overlay and overlap our more personal modes of storying.

It is only very recently that literature has begun to provide a non-declining story of life for those people between 40 and 60. As Margaret Gullette (1988) has recently argued in her elegant study of the invention of the midlife progress novel:

> The difference in the late 20th century is that the more optimistic minority view of the life course is beginning to appear, in the reiterated and gradually more self-conscious way that lets any new vision become visible. We are seeing the new paradigm – the new ideology – about the middle years shape itself under our reading eyes.
>
> (p. 24)

The new ideology, the new prior script speaks about a period of progress rather than decline through the years 40–60. She says:

> Perhaps, to have life-course sequences for a progressive kind in any numbers we had to wait until several favouring circumstances combined in the second half of the 20th century. Confessional literature became acceptable, while the novel form provided the illusion of privacy for authors who might otherwise have been reluctant to appear more confessional even than the poets.

Secondly, she argues:

> A demographic boom provided an audience getting readier, as it aged, to relinquish its original cult of youth and, thus prepared, to hear better news about its anxious aging. Indeed, like Juggernaut, some part of the midlife cohort is happy to crush old stereotypes of aging beneath its future-breasting cart. A postcard, a sweatshirt, and a mug keep before us a progressive slogan: 'Never trust anyone over 30, 36, 40, 45.' Where economic decline would have placed an intolerable strain on the reading public's willingness to assent to stories of midlife improvement, the post-war years have been a period of economic boom. Divorce laws and sexual revolution have expanded choices and attitudes open to adults, and the feminist revolution, those open to women.

What Gullette is, therefore, hinting at is that only now is literature, and literature is normally ahead of other cultural carriers of ideology, providing us with a different script for the way we story our life (Gullette, 1988, pp. 24–26).

The way these storylines are now being taken up can be adequately observed in the way women now talk about their lives. Angela Lambert recently commented on this in her newspaper column:

> Over the last few decades, largely triggered by feminism, there has been a real revolution in the lives of middle-aged women. My mother was typical of her generation: middle-aged at 35, old at 40. I can still remember how poignantly, on her 40th birthday, she wept – as though all the fun had gone out of her life. I'm old, was her cry; nobody will be interested in me, flirt with me, dance with me, ever again.
>
> It didn't cross my mind to think like that at 40, nor yet at 50, nor do I suppose it will at 60. Today's older women can have lives as vigorous and involved in the world and their jobs as older men. That central role is reflected in their faces: full of interest, energy, curiosity and confidence. My female contemporaries look wonderful. They have far too much intelligence to make themselves ridiculous by trying to look girlish, but what they do have is the beauty of an assured style, and control over their own lives.
>
> (Lambert, 1994, p. 17)

What I am searching for is a way of locating our scrutiny of stories to show that the general forms, skeletons, and ideologies that we employ in structuring the way we tell our individual tales, come from the wider culture. Hence, it is an illusion to think that we capture only the person's voice when we capture a personal story. What we capture, in fact, is a mediation between the personal voice and wider cultural imperatives. Hence, there is a need, not only to urge people to *narrate*, but to urge them to *collaborate*, also, so as to *locate* the narrative and the story in its wider cultural setting. We need, in short, three interlinked aspects: narration, collaboration and location.

It is, therefore, I think, a crucial part of our ethical position as researchers that we do not 'valorise the subjectivity of the powerless' in the name of telling 'their story'. This would be to merely record constrained consciousness – a profoundly conservative posture and one which no doubt explains the popularity of such work during the recent conservative political renaissance. In my view, stories should, where possible, provide not only a *narrative of action* but also a history of *genealogy of context*. I say this in full knowledge that this opens up substantial dangers of further changing the relationship to the academy.

Let me provide one other instance of a prior script that has become obsolescent, as social structures and political possibilities have changed. This is the script of the scholarship boy. Strangely, Bill Clinton, Whitewater notwithstanding, may resurrect this cultural dinosaur. Of course, scholarships were won by both male and female students. But given the cultural and gender politics of the time, it was the 'scholarship boy' who was most commonly celebrated, storied and scripted.

Richard Hoggart in his influential *Uses of Literacy* was an important inscriber of the 'scholarship boy' storyline. In his chapter 'Unbent Springs: A Note on the Uprooted and Anxious' he begins by quoting Chekhov and, later, George Eliot on scholarship boys.

> Do, please, write a story of how a young man, the son of a serf, who has been a shop boy, a chorister, pupil of a secondary school, and a university graduate, who has been brought up to respect rank and to kiss the priest's hand, to bow to other people's ideas, to be thankful for each morsel of bread, who has been

thrashed many a time, who has had to walk about tutoring without galoshes, who has fought, tormented animals, has been fond of dining at the house of well-to-do relations, and played the hypocrite both to God and man without any need but merely out of consciousness of his own insignificance – describe how that young man squeezes the slave out of himself, drop by drop, and how, awakening one fine morning, he feels running in his veins no longer the blood of a slave, but genuine human blood (Chekhov).

For my part I am very sorry for him. It is an uneasy lot at best, to be what we call highly taught and yet not to enjoy: to be present at this great spectacle of life and never to be liberated from a small hungry shivering self (George Eliot).

(Hoggart, 1958, p. 241)

From these quotes, Hoggart begins his exploration of the agony and the ecstasy of the scholarship boy. Writing in 1957, he must be situated in a time and place where in Britain socialist governments had been trying to build a post-war 'New Jerusalem' based on certain selective versions of social justice and equity. The 'scholarship boy' story, then, stands testimony to a particular version of the progress narrative – one which now stands devalued as reminiscent of outmoded models of meritocracies, masculinisms, and Marxisms. These factors give Hoggart's text a strangely dated flavour, even though he was writing less than 40 years ago:

It will be convenient to speak first of the nature of the uprooting which some scholarship boys experience. I have in mind those who, for a number of years, perhaps for a very long time, have a sense of no longer really belonging to any group. We all know that many do find a poise in their new situations. There are 'declassed' experts and specialists who go into their own spheres after the long scholarship climb has led them to a Ph.D. There are brilliant individuals who become fine administrators and officials, and find themselves thoroughly at home. There are some, not necessarily so gifted, who reach a kind of poise which is yet not a passivity nor even a failure in awareness, who are at ease in their new group without any ostentatious adoption of the protective colouring of that group, and who have an easy relationship with their working-class relatives, based not on a form of patronage but on a just respect. Almost every working-class boy who goes through the process of further education by scholarships finds himself chafing against his environment during adolescence. He is at the friction-point of two cultures; the test of his real education lies in his ability, by about the age of twenty-five, to smile as his father with his whole face and to respect his flighty young sister and his slower brother. I shall be concerned with those for whom the uprooting is particularly troublesome, not because I wish to stress the more depressing features in contemporary life, but because the difficulties of some people illuminate much in the wider discussion of cultural change. Like transplanted stock, they react to a widespread drought earlier than those who have been left in their original soil.

I am sometimes inclined to think that the problem of self-adjustment is, in general, especially difficult for those working-class boys who are only moderately endowed, who have talent sufficient to separate them from the majority of their working-class contemporaries, but not to go much farther. I am not implying a correlation between intelligence and lack of unease; intellectual people have their own troubles: but this kind of anxiety often seems most to afflict those in the working classes who have been pulled one stage away from their original culture and yet have not the intellectual equipment which would then cause them to move on to join the 'declassed' professionals and experts. In one sense, it is true, no one is ever 'declassed'; and it is interesting to see how this occasionally obtrudes (particularly today, when ex-working-class boys move in all the managing areas of society) – in the touch of insecurity, which often appears as a undue concern to establish 'presence' in an otherwise quite professional professor, in the intermittent rough homeliness of an important executive and committee-man, in the tendency to vertigo which betrays a lurking sense of uncertainty in a successful journalist.

(Hoggart, 1958, pp. 242–243)

The scholarship boy's script was employed by a wide range of young men in a variety of different social situations. I have previously written of my own experience of this, but here it is important to focus on the enormous 'outreach' of this prior script. What follows is a life story narrated by a 50-year-old black male teacher who grew up in Belize in Central America. Besides its importance in analysing the prior scripting of storylines, it is a valuable example of the texture of life story narrations.

I suppose that the significant figures that we looked up to were always educated people. Not sports figures or particularly wealthy people who had made their mark by amassing vast fortunes. When I was growing up, we had a notion of what a good job was: always a job with the civil service. This was British Colonial rule and the civil service was very attractive to us because you got to wear nice clean white shirt and a tie to go to work, as opposed to coming out from under the bottom of a car all grimy and besmirched. But, of course, for a civil service job you need at least a high school education. But in Belize, where I was growing up, a high school education was not a foregone conclusion. You had to pay for high school unless you won a government scholarship. It wasn't a case of applying, everyone who went to elementary school would take the government scholarship exam in grade six. I'm not sure exactly what standards they applied, but very few people won those scholarships. I distinctly recall, because it was a significant item in my life, that there were 33 of us in my grade six class, and I was the only one who got a scholarship. There was also a church scholarship, but in order to win it you had to be a regular churchgoer. I also won a church scholarship, together with another pupil. James Roby. Apparently, I had done slightly better than him. I distinctly remember our meeting with some 'authority figures', who explained to me that this was James's last chance because he was older than I was, and that I had a very good chance of getting a government scholarship.

When I went to St. Paul's College, the Anglican high school I attended, which was run according to the British system, with forms, there were about 25–30 of us in the first form. There were about five scholarship winners, but these had come from all over the country. They were all Anglicans, of course. The others were paid for by their parents. The government scholarship was a good thing, because your family just had to provide the uniform: khaki shorts or long pants, a white shirt with short sleeves and a green tie. The school sold the tie. We all went around with green ties, white shirts and khaki pants. When I look back now it cuts a funny sort of picture, but at that time it was a significant move in your life. At that time, we felt privileged to go to high school, because for many of our elementary classmates, that was it – grade six.

In Belize, parents, regardless of a child's academic potential, always felt that a son should have some sort of trade to fall back on. So during my elementary years, along with, I suppose, all my contemporaries, I went to learn a trade. My mother packed my younger brother and myself off to a tailor. But in my mind, even though I was very young, I knew very well that I was not going to be a tailor. I didn't know what I was going to be, but I was not going to sit in some gloomy tailor's shop and sew clothes for people all my life, and come out hunch-backed after 20 years of this, looking for and picking up pieces of thread. I wasn't going to do that; it would be too stultifying. I suppose way back then I saw myself as an academic person. As it turned out, this was confirmed by my experiences.

I did very well in elementary school, I suppose it's the same all over the world, doing well in high school does a whole lot for your self esteem and your popularity. People respect you because you are smart, and that meant all kinds of things. For example, one of the so-called smart things I displayed was the ability to memorise things. The school always put on plays, and my fantastic memory enabled me to get parts. I was very well respected – Johnson, he's very smart, he's got a future – that type of thing. I remember, earlier than grade four, that I was taken to some classroom where there were some other people, and we had to do a little test. The end result was that I skipped grade five, and went from grade four into grade six. I was very young in grade six. During the first couple of recesses, and old grade four classmate taunted me with: 'Get away from me, you smart Alec!' It's funny how we remember these things while forgetting what happened more recently.

My school experiences have always been imprinted on my mind. They were always really encouraging experiences because I was so enthusiastic and so keen. Teachers loved me. When I look back now this was inevitable, I got along with them quite well. In grade four you have a crush on your teacher, and I distinctly recall having a crush on this teacher, Miss Janet Jones. She liked me very much. My big thrill was that I would go to her house on Saturdays and wash her bicycle. Bicycles, then, were the way of getting around, and as a result, people took exceedingly good care of them. They would polish them and clean every spoke. After I had washed her bicycle, I could ride it. So there I was, quite proudly tooling around the city riding Miss Jones's bicycle. In a different environment it would be the equivalent of a teacher lending a car. We didn't have bicycles ourselves, so I would visit my classmates and friends – they knew I was riding teacher's bicycle.

Education officers visited our school, and they appeared to us as powerful figures. They went beyond the white shirt and tie to suit jackets. Very nice. To us, these guys were the pinnacle of professional achievement. We looked up to them. After that, it was on to St. Paul's College. That was also a very good experience as I continued to be quite enthusiastic and hard working. St. Paul's College had speech night at the end of every school year. There was a prize for every subject area. Of course, being the academic, highly competitive person I was, I always tried to get a couple of prizes, and always did, at least win something. I never forget how proud I always made my mother, God rest her soul. It was her son, and this is St. Paul's College. I mean, after all we are talking about a place that had no university.

Years after I graduated from high school, there was still no university, which is why I didn't go to university until I left the country. Of course, some people did stick their noses to the grindstone and go to university from there, but

I didn't. Speech night was very important because in a class of 20 or 30 boys, two or three would be getting all the prizes. It wasn't that spread out because it was mainly an Arts School: History, Geography, Language, Health Science, Mathematics – but Algebra and Physical Geometry, not Trigonometry, no Science. Our school didn't have a science programme at all. Later on, when the government opened a technical school in the north part of the city, some of us were encouraged, because they thought we could do it, half way along, to drop a couple of subjects from our regular curriculum. So, for example, I dropped Health Science and Geography and in the evenings I went over to this school and took Chemistry and Physics. But, anyway, that programme didn't work out well because we were well along in our exercises when we had to take the GCE. At that time it was called the Cambridge School Certificate.

High school was very enjoyable. A person who has been a prominent person in my life is my high school English teacher, Howard Robinson. He has since gone on to be one of the outstanding intellectuals in the country. He received his BA in English from UCW, and PhD, with a thesis on the Creole language as spoken in Belize, in England. He was my mentor throughout my high school years.

After I finished high school I got into teaching. At that time you could enter teaching in two different ways. You could stay on after elementary school and become a teacher's aid, then by taking exams, obtain your first-class teacher's certificate. This would take about five years. Alternatively, you could teach once you completed high school. I graduated high school in November and started teaching in January. It makes sense, as far as content is concerned. You certainly learn enough in high school to teach elementary school. In university PhD's teach MA's. There's not that much difference. Once I started teaching, I did in-service training, with courses in methodology, psychology, and class-room methods and management. I travelled to the district capital once or twice a week to attend classes.

After two years I received my first class teacher's certificate. About that time a teacher's college opened, but most who went there didn't have high school. I think there was a certain elitist attitude there about high school. I taught elementary for three years from the time I was 18...I taught elementary for three years in two rural schools. In the second I was the vice principal. An older woman was the principal and I think the powers that be wanted me to stay on and eventually take over the school. But I don't think it was meant to be; I didn't see that as what I really wanted to do, but I think that was back in my head was always the notion that I would leave Belize, and that I would never want to stay there. It always struck me that it was a place that would eventually end up being quite stifling. That may not be so. I know a lot of my ex-classmates who ended up getting a university education and are quite well-placed and they seem to love it. But I think I'm the kind of person who prefers to swim in a larger pond even though I might be anonymous in that pond, than to rule in a very, very, small little puddle and to move in a sort of almost claustrophobic world. That had never appealed to me.

Education is very important in Belize. There is one radio station, Radio Belize. Since there was no university there, anyone leaving the country to study was a news item. The radio would announce: departing from Belize Airport today is A, son of B and C of no.1 D street, he is making his way to E to study R. Then four years later, when he returned the event was announced. Conquering Hero. This was a very important thing, because in a country where high school education couldn't be taken for granted, a person with a degree was a deity, really! You could get a degree in anything and be considered super smart. So when a person returned to Belize International Airport! Even Cambridge School Certificates were announced on the radio. Students from all over the country got together in Belize City to take the exam in this huge hall, with proctors walking up and down. The exams were then sent to England to be graded and marked. Several months later the results were announced on Radio Belize, they would state the school and the class of the certificate. This radio station was the only one in the whole country, education is a very powerful thing to Belizians; they give education very high value. You want to be one of those announced on the radio for passing your school certificate, and, maybe, one day announced as departing the International Airport.

I'm just making this connection right now, this powerful thing, imagining the poor guys who didn't make it through high school. You know there is a certain class there, there's a definite thing, you either have a high school education or you don't! You either have a university education or you do not. It's like that. Its funny though, much as they had a university education, obviously something I dreamed of in a way, my not having a university education made it seem too out of reach for me. Because if you wanted to go to university, there were two ways of doing it, you could win a government scholarship or you could have your parents pay for you. Our family couldn't afford it, in fact if I had not won a scholarship to high school I wouldn't have had a high school education.

(Interview, George Johnson, 1993)

In the initial narration, George Johnson provides a rich commentary on the power of the scholarship boy script in organising a life story. As with Reagan, we note how in a real sense the script of a life story narration represents reality in certain ways. If we view the self and identity as ongoing narrative projects, we begin to see the sheer power of the script in organising and representing reality – both to the self and to others.

But as we noted earlier, the recent scholarship boy storyline grew out of a social and political milieu of optimistic meritocracy following the Second World War. Resources were limited but growing, and for a minority of the working class, there was the potential for social mobility. This potential, this window of opportunity, was celebrated in the scholarship boy story. The scholarship boy represented a particular selectivity of class, gender, and race at a particular historical moment.

In the event, this moment passed and in the hiatus of the 1960s was effectively deconstructed. But for those who had scripted their lives on this storyline, the story continued as their chosen representation of reality. One of the fascinations of collaborating on life story narrations is to see how intensive 'grounded conversations' and introspective reflection combine to allow the life story-tellers to *locate* their stories. George Johnson spoke of this towards the end of the process of collaborating on his life story, when historical and sociological insights began to provide the material for him to locate his story.

Looking back, I feel I betrayed the academic promise I showed as a child. Examining the tapes and transcripts had dislodged a number of memories and subsequent feelings. On Monday, I felt quite depressed, I realise that life had passed by. I was troubled by thoughts of what should have been. At this stage,

I should be a professor or an executive with a house and car. Where have 25 years gone?

A university degree is very important to me; I always envied those who returned to Belize with one. I appreciate there are complex reasons behind this. Part of me doubts my ability to do university studies. I don't know if I've got what it takes. However, at some point I made choices. I avoided putting my abilities to the test. Although I didn't articulate it at the time, now, on reflection – I escaped. I chose a different path. I was a womaniser who ignored my intellectual potential. Eventually I chose marriage over studies. Within my own family, my stepfather, a driver, was an incorrigible womaniser. In high school, despite my academic success, I was rebellious and made trouble for the teacher, largely through my quick wit. I avoided further education, but felt frustrated. I now perceive leaving St. Paul's for Honduras as running away because I didn't want to be trapped. I knew I wanted a university degree, but wasn't prepared to face the challenge so I quit. I didn't want to be edged out; I didn't want to be an anachronism.

Honduras seemed the logical choice, since I was born there. I now see this journey as a flight from self, or from destiny. Only be attending university could I be announced: arriving at the airport...I don't really know whether I wanted that, living out a culturally provided script.

(Interview, George Johnson, 1993)

Only as he talked and re-examined his life story over many months of interview, casual conversation, transcript commentary, and general reflection did George begin to focus on the limits of the 'culturally prepared script'. In the later stages, he began to comment on his 'absurdity' in career terms, of abandoning teaching to pursue a long held dream of a university career. Given the retrenchment in Canadian universities, he knew his chances of getting a university post were minimal, but until then the story, the script, 'had driven him onwards'. For the scholarship boy the motif is always 'onwards and upwards', but in the end we find him confronting the lonely pathways of this script.

Scripts and storylines

These examples of mid-life progress narratives and scholarship boy stories show the intimate relationship between social and political circumstances and cultural storylines. In a real sense, social structures push storylines in particular directions and the stories then legitimate the structures – and, so on, in a self-legitimating circle. The relationship between social structure and story is loosely-coupled and stories can resist as well as enhance the imperatives of structure. The scholarship boy story is a particular example of this – a 'celebration' of a particular historical moment of opportunity for a selective group of male students, sometimes of working class origin. The storyline then privileges some; more significantly, however, it silences whole nations and racial groups where such windows of opportunity do not exist. With the passing of the scholarship boy, we see the long overdue end of a storyline, but, as we have seen, when life storylines become obsolescent in the wider cultural setting, this leaves a good deal of rehabilitation and reformulation to be undertaken at the level of the narrative project of the self.

The collection of stories, then, especially the mainstream stories that live out a 'prior script', will merely fortify patterns of domination. We shall need to move from life stories to life histories, from narratives to genealogies of context, towards a modality that embraces 'stories of action within theories of context'. In so doing, stories can be located, seen as the social constructions they are, fully implicated their location within power structures and social milieu. Stories then provide a starting point for active collaboration, 'a process of deconstructing the discursive practices through which one's subjectivity has been constituted' (Middleton, 1992, p. 20). Only if we deal with stories as the *starting point* for collaboration, as the *beginning* of a process of coming to know, will we come to understand their meaning; to see them as social constructions which allow us to locate and interrogate the social world in which they are embedded.

References

Draper, T., 1993, Iran-Contra: The Mystery Solved. *New York Review* of *Books*, XL(11) (June 10).

Gullette, M., 1988, *Safe at Last in the Middle Years* (Berkeley, CA and London: University of California Press).

Hoggart, R., 1958, *The Uses of Literacy* (Harmondsworth, Middlesex: Penguin Books in association with Chatto and Windus).

Johnson, G., 1993, Interview.

Lambert, Angela, 1994, A Very Dodgy Foundation. *The Independent* (June 1).

Levinson, D.J., 1978, *Seasons of a Man's Life* (New York: Knopf).

Middleton, S., 1992, Developing a Radical Pedagogy. In I.F. Goodson (ed.), *Studying Teachers' Lives* (London and New York: Routledge).

Schachtel, E. (ed.), 1959, On Memory and Childhood Amnesia. In *Metamorphosis* (New York: Basic Books).

CHAPTER 17

REPRESENTING TEACHERS
Bringing teachers back in

Teaching and Teacher Education: An International Journal of Research and Studies, 1997, 13(1)

The representational crisis

Educational study is again undergoing one of those recurrent swings of the pendulum for which the field is noted. But, as the contemporary world and global economies are transformed by rapid and accelerating change, such pendulum swings in scholarly paradigms seem to be alarmingly exacerbated.

Hence, we see a set of responses to a specific structural dilemma in which educational study has become enmeshed. But alongside this, the field is becoming engulfed (though more slowly than in many fields) by a crisis of scholarly representation. A specific structural dilemma now becomes allied with a wider representational crisis. Jameson (1984, p. viii) has summarized the latter crisis succinctly, as arising from the growing challenge to 'an essentially realistic episte- mology, which conceives of representation as the production, for subjectivity, of an objectivity that lies outside it'. Jameson wrote this in the foreword to Lyotard's *The Postmodern Condition*. For Lyotard, the old modes of representation no longer work. He calls for an incredulity towards these old canonical meta-narratives and says, 'the grand narrative has lost its credibility, regardless of what mode of unifi- cation is used, regardless of whether it is a speculative narrative or a narrative of emancipation' (Lyotard, 1984, p. 37).

Returning to the field of educational study, we see that in response to the distant, divorced and disengaged nature of aspects of educational study in univer- sities, some scholars have responded by embracing the 'practical', by celebrating the teacher as practitioner.

My intention here is to explore in detail one of these movements aiming to focus on teachers' knowledge – particularly the genre which focuses on teachers' stories and narratives. This movement has arisen from the crises of structural displacement and of representation briefly outlined. Hence the reasons for this new genre are understandable, the motivations creditable. As we see, the represen- tational crisis arises from the central dilemma of trying to capture the lived experi- ence of scholars and of teachers within a text. The experience of other lives is, therefore, rendered textual by an author. At root, this is a perilously difficult act and Denzin has cogently inveighed against the very aspiration:

> If the text becomes the agency that records and represents the voices of the other, then the other becomes a person who is spoken for. They do not talk, the text talks for them. It is the agency that interprets their words, thoughts,

intentions, and meanings. So a doubling of agency occurs, for behind the text as agent-for-the-other, is the author of the text doing the interpreting.

(Denzin, 1993, p. 17)

Denzin, then, is arguing that we have a classic case of academic colonization, or even cannibalization: 'The other becomes an extension of the author's voice. The authority of their "original" voice is now subsumed within the larger text and its double-agency' (1993, p. 17).

Given the scale of this representational crisis, one can quickly see how the sympathetic academic might wish to reduce interpretation, even collaboration, and return to the role of 'scribe'. At least in such passivity sits the aspiration to reduce colonization. In this moment of representational crisis, the doors open to the educational scholar as facilitator, as conduit for the teacher, to tell her/his story or narrative. The genuine voice of the oppressed subject, uncontaminated by active human collaboration; teachers talking about their practice, providing us with personal and practical insights into their expertise.

Here, maybe, is a sanctuary, an inner sanctum, beyond the representational crisis, beyond academic colonization. The nirvana of the narrative, the Valhalla of voice; it is an understandable and appealing project.

The narrative turn/the turn to narrative

So the turn to teachers' narratives and stories is, at one level, a thoroughly understandable response to the way in which teachers have tended to be represented in so much educational study. The teacher has been represented to serve our scholarly purposes.

Given this history and the goal displacement of educational study noted, it is therefore laudable that new narrative movements are concentrating on the teachers' presentation of themselves. This is a welcome antidote to so much misrepresentation and representation in past scholarship, and it opens up avenues of fruitful investigation and debate. The narrative movement provides then a catalyst for pursuing understandings of the teacher's life and work. In many ways, the movement reminds me of the point raised by Molly Andrews in her elegant study of elderly political activists. She summarizes the posture of those psychologists who have studied such activists:

> When political psychology has taken to analysing the behaviour of political activists it has tended to do so from a thoroughly external perspective That is to say, that rarely have their thought processes been described, much less analysed, from their own point of view. Yet it is at least possible that a very good way to learn about the psychology of political activists is to listen to what they have to say about their own lives.
>
> (Andrews, 1991, p. 20)

What Andrews says can be seen as analogous to a good deal of our scholarly representation of teachers where they are seen as interchangeable and essentially depersonalized. In 1981, I argued that many accounts presented teachers as timeless and interchangeable role incumbents. But that:

> The pursuit of personal and biographical data might rapidly challenge the assumption of interchangeability. Likewise, by tracing the teachers' life as it evolved over time – throughout the teachers' career and through several generations – the assumption of timelessness might also be remedied. *In understanding something so intensely personal teaching it is critical we know*

about the person the teacher is. Our paucity of knowledge in this area is a manifest indictment of the range of our sociological imagination.

(Goodson, 1981, p. 69)

The argument for listening to teachers is, therefore, a substantial and long overdue one. Narratives, stories, journals, action research and phenomenology have all contributed to a growing movement to provide opportunities for teacher representations. In the case of stories and narratives, Kathy Carter has provided a valuable summary of this growing movement *in the early years of its educational incarnation:*

> With increasing frequency over the past several years we, as members of a community of investigator – practitioners, have been telling stories about teaching and teacher education rather than simply reporting correlation coefficients or generating lists of findings. This trend has been upsetting to some who mourn the loss of quantitative precision and, they would argue, scientific rigour. For many of us, however, these stories capture, more than scores or mathematical formulae ever can, the richness and indeterminacy of our experiences as teachers and the complexity of our understandings of what teaching is and how others can be prepared to engage in this profession.
>
> It is not altogether surprising, then, that this attraction to stories has evolved into an explicit attempt to use the literatures on 'story' or 'narrative' to define both the method and the object of inquiry in teaching and teacher education. Story has become, in other words, more than simply a rhetorical device for expressing sentiments about teachers or candidates for the teaching profession. It is now, rather, a central focus for conducting research in the field.
>
> (Carter, 1993, p. 5)

Story and history

The emphasis upon teachers' stories and narratives encouragingly signifies a new turn in presenting teachers. It is a turn that deserves to be taken very seriously, for we have to be sure that we are turning in the right direction. Like all new genres, stories and narratives are Janus-faced; they may move us forward into new insights or backwards into constrained consciousness – and sometimes simultaneously.

This uncertainty is well stated in Carter's summary of 'The place of story in the study of teaching and teacher education':

> Anyone with even a passing familiarity with the literatures on story soon realizes, however, that these are quite turbulent intellectual waters and quickly abandons the expectation of safe passage toward the resolution, once and for all, of the many puzzles and dilemmas we face in advancing our knowledge of teaching. Much needs to be learned about the nature of story and its value to our common enterprise, and about the wide range of purposes, approaches, and claims made by those who have adopted story as a central analytical framework. What does story capture and what does it leave out? How does this notion fit within the emerging sense of the nature of teaching and what it means to educate teachers? These and many other critical questions need to be faced if story is to become more than a loose metaphor for everything from a paradigm or world view to a technique for bringing home a point in a lecture on a Thursday afternoon.
>
> (Carter, 1993, p. 5)

But what is the nature of the turbulence in the intellectual waters surrounding stories, and will they serve to drown the new genre? The turbulence is multi-faceted, but here I want to focus on the relationship between stories and the social context in which they are embedded. For stories exist in history – they are, in fact, deeply located in time and space. Stories work differently in different social contexts and historical times – they can be put to work in different ways. Stories then should not only be *narrated* but also *located*. This argues that we should move beyond the self-referential individual narration to a wider contextualized, collaborative mode. Again, Carter hints at both the enormous appeal and the underlying worry about narrative and story. At the moment, the appeal is substantial after long years of silencing, but the dangers are more shadowy. I believe that unless those dangers are confronted now, narrative and story may end up silencing, or at least marginalizing in new ways, the very people to whom it appears to give voice.

> For many of us, these arguments about the personal, storied nature of teaching and about voice, gender, and power in our professional lives ring very true. We can readily point to instances in which we have felt excluded by researchers' language or powerless in the face of administrative decrees and evaluation instruments presumably bolstered by scientific evidence. And we have experienced the indignities of gender bias and presumptions. We feel these issues deeply, and opening them to public scrutiny, especially through the literature in our field, is a cause for celebration.
>
> At the same time, we must recognize that this line of argument creates a very serious crisis for our community. One can easily imagine that the analysis summarized here, if pushed ever so slightly forward, leads directly to a rejection of all generalizations about teaching as distortions of teachers' real stories and as complicity with the power elite, who would make teachers subservient. From this perspective, only the teacher owns her or his story and its meaning. As researchers and teacher educators, we can only serve by getting this message across to the larger society and, perhaps, by helping teachers to come to know their own stories. Seen in this light, much of the activity in which we engage as scholars in teaching becomes illegitimate if not actually harmful.
>
> (Carter, 1993, p. 8)

Carolyn Steedman, in her marvellous work, *Landscape for a Good Woman*, speaks of this danger. She says, 'Once a story is told, it ceases to story: it becomes a piece of history, an interpretative device' (Steedman, 1986, p. 143). In this sense, a story 'works' when its rationale is comprehended and its historical significance grasped. As Bristow (1991, p. 117) has argued, 'The more skilled we become at understanding the history involved in these very broadly defined stories, the more able will we be to identify the ideological function of narratives – how they designate a place for us within their structure of telling'. In reviewing Steedman's work and its power to understand patriarchy and the dignity of women's lives, Bristow talks about her unswerving attention to:

> the ways in which life writing can bring its writers to the point of understanding how their lives have already been narrated – according to a pre-figurative script, Steedman never loses sight of how writers may develop skills to rewrite the life script in which they find themselves.
>
> (Bristow, 1991, p. 114)

This, I think, focuses acutely on the dangers of a belief that merely by allowing people to 'narrate', we in any serious way give them voice *and* agency. The narration of a pre-figurative script is a celebration of an existing power relation. More often, and this is profoundly true for teachers, the question is how to 'rewrite the life script'. Narration, then, can work in many ways, but clearly it can work to give voice to a celebration of scripts of domination. Narration can both reinforce domination or rewrite domination. Stories and narratives are not an unquestioned good: it all depends. And above all, it depends on how they relate to history and to social context.

Again, Andrews's work on the lives of political activists captures the limitation of so much of the developmental psychologists' study of lives, and it is analogous to so much work on teacher narratives:

> In Western capitalist democracies, where most of the work on development originates, many researchers tend to ignore the importance of the society–individual dialectic, choosing to focus instead on more particularized elements, be they personality idiosyncrasies, parental relationships, or cognitive structures, as if such aspects of the individual's make-up could be neatly compartmentalized, existing in a contextual vacuum.
>
> (Andrews, 1991, p. 13)

The version of 'personal' that has been constructed and worked for in some Western countries is a particular version, an individualistic version, of being a person. It is unrecognizable to much of the rest of the world. But so many of the stories and narratives we have of teachers work unproblematically and without comment with this version of personal being and personal knowledge. Masking the limits of individualism, such accounts often present 'isolation, estrangement, and loneliness...as autonomy, independence and self-reliance' (Andrews, 1991, p. 13). Andrews concludes that if we ignore social context, we deprive ourselves and our collaborators of meaning and understanding. She says:

> it would seem apparent that the context in which human lives are lived is central to the core of meaning in those lives. Researchers should not, therefore, feel at liberty to discuss or analyse how individuals perceive meaning in their lives and in the world around them, while ignoring the content and context of that meaning.
>
> (Andrews, 1991, p. 13)

This, I believe, has been all too common a response among these educational researchers working with teachers' stories and narratives. Content has been embraced and celebrated, context has not been sufficiently developed. Cynthia Chambers has summarized this posture and its dangers in reviewing work on teachers' narratives:

> These authors offer us the naive hope that if teachers learn 'to tell and understand their *own* story' they will be returned to their rightful place at the centre of curriculum planning and reform. And yet, their method leaves each teacher a 'blackbird singing in the dead of night'; isolated, and sadly ignorant of how his/her song is part of a much larger singing of the world. If everyone is singing their own song, who is listening? How can we hear the larger conversation of humankind in which our own history teacher is embedded and perhaps concealed?
>
> (Chambers, 1991, p. 354)

Likewise, Salina Shrofel, in reviewing the same book, highlights the dangers:

> Focus on the personal and on practice does not appear to lead practitioners or researchers/writers to analyse practice as theory, as social structure, or as a manifestation of political and economic systems. This limitation of vision implicit in the narrative approach serves as a constraint on curriculum reform. Teachers will, as did the teachers cited by Connelly and Clandinin, make changes in their own classroom curricula but will not perform the questioning

and challenging of theory, structure, and ideology that will lead to radical and extensive curriculum reform.

It can be argued that the challenge of running a classroom fully occupies the teachers and that questions of theory, structure, and ideology don't affect the everyday lives (practical knowledge) of teachers and are relegated to 'experts'. However, there are many dangers in separating practice from these other questions. First, as Connelly and Clandinin point out, it ignores the dynamic relationship of theory and practice. Second, it ignores the fact that schools are intricately and inextricably part of the social fabric and of the political and economic system which dominates. Third, because curriculum reform is implemented in the classroom by teachers, separating teachers from these other aspects might negatively affect radical and widespread curriculum reform. To avoid these dangers, either the narrative method will have to be extended, or it will need to be supplemented with a process that encourages teachers to look beyond the personal.

(Shrofel, 1991, pp. 64–65)

In summary, should stories and narratives be a way of giving voice to a particular way of being, or should the genre serve as an introduction to alternative ways of being? Consciousness is constructed rather than autonomously produced; hence, giving voice to consciousness may give voice to the constructor at least as much as the speaker. If social context is left out this will likely happen.

The truth is that many times a life storyteller will neglect the structural context of their lives, or interpret such contextual forces from a biased point of view. As Denzin (1989, p. 74) says, 'Many times a person will act as if he or she made his or her own history when, in fact, he or she was forced to make the history he or she lived'. He gives an example from his 1986 study of alcoholics: 'You know I made the last four months by myself. I haven't used or drank. I'm really proud of myself. I did it' (Denzin, 1989, pp. 74–75). A friend, listening to this account commented:

> You know you were under a court order all last year. You didn't do this on your own. You were forced to, whether you want to accept this fact or not. You also went to AA and NA. Listen Buster, you did what you did because you had help and because you were afraid and thought you had no other choice. Don't give me this, 'I did it on my own' crap.
>
> (1989, pp. 74–75)

The speaker replies, 'I know. I just don't like to admit it'. Denzin concludes:

> This listener invokes two structural forces, the state and AA, which accounted in part for this speaker's experience. To have secured only the speaker's account, without a knowledge of his biography and personal history, would have produced a biased interpretation of his situation.
>
> (1989, pp. 74–75)

The great virtue of stories is that they particularize and make concrete our experiences. This, however, should be the *starting point* in our social and educational study. Stories can so richly move us into the terrain of the social, into insights into the socially constructed nature of our experiences. Feminist sociology has often treated stories in this way. As Hilary Graham says, 'Stories are pre-eminently ways of relating individuals and events to social contexts, ways of weaving personal experiences into their social fabric' (see Armstrong, 1987, p. 14). Again, Carolyn Steedman speaks of this two-step process. First the story particularizes, details and historicizes – then at second stage, the 'urgent need' to develop theories of context:

> The fixed townscapes of Northampton and Leeds that Hoggart and Seabrook have described show endless streets of houses, where mothers who don't go out to work order the domestic day, where men are masters, and children, when they grow older, express gratitude for the harsh discipline meted out to them. The first task is to particularize this profoundly a-historical landscape (and so this book details a mother who was a working woman and a single parent, and a father who wasn't a patriarch). And once the landscape is detailed and historicized in this way, the urgent need becomes to find a way of theorizing the result of such difference and particularity, not in order to find a description that can be universally applied (the point is *not* to say that all working-class childhoods are the same, nor that experience of them produces unique psychic structures) but so that the people in exile, the inhabitants of the long streets, may start to use the auto-biographical 'I', and tell the stories of their life.
>
> (Steedman, 1986, p. 16)

The story, then, provides a starting point for developing further understandings of the social construction of subjectivity. If the teachers' stories stay at the level of the personal and practical, we forego that opportunity. Speaking of the narrative method focusing on personal and practical teachers' knowledge, Willinsky writes: 'I am concerned that a research process intended to recover the personal and experiential (aspects or not?) would pave over this construction site in its search for an overarching unity in the individual's narrative' (Willinsky, 1989, p. 259).

Personal and practical teachers' stories may, therefore, act not to further our understandings, but merely to celebrate the particular constructions of the 'teacher' which have been wrought by political and social contestation. Teachers' stories can be stories of particular political victories and political settlements. Because of their limitation of focus, teachers' stories – as stories of the personal and practical – are likely to be limited in this manner.

A story of action within a story of context

This section comes from a phrase often used by Lawrence Stenhouse (1975), who was concerned in much of his work to introduce a historical dimension to our studies of schooling and curriculum. While himself a leading advocate of the teacher as researcher and pioneer of that method, he was worried about the proliferation of practical stories of action, individualized and isolated, unique and idiosyncratic, as our stories of action and our lives are. But as we have seen, lives and stories link with broader social scripts – they are not just individual productions, they are also social constructions. We must make sure that individual and practical stories do not reduce, seduce and reproduce particular teacher mentalities, and lead us away from broader patterns of understanding.

Let us try to situate the narrative moment in the historical moment – for the narrative movement itself could be located in a theory of context. In some ways the movement has analogies with the existential movement of the 1940s. Existentialists believed that only through our actions could we define ourselves. Our role, existentialists judged, was to invent ourselves as individuals, then, as in Sartre's (1961) trilogy *Les Chemins de la Liberté*, we would be 'free', especially from the claims of society and the 'others'.

Existentialism existed at a particular historical moment following the massive trauma of the Second World War, and in France, where it developed most strongly, of the protracted German occupation. George Melly judges that existentialism grew out of this historical context.

> My retrospective explanation is that it provided a way of exorcising the collective guilt of the occupation, to reduce the betrayals, the collaboration, the blind eye, the unjustified compromise, to an acceptable level. We know now that the official post-war picture of France under the Nazis was a deliberate whitewash and that almost everyone knew it, and suppressed the knowledge. Existentialism, by insisting on the complete isolation of the individual as free to act, but free to do nothing else, as culpable or heroic but *only* within those limits, helped absolve the notion of corporate and national ignominy.
>
> (Melly, 1993, p. 9)

Above all, then, an individualizing existentialism freed people from the battle of ideologies, freed them from the awfulness of political and military conflict. Individualized existentialism provided a breathing space away from power and politics.

But the end of the Second World War did not provide an end to politics, only a move from hot war to cold war. As we know, ideologies continued their contest in the most potentially deadly manner. During this period, narratives of personal life began to blossom. Brightman (see Sage, 1994) has developed a fascinating picture of how Mary McCarthy's personal narratives grew out of the witch-hunting period of Joe McCarthy. Her narratives moved us from the 'contagion of ideas' to the personal 'material world'. Mary McCarthy could 'strip ideas of their abstract character and return them to the social world from whence they came' (quoted in Sage, 1994, p. 5). In Irving Howes's memorable phrase, as 'ideology crumbled, personality bloomed' (Sage, 1994, p. 5).

And so with the end of ideology, the end of the cold war, we see the proliferate blooming of personality, not least in the movement towards personal narratives and stories. Once again, the personal narrative, the practical story, celebrates the end of the trauma of the cold war and the need for a human space away from politics, away from power. It is a thoroughly understandable nirvana, but it assumes that power and politics have somehow ended. It assumes, in that wishful phrase, 'the end of history'.

In educational bureaucracies, power continues to be hierarchically administered. I have often asked administrators and educational bureaucrats why they support personal and practical forms of knowledge for teachers in the form of narratives and stories. Their comments often echo those of the 'true believers' in narrative method. But I always go on, after suitable pause and diversion to ask: 'What do you do on your leadership courses?' There, it is always 'politics as usual' management skills, quality assurance, micro-political strategies, personnel training. Personal and practical stories for some, cognitive maps of power for others. So while the use of stories and narratives can provide a useful breathing space away from power, it does not suspend the continuing administration of power; indeed, it could well make this so much easier. Especially as, over time, teachers' knowledge would become more and more personal and practical – different 'mentalities'. Wholly different understandings of power would emerge, as between, say, teachers and school managers, teachers and administrators, teachers and some educational scholars.

Teachers' individual and practical stories certainly provide a breathing space. However, at one and the same time, they reduce the oxygen of broader understandings. The breathing space comes to look awfully like a vacuum, where history and social construction are somehow suspended.

In this way, teachers become divorced from what might be called the 'vernacular of power', the ways of talking and knowing which then become the prerogative of managers, administrators and academics. In this discourse, politics and micro-politics are the essence and currency of the interchange. Alongside this and in a sense facilitating this, a new 'vernacular of the particular, the personal and the practical' arises, which is specific to teachers.

This form of apartheid could easily emerge if teachers' stories and narratives remain singular and specific, personal and practical, particular and apolitical. Hence, it is a matter of some urgency that we develop stories of action within theories of context – contextualizing stories, if you like – which act against the kinds of divorce of the discourses that are all too readily imaginable.

Carter had begun to worry about just such a problem in her work on 'The Place of Story in the Study of Teaching and Teacher Education':

> And for those of us telling stories in our work, we will not serve the community well if we sanctify story-telling work and build an epistemology on it to the point that we simply substitute one paradigmatic domination for another *without challenging domination itself*. We must, then, become much more self conscious than we have been in the past about the issues involved in narrative and story, such as interpretation, authenticity, normative value, and what our purposes are for telling stories in the first place.
>
> (Carter, 1993, p. 11)

Some of these worries about stories can be explored in scrutinizing the way in which powerful interest groups in society actually promote and employ storied material.

References

Andrews, Molly, 1991, *Lifetimes of Commitment: Aging, Politics, Psychology* (Cambridge, UK and New York: Cambridge University Press).

Armstrong, P.F., 1987, *Qualitative Strategies in Social and Educational Research: The Life History Method in Theory and Practice*. Newland Papers No. 14, The University of Hill, School of Adult and Continuing Education.

Bristow, J., 1991, Life Stories. Carolyn Steedman's History Writing. *New Formations*, (13), 113–130, (Spring).

Carter, Kathy, 1993, The Place of Story in the Study of Teaching and Teacher Education. *Educational Researcher*, 22(1), 5–12, 18.

Chambers, Cynthia, 1991, Review of Teachers as Curriculum Planners: Narratives of Experience. *Journal of Education Policy,* 6(3), 353–354.

Denzin, Norman, K., 1989, Interpretive Biography. *Qualitative Research Methods Series 17.* (Newbury Park, CA, London and New Delhi: Sage Publications).

Denzin, Norman K., 1993, Review Essay – On Hearing the Voices of Educational Research (Mimeo, University of Illinois at Urbana, IL – Champaign).

Goodson, I.F., 1981, Life History and the Study of Schooling. *Interchange*, II(4).

Jameson, F., 1984, Forward. In J.F. Lyotard (ed.), *The Postmodern Condition: A Report on Knowledge* (Minneapolis, MN: University of Minnesota Press), pp. vii–xxi.

Lyotard, J.F., 1984, *The Postmodern Condition: A Report on Knowledge* (Minneapolis, MN: University of Minnesota Press).

Melly, George, 1993, Look Back in Angst. *The Sunday Times* (June 13).

Sage, L., 1994, How to do the Life. Review of C. Brightman's *Writing Dangerously: Mary McCarthy and Her World*. London Review of Books.

Shrofel, Salina, 1991, Review Essay: School Reform, Professionalism, and Control. *Journal of Educational Thought*, 25(1), 58–70.

Steedman, Carolyn, 1986, *Landscape for a Good Woman* (London: Virago Press).

Stenhouse, L., 1975, *An Introduction to Curriculum Research and Development* (London: Heinemann).

Willinsky, J., 1989, Getting Personal and Practical with Personal Practical Knowledge. *Curriculum Inquiry*, 19(3), 247–264.

CHAPTER 18

SPONSORING THE TEACHER'S VOICE

Cambridge Journal of Education, 1991, 21(1): 35–45

Some time ago, I became convinced that the study of teachers' lives was central to the study of curriculum and schooling. In reflecting on the development of my conviction two episodes stand out. Were this merely a reminiscence of personal conversion it would be of little interest, but the two episodes do speak to a number of salient issues in the argument for greatly extended study of teachers' lives.

The first episode took place in the year of post-graduate certification when I was training to be a teacher. I returned to spend the day with a teacher at my secondary school who had been a major inspiration to me, a mentor. He was a radical Welshman. Academically brilliant, he had a BSc in Economics and a PhD in History. He was open, humorous, engaging, stimulating – a superb and popular teacher. But he faced me with a paradox because when the school changed from a grammar school to a comprehensive, it was he who opposed all the curriculum reforms which sought to broaden the educational appeal of the school to wider social groups. He was implacably conservative and traditionalist on this, and so far as I know only this, issue. But he, it should be remembered, was a man who had personally visited the factory to which I had gone after leaving school early at 15. He had implored me to return to school. He had spoken then of his commitment to public schooling as an avenue to working class emancipation. He no doubt saw me, a badly behaved working class pupil, as some sort of test case. I knew personally then that he was very deeply concerned to keep working class pupils in school. So why did he oppose all those curriculum reforms which had that objective?

During the day back visiting my old school, I continually probed him on this issue. At first he stonewalled, giving a series of essentially non-committal responses, but at the end of the day, in the pub, over a beer, he opened up. Yes, of course he was mainly concerned with disadvantaged pupils; yes, of course that's why he had come to the factory to drag me back to school. Yes, he was politically radical and yes, he had always voted Labour. But, and here I quote:

> you don't understand my relationship to the school and to teaching. My centre of gravity is not here at all. It's in the community, in the home – that's where I exist, that's where I put my effort now. For me the school is nine to five, I go through the motions.

In short, in the school he sought to minimise his commitment, he opposed any reform which dragged him into more work. His centre of gravity was elsewhere.

The point I am making is that to understand teacher development and curriculum development and to tailor it accordingly we need to know a great deal more about teachers' priorities. We need in short to know more about teachers' lives.

The second episode began in the late 1970s. I was interested in some work on folk music being conducted at the University of Leeds. At the same time, I was exploring some themes for an ethnography conference that was coming up at the St Hilda's in Oxford. The work of a folklorist Pegg suddenly opened up again the line of argument which I had been pondering since 1970. Pegg says:

> The right to select lies not with the folklorist ('Sorry old chap, can't have that – it's not a folk song'), but with the singer. Today's collector must have no preconceptions. His job is to record a people's music, whether it is a traditional ballad or a hymn or a musical song or last week's pop hit!

With this basic attitude comes another revelation:

> I began to realise that, for me, the people who sang the songs were more important than the songs themselves. The song is only a small part of the singer's life and the life was usually very fascinating. There was no way I felt I could understand the songs without knowing something about the life of the singer, which does not seem to apply in the case of most folklorists. They are quite happy to find material which fits into a preconceived canon and leave it at that. I had to know what people thought about the songs, what part they played in their lives and in the lives of the community.
>
> (Pegg, 1991, p. 138)

A similar point is made by the folksong collector Robin Morton:

> The opinion grew in me that it was *in* the singer that the song becomes relevant. Analyzing it in terms of motif, or rhyming structure, or minute variation becomes, in my view, sterile if the one who carries the particular song is forgotten. We have all met the scholar who can talk for hours in a very learned fashion about folksongs and folklore in general, without once mentioning the singer. Bad enough to forget the social context, but to ignore the individual context castrates the song. As I got to know the singers, so I got to know and understand their songs more fully.
>
> (Morton, 1991, p. 139)

The pre-occupation with 'the singer, not the song' needs to be seriously tested in our studies of curriculum and schooling. What Pegg and Morton say about folklorists and implicitly about the way their research is received by those they research, could be said also about most educational research.

The project I am recommending is essentially one of re-conceptualizing educational research so as to assure that 'the teacher's voice' is heard, heard loudly, heard articulately. In this respect the most hopeful way forward is, I think, to build upon notions of the 'self-monitoring teacher', 'the teacher as researcher', the teacher as 'extended professional'. For instance, in the early 1970s at The Centre for Applied Research in Education at the University of East Anglia in England, a good deal of work was conducted into how to operationalize this concept. Perhaps the most interesting developments were within the Ford Teaching Project conducted by John Elliott and Clem Adelman in the period 1973–75. They sought to rehabilitate the 'action-research' mode pioneered by Kurt Lewin in the post-war period. In the interim period educational action research had fallen into decline. Carr and Kemmis, who have done a good deal to extend and popularise the concept, give a number of reasons for the resurgence of action-research:

> First, there was the demand from within an increasingly professionalized teacher force for a research role, based on the notion of the extended professional

investigating his or her own practice. Second, there was the perceived irrelevance to the concerns of these practitioners of much contemporary educational research. Third, there had been a revival of interest in 'the practical' in curriculum, following the work of Schwab and others on 'practical deliberation'. Fourth, action research was assisted by the rise of the 'new wave' methods in educational research and evaluation with their emphasis on participants' perspectives and categories in shaping educational practices and situations. These methods place the practitioners at centre stage in the educational research process and recognize the crucial significance of actors' understandings in shaping educational action. From the role of critical informant helping an 'outsider' researcher, it is but a short step for the practitioner to become a self-critical researcher into her or his own practice. Fifth, the accountability movement galvanized and politicized practitioners. In response to the accountability movement, practitioners have adopted the self-monitoring role as a proper means of justifying practice and generating sensitive critiques of the working conditions in which their practice is conducted. Sixth, there was increasing solidarity in the teaching profession in response to the public criticism which has accompanied the post-expansion educational politics of the 1970s and 1980s; this, too, has prompted the organization of support net-works of concerned professionals interested in the continuing developments of education even though the expansionist tide has turned. And, finally, there is the increased awareness of action research itself, which is perceived as providing an understandable and workable approach to the improvement of practice through critical self-reflection.

(Schwab, 1969)

The focus of action-research has however tended to be very practice-oriented. In introducing a survey of action-research for instance Carr and Kemmis note:

A range of practices have been studied by educational action-researchers and some examples may suffice to show how they have used action research to improve their practices, their understandings of these practices, and the situations in which they work.

(Carr and Kemmis, 1986, pp. 166–167)

Not surprisingly with the notion of an extended professional in mind workers have 'used action-research to improve their practice'. Other developments in teacher education have similarly focussed on practice. The work of Clandinin and of Connelly has argued in innovative and interesting ways that would seek to understand teachers' *personal practical knowledge*. The addition of the personal aspect in this formulation is a welcome move forward hinting as it does at the importance of biographical perspectives. But again the personal is being linked irrevocably to practice. It is as if the teacher *is* his or her practice. For teacher educators, such specificity of focus is understandable but I wish to argue that a broader perspective will achieve more: not solely in terms of our understandings but ultimately in ways that feed back into changes in practical knowledge.

In short what I am saying is that it does not follow logically or psychologically that to *improve* practice we must initially and immediately *focus* on practice. Indeed I shall argue the opposite point of view.

Taking the 'teacher as researcher' and 'action-research' as expressing defensible value positions and viable starting points, I want to argue for a broadened sense of purpose. In particular I am worried about a collaborative mode of research which seeks to give full equality and stature to the teacher but which employs as its initial and predominant focus the practice of the teacher. It is, I believe, a profoundly unpromising point of entry from which to promote a collaborative enterprise. For the university researcher, aspiring to collaborative and equalitarian partnership, it may seem quite unproblematic, for the teacher it might seem far less so. In fact it may seem to the teacher that the starting point for collaboration focuses on the maximum point of vulnerability.

We must, I think, constantly remind ourselves how deeply uncertain and anxious most of us are about our work as teachers whether in classrooms or in (far less contested) lecture halls. These are often the arenas of greatest anxiety and insecurity – as well as, occasionally, achievement.

Hence I wish to argue that to place the teachers' classroom practice at the centre of the action for action-researchers is to put the most exposed and problematic aspect of the teachers' world at the centre of scrutiny and negotiation. In terms of strategy, both personally and politically, I think it is a mistake to do this. I say it is a mistake to do this – and this may seem a paradox – particularly if the wish is to ultimately seek reflection about and change in the teachers' practice.

A more valuable and less vulnerable entry point would be to examine teachers' work in the context of the teacher's life. Much of the emerging study in this area indicates that this focus allows a rich flow of dialogue and data. Moreover, the focus may (and I stress may) allow teachers greater authority and control in collaborative research than has often appeared to be the case with practice-oriented study. What I am asserting here is that, particularly in the world of teacher development, the central ingredient so far missing is the *teacher's voice*. Primarily the focus has been on the teacher's practice, almost the teacher *as* practice. What is needed is a focus that listens above all to the person at whom 'development' is aimed. This means strategies should be developed which facilitate, maximize and in a real sense legislate the capturing of the teacher's voice.

Bringing substance and strategy together points us in a new direction for re-conceptualising educational research and development. In the first section, I provided two somewhat episodic arguments for seeking to understand teachers' lives as part of the educational research and development enterprise. In the second section, I argued that the 'teacher as researcher' and 'action research' modes were productive and generative ways forward but that the initial and immediate focus on practice was overstated and undesirable. Strategically a broader focus on life and work is hereby recommended. Hence for substantive and strategic reasons I would argue for a broadening of focus to allow detailed scrutiny of the teacher's life and work.

Broadening our data base for studying teaching

So far I have argued in somewhat anecdotal fashion that data on teachers' lives is an important factor for our educational research studies. I have argued that *strategically* this is desirable; so as to involve teachers as researchers and to develop a collaborative mode. But there is also a *substantive* reason. The primary reason is that in my experience when talking to teachers about issues of curriculum development, subject teaching, school governance and general school organisation they constantly import data on their own lives into the discussion. This I take to be *prima facie* evidence that teachers themselves judge such issues to be of major importance. One of the reasons that these data have not been much used however is that researchers edit out such data viewing it as too 'personal', 'idiosyncratic' or 'soft'. It is, in short, yet another example of the selective use of the 'teacher's voice'.

The researcher only hears what he/she wants to hear and knows will sound well when replayed to the research community.

There may of course be perfectly valid reasons for not employing data on teachers' lives in our educational research studies. But this would require a sequence of reasoning to show why such data were irrelevant or of no importance. The normal research strategy is however to simply purge such data. I have not come across any accounts which give reasoned explanations as to why such data are not employed. The most commonsensical explanation seems to be that data on teachers' lives simply do not fit in with existing research paradigms. If this is the case then it is the paradigms that are at fault, not the value and quality of this kind of data.

The arguments for employing data on teachers' lives are substantial, but given the predominance of existing paradigms should be spelt out:

1   In the research on schools in which I have been involved – covering a wide range of different research foci and conceptual matrixes – the consistency of teachers talking about their own lives in the process of explaining their policy and practice has been striking. Were this only a personal observation it would be worthless but again and again in talking to other researchers they have echoed their point. To give one example: David Hargreaves in researching for *Deviance in Classrooms* noted in talking about the book that again and again teachers had imported autobiographical comments into their explanations. He was much concerned in retrospect by the speed with which such data had been excised when writing up the research. The assumption, very much the conventional wisdom, was that such data was too 'personal', too 'idiosyncratic', too 'soft' for a fully-fledged piece of social science research.

Of course in the first instance (and some cases the last instance) it is true that personal data can be irrelevant, eccentric and essentially redundant. But the point that needs to be grasped is that the features are not the inevitable corollary of that which is personal. Moreover that which is personal at the point of collection may not remain personal. After all a good deal of social science is concerned with the collection of a range of often personal insights and events and the elucidation of more collective and generalisable profferings and processes.

The respect for the autobiographical, for 'the life', is but one side of a concern to elicit the teachers' voice. In some senses like the anthropologist this school of qualitative educational research is concerned to listen to what the teacher says, and to respect and deal seriously with that data which the teacher imports into accounts. This is to invert the balance of proof. Conventionally that data which does not service the researcher's interests and foci is junked. In this model the data the teacher provides has a more sacred property and is only dispensed with after painstaking proof of irrelevance and redundancy.

Listening to the teacher's voice should teach us that the autobiographical, 'the life', is of substantial concern when teachers talk of their work. And at a commonsensical level I find this essentially unsurprising. What I do find surprising, if not frankly unconscionable, is that for so long researchers have ruled this part of the teachers account out as irrelevant data.

2   Life experiences and background are obviously key ingredients of the person that we are, of our sense of self. To the degree that we invest our 'self' in our teaching, experience and background therefore shape our practice.

A common feature in many teachers' accounts of their background is the appearance of a favourite teacher who substantially influenced the person as a young school pupil. They often report that 'it was this person who first sold me on teaching'; 'it was sitting in her classroom when I first decided I wanted to be a teacher'. In short such people provide a 'role model' and in addition they most probably influence the subsequent vision of desirable pedagogy as well as possibly choice of subject specialism.

Many other ingredients of background are important in the teacher's life and practice. An upbringing in a working class environment may for instance provide valuable insights and experience when teaching pupils from a similar background. I once observed a teacher with a working class background teach a class of comprehensive pupils in a school in the East End of London. He taught using the local cockney vernacular and his affinity was a quite startling aspect of his success as a teacher. In my interview I spoke about his affinity and he noted that it was 'coz I come from round "ere don't I?"' Background and life experience were then a major aspect of his practice. But so they would be in the case of middle class teachers teaching children from the working class or teachers of working class origins teaching middle class children. Background is an important ingredient in the dynamic of practice (see Hargreaves, 1986; Lortie, 1975).

Of course class is just one aspect as are gender or ethnicity, teachers' backgrounds and life experiences are idiosyncratic and unique and must be explored therefore in their full complexity. (Treatment of gender issues has often been inadequate – see Sikes *et al.*, 1985.) Recent work is more encouraging – see Nelson (in Goodson, 1992) and Casey (in Goodson, 1992).

3   The teacher's *Life style* both in and outside school, his/her latent identities and cultures, impact on views of teaching and on practice. Becker and Geer's work on latent identities and cultures provide a valuable theoretical basis (Becker and Geer, 1971). Life style is of course often a characteristic element in certain cohorts; for instance, work on the generation of sixties teachers would be of great value. In a recent study of one teacher focussing on his life style Walker and myself stated:

> How the connections between Youth Culture and the curriculum reform movement of the 60's is more complex than we first thought. For Ron Fisher there definitely is a connection, he identifies strongly with youth culture and feels that to be important in his teaching. But despite his attraction to rock music and teenage life styles it is the school he has become committed to, almost against his own sense of direction. Involvement in innovation, for Ron at least, is not simply a question of technical involvement, but touches significant facets of his personal identity. This raises the question for the curriculum developer, what would a project look like if it explicitly set out to change the teachers rather than the curriculum? How would you design a project to appeal to the teacher-as-person rather than to the teacher-as-educator? What would be the effects and consequences of implementing such a design?
>
> (Goodson and Walker, 1991, p. 139)

This I think shows how work in this area begins to force a re-conceptualization of models of teacher development. We move in short from the teacher-as-practice to the teacher-as-person as our starting point for development.

4   Focus on the *life cycle* will generate insights therefore into the unique elements of teaching. Indeed so unique a characteristic would seem an obvious starting point for reflection about the teachers' world. Yet our research paradigms face so frankly in other directions that there has been little work to date in this area.

Fortunately work in other areas provides a very valuable framework. Some of Gail Sheehy's somewhat populist work in '*Passages*' and '*Pathfinders*' is I think important (Sheehy, 1976). So also is the research work on which some of her publications are based carried out by Levinson. His work, whilst regrettably focussed only on men does provide some very generative insights into how our perspectives at particular stages in our life crucially affect our professional work.

Take for instance the case study of John Barnes, a university biologist. Levinson is writing about his 'dream' of himself as a front-rank prize-winning biological researcher:

> Barnes's Dream assumed greater urgency as he approached 40. He believed that most creative work in science is done before then. A conversation with his father's lifelong friend around this time made a lasting impression on him. The older man confided that he had by now accepted his failure to become a 'legal star' and was content to be a competent and respected tax lawyer. He had decided that stardom is not synonymous with the good life; it was 'perfectly all right to be second best.' At the time, however, Barnes was not ready to scale down his own ambition. Instead, he decided to give up the chairmanship and devote himself fully to his research.
>
> He stepped down from the chairmanship as he approached 41, and his project moved into its final phase. This was a crucial time for him, the culmination of years of striving. For several months, one distraction after another claimed his attention and heightened the suspense. He became the father of a little boy, and that same week was offered a prestigious chair at Yale. Flattered and excited, he felt that this was his 'last chance for a big offer'. But in the end Barnes said no. He found that he could not make a change at this stage of his work. Also, their ties to family and friends, and their love of place, were now of much greater importance to him and Ann. She said: 'The kudos almost got him, but now we are both glad we stayed'.
>
> (Levinson, 1979, p. 267)

This quotation I think shows how definitions of our professional location and of our career direction can only be arrived at by detailed understanding of people's lives.

5   Likewise, *career stages* and *career decisions* can be analysed in their own right. Work on teachers' lives and careers is increasingly commanding attention in professional development workshops and courses. For instance, The Open University in England now uses our *Teachers Lives and Careers* book as one of its course set books (Ball and Goodson, 1989). This is symptomatic of important changes in the way that professional courses are being reorganised to allow concentration on the perspective of teachers' careers.

Besides the range of career studies in *Teachers Lives and Careers* a range of new research is beginning to examine this neglected aspect of teachers' professional lives. The work of Sikes, Measor and Woods has provided valuable new insights into how teachers construct and view their careers in teaching and of course the work of Michael Huberman reported in this volume (Sikes *et al.*, 1985).

6   Moreover, the new work on teachers' careers points to the fact that there are *critical incidents* in teachers' lives and specifically in their work which may crucially affect perception and practice. Certainly work on beginning teachers has pointed to the importance of certain incidents in moulding teachers' styles and practices. Lacey's work has pointed to the effects on teachers' strategies and the work of Woods, Pollard, Hargreaves and Knowles has further elucidated the relationship to evolving teacher strategies (Knowles, 1992).

Other work on critical incidents in teachers' lives can confront important themes contextualised within a full life perspective. For instance, Kathleen Casey has employed 'life history narratives' to understand the phenomenon of teacher dropout, specifically female and activist teacher drop-out (Casey, 1988). Her work is exceptionally illuminating of this phenomenon which is currently receiving a great deal of essentially uncritical attention given the problem of teacher shortages. Yet few of the countries at the hard edge of teacher shortages have bothered to fund serious study of teachers' lives to examine and extend our understanding of the phenomenon of teacher drop-outs. I would argue that only such an approach affords the possibility of extending our understanding.

Likewise with many other major themes in teachers' work. The question of teacher stress and burn-out would, I believe, be best studied through life history perspectives. Similarly, the issue of effective teaching and the question of the take-up innovations and new managerial initiatives. Above all, in the study of teachers' working conditions this approach has a great deal to offer.

7   Studies of teachers' lives might allow us to see the individual in relation to the history of his or her time allowing us to view the intersection of the life history with the history of society thus illuminating the choices, contingencies and options open to the individual. 'Life histories' of schools, subjects and the teaching profession would provide vital contextual background. The initial focus on the teachers' lives therefore would re-conceptualise our studies of schooling and curriculum in quite basic ways.

Essentially collaborative study of teachers' lives at the levels mentioned constitutes a new way of viewing teacher development; a way which should re-direct the power relations underpinning teachers lives in significant and generative ways.

Collaboration and teacher development

Strategically I have argued that to promote the notion of teachers as researchers and to develop an action research modality where collaboration with externally situated researchers was fostered we need to avoid an immediate and predominant focus on practice. I have further argued that this focus on practice should, at least partially, be replaced by a focus on the teacher's life.

What is at issue here seems to me almost anthropological: we are looking for a point for teachers (as researchers) and externally located researchers to 'trade'. Practice promises maximum vulnerability as the 'trading point'. This is a deeply unequal situation in which to begin to 'trade' – for it could be argued that the teacher may already feel vulnerable and inferior in the face of a university researcher.

Talking about his/her own life the teacher is, in this specific sense, in a less immediately exposed situation; and the 'exposure' can be more carefully, consciously and personally controlled. (This is not, it should be noted, to argue that once again 'exploitation' might not take place, nor that there are no longer major ethical questions to do with exposure.) But I think this starting point has substantive as well as strategic advantages. Some have already been listed, however, in terms of the 'trade' between teacher/researcher and external researcher, this focus seems to me to provide advantages.

Much of the work that is emerging on teachers' lives throws up structural insights which locate the teacher's life within the deeply structured and embedded environment of schooling (Goodson, 1992). This provides a prime 'trading point' for the external researcher. For one of the valuable characteristics of a collaboration between teachers as researchers and external researchers is that it is a collaboration between two parties that are differentially located in structural terms. Each see the world through a different prism of practice and thought. This valuable difference may provide the external researcher with a possibility to offer back goods in 'the trade'. The teacher/researcher offers data and insights; the external researcher, in pursuing glimpses of structure in different ways, may now also bring data and insights. The terms of trade, in short, look favourable. In such conditions collaboration may at last begin.

I noted earlier that this possible route to collaboration does not suspend issues of ethics and exploitation. This is above all because the collaboration between teacher/researcher and external researcher takes place in an occupational terrain which is itself inequitably structured. In terms of power, the external researcher still holds many advantages. Moreover the conditions of university careers positively exhort researchers to exploit research data: the requirements of publications and peer review have their own dynamics.

So whatever the favourable aspects of a focus on teachers' lives we must remain deeply watchful. For if the teacher's practice was a vulnerable focus, the teacher's life is a deeply intimate, indeed intensive, focus. More than ever procedural guidelines are necessary over questions relating to the ownership and publication of the data. These issues themselves must be conceived of in terms of a collaboration in which each party has clear rights and in this case the teacher's power of veto should be agreed on early and implemented, where necessary, late.

References

Ball, S.J. and Goodson, I., 1989, *Teachers Lives and Careers* (London and New York: Falmer Press/Open University set book).

Becker, H.S. and Geer, B., 1971, Latent Culture: A Note on the Theory of Latent Social Roles. In B.R. Cosin *et al.* (eds), *School and Society: A Sociological Reader* (London: Routledge and Kegan Paul), pp. 56–60.

Carr, W. and Kemmis, S., 1986, *Becoming Critical: Education Knowledge and Action Research* (London and Philadelphia, PA: Falmer Press).

Casey, K., 1988, Teacher as Author: Life History Narratives of Contemporary Women Teachers Working or Social Change, PhD dissertation (Madison, WI: University of Wisconsin).

Casey, K., 1992, Why do Progressive Women Activists Leave Teaching? Theory, Methodology and Politics in Life History Research. In I.F. Goodson (ed.), *Studying Teachers' Lives* (London: Routledge).

Casey, K. and Apple, M.W., 1989, Gender and the Conditions of Teachers' Work: The Development of Understanding in America. In S. Acker (ed.), *Teachers, Gender and Careers* (New York: Falmer).

Goodson, I.F. (ed.), 1992, *Studying Teachers' Lives* (London and New York: Routledge).

Hargreaves, D.H., 1986, *Deviance in Classrooms* (London: Routledge).

Knowles, J.G., 1992, Models for Understanding Preserving and Beginning Teachers' Biographies: Illustrations for Case Studies. In I.F. Goodson (ed.), *Studying Teachers' Lives* (London: Routledge).

Levinson, D.J., 1979, *The Seasons of a Man's Life* (New York: Ballantine Books).

Lortie, D., 1975, *School Teacher* (Chicago, IL: University of Chicago Press).

Morton, R., quoted in Goodson, I. and Walker, R., 1991, *Biography, Identity and Schooling* (New York, Philadelphia, PA and London: Falmer Press).

Nelson, M., 1992, Using Oral Histories to Reconstruct the Experiences of Women Teachers in Vermont, 1900–1950. In I.F. Goodson (ed.), *Studying Teachers' Lives* (London: Routledge).

Pegg, J., quoted in Goodson, I. and Walker, R., 1991, *Biography, Identity and Schooling* (New York and London: Falmer Press).

Schwab, J.J., 1969, The Practical: A Language for Curriculum, *School Review*, 78, 1–24.

Sheehy, G., 1976, *Passages: Predictable Crises of Adult Life* (New York: Dutton).

Sheehy, G., 1981, *Pathfinders* (London: Sidgwich and Jackson).

Sikes, P., Measor, L. and Woods, P., 1985, *Teachers Careers* (London and Philadelphia, PA: Falmer Press).

CHAPTER 19

THE PERSONALITY OF EDUCATIONAL CHANGE

Professional Knowledge, Professional Lives: Studies in Education and Change, Maidenhead: Open University Press, 2003

Many current school reforms and change theories start from the assumption that since all is not well with the schools (*true*), reform and change can only help the situation (*false*). The assumption is held that the clear enunciation of objectives, backed by a battery of tests, accompanied by accountability strategies, and confirmed by a range of financial incentives and payments by results, will inevitably raise school standards. The teacher is positioned as a key part of this delivery system, but the technical aspects of teacher professionalism are stressed, rather than the *professional biography* – the personal missions and commitments that underpin the teacher's sense of vocationalism and caring professionalism.

We can over stress this growing technicalisation element which is far from universal, and we can overstate the attack on the teacher's sense of vocation. Nonetheless, what is irrefutable is that there has been little work on the 'personality of change'. In very few instances have school reforms or change theories been promulgated which place personal development and change as central 'building blocks' in the process. Instead, changes have been pursued in ways that seem to insist this will happen, *in spite* of the teacher's personal beliefs and missions. All too often, the 'personality of change' has been seen as the 'stumbling block' of real reform, rather than as a crucial 'building block'.

In this section, I want to evidence why such a view is potentially catastrophic for the current wave of reforms and change initiatives. Before I do this, however, let us examine a common myth in current school restructuring. It has a number of different embodiments, but goes something like this: in the old days (the 1960s and 1970s) in many Western countries, we operated loosely organised democratic social services and welfare states. Because the economies were affluent, discipline was fairly casual, and schoolteachers (like other professionals) were allowed uncommon degrees of autonomy and professional self-direction. The result was a weak sense of social discipline and low school standards.

Now those days are over, governments are now firmly in control of the schools – objectives and tests are being clearly defined, and school standards and discipline will steadily improve.

With regard to the teachers, the story goes this way. The old days of professionals as autonomous and self-directed are over: the 'new professional' is technically competent, complies with new guidelines and ordinances, and views teaching as a job where, like others, he/she is managed and directed and delivers what is asked. Educational change at the level of teaching means replacing, as soon as possible, the 'old professionals' with the 'new professionals'. Once this task is completed and the 'old professionals' have been 'mopped up', a new, more efficient and improved schooling system will emerge.

In some ways, this story is similar to the restructuring initiatives pursued in a range of industries and services, but I want to suggest that in education, in particular, it is proving a dangerous package to pursue. Let us look at this from the perspective of teachers. From the point of view of the 'old professionals', the pattern is clear – 'the game is up', they are told. Either they abandon their dreams of a professional autonomy, or they take early retirement. The results have been predictable everywhere – a huge rush of 'early retirements', alongside a group of teachers who 'hang in' in a state of despair and disenchantment.

For the reformers, this might be deemed a small transitional price to pay for replacing the 'old professionals' with 'new delivery conscious professionals'. But there we must stop – is it really that simple? Even in business, restructuring has proved more complex and contradictory than expected. In schools, the business is messily human and personal. Here, despair and disenchantment lead directly to uninspired teaching and spoilt student life-chances.

Ignoring the 'personality of change' might prove highly dangerous.

Talking to teachers, you can see what happens to their commitments. Here a prize-winning teacher of the 'old professional' sort talks:

> I could probably break down my 30 years into little maybe five to six year blocks. The first few years, maybe five years, I floundered. I was trying to figure this out. There were some things I did very well and other times I was a total disaster. But in that time, I was accumulating stuff. So there was that touchy feely sort of floundering person. And then when I got my creative writing class in 1975 and then when I got my first honours class in '79. From '75 until probably '85 was a kind of golden age where the kids I was getting and my own intellectual curiosity were at a peak. And I was living off energy that was coming from outside and from inside. And I was constantly just looking for new stuff, finding new material, building up new stuff, and testing things out. And it was a great time period.
>
> About 1985/1986, I think, I entered a period of real competence where I felt like I was someone with tools that I could use well and at will. I was a ... I became a much more rigorous teacher. I began assigning a term paper, a 15-page term paper where the students had to read five novels by a particular author, do biographical research, do critical research, create a thesis and argue that thesis. A very, very rigorous, tough assignment and I knew how to teach it and I knew how to get it out of the kids. And I was ... I became an expert, I think, in that time period. I was living on ... it was probably more fun to be in that middle period class. But I think in terms of what I actually was teaching or what the kids were actually learning and the skills they were acquiring, I think that third period was probably the best when I was most skilful and I was giving the most to the kids.
>
> Then I'd say in the last few years when I got involved in TLI and just a number of things have changed: the new Regents exam started popping up; the administration began to have more particular demands on what I was supposed to be doing.

What the teacher has talked to me about in length is how the new guidelines and texts have, over time, almost completely destroyed his commitment and ideals.

This is a personal disaster, but I want to suggest that such a perception among 'old professionals' is a much wider disaster for the complex ecology of schools.

The term 'old professional' needs to be further elucidated. I do not mean this to imply a particular professional of a certain age and stage, rather it means a view of teaching where the professionalism is expressed and experienced as more than just a job, but as a caring vocationalism. At heart, it means viewing the work of teaching as comprising more than material reward and technical delivery, as a form of work overlaid with purpose, passion and meaning. This sounds too pious (for it is not always – not in all circumstances – as we all have bad days, bad periods; we do mundane materialist things, of course), but it means a kind of professionalism where 'vocation' is part of the package, where 'ideals' are held and pursued. 'Old professional' then, captures an aspiration that is felt by both old and new teachers – it refers to a kind of professionalism and it is called 'old' merely because it was once more common and easier to pursue than it is in current circumstances.

In schools, the attack on 'old professional' vocationalism becomes a problem for a number of reasons:

1   Memory loss
2   Mentoring loss
3   Teacher retention and recruitment.

Let me take these in turn.

Memory loss

I have become very interested in what happens when the more mature members of an industry or community are given early retirement or subjected to change and reform that they disagree with, as is the case in so many of our schools. Interestingly, a range of new studies in Britain is looking at what happened to another delicate service industry – the railways. Tim Strangleman, himself a railway signalman, has been doing a PhD on the railway industry. He has been particularly interested in the occupational identity that railway workers have, and their skill and pride in 'running the railways' – a complex task with a wide range of skills and techniques learned on the job and passed on from worker to worker. The railways are being restructured and divided into separate, self-managing regional companies, each with their own budgets. The workers' skill and pride in their jobs has been a central ingredient in the old national service – a feature of old railway professionals, one might say. But now with the restructuring:

> Any residual pride in the job is wearing thin as new managers, with no railway background themselves, foster the notion that 'it's just another job, like shelling peas'.
>
> (Newnham, 1997, p. 28)

This reflects a similar phrase used again and again by younger teachers in our studies, 'after all, teaching is only a job, like any other'. In his railway study, Strangleman also makes connections. For instance, he:

> makes a surprising comparison with the banking industry, where the term 'corporate memory loss' has been coined to describe the process whereby layers of unquantifiable knowledge, acquired through years of experience, were

swept aside during the Eighties by an over-confident managerial class with no sense of the past. In the banking context, such tacit knowledge – 'rule of thumb, finger-in-the-air stuff' – might be the difference between sound and unsound investment. On the railways, it might be the difference between life and death.

(Newnham, 1997, p. 28)

This was written in 1997. Since then, Britain has witnessed a number of horrendous railway accidents, culminating in the Hatfield crash, which led to the whole railway system being almost shut down for weeks.

Perhaps then, in school reform, the purging of the 'old professionals' in the face of new change and reform might be a similarly catastrophic move. All too clearly, attention to these aspects of the 'personality of change' is worth much greater attention.

Mentoring loss

Each school is a carefully constructed community: if the elders in that community feel disenchanted and disvalued, this is a problem for the community of the school. It then becomes a problem for the successful delivery of the educational services the school provides – in short, a problem of school performance and educational standards.

Robert Bly (1991) has written about the problems for any community when the 'elders' of that community are disenchanted, disorientated and disregarded.

Let me give a specific example of what is lost when a whole cohort or section of teachers becomes disenchanted, disaffected and disorientated. In our studies, we have witnessed a number of schools where the sense of drift, of anarchy, of a lack of direction is palpable. In one of the schools – an innovative, landmark school in Toronto, founded in the 1960s – the ex-headmaster judged the problem to be exactly as with the railways.

The old cohort of founding professionals had become disenchanted by the new changes and reforms. As a result, they either took early retirement or remained at work in a disaffected, disengaged way. The problem this posed, according to the ex-headmaster, was that nobody therefore took on the mentoring of young teachers. They just arrived and went to work; it was just a job and they followed management instructions and state guidelines as best they could. As a result, the 'old professionals' (in this specific case, mainly the elders) kept their professional knowledge to themselves and the chain of professional transmission was broken – the 'layers of unquantifiable knowledge, acquired through years of experience' remained untransmitted to the new generation of teachers. The school then suffered 'corporate memory loss'.

The result, apparently, was a school without passion or purpose, without direction. People turned up to do a job like any other job without a sense of over-riding vocation or ideals and, as soon as they could, went home to their other life where, presumably, their passion and purpose resided and revived.

Teacher retention and recruitment

In the first two sections, we have seen how 'old professional' vocationalism has declined in teaching, either formally through early retirement, or spiritually because a wider cohort of teachers has become detached and disillusioned. At one stage, reform advocates and change theorists thought this evacuation by 'old professionals' a sign of the success of their strategy. As a result, they argued schools would be rejuvenated and filled with eager advocates of the new reforms.

This has proved both wildly optimistic and misguided. The problem of retention (or the non-problem in the eyes of reformers) has quickly shifted to the problem of recruitment. The second is seen as a problem, because even the wildest change advocates recognise that schools have to be staffed!

What research is showing is that, in many ways, the problems of retention and of recruitment are related and have the same root cause. It seems that many of the younger cohorts of would-be teachers are looking at the job and making similar judgements to their 'old professional' elders. The 'purging of the old' stands alongside the 'turning-off' of the young.

To sum up the reasons, it is because, in Bob Hewitt's felicitous phrase, in teaching now 'initiative and resourcefulness are banned' and, in his farewell article 'I Quit', he says:

> To see schools these days as filled just with bureaucratic bullshit is to seriously miss the point, however. Education has traditionally been about freedom. But there is no freedom anymore. It's gone. Initiative and resourcefulness are banned. Every school has become a part of the gulag. How else could inspectors time the literacy hour with stopwatches, or a teacher be dismissed over a bit of missing paperwork?
>
> (Hewitt, 2001, p. 3)

Whilst some younger recruits accept this form of occupational identity, far more are judging that they will take their initiative and resourcefulness into occupations that value rather than denigrate these characteristics. For example, Carmel Fitzsimons has just qualified as a teacher, but sees no possibility of actually practising. In the article 'I Quit', she says:

> I don't think teachers are uncreative – but creativity is being crushed out of them by the grinding cogs of bureaucracy and filing.
>
> To give you a glimpse: for every lesson a teacher is supposed to prepare assessment sheets from the previous lesson; they must then reflect upon the issues the assessment throws up. Then they must prepare a lesson plan – based on long-term, medium-term and short-term objectives from the curriculum; and having delivered the lesson, they must write up an evaluation of how the lesson went and then individually assess the progression of each child's learning. This can mean five sheets of written paper per lesson for each of the five lessons a day. Add the individual record of each child, the reading records and the collection of money for the school trip and you start to wonder whether there is any time left for getting your coat on before legging it across the playground.
>
> (Fitzsimons, 2001, p. 2)

Interestingly, the same kind of transition from 'old professionalism' to 'new professionalism' seems to be at work in nursing. In a recent study of NHS nurses, Kim Catcheside found that patterns of professionalism were transforming themselves:

> Modern nurses are a health hazard, the old-fashioned TLC-trained ones have all retired or resigned and the new lot, badly trained and poorly motivated, could not care less and are as likely in their ignorance to kill as to cure.
>
> (Arnold, 2001, p. 12)

Alistair Ross and a team of researchers have been studying teacher recruitment and retention for the past three years. Their findings make salutary reading for the advocates of reform and change:

> We asked those who were leaving for other careers what it was that they saw as attractive in their new work.
>
> Three-fifths of all teachers taking up work outside the profession do not find that teaching allows them to be creative and resourceful. These factors used to be one of the key defining elements of the teaching profession: people joined the profession because it used to offer them autonomy, creativity and the ability of use one's initiative.
>
> What has happened to the profession that has caused these teachers, at least, to become so disillusioned that they seek alternative careers? This question, to teachers, is rhetorical. The ways in which teaching has become managed, has become 'accountable' and has been subjected to control and direction, have contributed to demotivation.
>
> (Ross, 2001, p. 9)

They found also that the problems of recruitment and retention were not primarily economic as has so often been argued:

> We have also found that for teachers leaving the profession, it isn't high alternative salaries that are attracting them out. Of our sample of teachers leaving for other careers, only 27% would be earning more than they earned as teachers; 27% said that they would earn the same as they had earned as in their previous teaching post; and 45% were going to posts paying *less* than they had earned in their last teaching post.
>
> It is the change in the nature of teaching that is behind the crisis points we have described.
>
> (Ross, 2001, p. 9)

Conclusion

Behind the question of the 'personality of change' stands the complex issue of what constitutes professional knowledge and action; what characterises teacher professionalism? In our book, *Teachers' Professional Lives* (Goodson and Hargreaves, 1996), we defined five kinds of professionalism as classical, flexible, practical, extended and complex. We predicted in the twenty-first Century that a complex, post-modern, professionalism would emerge, based on a range of characteristics, most notably 'the creation and recognition of high task *complexity*, with levels of status and reward appropriate to such complexity' (Goodson and Hargreaves, 1996, p. 21). We argued that this would lead to a more personalised notion of professionalism emerging and based upon:

> a self-directed search and struggle for *continuous learning* related to one's own expertise and standards of practice, rather than compliance with the enervating obligations of *endless change* demanded by others.
>
> (Goodson and Hargreaves, 1996, p. 21)

Geoff Troman (1996) has examined the rise of what he calls the 'new professionals'. This group accepts the new political dispensation and hierarchies of the reform process, new governmental guidelines, and national objectives and curriculum. However, some members of the group have taken aspects of the 'old professionals' view of the world. The 'old professionals' believed in the teachers' collective control of their work, in professional and personal autonomy. In some ways, the 'new professionals' have found some way to continue being semi-autonomous and, in this sense, are pioneering a new complex professionalism which may moderate the bad effects of over zealous reform initiatives.

But Troman was studying schools in the UK from the 1980s, through to the 1990s, before the excesses of the reform process noted above began to bite. He argued:

> The strategy of resistance within accommodation is possible, at this time, only because spaces exist within the work of teaching and management-teacher relations.
>
> (Troman, 1996, p. 485)

In fact, recent reforms in a number of countries have sought to close these spaces for semi-autonomous personal and professional action. In doing so, they are tightening the screw too much and threatening to turn teaching into a profession attractive only to the compliant and docile, and conversely unattractive to the creative and resourceful. By pushing too far, they threaten to turn our schools into places of uniformity and barrenness – hardly a site on which standards will rise and educational inspiration flourish.

One way to view these changes and reforms is through the clear signs that it is most creative and resourceful of our teachers who are the most disenchanted with new prescriptions and guidelines. In a recent survey, teachers generally have listed 'government initiatives' as a major reason why they wish to leave teaching. It is instructive to view any profession or workforce not as a monolithic entity but as made up of a number of segments. Looking at the teaching profession, we might distinguish three segments:

- An elite or vanguard made up of the top 10–20 per cent.
- A mainstream 'backbone' group comprising 60–70 per cent.
- A borderline group comprising 10–20 per cent.

The elite group are the most creative and motivated group and often help define, articulate and extend the 'mission of teaching' generally, and of a school in particular. Their commitment to change and reform is a basic prerequisite for successful implementation: their disenchantment and disengagement leave change and reform as a hollow rhetoric. This is not least because of their mentorship and leadership of the mainstream group of teachers. This group, comprising 60–70 per cent of honest, hardworking professionals, makes up the backbone of the teaching profession. The interplay of mentorship and leadership between elite and the backbone is reciprocal and vital in motivating and defining the teaching workforce. It is also central in the maintenance of a sense of vocation and mission.

The third group of any profession is the 10–20 per cent. who are minimally involved: for them it is 'just a job' and some border on the competence level. This group has been the focus of many of the reforms and accountability strategies articulated by Western governments recently, yet one senses that like the poor they are 'always with us'. By focusing the reforms on this group, little is actually changed with regard to the performance and motivation of the group. However, and paradoxically, the world is transformed for the elite and the backbone. By attacking the small substandard groups, which all professions contain, many of the reforms have encountered a colossal downside by demotivating the vanguard and the backbone. Frankly, to use a business jargon, the balance sheet's costs and benefits are deeply unsatisfactory – the benefits are minimal and the costs colossal. If it were a simple question of financial bottom lines and profits, action would be taken immediately: the reforms would be aborted and new, more motivating and sensitive initiatives undertaken. However, since in education it is a question of human judgement and political face, one senses a long war of attrition before sensible judgements are made. In the meantime, the system continues its downward spiral.

The signs of disaffection grow daily, not just problems of teacher recruitment, but problems of student disaffection and recruitment, and the number of students being educated at home rather than at school continues to rocket under the National Curriculum in England. Meanwhile, in more vital and entrepreneurial environments like Hong Kong, the government is moving away from a rigid syllabus-defined subject-centred curriculum to a loose facilitating framework of 'key learning areas'. Each school defines its own curriculum within that facilitating framework, and the teacher's personal and professional judgement is given greater provenance. Here, respect for the 'personality of change' is built in to encourage greater creativity and competitiveness.

Above all, the reforms return some personal and professional discretion to the teacher; to the 'layers of unquantifiable knowledge acquired through years of experience which only a foolish management group sort to expunge in the schools (as in the railways). In the railways, the result of the over zealous pursuit of reform was a death-dealing dysfunctional system. In the school, the effect on student life-chances will amount to the same thing.

References

Arnold, S., 2001, Savage Angels. *The Observer Review* (February 4).

Bly, R., 1991, *Iron John* (Shaftesbury: Element Books Ltd).

Fitzsimons, C., 2001, I Quit. *Guardian Education*, 2–3 (January 9).

Goodson, I.F. and Hargreaves, A., 1996, Teachers' Professional Lives: Aspirations and Actualities. In I.F. Goodson, and A. Hargreaves, (eds), *Teachers' Professional Lives* (London and Washington, DC: Falmer Press), 1–27.

Hewitt, B., 2001, I Quit, *Guardian Education*, 2–3 (January 9).

Newnham, D., 1997, Going Loco. *The Guardian Weekend*, 20–31 (March 1).

Ross, A., 2001, Heads will Roll. *Guardian Education*, 8–9 (January 23).

Troman, G., 1996, The Rise of the New Professionals? The Restructuring of Primary Teachers' Work and Professionalism. *British Journal of Sociology of Education*, 17(4), 473–487.

LIST OF RECENT WORKS

Books

Learning Curriculum and Life Politics: Selected Works (Routledge: England, 2005).

Social Geographies of Educational Change, with F. Hernandez (ed.) (Kluwer: Dordrecht, 2004).

Life History and Professional Development: Stories of Teachers' Life and Work, with U. Numan (Studentlitteratur: Lund, 2003).

Professional Knowledge, Professional Lives: Studies in Education and Change (Open University Press: Maidenhead and Philadelphia, PA, 2003).

Estudio del Curriculum: Casos y Métodos (Amorrortu Editores: Buenos Aires, 2003).

Cyber Spaces/Social Spaces: Culture Clash in Computerized Classrooms, with M. Knobel, C. Lankshear and M. Mangan (Palgrave Macmillan: New York, 2002).

Life Histories of Teachers: Understanding Life and Work (Koyo Shobo: Japan, 2001).

The Birth of Environmental Education (East China Normal University Press: P.R. China, 2001).

O Currículo em Mudança: Estudos na construção social do currículo (Porto Editora: Portugal, 2001).

Life History Research in Educational Settings: Learning from Lives, with P. Sikes (Open University Press: Buckingham and Philadelphia, PA, 2001).

Currículo: Teoria e História, 4th edn (Editora Vozes: Petrópolis, Brazil, 2001).

Opetussuunnitelman Tekeminen: Esseitä opetussuunnitelman ja oppiaineen sosiaalisesta rakentumisesta (Joensuu University Press: Finland, 2001).

La enseñanza y los profesores, III, La reforma de la enseñanza en un mundo en transformación, with B.J. Biddle and T.L. Good (eds) (Ediciones Paidós Ibérica: Barcelona, 2000).

La enseñanza y los profesores, II, La enseñanza y sus contextos, with B.J. Biddle and T.L. Good (eds) (Ediciones Paidós Ibérica: Barcelona, 2000).

La enseñanza y los profesores, I, La profesión de enseñar, with B.J. Biddle and T.L. Good (eds) (Ediciones Paidós Ibérica: Barcelona, 2000).

Livshistorier – kilde til forståelse av utdanning (Fagbokforlaget: Bergen, Norway, 2000).

El Cambio en el Currículum (Ediciones Octaedro: Spain, 2000).

Currículo: Teoria e História, 3rd edn (Editora Vozes: Petrópolis, Brazil, 1999).

Subject Knowledge: Readings for the Study of School Subjects, with C. Anstead and J.M. Mangan (Falmer Press: London and Washington DC, 1998).

Currículo: Teoria e História, 2nd edn (Editora Vozes: Petrópolis, Brazil, 1998).

An International Handbook of Teachers and Teaching, Vol. 1, with B. Biddle and T. Good (eds) (Kluwer, 1998).

An International Handbook of Teachers and Teaching, Vol. 2, with B. Biddle and T. Good (eds) (Kluwer, 1998).

A Construçâo Social do Currículo (EDUCA: Lisboa, Portugal, 1997).

The Changing Curriculum: Studies in Social Construction (Peter Lang: New York, 1997).

Studying School Subjects: A Guide, with C. Marsh (Falmer Press: London and Washington DC, 1996).

Att Stärka Lärarnas Röster: Sex essäer om lärarforskning och lärar-forskarsamarbete (HLS Förlag: Stockholm, 1996).

Making a Difference about Difference, with N. Bascia and D. Thiessen (Garabond Press: Toronto, 1996).

Teachers' Professional Lives, with I.F. Goodson and A. Hargreaves (eds) (Falmer Press: London, New York and Philadelphia, PA, 1996).
The Making of Curriculum: Collected Essays, 2nd edn (Falmer: London, New York and Philadelphia, PA, 1995).
Currículo: Teoria e História, 1st edn (Editora Vozes: Petrópolis, Brazil, 1995).
Historia del Currículum: La construcción social de las disciplinas escolares (Ediciones Pomares-Corredor: Barcelona, Spain, 1995).

Journal articles

'Onderwijsvernieuwers vergeten de leerkracht', *didaktief*, Jaargang 34, No. 3/Maart 2004.
'Changements de l'éducation et processus historiques: une perspective internationale', *Éducation et Sociétés*, No. 11/1, pp. 105–118, 2003.
'Hacia un desarrollo de las historias personales y profesionales de los docentes', *Revista Mexicana de Investigacion Educativa*, Vol. VIII, No. 19, September–December 2003.
'Teacher's Life Worlds, Agency and Policy Contexts', with U. Numan, *Teachers and Teaching: Theory and Practice*, Vol. 8, No. 3/4, pp. 269–277, August/November 2002.
'La personalidad de las reformas', *Cuadernos de Pedagogía*, No. 319, pp. 34–37, December 2002.
'De la historia al futuro: Nuevas cadenas de cambio', Entrevista a Ivor Goodson, *Revista Páginas de la Escuela de Ciencias de la Educación U.N.C.*, Vol. 2, No. 2 y3, pp. 9–17, Córdoba, September 2002.
'Un curriculum para una sociedad democrática y plural', Entrevista con...Ivor Goodson, *KIKIRIKI-62/63*, pp. 25–30, September 2001/February 2002.
'Med livet som innsats (faktor)', *Bedre Skole: Norsk Lærerlags Tidsskrift for Pedagogisk Debatt*, No. 1, pp. 49–51, Oslo, 2001.
'Testing Times: A School Case Study', with M. Foote, *Education Policy Analysis Archives*, Vol. 9, No. 2, January 2001. (http://epaa.asu.edu/epaa/v9n2.html)
'Social Histories of Educational Change', *Journal of Educational Change*, Vol. 2, No. 1, pp. 45–63, 2001.
'The Story of Life History: Origins of the Life History Method in Sociology', *Identity: An International Journal of Theory and Research*, Vol. 1, No. 2, pp. 129–142, 2001.
'The Crisis of Curriculum Change', *Taboo: The Journal of Culture and Education*, Vol. 4, No. 2, pp. 109–123, Fall–Winter 2000.
'La mediación es el mensaje', *La revista del IICE*, Vol. IX, No. 17, pp. 53–61, December 2000.
'Developing Chains of Change', *Resources in Education*, ERIC, Issue RIEDEC00, I.D: 442 718.
'Recuperar el poder docente', *Cuadernos de Pedagogía*, No. 295, pp. 44–49, Barcelona, October 2000.
'The Principled Professional', *Prospects*, UNESCO, pp. 198–208, Geneva, January 2000.
'Life Histories and Professional Practice', *Curriculum and Teaching*, Vol. 16, No. 1, pp. 11–20, 2000.
'Professionalism i reformtider', *Pedagogiska Magasinet*, No. 4, pp. 6–12, December 1999.
Entrevista, Ivor Goodson, with V. Baraldi, *Revista El Cardo*, UNER, 1999.
'Møte med Ivor F. Goodson', with R. Ådlandsvik, *Norsk PEDAGOGISK ttidsskrift*, Vol. 82, No. 2, pp. 96–102, 1999.
'The Educational Researcher as a Public Intellectual', *British Educational Research Journal*, Vol. 25, No. 3, pp. 277–298, 1999.
'Preparing for Postmodernity: Storying the Self', *Educational Practice and Theory*, Vol. 20, No. 1, pp. 25–32, 1998.
'Exchanging Gifts: Collaboration and Location', with C. Fliesser, *Resources in Education*, February 1998.
'Heroic Principals and Structures of Opportunity: Conjoncture at a Vocational High School', with C. Anstead, *International Journal of Leadership in Education*, Vol. 1, No. 1, pp. 61–73, January 1998.
'Action Research and the Reflective Project of Self', *Taboo, The Journal of Culture and Education*, Spring, 1997.

'Distinction and Destiny', with P. Cookson, Jr and C. Persell, *Discourse*, Vol. 18, No. 2, pp. 173–182, 1997.
'Trendy Theory and Teacher Professionalism', *Cambridge Journal*, Spring, pp. 7–22, 1997.
'Representing Teachers', *Teaching and Teacher Education: An International Journal of Research and Studies*, Vol. 13, No. 1, 1997.
'Towards an Alternative Pedagogy', *Taboo, International Journal of Culture and Education*, Fall, 1996.
'New Prospects/New Perspectives: A Reply to Wilson and Holmes', with J.M. Mangan, *Interchange*, Vol. 27, No. 1, pp. 71–77, 1996.
'Exploring Alternative Perspectives in Educational Research', with J.M. Mangan, *Interchange*, Vol. 27, No. 1, pp. 41–59, 1996.
'Talking Lives: A Conversation About Life History', with P. Sikes and B. Troyna, *Taboo: The Journal of Culture and Education*, Vol. 1, pp. 35–54, Spring 1996.
'Computer Literacy as Ideology', with J.M. Mangan, *British Journal of Sociology of Education*, Vol. 17, No. 1, 1996.
'Curriculum Contests: Environmental Studies Versus Geography', *Environmental Education Research*, Vol. 2, No. 1, pp. 71–88, 1996.
'Storying the Self: Life Politics and the Study of the Teacher's Life and Work', *Resources in Education*, ERIC, Issue RIEJAN96, I.D: 386 454, 1996.
'Developing a Collaborative Research Strategy with Teachers for the Study of Classroom Computing', with J.M. Mangan, *Journal of Information Technology for Teacher Education*, Vol. 4, No. 3, pp. 269–286, 1995.
'Subject Cultures and the Introduction of Classroom Computers', with J.M. Mangan, *British Educational Research Journal*, Vol. 21, No. 5, pp. 587–612, December 1995.
'The Story So Far: Personal Knowledge and the Political', *Resources in Education*, ERIC Issue RIEMAR95, I.D.: ED 376 160, 1995.
'Developing a Collaborative Research Strategy with Teachers for the Study of Classroom Computing', with J.M. Mangan, *Journal of Information Technology for Teacher Education*, Vol. 4, No. 3, pp. 269–287, 1995.
'Negotiating Fair Trade: Towards Collaborative Relationships Between Researchers and Teachers in College Settings', with C. Fliesser, *Peabody Journal of Education*, Vol. 70, No. 3, pp. 5–17, 1995.
'Schooldays are the Happiest Days of Your Life', with C. Anstead, *Taboo: The Journal of Culture and Education*, Vol. 11, pp. 39–52, Fall 1995.
'The Historical Study of the Curriculum', with C. Anstead, *Curriculum and Teaching*, Vol. 10, No. 2, pp. 33–44, 1995.
'The Story So Far: Personal Knowledge and the Political', *The International Journal of Qualitative Studies in Education*, Vol. 8, No. 1, pp. 89–98, 1995.
'Education as a Practical Matter', *Cambridge Journal of Education*, Vol. 25, No. 2, pp. 137–148, 1995.

Chapters in encyclopedia

'Curriculum History', in D. Levinson, P. Cookson and A. Sadovnik (eds), *Education and Sociology: An Encyclopedia* (Routledge Falmer: London and New York, 2002), pp. 133–150.
'Testing Times: A School Case Study', with M. Foote, *Schooling and Standards in the U.S.: An Encyclopedia* (Lawrence Farlbaum: London and New York, 2001).

Chapters in books

'The Personality of Change', in W. Veugelers and R. Bosman (eds), *De strijd om het curriculum (The Struggle Around the Curriculum)* Antwerpen/Apeldoorn: Garant (series *Sociology of Education*) 2005.
'Change Processes and Historical Periods: An International Perspective', in C. Sugrue (ed.), *Curriculum and Ideology: Irish Experiences International Perspectives* (The Liffey Press: Dublin, 2004).

'Afterword – International Educational Research: Content, Context, and Methods', in L. Bresler and A. Ardichvili (eds), *Research in International Education: Experience, Theory, and Practice*', Vol. 180, pp. 297–302 (Peter Lang: New York, 2002) (ISBN 0–8204–5215–7).

'Basil Bernstein, F., 1925–2000', in J. Palmer (ed.), *Fifty Modern Thinkers on Education: From Piaget to the Present*, pp. 161–169 (Routledge: London and New York, 2001).

'Foreword – Contextualizing the Curriculum' in B. Adamson, T. Kwan and K.K. Chan (eds), *Changing the Curriculum: The Impact of Reform on Primary Schooling in Hong Kong*, pp. xv–xvi (Hong Kong University Press: Aberdeen, HK, 2000).

'Curriculum Contests: Environmental Studies Versus Geography' in S. Ball (ed.), *The Sociology of Education: Major Themes* (Routledge Falmer: London and New York, 2000) (Hb: 0–415–19812–7).

'Professional Knowledge and the Teacher's Life and Work' in C. Day, A. Fernandez, T. E. Hauge and J. Møller (eds), *The Life and Work of Teachers: International Perspectives in Changing Times* (Falmer Press: London and New York, 2000) (ISBN 0–750–70944–8).

'Schulfächer und ihre Geschichte als Gegenstand der Curriculumforschung im angelsächsischen Raum' in I. Goodson, S. Hopmann and K. Riquarts (eds), *Das Schulfach als Handlungsrahmen: Vergleichende Untersuchung zur Geschichte und Funktion der Schulfächer*, pp. 29–46 (Böhlau Verlag GmbH and Cie: Köln, Weimar, Wien, Böhlau, 1999) (ISBN 3–412–04295–1).

'Entstehung eines Schulfaches' in I. Goodson, S. Hopmann and K. Riquarts (eds), *Das Schulfach als Handlungsrahmen: Vergleichende Untersuchung zur Geschichte und Funktion der Schulfächer*, pp. 151–176 (Böhlau Verlag GmbH and Cie: Köln, Weimar, Wien, Böhlau, 1999) (ISBN 3–412–04295–1).

'A crise da mudança curricular: algumas advertências sobre iniciativas de reestruturação' in L. Peretti and E. Orth (eds), *Século XXI: Qual Conhecimento?Qual Currículo?*, pp. 109–126 (Editora Vozes: Petrópolis, Brazil, 1999) (ISBN 85.326.2202–X).

'Representing Teachers' in M. Hammersley (ed.), *Researching School Experience: Ethnographic Studies of Teaching and Learning* (Falmer Press: London and New York, 1999) (ISBN 0–7507–0914–6).

'Education as a Practical Matter: Some Issues and Concerns' in C. Sugrue (ed.), *Restructuring Initial Teacher Education: A focus on Preservice and Induction at Primary Level* (St Patrick's College: Dublin, 1998) (ISBN 1–872327–18–4).

'Holding on Together: Conversations with Barry' in P. Sikes and F. Rizvi (eds), *Researching Race and Social Justice Education – Essays in Honour of Barry Troyna* (Trentham Books: Staffordshire, 1997).

'Action Research and the Reflexive Project of Selves' in S. Hollingsworth (ed.), *International Action Research: A Casebook for Educational Reform* (Falmer Press: London and Washington, 1997).

'Towards an Alternative Pedagogy' in S. Steinberg and J. Kincheloe (eds) (Routledge: New York and London, 1998).

'Trendy Theory and Teacher Professionalism' in A. Hargreaves and R. Evans (eds), *Beyond Educational Reform*, pp. 27–41 (Open University Press, 1997).

'New Patterns of Curriculum Change' in A. Hargreaves (ed.), *A Handbook of Educational Change* (Kluwer: Dordrecht, Boston and London, 1997).

'Storying the Self' in W. Pinar (ed.), *New Curriculum Identities*, pp. 3–20 (Westview: New York and London, 1997).

'The Life and Work of Teaching' in B. Biddle, T. Good and I. Goodson (eds), *A Handbook of Teachers and Teaching*, Vols 1 and 2 (Kluwer: Dordrecht, Boston and London, 1997).

'Writing for Bjorg Gundem: On Curriculum Form' in B. Karseth, S. Gudmundsdottir and S. Hopmann (eds), *Didaktikk: Tradisjon og fornyelse: Festskrift til Bjorg Bradntzaeg Gundem*, pp. 35–51 (University of Oslo, Institute for Educational Research: Norway, 1997).

'Representing Teachers: Bringing Teachers Back In' in M. Kompf (ed.), *Changing Research and Practice: Teachers Professionalism, Identities and Knowledge* (Falmer Press: London, New York and Philadelphia, PA, 1996).

'Studying the Teacher's Life and Work' in J. Smyth (ed.), *Critical Discourses on Teacher Development*, pp. 56–65 (Cassell: London, 1996).

'The Personal and Political' in T. Tiller, A. Sparkes, S. Karhus and F. Dowling Naess (eds), *Reflections on Educational Research: The Qualitative Challenge*, pp. 55–77 (Landas, Norway: Caspar Forlag A/S, 1996).

'Scrutinizing Life Stories: Storylines, Scripts and Social Contexts' in D. Thiessen, N. Bascia and I. Goodson (eds), *Making a Difference About Difference*, pp. 123–138 (Garamond Press: Canada, 1996).

'Materias Excolares y la Construccion del Curriculum: Texto y contexto' in J.G. Minguez and M. Beas (eds), *Libro de Texto y Construccion de Materiales Curriculares*, pp. 183–199 (Granada, Spain: Proyecto Sur de Ediciones S.A.L, 1995).

'A Nation at Rest: The Contexts for Change in Teacher Education in Canada' in N.K. Shimahara and I.Z. Holowinsky (eds), *Teacher Education in Industrialized Nations*, pp. 125–153 (Garland Press: New York and London, 1995).

'Telling Tales' in H. McEwan and K. Egan (eds), with Walker, R., *Narrative in Teaching, Learning, and Research*, pp. 184–194 (Teachers College Press: New York, 1995).

'The Context of Cultural Inventions: Learning and Curriculum' in P. Cookson and B. Schneider (eds), *Transforming Schools*, pp. 307–327 (Garland Press: New York and London, 1995).

'Basil Bernstein and Aspects of the Sociology of the Curriculum' in P. Atkinson, B. Davies and S. Delamont (eds), *Discourse and Reproduction*, pp. 121–136 (Hampton Press: Cresskill, NJ, 1995).

'A Genesis and Genealogy of British Curriculum Studies' in Alan Sadovnik (ed.) *Knowledge and Pedagogy: The Sociology of Basil Bernstein*, pp. 359–370 (Ablex: Norwood, NJ, 1995).

INDEX